SALVAGE POETICS

SALVAGE POETICS

Post-Holocaust
American Jewish
Folk Ethnographies

SHEILA E. JELEN

WAYNE STATE UNIVERSITY PRESS
DETROIT

ISBN (hardcover): 978-0-8143-4318-0
ISBN (e-book): 978-0-8143-4319-7

Library of Congress Control Number: 2019947683

Wayne State University Press
Leonard N. Simons Building
4809 Woodward Avenue
Detroit, Michigan 48201-1309

Visit us online at wsupress.wayne.edu.

For My Parents

Henry (Chaim) Jelen (b.1945)

Syma Rose Ralston (b.1949)

Born in the Aftermath

CONTENTS

ACKNOWLEDGMENTS

I acknowledge, with gratitude, all those institutions and individuals who have made the writing of this book possible. Thank you to the Meyerhoff Center for Jewish Studies at the University of Maryland for several summer grants that enabled me to write and research in Jerusalem. Thank you to the Department of Modern and Classical Languages, Literatures, and Cultures at the University of Kentucky for helping to defray the cost of rights to the Vishniac Illustrations, provided by the International Center for Photography, which appear in chapter 5. I am grateful as well to Maya Benton of the ICP who read the chapter on Vishniac, providing comments and insights in order to help me obtain rights to the photographs from the Vishniac estate. Thank you to the department of English at the University of Maryland for providing me with research money to help defray the cost of rights to the illustrations in the YIVO Archives for publication in chapter 4. Thank you to Barbara Kirshenblatt-Gimblett, chief curator of the core exhibition at the POLIN Museum of the History of Polish Jews in Warsaw and professor emerita at New York University for sharing her father's Mayer Kirshenblatt's paintings with me and for allowing them to appear in chapter 6. Thank you as well to Yossi Raviv for permission to republish images taken by his father, Moshe Vorobeichic-Raviv, in chapter 4. Magnum Photos graciously provided rights for the images that appear in the Introduction, while VAGA allowed me to reprint all the images by Ben Shahn that appear in chapter 4. The Modern Art Museum of Fort Worth and the Amon Carter Museum of Modern Art both provided high quality prints of the

Shahn paintings that appear in chapter 4 as well. Artist and teacher Mira Schor, Ilya Schor's daughter, read chapter 2 and made valuable comments and corrections. She also gave me permission to reproduce her father's drawings and images of several of his Jewish ritual objects, and for that I am grateful. Suzanna Heschel, daughter of Abraham Joshua Heschel and professor of Jewish history at Dartmouth University, also read a version of chapter 2 and helped me shape that chapter with her insights. I am grateful to the editors at the Wayne State University Press, Kathryn Peterson Wildfong and Annie Martin, for ushering this book to publication, alongside all the other staff of the press, as well as to my anonymous readers whose valuable comments helped me make badly needed improvements. My gratitude goes out to Michelle Alperin, an early reader and editor of this entire text, and to my students and colleagues in the comparative literature program and in the English department at the University of Maryland for reading parts of this over a period of many years and providing me with valuable feedback. I acknowledge as well that a much abbreviated version of chapter 4 appeared in an anthology of essays, *Reconstructing the Old Country: American Jewry in the Post-Holocaust Decades* (Detroit: Wayne State University Press, 2017), 137–51, under the title "A Treasury of Yiddish Stories: Salvage Montage and the Anti-Shtetl." Thank you to Obie, for learning to sit still during my year of sabbatical so we could write together on the couch. I am, as always, grateful to my children Malka, Nava, Akiva, and Meirav for always putting everything into perspective. Their struggles are my struggles and their triumphs my triumphs. I can't imagine reading or writing or thinking or living without them always by my side. Thank you to my husband, Seth Himelhoch, who believes in me unconditionally and whose love has sustained me and taught me through many years of a shared life. And finally, I dedicate this book to my parents, Henry (Chaim) Jelen and Syma Rose Ralston, who have taught me that life is blessedly complicated, whether you are living it or writing about it, and who have always supported me through all my impractical pursuits.

PROLOGUE

In Search of a Postwar Jewishness

Judaism's essence, as developed over a period of two thousand years, was a complete pattern of life in which a daily round of prayers and observances, punctuated by the more intense observances of the Sabbath and the festivals, reminded all Jews that they were a holy people. This pattern of life was Judaism; today it is maintained by a small minority, and, since only a minority observe it, it has changed its character . . . This creates a more serious break in the continuity of Jewish history than the murder of six million Jews. Jewish history has known, and Judaism has been prepared for, massacre; Jewish history has not known, nor is Judaism prepared for, the abandonment of the law.[1]

In 1957, Nathan Glazer, a thirty-four-year-old up-and-coming sociologist, published *American Judaism*, part of a University of Chicago series on America's major religions, which included volumes on American Protestantism and American Catholicism. A member of the cadre of "New York Intellectuals," which coalesced at City College during the 1930s, Glazer was also a frequent contributor to *Commentary*, a mouthpiece for American Jewish literati beginning in 1945. Written during the era of what had been called a "renascence of Judaism,"[2] Glazer's *American Judaism* galvanized American Jews with its mixed review of their prospects for survival as a distinct community in America after the Holocaust.

Here, in his striking correlation between the abandonment of the law and the loss of six million Jews, Glazer does not sound like a young intellectual, secular in his outlook and in his own Jewish practices. Rather, he sounds like a traditionalist, astonished in the face of East European Jewry's recent destruction at his own American coreligionists' abandonment of Jewish law. That is one of the interesting dynamics that we will explore together in *Salvage Poetics*. Through a study of the texts produced by and for American Jews in the half century following the Holocaust of East European Jewry, we will consider the fraught relationship with Jewish "tradition," whether religious or ethnic, that many felt in the aftermath of the war. We begin our discussion with Nathan Glazer's conflicted approach to this matter in *American Judaism* as a case study in the complexities of the relationship between nonreligious, ethnic Jewish identity and a sense of responsibility to uphold the memory and culture of East European Jewry through some obeisance to and recognition of the primacy of Jewish law.

To begin, let us consider the specific language used by Glazer in the above quotation. What is this "complete pattern of life" that he perceives to have been abandoned by the majority of American Jews by 1957? In Glazer's analysis, a complete pattern of life certainly alludes to religious law. The law indeed creates a comprehensive approach to living that encompasses the Jew and differentiates the Jewish community from other communities; it is a way of putting on your shoes and eating your food, a way of keeping time by the moon and not the sun, a way of educating your children and teaching them history through ritual and experience as opposed to textbooks. It is a way of waking up with prayers on your lips and going to sleep with prayers as well. But once Jews have moved away from "the law," as Glazer puts it, a "complete Jewish pattern of life" must still be preserved. It must be an accent, a political sensibility, a taste for foods, a memory of oppression, faith in the coming of the messiah, be he a man or a political moment, sacred or secular. In Glazer's words:

> What binds all these shifting manifestations of Judaism and Jewishness together is the common refusal to throw off the yoke. The refusal to become non-Jews stems from an attitude of

mind that seems to be, and indeed in large measure is, a stubborn insistence on remaining a Jew, enhanced by no particularly ennobling idea of what that means. And yet it has the effect of relating American Jews, let them be as ignorant of Judaism as a Hottentot, to a great religious tradition. Thus, the insistence of the Jews on remaining Jews, which may take the religiously indifferent forms of liking Yiddish jokes, supporting Israel, raising money for North African Jews, and preferring certain kinds of food, has a potentially religious meaning.[3]

According to Glazer, Jewishness, as distinct from Judaism, is more than a religious commitment. It is something that may come to resonate with religious meaning through its association with Judaism, but it does not necessarily originate in "the law." By Glazer's reckoning, Jewishness constitutes a way of life that is not necessarily compatible with American middle-class values in the 1950s. In their move to the suburbs in the third generation that has been exhaustively studied and theorized, American Jews, Glazer claims, transformed their ethnic "Jewishness" into "Judaism," limiting their Jewish commitments to the synagogue and the religious school, and letting most of the Jewish laws that controlled the daily lives of Jews for millennia fall by the wayside.

But Glazer's concern about Jewishness in America after the war goes beyond what the Jews are doing to themselves. He wonders at the appointment of Judaism as one of the three major religions in America. In the first paragraph of *American Judaism*, Glazer fleshes out his skepticism as not simply a matter of Jewish continuity but as a disciplinary concern with the classification of Judaism:

> It would be an interesting essay in the history of ideas to determine just how the United States evolved in the popular mind from a "Christian" nation into a nation made up of Catholics, Protestants and Jews. The most interesting part of such a study—which I do not plan to undertake here—would be to discover how it came about that the Jewish group, which through most of the history of the US has formed an insignificant percentage of the American people, has come to be granted the status of a "most favored religion."[4]

Differentiating between what he calls "Jewishness" and "Judaism," Glazer identifies Jewishness as an ethnicity and Judaism as a religion. Until the 1950s, he argues, the Jews had always been an ethnicity. Religion was clearly a piece of that ethnicity, but it was not the sum total of it. What then happened in the 1950s when the majority of American Jews gravitated toward synagogues that served, in many cases, as Jewish community centers where you could swim, throw a party, hold a movie night or a bingo game, while the rabbi in the sanctuary struggled to find ten men for a minyan on a regular weeknight? The brick-and-mortar building was an emblem of the Jewish religion, but there seemed to be a surprising lack of religious commitment expressed there. This wouldn't be a problem, Glazer implies, if Jews weren't suddenly viewed as one of the major "religions" in America.

For Glazer, arguing for Jewishness instead of Judaism, or for an ethnic identification as opposed to a religious one, was his way of rejecting the American conception of what should constitute a religious community. As a young sociologist called upon to bring Judaism to the American table, he bridled at the assumption that Judaism was somehow parallel to Catholicism and Protestantism. He was critical of the Jews who had enabled that perception by taking on the trappings of American religious systems through their overwhelming investment in synagogue life, but he was also critical of the academic establishment, which had invited him to participate in their discussion. He decries what he calls the "protestantization" of American Judaism, arguing that Judaism, unlike Christian denominations, is not a religion of dogma or institution, but is a religion of action and experience.[5] Don't ask Jews what they believe, he says, because Judaism has no catechism (with the exception of the Shema). Judaism, indeed, is about lifestyle, life cycle, and the vernacular experience of the day to day within a community of like-minded people. By building synagogue after synagogue in the suburbs and limiting one's Jewish experience to affiliation (or lack thereof) with that synagogue, one becomes a devotee of Judaism while losing one's Jewishness.

Glazer's voice was not alone. Many others were profoundly anxious about the direction that American Jewish life was taking in what has been called the "suburban Jewish paradox" of the moment: Jews were doing more but knew so much less; the parents were building synagogues to which the children never went. Like Glazer, Marshal Sklare was powerfully attuned to the different valences of ethnic and religious identification. A leading sociologist of postwar American Jews, Sklare wrote that "in the Conservative synagogue ties of ethnicity really brought Jews together under the guise of religion."[6] In denying their ethnic identity and cloaking it as a strictly religious one, what would the future of American Judaism look like?

These concerns continue to pertain. In his 2018 survey of how "ordinary Jews"—as he calls them—express their Jewish identity in America today, Jack Wertheimer, quoting Leora Batnitzky's study, *How Judaism Became a Religion*, notes that "for much of their history, Jews did not have a word for their religion, and the characterization of Judaism as a religion is itself a modern invention."[7] For much of Jewish history, he concludes, "Jews have understood matters differently; religion was intertwined with folk culture." Wertheimer further asserts that "those who contend that the ethnic dimension of Jewishness is passé but also unnecessary ignore the power of Jewish peoplehood to provide religious meaning."[8] For Wertheimer, "the power of Jewish peoplehood" is his own variation on Glazer's notion of Jewishness, in contrast to Judaism, or "Judaism," in America as it emerged from the "procrustean bed of Protestantism."[9]

Declaring themselves members of a religion like other religions in America in the 1950s was the means that American Jews, according to Glazer, minimized their ethnic associations with the racial connotation that had proven to be such a barrier to the middle class for other ethnic minorities during the postwar era. In *How Jews Became White Folks and What That Says about Race in America*, Karen Brodkin has written extensively about the "whitening" of American Jews at mid-century because of the GI Bill, among other factors, and the role this whitening played in their rise into the middle class.[10] Alongside this move to the suburbs was a boom in the building of suburban synagogues as a way for Jews to identify themselves as upstanding middle-class citizens within a predominantly religious American culture.

Ethnicity among Jews in America was best manifested, according to Deborah Dash Moore and others, in the first- and second-generation urban neighborhoods of East European Jews in America—on the Lower East Side of New York or the South Side of Chicago, for example. There, the consensus is, one could be a Jew without being religious.[11] Irving Howe famously describes the neighborhood and milieu in which he grew up as one in which he expressed his Jewishness through his attitude, the tone of his voice, the rejection of his parents' languages and literatures. It was not expressed through attendance at a synagogue.[12] It was in the riot of ideologies and organizations that took shape in Jewish urban neighborhoods—socialism, Zionism, communism, Yiddishism, to name just a few—that Jewish ethnicity could be articulated on the American street. With the move to the suburbs, the narrative goes, Jews shed their racialized ethnicity and proved their whiteness. In the process, their ethnic Jewishness dwindled, and religious Judaism became the predominant means by which America understood them and they understood themselves. Paradoxically, however, though the religious element of Jewish experience was trumpeted, Jewish observances and Jewish knowledge were not. Affiliation replaced memory in the Jewish experience, community replaced culture, and activity replaced knowledge.

Despite its racial connotations, ethnicity is a useful category for collective self-definition in an era of multiculturalism. Jews were at a critical point in their history in America when it became possible for them to shed their ethnic identification along with their racialized one. They had moved from the sweatshops to the universities by the second generation and from the working-class ranks into the ranks of the professions by the third generation. They had fought in the armed forces during the Second World War, cementing their "American identity," and qualified for education and housing through the GI Bill with the rest of the white middle class in the years following it.[13] Therefore, just as they were moving into the middle class they were also able to differentiate themselves racially from those who were more rigorously discriminated against in housing, in hiring, and in education. This was an economic blessing for them, but a cultural disaster according to theorists like Glazer, because along with their ethnicity they lost their Jewishness. With the rise of voices such as Horace Kallen's, who argued against the melting pot on behalf of all ethnics, but particularly

Jews, in the early part of the twentieth century,[14] and in recognition of the value of communal "difference" in America as a means of creating community cohesion,[15] one can better understand Glazer's eagerness to lament the loss of Jewish ethnicity.

What I do in this study is try to understand the role played by a variety of different hybrid texts—or texts that exist on the border between the literary and the ethnographic, whether re-workings and translations of fiction, works of nonfiction, or photo collections—in the reconstitution of an American Jewish ethnicity, or a sense of "Jewishness," during the postwar era from the mid-1940s through the turn of the twenty-first century. I contend that literary culture plays a monumental role in the invention of "ethnicity." The creation of a folk-ethnographic movement in the 1940s—as part of the movement to reclaim a Jewish ethnicity that enabled Jews to cast an ethnographic eye on the specific folk formations of the Jewish religion without necessarily ascribing to them—can be attributed to the constellation of forces described and lamented by Glazer, as explained above.

As part of the movement to reclaim their ethnicity, perhaps as a tribute to their awareness of the very recent loss of a European Jewish world that had, in Glazer's terms, been suffused with a more integrated "Jewishness" than was available among the non-Orthodox in America, American Jews sought to construct a folk ethnography of East European pre-Holocaust Jewry in order to map out future directions for their own de-racialized ethnic consciousness. As Jewish ethnicity dwindled with the move out of urban centers and into the suburbs, what kinds of possibilities for ethnic identification did pre-Holocaust East European Jewry hold out to third-generation American Jews and beyond?

One basic example of how hybrid literature could create a de-racialized ethnic framework for American Jews from the 1940s to the present can be found in the development of the shtetl trope. The *shtetl*, or the small Jewish town in Eastern Europe, was popularized significantly with its appearance in 1964 on Broadway in *Fiddler on the Roof*. It provided a locus for American Jews to idealize as an insular haven where Jews had the freedom to pursue their own language, their own lifestyle, and their own culture. We all know that no shtetl was comprised entirely of Jews, but in the popular imagination, as it developed in America beginning in the 1940s, the shtetl was just that—an isolated place where Jews were not "othered" by the majority population and therefore did not take on any kind of racial identity. Jews in these fictionalized shtetls were racially neutralized for American Jews even as they embodied the "complete pattern of [Jewish] life," as Glazer put it.

Rachel Kranson has argued that interest in the shtetl spiked during the postwar period because it operated as a kind of anti-suburb, the opposite of the kind of prosperous, privileged existence that had deprived the Jews of their impetus to build alliances and communities beyond the synagogue. Furthermore, it served to reactivate the repressed ethnicity of the Jews who had fled to the suburbs. She points out:

> The tendency to idealize the shtetl reached new levels of poignancy after the Holocaust wreaked its abrupt and complete destruction of Jewish life as it had existed in Eastern Europe. In fact the word shtetl did not enter common English parlance until 1949 when the YIVO Annual of Jewish Social Science translated and published Abraham Ain's 1944 study of the Belorussian town of Swislocz. The translator's decision to retain the Yiddish world shtetl instead of translating it into English offered American Jews a new vocabulary through which to commemorate the destroyed culture of East European Jews.[16]

While the shtetl as an emblem of East European Jewish life has been studied from the perspective of its fictionality, and its impossibly saccharine dimensions within the discourse and the literature of postwar America, it has not been probed for its role in the reclamation of an ethnic identity among American Jews. Rather than viewing it as a damaging token of American Jewry's limited and limiting imagination, it might be useful to consider the way in which representations of the shtetl—such as can be found in *Life Is with People*, *The Earth Is the Lord's*, and *The World of Sholem Aleichem*[17]—contributed to the reclamation of a de-racialized ethnic identity among American Jews after the Holocaust. It was the Holocaust, it seems, that created the need for American Jews to identify themselves with more than just a formal, religious Judaism. Their sense of loss and disorientation was palpable in the postwar years as they realized that they were the last remnant of a distinct culture, and not just one of the favored religions of their newfound home.

Riv Ellen Prell has questioned the rather elegiac tone employed in the popular writings of the immediate postwar period in America and echoed in the historical accounts of that time. She has challenged this narrative by pointing out that the shifting landscape of American Jewry during the postwar years did not necessarily reflect a denaturing of Jewishness as much as it reflected a redefinition of it. In an essay titled "Community and the Discourse of Elegy: The Postwar Suburban Debate," Prell states that the historical writing on the period under discussion echoes the discourse of the period itself:

> The mordant tone of much of the popular literature of this time has found its way into historical writing. What the historiography appears to share with the 1950s discourse about American Jewish viability is the inability to envision the extent to which change is organic to culture and how communities develop in response to those changes. The elegiac ode offers a language of nostalgia and limits the ability to envision a vital future.[18]

American Jewish popular discourse from the postwar period was, according to Prell, misplacing its anxiety over the Holocaust onto its own demographic patterns and community behaviors. Prell recommends that instead of accepting the truisms of the postwar period about the loss of Jewish authenticity with the move to the suburbs, we engage in the study of "cultural logics," or

> complex consideration of in what settings are American Jews made Jews? What must they do and with whom must they do it to become Jewish and American? What authenticates their experiences and what denies them?[19]

The cultural logics of the moment under investigation here demand that we ask specific questions concerning what American Jewry was thinking about its Judaism, its ancestry in Eastern Europe, and its future in America during the post-Holocaust period. What were Jews writing about East European Jewish culture in the aftermath of its destruction and what were they reading? What media seemed to dominate the post-Holocaust response of American Jews? I hope to engage in a kind of cultural logics instead of expanding the discourse of despondency and disappointment that seems to have dominated our understanding of the postwar period among American Jews.

Kranson, in her study of American prosperity during those years, has addressed the Jewish American self-perception at the time:

> While the preservation of an authentic Jewish culture in its encounter with a prosperous American society had long been a concern for American Jewish leaders, the genocide of European Jews during the Second World War intensified this impulse. After the vibrant Jewish communities of Europe had been annihilated in the Holocaust, they came to believe that the enormous responsibility of sustaining Jewish life and providing leadership for the rest of the Jewish world rested on their shoulders.[20]

In his 1954 history of American Jews, for example, Isaac Goldberg declared that the Jewish population of America had become "the most influential and also the largest in the world. The war made it a dominant factor in the destiny of the Jewish people as a whole."[21]

How did hybrid texts encourage American Jews in the post-Holocaust period to reclaim their "Jewishness," that broader ethnic category that takes into consideration a whole range of practices and norms? Through an exploration of a sampling of canonic hybrid texts from a range of periods in a range of genres, I ask the following questions: What role did these texts play in the construction of a post-Holocaust American-Jewish folk ethnography of pre-Holocaust East European Jewish life? What do we learn about the American Jewish community in the post-Holocaust years—its relationship to its East European Jewish past, its sense of the present in America, and the future—through its production and reception of these hybrid texts? Why do the texts become increasingly more focused on visual images over time, and what does that tell us about American Jewish textual literacy, linguistic proficiency in Jewish languages, and their attitude toward their own place within American culture? Rather than seeing the texts as a homogenous unit, can one see a progression in them, from the 1940s through the early 2000s? What can a literature scholar reading these texts closely accomplish that the historians and the sociologists of American Jewry do not?

In this study, we will be observing the shift from the second to the third generation—from the generation of the urban neighborhood to the generation that grew up in the suburbs. After the war, how did the third generation grapple with the fact that they did more but knew less? How do the texts presented here reflect the kinds of anxiety over literacy, and also the sense of security over upward mobility in that generation? And what does the relationship between the textual and the visual tell us about the nature of American Jewish ethnic identification as opposed to religious identification?

In his study of ethnicity in American culture, Werner Sollors uses literature as the primary text by which he develops his notion of the "invention" of an American ethnic literature.[22] In *Salvage Poetics*, through an analysis of the appearance of primary texts and commentaries in hybrid literature, I consider whether there is a uniquely post-Holocaust Jewish American ethnicity modeled on traditional Jewish textuality. The primary texts are the "artifacts," such as Yiddish literature, documentary photography, and programmatic essays, that provide a window into East European pre-Holocaust Jewish ethnicity, while the frame for those texts, written by American Jews for American Jews in terms that are comprehensible and comprehensive, reflect the hermeneutics of Jewish study. In other words, hybrid texts provide a folk ethnographic frame for texts from the Jewish "tradition" that help American Jews get a better sense of "a complete pattern of life" in an ethnic sense. I put "tradition" in quotation marks because the texts that are considered "traditional" in that generation tend to be modern texts—like Yiddish literature and documentary photographs—not religious texts such as the Torah, the Talmud, or the prayer book. These modern texts, as we will discuss at greater length in the body of *Salvage Poetics*, are pre-Holocaust texts of a particular sort. They themselves are highly self-conscious of the confrontation between tradition and modernity, as are American Jews. Since they are pre-Holocaust, however, they strike American Jews as being "traditional" and representative "artifacts" of the destroyed world. In translation, framed with narrative, and/or supplemented or wholly constituted by visual elements, these texts are construed as highly accessible to American Jews in the postwar era. At the same time, like traditional Jewish texts, they are layered with explanatory discourse that makes them feel authentically and ethnically Jewish.

Like Sollors, I see the invention of ethnicity (American Jewish ethnicity) as dependent in part on the cultural formations of American-Jewish literature—based on images of Jews in another time and place but framed by uniquely American concerns and projections in a traditional Jewish constellation. The ethnic American Jewish narratives of the early part of the twentieth century are based on an ambivalent disavowal of the past, as stated by Mary Antin in her introduction to *The Promised Land* (1912): "I was born, I have lived, and I have been made over . . ."[23] Sarah Wilson has written eloquently about the advantages of claiming a kind of Darwinian ethnic survival of the fittest among Jewish immigrant writers of Antin's generation.[24] By that logic, those Jews who made it through the Old Country and the process of immigration are clearly a better developed ethnic specimen than those who did not. They are adaptable and they can become exemplary Americans. But how does this disavowal of the past change in the post-Holocaust generations?

The texts we will study together here are part of the construction of a new kind of ethnic Jew, bridging the second and third generation of Jewish American immigrants. They represent the consolidation of ethnic categories for Jews in America by following the model of traditional Jewish textuality, of primary text and commentary. Their hybrid nature, as we will discuss, is a sign of engagement with matters of Jewish literacy, of the anxiety prevalent despite the seeming healthiness of the community in those years—redefining the terms of ethnic identification, without its racial implications, and Judaizing it to whatever extent possible, in the process.

AN INTRODUCTION TO SALVAGE POETICS

Anecdotes, Artifacts, Antidotes, and Art

How do American Jews know what they think they know about pre-Holocaust East European Jewish life? On what do they base their impressions, assumptions, and suppositions about the world destroyed in the Holocaust? This book explores how American-Jewish post-Holocaust writers, scholars, and editors adapt pre-Holocaust works, such as Yiddish fiction and documentary photography, for popular consumption, in the form of folk ethnography, with the hope of clarifying the role of East European Jewish identity in the construction of a post-Holocaust American one.

Understanding the particular "salvage poetics" that govern the ways in which pre-Holocaust East European Jewish experience is reconstituted from aesthetic artifacts of that world in a post-Holocaust American context is central to understanding the questions posed above. Salvage poetics are a series of framing devices wherein primary cultural materials in the form of text or image are mediated, translated, explicated, personalized, and/or valorized in an effort to create an accessible description of a lost culture. Salvage poetics represent a marriage of aesthetic and ethnographic impulses, a streamlining of popular desire on the part of an audience and specialized linguistic and cultural knowledge on the part of authors who seek to educate that audience. A variation on salvage poetics, for example, is readily identifiable in the 1971 Hollywood production of *Fiddler on the Roof* wherein a religious, Yiddish-speaking population in Eastern Europe before the war is presented to an audience with only one Yiddish word (*l'chaim*) and a general overview of two religious rituals (the Sabbath and a wedding). Based on the Yiddish stories of Sholem Aleichem (the pseudonym of Sholem Rabinowitz, 1859–1916), *Fiddler on the Roof* also articulates an important element of salvage poetics in that it appoints a literary text (the *Tevye the Milkman* stories, 1894–1914) as the basis for its bridge to an American public, translating it from Yiddish to English, from text to cinema, and even from a Russian sensibility to an American one.[1] Salvage poetics, therefore, as they are articulated in *Fiddler* can be summed up in the following way: First, they fulfill a popular desire to salvage a dead or dying world. Second, they base themselves on cultural "artifacts," in this case, literary, which are consciously and actively glossed, translated, and rendered accessible or "relatable" by transformative mediation of some variety or another.

Fiddler on the Roof is an ideal example of other aspects of salvage poetics as well, when we consider the genesis of the 1964 Broadway play from the perspective of its producer, Jerome Robbins, alongside its transformation from a text to a dramatic spectacle through the mediation of a variety of other visual articulations of East European Jewish experience. When asked in 1962 by Sheldon Harnick and Jerry Bock to direct a play that would be based on Sholem Aleichem's Tevye stories, Robbins overcame his sense of revulsion and alienation toward the world represented therein, and became excited at the possibility of doing a play about "our people." It "should really star my father," he said in his early correspondence about the project.[2] In anatomizing his disgust for Orthodox Jewry, and his indifference to the East European background from which his own immigrant parents had emerged, Jerome Robbins pointed to the experience of studying for his bar mitzvah with an Orthodox man who represented nothing of interest or relevance to him in Weehawken, New Jersey, where he grew up. His commitment to the project therefore was to some extent, a means of salvaging his own background, of revisiting it and reconciling himself to it.

Robbins's research on background for the play began with his "search for a photograph" that could define the world he felt that he needed to capture and become reconciled to—a world of infinite poverty and obsessive study, as he saw it.[3] Cornell Capa's 1955 *Hebrew Lesson* features a man in traditional Hasidic dress hovering over a table full of little boys, pointing to the texts that lay before them (figure I.1). This photograph became Jerome Robbins's muse. He hung *Hebrew Lesson* on the wall in his office (figure I.2), and it accompanied him throughout the journey that was to be the *Fiddler* phenomenon. Significantly, the photograph was taken in Brooklyn, New York, not in Eastern Europe. It testified to the revival of Hasidic communities largely decimated in Europe but transplanted bit by bit to the United States in the decades after the war. Said to be more of a reflection of the American audiences who celebrated it than the East European Jewish world featured in it, the fact that *Fiddler on the Roof* was directed by a man inspired by a picture of Hasidim taken in Brooklyn speaks profoundly to the fascinating interplay of American Jews and their fantasies about Jewish Eastern Europe during the postwar era.

Hebrew Lesson was only one of many visual "aids" that helped Robbins familiarize himself with what he perceived to be East European Jewry in order to direct what was to become the most widely disseminated and celebrated representation of pre-Holocaust East European Jewish experience in America and arguably the world. Nineteen fifty-five seems to have been the year of junctures between Sholem Aleichem and visual art, with Cornell Capa becoming the inspiration for the stage adaptation of his *Tevye the Milkman* stories as *Fiddler on the Roof*, and Marc Chagall as the inspiration for the image of the fiddler itself. The same year that the Capa photograph was made, Sholem Aleichem's autobiography, *The Great Fair*, was translated from Yiddish into English and published by the author's granddaughter, Tamara Kahana. The book featured a Chagall drawing as its frontispiece. Translating a Yiddish literary work whose charm and genius was comprised of intertextual faux pas, with Tevye pretending to be a Torah scholar while misquoting "the Holy Books" left and right, into a stage play in English might have been impossible had it not been for the replacement of the figure of Sholem Aleichem, Tevye's interlocutor in the short story

FIGURE I.1. *Hebrew Lesson.* Cornell Capa ©/Magnum Photos (1955).

FIGURE I.2. *Jerome Robbins, chorégraphe américain.* Henri Cartier-Bresson/ Magnum Photos (1960).

cycle, with a Fiddler who did not interact with Tevye at all, but served to punctuate the ethnographic rhythms of the play. Therefore, a play on words that would have been appreciated and recognized by Sholem Aleichem's first readers was replaced for an American audience unfamiliar with Yiddish, Torah, and Jewish liturgy—all the building blocks of Tevye's intertextual humor—by a visual marker, drawn from Chagall, of time's passage and of Jewish cultural institutions.

In educating his staff—his costume designer and lighting designer and others who had no acquaintance with Jewish life, Robbins had them view Albert Barry's 1960 film *Ghetto Pillow*. An overview of the "daily life and folk customs of East European Jewish ghettos," the film was organized around 215 watercolor paintings by Samuel Rothbort, a Lithuanian-born painter (1882–1971) who made his home in New York as a young man, immigrating in 1904. In addition to viewing *Ghetto Pillow* with them, Robbins purchased for his company and staff copies of Roman Vishniac's 1947 *Polish Jews*, a collection of images of East European Jews taken in the 1930s, which we will discuss in chapter 5.[4] On opening night, September 22, 1964, Robbins gave art books—either by Ben Shahn or Marc Chagall—to all the company members. To his art director, Boris Aronson, the Kiev-born son of a rabbi, the former art director of the Moscow art theater, and the author of a book on Chagall, Robbins gave a plant, with apologies.[5] Aronson had nothing to learn from Jewish art, Robbins felt, that he didn't already know. To Robbins, it seems, Jewish art and photography served to fill in the blanks left by the script of the play and the text of the original short story cycle upon which the play was based. For Americans seeking to bring those texts to life, visual representations of that world provided crucial context and flavor.

The visual expansions of Sholem Aleichem's literary text in order to produce it for the stage speak to the intersection of the visual and the textual that will be documented throughout *Salvage Poetics*, an exploration of the cross between ethnographic and literary texts that introduced East European Jewry to American Jews in the post-Holocaust period, from the 1940s through the turn of the twenty-first century. These hybrid texts facilitated American Jews' reclamation of their ethnic "Jewishness" as a reaction against what came to be known as the "protestantization" of American Jewish culture through its postwar emphasis on synagogue culture and identification with institutionally centered "Judaism." Maintaining their ethnic identity was an essential alternative to morphing into a community that viewed itself in strictly religious terms. To the minds of many sociologists of the moment and historians of a later one, this reacquaintance with an ethnic Jewish self required engagement with the artifacts and evidence of a fully ethnic Jewish past. For American Jewish authors, artists, and intellectuals, the only way to reach American Jews with an "authentic" representation of the world that had been destroyed during their own lifetimes, was to shower them with a variety of media that could reflect the richness and variety of an ethnic identity: fiction and photography and film and painting and drama all feeding off one another in order to create a comprehensive, multidimensional representation.

The "ethnic," as Jonathan Freedman points out, is a "space of category confusion and hybridizing reinvention";[6] it is, according to Werner Sollors, a dynamic process as opposed to a static product.[7] As we move through the texts, arranged here chronologically, that present the possibility of ethnic American Judaism to an audience of Jewish Americans, we see an increasing reliance on the visual over the textual. Indeed, Robbins did not do a deep study of Sholem Aleichem in order to produce *Fiddler*. Instead, he supplemented his own and his company's experience of Anatevka through visual props. So too, in our exploration of the hybrid texts presented here, do we witness a deep contextualization of the texts presented by images until the ratio of image to text switches by the turn of the twenty-first century. This is as much a testament to the lack of Jewish textual literacy of American Jews as to the abundance of visual literacy that they acquired in the course of the second half of the twentieth century.

Today, with the nearly complete shift to the visual in salvage poetics, we are witnessing a further shift, as demonstrated by the most recent incarnation of the *Fiddler* phenomenon. Since July 2018, a Yiddish production of *Fiddler on the Roof* has been produced in Yiddish by The National Yiddish Theater Folksbiene (NYTF) first off and then on Broadway. *Fidler afn Dakh* was written by the late Shraga Friedman and directed by Joel Grey (of *Cabaret* fame). The play's success speaks to a shift, I would argue, in the quest for Jewish ethnicity, "Jewishness," and the creation of a contemporary folk ethnography, in keeping with Jeffrey Shandler's notion of a "post-vernacular." Moving from fascination with images of East European life, to a fixation on the remnants of the language of East European Jewry, Jewish Americans today are identifying, for themselves, new artifacts of East European Jewish experience in the form of discourse and language. *Fiddler*, it seems, has become a comfortable, "traditional," and accessible frame for a new kind of artifact, the Yiddish language as specially tailored for an American Jewish audience that doesn't really know it but is eager to embrace it.

Having been watched and shared by several generations of the same family since it was first produced on Broadway in 1964, *Fiddler on the Roof* has become its own form of authentic Jewish "tradition" for Americans. The original language of the world it represents has now become the focus of popular fascination, and comprehensible not as an actual vernacular, but as a post-vernacular, signifying loss and cultural reclamation, and rendered accessible through various forms of mediation. The mediation that made this latest, and Yiddish, *Fiddler* accessible to a contemporary audience is translation texts on side panels, alongside the fact that the play was produced, directed, and performed by non-Yiddish speakers. Yiddish, therefore, it seems, need not be used only by the initiated. It can be deployed by the uninitiated and to "authentic" effect. Press coverage of the play emphasized that "this production [was] directed by Joel Grey who does not speak Yiddish, and performed by a cast of 26, three quarters of whom also do not speak the language."[8] According to Joseph Berger, the actors learned their Yiddish parts in "barely three weeks of Yiddish coaching and four weeks of rehearsals."[9]

Yiddish in the newest *Fiddler* has become the artifact, and the play the frame that gives the audience its contemporary context; because *Fiddler* has become a staple of the Jewish American imagination of East European Jewish life, it is no longer sufficient as a vehicle for folk ethnography by itself. It needs to contain something deeper, something more "authentic," and that thing is Yiddish. In this spirit, Alisa Solomon titled a review of the play in the English-language

Forward, "A 'Fiddler on the Roof' in Yiddish—The Way It Ought to Be."[10] But it is a uniquely American Yiddish, a Yiddish that Americans can assimilate—a post-vernacular Yiddish that is unthreatening in its grammar and its vocabulary. It is a Yiddish that can be translated and performed on the stage by those for whom the language is appropriately foreign, connecting its performers to its viewers, its audience to its purveyors, and building a new bridge between the world destroyed in Europe and the world of American Jewry trying, in the latest generation, to connect to that world.

Salvage poetics are not an invention of the post-Holocaust period. Martin Buber's work of collecting, translating, and adapting Hasidic tales serves as an excellent model for the types of salvage poetics we will document and analyze here. Beginning in 1907 and extending until the end of his life, Martin Buber (1878–1965) published translations and commentaries on the anecdotes, legends, and epigraphs of the Hasidim. By most accounts, Buber's work on the Hasidim, spanning the bulk of six decades and translated into numerous languages, served as the single most important introduction to Hasidism for the uninitiated. In his introduction to one of his later collections of Hasidic anecdotes, translated in 1947 as *Tales of the Hasidim: The Early Masters*, Buber describes his process of mediation as translator and editor of the stories he collected:

> One like myself, whose purpose it is to picture the *zaddikim* [righteous leaders] and their lives from extant written (and some oral) material, must above all, to do justice simultaneously to legend and to truth, supply the missing links in the narrative. In the course of this long piece of work I found it most expedient to begin by giving up the available form (or rather formlessness) of the notes with their meagerness or excessive detail, their obscurities and digressions, to reconstruct the events in question with the utmost accuracy (wherever possible, with the aid of variants and other relevant material), and to relate them as coherently as I could in a form suited to the subject matter. Then, however, I went back to the notes and incorporated in my final version whatever felicitous turn of phrase they contained.[11]

Through the medium of his adapted Hasidic tales, Buber sought to transmit and to "salvage" for popular audiences a model of spirituality and a way of life that could serve as an antidote to the ravages of modernity within the German Jewish community. He viewed Hasidic tales as "anecdotes" that express Hasidic belief and depended exclusively on these tales for his presentation of a wide range of philosophical and cultural essays on Hasidism. Working with un-stylized and sometimes oral materials drawn exclusively from Hasidic anecdotes rather than from more formally textualized and canonized Hasidic philosophical and theological treatises, such as the *Toledoth Yaacov Yosef* (1780) or the *Maggid Devarav La'Yaakov* (1810), does present a dilemma, which Buber addresses elsewhere.[12] But because he believed the legends of the Hasidim would be more accessible and have a more powerful effect on the general reader, he became a "filter," he says, for raw materials drawn from the legendary and the mythical narratives of Hasidism, and not the philosophical or theological treatises that flowered during the first several generations of Hasidic masters. He chose his primary texts carefully and deliberately excluded anything not "anecdotal," anything that was not a "little story" from the mix. Buber's description of his process of filtering—his identification, translation, adaptation, and mediation of a particular aesthetic form as the catalyst for the renewal of Jewish identity and spirituality in a post-Enlightenment moment serves as a good starting point for our discussion of salvage poetics.

The process Buber describes is one of "do[ing] justice" to a particular group of texts and "supply[ing] missing links." To do so, Buber suggests above, he found it necessary to "giv[e] up the available form" or to rectify what he parenthetically refers to as the "formlessness" of those narratives in order to "reconstruct" the events behind the narratives as accurately and as coherently as possible. Buber's unique articulation of his process of mobilizing, translating, and adapting a particular set of texts in order to turn them into a palatable literary form for the purposes of rejuvenating the spiritual lives and Jewish identity of a generation of German Jews in the first part of the twentieth century sets the stage for a similar development among American Jews a generation later, after the Holocaust. Buber treats Hasidic stories as an essential artifact of Jewish spirituality to be adapted at whatever formal cost to the original, granting German readers, with their particular aesthetic and modern sensibilities, access to them.

The Jews of Europe had, throughout the twentieth century, been aware of the decline of traditional Jewish folkways, in particular due to mass migration and to the shifting borders and destruction of World War I. Jews in confrontation with modernity were encouraged to become collectors, documenters, and preservers of traditional Jewish experience in service to the creation of a modern, secular Jewish art. Buber was not the first European Jew at the beginning of the twentieth century to seek out an artifact of traditional Jewish culture that could turn the tide of Jewish assimilation in Europe, from a cultural if not a religious perspective. Chaim Nachman Bialik (1873–1934), M. Y. Berdischevsky (1865–1921), and Louis Ginzberg (1873–1953), working like Buber with literary texts, engaged in anthology projects aimed, in different ways, at preserving Talmudic, biblical, or Hasidic narratives and modernizing them for consumption in Modern Hebrew or German, primarily by secular Jews.[13] Efforts to bridge tradition and modernity were also evident among ethnographers of Jewish culture at the turn of the twentieth century. The best known, S. Ansky (pen name of Shloyme Zanvil Rappaport, 1863–1920), most famously (and rather belatedly) sought a way, on his 1912–14 ethnographic expeditions throughout Podolia and Volhynia, to collect folklore, folk songs, ritual objects, and images, among thousands of other ethnographic artifacts, in order to help contemporary Jews find "authentic" Jewish models for a modern Jewish art.[14] European auto-ethnographic and folk ethnographic work also influenced the Jewish community. In particular, the *landkantenesch* movement, which encouraged individuals to acquaint themselves with the provincial towns they or their forebears had left behind, motivated YIVO to introduce contests in 1926 and 1929 to see how many artifacts, photographs, and stories of their European origins American Jews could produce for archiving at YIVO.[15]

Buber, with his appointment of Hasidic tales and anecdotes as the antidote to assimilation, and Ansky, with his quest for artifacts that could inspire modern Jews to reclaim their cultural roots, are the authorizing spirits for this exploration of salvage poetics in the work of Americans in the post-Holocaust period. The juncture of ethno-graphic and literary concerns articulated in the juxtaposition of these two early twentieth-century advocates for the marriage of traditional Jewish culture and modern Jewish experience provides us with a strong foundation for mapping out the discourse of salvage poetics. In what follows, I will present a particular moment in Buber's intellectual history as a jumping-off point for our discussion. I focus particularly on Buber because of the singularity of his artifact pool for purposes of spiritual and cultural reconstruction. Although Ansky's ethnographic project is important in helping us to characterize the moment, it is Buber's method of adopting and adapting Hasidic tales that is of pri-mary interest here as we begin to consider a parallel American devel-opment in a later period.

According to Ran HaCohen, "Buber successfully changed the image of Hasidism from the incarnation of superstition and oriental backwardness ... into a literarily presentable phenomenon, by dress-ing it in the state of the art neo-romantic, later expressionistic lan-guage and style."[16] Buber created a new literary genre out of early literary materials in order to, in his own words, "restore a great buried heritage of faith to the light."[17] To do so, he claimed, he needed to "recapture a sense of the power that once gave it the capacity to take hold of and vitalize the life of diverse classes of people."[18] Gershom Scholem, in a well-known scathing 1961 response to Buber's treat-ment of Hasidism, asserts:

> Buber's influence is not hard to account for ... Buber has a deep
> and penetrating mind which not only admires intuition in others
> but has it at its own command. The earnest manner in which a
> writer of such literary refinement and intellectual subtlety pro-
> pounded what to him seemed the very soul of Hasidism could
> not fail to produce a deep impression on our generation.[19]

Buber, according to Scholem, is the cipher through which moderns have accessed Hasidism, and his primary source material was Hasidic anecdote, legend, and epigraph. In something of a tongue-in-cheek manner, Scholem acknowledges Buber's important role as a well-known philosopher and scholar in creating a field of neo-Hasidic discourse among moderns. The man Buber played as much of a role in the revolution in Hasidic thought as the texts themselves. Buber's mediation was as important, if not more, than the inherent value of the texts themselves.

Buber's approach to Hasidic anecdote, legend, and epigraph developed and changed over the course of his work with the material. In his earlier work, such as his *The Legend of the Ba'al Shem* (1907), Buber took short, orally inflected anecdotes and fleshed them out significantly, weaving them into a highly formalized narrative fabric; however, his later anthologies, such as *Tales of the Hasidim* (1947), retain the brevity and the atomization of different narratives built around original, oral Hasidic anecdotes upon which the transcription, translation, and adaption were based. Of the transformation—from the impulse to streamline and embellish to the impulse to retain the fragmentation and the oral register of the original tales—Buber says:

> Only some time after the original German edition appeared in 1907 was a stricter binding imposed on the relation which I had as an author to the tradition of the Hasidic legends—a binding that bid me reconstruct the intended occurrence of each individual story, no matter how crude and unwieldly it was in the form in which it had been transmitted to us.[20]

Thus Buber acknowledges his original impulse to change, as much as possible, the raw material of the rather un-stylized traditional tales in order to better accommodate a modern literary audience concerned as much with form as with content. Also acknowledged, however, is his later ambivalence over those choices. Awareness of the considerable responsibility that he must accept as mediator of these works seems to have become a larger part of his consciousness later in his career.

When Scholem, as quoted above, acknowledges the influence of Buber on the popular sense of Hasidism, he does so within an essay whose main purpose is to seriously criticize what he perceives to be Buber's ahistoric and philosophically unbalanced approach to Hasidism, fostered primarily by his exclusive selection of myths and anecdotes as his source materials.

But while Buber's magnetic attraction primarily to the narrative and mythic components of Hasidic culture was the very thing that set Scholem's teeth on edge, Buber himself was highly critical of the trend among German Jewish youth to valorize the East European Jew on the basis of what he perceived to be a rather impressionistic sense of that world. In 1919, he issued this warning:

> [Youth] must no longer permit itself the illusion that it can establish a decisive link to its people merely by reading Bialik's poems or by singing Yiddish folksongs, nor by the addition of a few quasi-religious sentiments and lyricism . . . something bigger is at stake . . . one must join, earnest and ready for much struggle and work, in Judaism's intense creative process . . . one must recreate this process from within.[21]

In this statement Buber was responding, according to Steven Aschheim, to the fact that the cult of the *Ostjude*, a German Jewish fascination with East European Jews, was "more a mood, a literary feeling, than an attempt to establish real contact with the ghetto masses and put into practice theoretical notions of East-West Jewish symbiosis."[22] Buber stands accused by Scholem of the very thing that Buber attempted to rectify earlier in the century in his own deep engagement not simply with the "sense" of a culture, but in the creative process of that culture through his embrace and adaptation of Hasidic narratives. Because Buber was inclined almost exclusively toward Hasidic tales and anecdotes, Scholem was highly critical of Buber's claim to represent the culture as a whole.

Several strands of the Buber-Scholem controversy over the representation of Hasidism to popular audiences are relevant to our discussion of salvage poetics. Buber's inclination not only to interpret but also to embrace, adapt, and reconfigure the narratives of the Hasidim for modern literary consumption is very much in keeping with the work of the writers, photographers, and scholars, all purveyors of salvage poetics, that we will focus on here. These writers, like Buber in their choice of textual or visual artifacts as the basis for their own variations on the East European Jewish legacy for American Jews, articulate an interest in participating in the unfolding of an important Jewish narrative of modernization. Lucy Dawidowicz writes:

> Tradition, Talmud, piety—these are both the stereotype and the reality. Tradition, Talmud, piety are the heritage that East European Jewry passed on to the Jews of America and in Israel. But they are only part of the reality of East European Jewish life and culture, and only part of the heritage bequeathed to us. There was also another reality and another heritage—the experience of Jewish modernity as it worked itself out in Eastern Europe and as it was transmitted to subsequent generations.[23]

In fact, like Buber, the work of all the authors we will discuss have this in common: they are trying to create a new Jewish narrative for post-Holocaust American Jewry out of pre-Holocaust materials—just as Buber created a post–East European Jewish Enlightenment narrative out of pre-Enlightenment artifacts—in order to both salvage those materials and also to create a modern, "authentically" Jewish articulation of Jewish traditions. Like Buber, all the writers and compilers of the texts we will be studying in depth recognize their own crucial role as mediators of the artifacts they have elected as a basis for their salvage poetic texts. Also like Buber, they have some concerns about the propriety of their adaptations; the intensity of their role in mediating the text for an American readership; and the impossibility, in the final analysis, of ever entering the world they represent sufficiently to actually meet their audiences in a comfortable place. Finally, the hermeneutics of reading traditional texts implied in Buber's style of adapting Hasidic tales will prove important to our overview of the post-Holocaust American Jewish style of adapting pre-Holocaust works because many of the authors presented here adopt hermeneutics intrinsic to the very works they adapt in order to meld their voices and their texts with those earlier works. In so doing, they hope to minimize what they perceive to be a significant gap between the primary, pre-Holocaust "artifacts," be they textual or visual, that are mobilized in salvage poetic texts, and the salvage poetic texts themselves. In other words, the frame and their content are often forcibly married through hermeneutic means.

Some of the works we will explore together have been accused of "falsifying" East European Jewish experience, rendering it puerile or overly simplistic, in an attempt to memorialize and make accessible the lost world of pre-Holocaust European Jewry. However, I would argue that the salvage poetic impulses underlying the reframing, retelling, and embellishments of which their authors have been accused, are all closely related to Buber's own deeply thoughtful yet largely emotional and autobiographically inflected investment in Hasidic stories. In an essay, "My Way to Hasidim," Buber invokes early childhood visits to his grandfather in Bukovina:

> In my childhood I spent every summer on an estate in Bukovina. There my father took me with him at times to a nearby village of Sadagora . . . I realized at that time, as a child, in the dirty village of Sadagora from the "dark" Hasidic crowd that I watched—as a child realizes such things, not as thought, but as image and feeling—that the world needs the perfected man and that the perfected man is none other than the true helper . . . The palace of the rebbe, in its showy splendor, repelled me. The prayer house of the Hasidim with its enraptured worshipers seemed strange to me. But when I saw the rebbe striding through the rows of the waiting, I felt, "leader" and when I saw the Hasidim dance with the Torah, I felt "community." At that time there rose in me a presentiment of the fact that common reverence and common joy of soul are the foundations of genuine human community.[24]

Reminiscent of the way that Hasidic anecdotes best served Buber's sense of the needs of his German Jewish community and his own personal need to revisit the Hasidic court of his childhood, so too did certain textual and visual "artifacts" of pre-Holocaust East European Jewish life serve the needs of various post-Holocaust artists, writers, and scholars as they sought to bridge the pre-Holocaust East European Jewish world to the post-Holocaust American one.

The authors of the works we will explore in this study of salvage poetics were working quite self-consciously within a folk ethnographic Jewish continuum representing a new stage of Jewish folk ethnography that began in Europe before World War II. Whereas in Europe and in America in the 1920s Jews could still produce artifacts, stories, traditions, and documents from their own contact with the world under investigation, the period after the war, beginning in the mid-1940s, was one of geographic and temporal distance from Eastern Europe that had never before been experienced by Jews of East European origins. Maurice Samuel was among the first to respond to that reality, producing a series of folk ethnographic texts based on the work of Sholem Aleichem (*The World of Sholem Aleichem*, 1943) and Y. L. Peretz (*Prince of the Ghetto*, 1947). Irving Howe and Eliezer Greenberg followed suit with their anthologization of Yiddish stories in their 1954 *Treasury of Yiddish Stories*, and, surprisingly, Mark Zborowski and Elizabeth Herzog's 1952 ethnography of East European Jewish life, *Life Is with People*, also based its understanding of that world on readings of Yiddish literature by many of the authors' informants. Other artifacts that serve as the basis for folk ethnographic "retellings" include Hasidic stories, as in the different versions of Abraham Joshua Heschel's *The Earth Is the Lord's* (1945–50), as well as photographs in the YIVO Archives, as published both in the 1977 anthology *Image before My Eyes* and the 1999 *Poyln*. Ideological, autobiographical, and historical essays are treated as pre-Holocaust artifacts by Lucy Dawidowicz in *The Golden Tradition* (1967), where she contextualizes them and reframes them to try to diffuse some of the unrealistic mists surrounding the adaptations of Yiddish literature that were so common in the early years after the Holocaust. Photographs taken by Roman Vishniac in Eastern Europe just before the war and reframed and reshaped as narrative in a series of image books after the war (1947 and 1983) serve as the most unusual example of salvage poetics explored here, being, as they are, artifacts created by Vishniac himself in the prewar period and then reframed in the postwar period.

As discussed in the fifth chapter of this study, Vishniac's East European photographic oeuvre, commissioned by the Joint Distribution Committee (JDC) from 1935 to 1938 to raise consciousness among American Jews about the impoverishment of the Jews of Europe after World War I, captured a culture already facing extinction due to internal forces of modernity as well as the external impact of war. After the

Holocaust it was not hard for Vishniac to reframe these photographs as a final farewell to a culture already on the brink of extermination because even before the war that culture was imploding. To further emphasize his prewar cognizance of the historical nature of his photographs, Vishniac chose after the war to frame his photographs as the work of the consummate insider, or a native informant. His tendency to demonstrate his "insider" status articulates a crucial trend in salvage poetic works, one we will revisit again and again throughout this study.

Highlighting the unique and complicated beauty of Vishniac's narrative implication of himself into the photographs he published in *A Vanished World* (1983), Laura Wexler points to a particular moment in Vishniac's captions that reproduces a folktale about a coach driver in Chelm, a fictional city (real, although rendered in fictional terms) populated by mythic fools who border on genius in their naivete and self-confidence.[25] In the caption to a photograph of a coach driver, Vishniac tells about a visit to his father's birthplace, Slonim. The coach driver meets him at the train station, takes him to an inn, and refuses payment, telling Vishniac that he will collect payment from him at the end of his trip when he takes Vishniac back to the train. Vishniac, as would anyone, expects the coachman to work in the interim days. But, in fact, at the end of his journey, the coachman informs him that he has waited for Vishniac during his entire visit in Slonim. When Vishniac tries to pay him only for his trips, the coachman, in Vishniac's words says:

> "For the trips, only for the trips, is that all?" I was astonished—what else had he done for me? He wrung his hands and wailed, "Who will pay for the freezing nights I waited? For the nights when nobody came, and for my suffering? My wife was sick and my child died. I had to borrow money for the tiny coffin."[26]

In reproducing this Chelm story, according to Wexler, Vishniac personalizes the photograph of the coachman. The literary vehicle he employs to accomplish this, however, draws attention to the fundamentally literary quality of the narrative he writes in his photographic captions to *A Vanished World*. Choosing an East European literary artifact, he salvages it, as it were, within the body of his text, while linking it to a photograph and a personal vignette. His is not a fictional gesture as much as it is a gesture toward fiction. Vishniac's captions, in cases such as this, are cognizant of their role in the work of salvaging not just photographs of a culture, but other artifacts as well—fiction included.

In the course of this project on salvage poetics I have frequently asked myself what the difference is between contemporary American Jewish fiction focused on East European Jewish life and the "hybrid" works, as coined by Barbara Kirshenblatt-Gimblett, combining literary sources and folk ethnographic aspirations, that characterize salvage poetic texts in post-Holocaust America. Historical fiction, for better or for worse, plays a significant role in American Jewry's understanding of East European Jewish pre-Holocaust existence. Contemporary American works of shtetl fiction written sometimes in a historical and sometimes in a magical realist vein—such as *Mazel* (1995) by Rebecca Goldstein, *Everything Is Illuminated* (2002) by Jonathan Safran Foer, *Small Worlds* (1996) by Alan Hoffman, or *Stories of an Imaginary Childhood* (1992) by Melvin Bukiet—operate in a fundamentally different manner than the hybrid salvage poetic texts we will explore here. In a discussion of contemporary shtetl fiction, Jeffrey Shandler argues:

> Contemporary works of shtetl fiction are all somehow self-consciously counterfactual; they knowingly play with shtetl literature's tropes as well as with what is known of the actuality of the East European Jewish past. The counterfactual turns in these works point up their artifice and, with it, a defining ambivalence. They are the contrivances of writers who only know the shtetl vicariously, for whom the shtetl exists as a literary topos.[27]

While many hybrid works base themselves on the same early shtetl literature as does contemporary shtetl fiction, hybrid works treat those early texts as primary texts, not tropes, as alluded to above by Shandler, and salvage works build an explanatory, ethnographic frame around those primary texts. The ambivalence, as described by Shandler, may very well remain, but the self-conscious artifice does not.

What characterizes salvage poetic texts as an unmistakable "hybrid" genre of their own, unifying literary as well as ethnographic impulses, is the way in which pre-Holocaust literary and other aesthetic works (such as photography, for instance) are deployed after the Holocaust in order to provide an opportunity for "thick description," a description of a culture that provides a rich context for what is observed, so as to enable outsiders to better comprehend it.[28] The concept of "thick description" belongs to Gilbert Ryle, a British philosopher, but it was significantly popularized within the field of ethnography by Clifford Geertz. In his well-known essay "Thick Description: Toward an Interpretive Theory of Culture," Geertz argues:

> ... doing ethnography is establishing rapport, selecting informants, transcribing texts, taking genealogies, mapping fields, keeping a diary, and so on. But it is not these things, techniques and received procedures, that define the enterprise. What defines it is the kind of intellectual effort it is: an elaborate venture in, to borrow a notion from Gilbert Ryle, "thick description."[29]

According to Geertz, ethnography is distinguished from other social sciences through its employment of "thick description." And since 1972 when this essay was first published, literary scholars have drawn on this notion of "thick description" to justify and methodologically describe cultural histories based on literary texts. Drawing from Erich Auerbach's famous notion of literary "anecdotes" as presented in *Mimesis* (1942), advocates of New Historicism have attempted to wed New Criticism, or the practice of close reading to the exclusion of any contextual information, with classic Historicism, using rich historical and biographical contextualizations and ethnography, through its notion of "thick description"; they argue certain elements of literary texts can open doors and windows onto a culture without excessive digression or a lack of textual engagement.[30]

The concept of "thick description" as a link between literary and ethnographic discourse helps us to better understand texts like the ones explored in this study that recycle earlier texts in order to approximate the ethnic spirit of a culture, facilitating the transmission of

"Jewishness" as opposed strictly to religious Judaism, in Nathan Glazer's sense. Through the creation of "hybrids" between primary textual or visual sources and folk ethnographic ambitions, these earlier texts function as artifacts, or "anecdotes" writ large, that allow for expansion and contextualization, for "thick description" of a culture. In this sense, the works we will explore, to my mind, engage in ethnographic interventions as opposed to historical ones; whereas historical works need not be self-conscious about their representation of a world destroyed in ways that try to salvage what can still be salvaged in the aftermath of its destruction, "hybrid" texts do just that. They draw on earlier texts as artifacts of a culture, if not its sum total, that provide opportunities for glossing, exegesis, and explication in ways that can bring foreign worlds together. The need for linguistic and cultural translation, the need to bridge the gaps between the original literary and often intertextual context for those works and their new American Jewish readership, is what makes these adaptations ethnographic as opposed to historic.

Ethnography, as the study of culture, is the principle at work in the expansions and adaptations of pre-Holocaust fiction, photography, essays, and memoirs in the immediate post-Holocaust era. The texts explored in this book are texts that are being redeployed, reread, or "repurposed" in order to, in Maurice Samuel's words, "spread information on Jewish history, Jewish literature, Jewish folkways and Jewish thought."[31] Through translation and contextualization, through the creation of a narrative in which post-Holocaust authors become cocreators of pre-Holocaust works, writers like Samuel, photographers like Vishniac, and philosophers like Heschel, among the others we will be exploring, hope to build a bridge between American Jewry and East European Jewry; they hope to make the Jews of Europe less "other" to the Jews of the United States in the years immediately following the Holocaust.

As an academic discipline, ethnography has prioritized the study of human community and interaction and has downplayed the importance of literacy tools, particularly in the study of nonprint literate cultures. However, when considering Jewish culture, ethnographers such as Jonathan Boyarin and Harvey Goldberg have both argued that Jewish culture is text, not metaphorically, in the sense famously expounded by Clifford Geertz, but actually.[32] Karin Barber, in *The Anthropology of Texts*, has pointed out that it is "rather unusual for anthropological inquiry to treat literature as a key diagnostic device."[33] But in order to understand Jewish culture in large part, from ancient times to the present, you have to understand its relationship to texts as the origin of Jewish law, practice, exegesis, and literacy. While Jewish texts, just as in any literate culture, may not encompass the whole of Jewish experience in what they represent, their centrality to Jewish culture as the basis of Jewish praxis and Jewish discourse is fundamental. The everyday history of ancient Judaism is being written in part by Talmudic and biblical scholars as well as by archeologists working from Talmudic and biblical texts on the ground in the Middle East. There is no question that despite legitimate concerns about the historicity of those texts, as well as their elitist nature, one cannot possibly engage in the history of the Jews without a serious consideration of the Bible, the Talmud, and the whole rabbinic corpus that grew out of them.

For American Jews trying to find a way to communicate East European Jewish culture to popular audiences, Yiddish literature, for example, took on the role of the Bible and the Talmud as a sacred text that could serve as not just a representation of but an artifact of East European Jewish culture in the absence of traditional Jewish literacy in America.[34] American Jews, it seems, particularly during the post-Holocaust period, naturally sought out texts that could provide the substance of an ethnographic portrait in order to model for themselves the possibility of a return to a Jewish ethnic status in a generation of Jews without "Jewishness." Yiddish literature mediated by writers such as Maurice Samuel enabled American Jews to assimilate the "other" within themselves, to better understand those Jews they, in the best case scenario, found so foreign. Throughout *The World of Sholem Aleichem*, Samuel attempts to describe East European Jewry according to terms and categories that American Jews might comprehend.

In teaching students to write, I discouraged their use of the term "relatability" for many years. The term bothered me because it seemed an awkward and unsophisticated way to articulate the way in which texts find ways to speak directly to their audiences. However, in writing this book, it has become abundantly clear to me that the term "relatability," with its vernacular overtones and its clear articulation of the power of a text to connect, or not connect, with its readers, is the perfect term to describe the ultimate challenge of salvage poetics. Many authors of the works presented in this study were urgently and emergently, in the aftermath of the Holocaust, concerned with the relatability of their texts. They wanted to use whatever skills and artifacts were at their disposal to build a connection between their American audience and their East European coreligionists, either as a form of memorial or as a form of identity and nation building. To use Benedict Anderson's well-known formulation, it became crucial in the post-Holocaust era to build an "imagined community" for American Jews that included the now-defunct East European Jewish community, because so much of who they were and what they could become, Jewishly, spiritually, and communally, grew out of that far-distant world.[35] In a similar vein, it became crucial, outside of the urban strongholds of Jewish ethnicity enjoyed by Jews in earlier generations, to reinvent a Jewish ethnicity for the suburban third generation. The relatability of the texts we will explore together was designed to heighten that "imagined community" or that "invented ethnicity" that stretched from Eastern Europe to America for American Jews.

Perhaps the best example of a text that strives for relatability among those we will be exploring together is Maurice Samuel's *The World of Sholem Aleichem*. According to Cynthia Ozick, "through his writings and lectures [Samuel] became the voice of self-affirming American Jewry and a pre-eminent shaper of Jewish values among English speaking Jews the world over."[36] John Murray Cuddihy described him as "the great historian of the shtetl and of East European Jewry,"[37] and Harold U. Ribalow wrote that he could not think of a single English-language writer who had enriched Jewish literature as Samuel had done. He said that "it was Maurice Samuel's pioneering studies that prepared the way for the spate of notable expositions of East European Jewish culture that followed, from *Life Is with People* to *The Joys of Yiddish* and *Fiddler on the Roof*."[38] In light of our discussion of salvage poetics, the most important critical statement about Samuel's works was made by the ethnographer of American Jewish life,

Barbara Kirshenblatt-Gimblett, in "Imagining Europe: The Popular Arts of American Jewish Ethnography"; she wrote that his *The World of Sholem Aleichem* was a "hybrid" text, or a text that articulates the intersecting concerns and styles of literary and ethnographic writing.[39] In this essay, she points in particular to Samuel's *The World of Sholem Aleichem*, a gloss on pre-Holocaust East European Jewry based on the fiction of Sholem Rabinowitz (or "Sholem Aleichem"). "In *The World of Sholem Aleichem*," Kirshenblatt-Gimblett says, "Samuel fashioned a hybrid genre that mediates between literature and ethnography, between retelling the Tevye stories and providing an ethnographic gloss on them."[40] It was this observation of Kirshenblatt-Gimblett that served as the seed for this exploration of salvage poetics. How, I wondered, would a literary approach to a text described as "hybrid" change our perception not only of American Jewish responses to the Holocaust but also of the study of folk ethnography in a post-Holocaust universe? *The World of Sholem Aleichem* exemplifies the way in which, from the middle of the twentieth century and forward, literary texts became the main venue for American Jews to reconstruct the world of their East European forebears; and it is crucial, it seems to me, to understand this dynamic from a literary perspective that takes ethnographic concerns into consideration but is not limited by them.

While Samuel's book marked the debut of "hybrid" works, or marriages between folk ethnography and literary consciousness, Herzog and Zborowski's work marked the transformation of ethnography into a popular medium for American Jewish audiences. More succinctly, when an anthropologist like Barbara Kirshenblatt-Gimblett identifies "ethnographic" overtones in a work like Abraham Joshua Heschel's *The Earth Is the Lord's*, as she does in "Imagining Europe," she does so because *Life Is with People* (1952) established American Jewish ethnography as a popular art in its own right.[41] This is not to say that *Life Is with People* influenced Heschel. On the contrary, Heschel's text was published first. Rather, Kirshenblatt-Gimblett's observation comes out of several decades during which American Jews had grown accustomed to reading ethnography in places where ethnographers did not place their work, beginning with the surprisingly popular *Life Is with People*. Suddenly it became possible for nonanthropologists to be writing ethnographies of the lost culture because formal ethnographies themselves, like *Life Is with People*, had been authored by nonanthropologists and were viewed among popular audiences as culturally definitive. We will discuss Heschel's essay at greater length in the second chapter of this study, but this allusion to Barbara Kirshenblatt-Gimblett's 1991 essay is apt here because that essay indeed represents the germination of my concept of post-Holocaust folk ethnographies based on the fiction and images of pre-Holocaust East European Jewish life.

In "Imagining Europe," Kirshenblatt-Gimblett lists many of the major works explored in this book, by Samuel, Vishniac, and Heschel, among others, and refers to them as examples of the "popular arts of American Jewish ethnography."[42] Early in this project I wondered why she didn't simply call them examples of "popular ethnography," and I surmised, through years of research and writing, that popular ethnography is considered, among anthropology professionals, the formal study of a culture by nonprofessionals. It is not, as I originally thought, the imposition of ethnographic values on a non-ethnographic work. Hence, the "popular arts of ethnography" in Kirshenblatt-Gimblett's title as opposed to "popular ethnography," because most of the works she points to are not written or composed for ethnographic purposes as much as they are received in that vein. In her essay Kirshenblatt-Gimblett suggests that certain works (Samuel's, Heschel's, Bella Chagall's, and others) may not constitute popular ethnographies within ethnographic circles, but serve as ethnographies within popular circles; they began as cultural descriptions with aesthetic or other aspirations (not necessarily ethnographic), but they evolved into folk ethnographies because of their historical moment as well as their particular poetics. This is to be distinguished, of course, from the study of folklore, which is defined by the *Oxford English Dictionary* as "the study of traditional beliefs, legends, or customs current among the common people."[43] In my use of the term "folk ethnography" what is of interest is not the study of traditional beliefs and customs by professional ethnographers, but the informal study of traditional beliefs and customs of a culture by a popular audience or by scholars and writers in fields other than anthropology who are addressing a popular audience. My choice of the term "folk ethnography" rather than "popular ethnography" or "popular folklore" in this study is based on the idea of folk ethnography as an ethnography conducted by the folk in order to better understand the self. The works upon which I focus here are designed to build a bridge between pre-Holocaust East European Jewish culture and a post-Holocaust American audience as a means of encouraging that audience to better understand their own ethnic identities as American Jews.

The effect I was searching for throughout this project was a shifting understanding of what constitutes ethnographic materials in the face of a historical rupture. The Holocaust, in other words, forced the hand of many writers, scholars, and even painters and photographers to seek out ways to create a portrait of a culture, not for use by ethnographers, but for use by popular audiences, for a "folk" in need of ways to assimilate their sense of self with their sense of loss. Therefore, salvage poetics are to be understood as working toward a kind of "folk ethnography" or an ethnography created outside the world of professional anthropology.

As articulated by Jack Kugelmass, "folk ethnography is different from the purely intellectual pursuits and speculation of academic ethnography. It exists not to advance human knowledge but to focus group understanding of the self and thereby reinforce the cohesiveness of the population that sponsors it and consumes it."[44] In further defining "folk ethnography" in the American Jewish community, Kugelmass writes,

> American Jewish folk ethnography takes several distinct forms: the first is tourism; the second, which is closely related to the first, is the creation—and more typically, vicariously, the ownership— of these and similar coffee-table books; a third is humorous writing and stand-up comedy.[45]

I would venture to add to this categorization of folk ethnographic forms all those works that employ salvage poetics. Events such as the

Holocaust create the necessity for salvage poetics, serving, in Barthe-sian photographic parlance, as the "punctum" that turns a literary text, photograph, essay, or painting into an artifact for folk ethnographic purposes.[46] I am indebted to Jack Kugelmass in his formulation of Jew-ish folk ethnographies for giving me a term that I could use instead of "popular ethnographies" or "popular folklore" and thereby avoid the pitfalls of slipping into the parlance of professional anthropolo-gists. More importantly, he helped me identify a term that is reflex-ive, focused on the work of constructing a sense of self, community, and history for the Jewish population of East European provenance in post-Holocaust America.

My notion of salvage poetics as a concept grew out of the dis-crepancy I discerned between the kinds of observations Kirshenblatt-Gimblett was making as a professional anthropologist and the kinds of questions I was asking about the texts Kirshenblatt-Gimblett had led me to investigate: How do some texts come to be understood by popular audiences as comprehensively descriptive of a culture while others do not? Why do some creative works become linked in the pop-ular imagination with the sum total of a culture?

Bronislaw Malinowski, popularly considered the father of social anthropology, spoke of the disappearance of the ethnographic object at its moment of recognition: "ethnology is in a sadly ludicrous, not to say tragic position in that at the very moment when it begins to put its workshop in order . . . the material of study melts away with hopeless rapidity . . . dy[ing] away under our very eyes."[47] In a similar fashion, modern Yiddish literature's favorite and most popular subject—the shtetl—was designated as such at the turn of the twentieth century because it was in the process of disappearing. Therefore, the very lit-erature that immortalized the world of the shtetl is recycled in the post-Holocaust era as an artifact not only of its existence but also its disappearance. "Salvage" implies extinction and therefore those aes-thetic materials that operate as artifacts within a salvage poetic econ-omy are necessarily attuned to the extinction of their subject matter.

Salvage poetics arise out of the post-Holocaust deployment of aes-thetic works either produced in the pre-Holocaust period or based on memories of the pre-Holocaust period, by individuals who themselves are straddling several different worlds. In his fiction Sholem Rabinovitch, for example, living in a Russian Jewish upper-middle-class milieu in the metropolis of Odessa, with (more than) one foot outside of traditional Jewry, channels his voice through the character of Sholem Aleichem in order to bring his readers back into the rural shtetl while maintaining some critical and literary distance from it. His literary skill enabled him to create a vernacular voice that spoke to Jews who had left that world behind, whether religiously, geographically, or politically, and gave them a sense of recognition and familiarity, of simultaneously belonging and not belonging, of remembering the world but having moved beyond it. That dynamic tension—between the artist and his subject matter, between Sholem Aleichem as an insider conversing intimately with Tevye and as an outsider who can write down Tevye's story with an eye toward its novelty as an articulation of a culture facing extinction—is what makes Sholem Aleichem's stories so compelling in a post-Holocaust salvage context. His works are always already grappling with the inevitable extinction of the culture they embody.

In addition to the fiction we will discuss at length throughout this study, Elizabeth Edwards has pointed out that "much writing and practice of photography in anthropology in the late nineteenth and early twentieth centuries clusters around concerns with disappearance, presence and absence and the seen and the unseen."[48] In keeping with this, I argue here that image books are the most effective model of the dynamics and the impact of salvage poetics in American Jewish hybrid works. Of all the "artifacts" that constitute the basis for hybrid works, images provide the clearest, most concise, and most accessible channel for communicating the relationship between the art and culture of present and past in a post-Holocaust American Jewish milieu that seeks to understand its origins in East European Jewish communities before the war. Image books, which render East European pre-Holocaust Jewish life not exclusively in language, bypass the linguistic challenges presented by American Jews' generalized lack of literacy in the Jewish and European languages (Yiddish, Hebrew, Polish, Russian, German, etc.) that were so essential to East European Jewish experience. Even books that "translate" fiction into ethnic terms, such as

Life Is with People or *The World of Sholem Aleichem*, require intense mediation to compensate for their American audience's lack of Jewish literacy, on a linguistic as well as a cultural level. While image books also require some mediation by the photographer and the painter as well as the book's editor in order to contextualize an archive of what could be construed as rather disconnected or arbitrary artifacts, the visual's pretense to realism, its alleged correspondence with real-life referents, creates an impression of direct and unmediated expression. We conclude our discussion of salvage poetics by focusing on image books, which play a critical role in American Jewish folk ethnography. As articulated above, and as will be teased out throughout this study with each text progressively explored here, there is an increasing reliance on the visual, first as a supplement to text, and then as a replacement for text, in the hybrid works we are discussing. As authors sought to reinforce Jewish ethnicity, or Jewishness as opposed to Judaism, among the post-Holocaust generation, they came to define a new kind of "Yiddish" or "Hebrew" texts for their readers. Whereas Cynthia Ozick considers English the "new Yiddish" for American writers, tracing these hybrid works of salvage poetics here, I would argue that a "new Yiddish" in the construction of a post-Holocaust folk ethnography of pre-Holocaust East European Jewish life is the image. Drawing on Riv Ellen Prell's call for "cultural logics" which acknowledge the conditions for change and adaptation within the America Jewish community, the prevalence of images as articulations of a "new Yiddish" respects the fact that American Jews, over the course of the second half of the twentieth century, grew more and more distant from the kinds of Jewish literacy and linguistic fluencies that would have been required of them to try to approach ethnic "artifacts" on their own. Therefore, as images were incorporated more frequently into the hybrid texts we will be discussing, we can trace the movement away from a certain kind of textual literacy and into a kind of visual literacy enjoyed by American Jews as an arsenal and archive of images grew common. I would also suggest that basing a renewed sense of Jewish ethnicity or "Jewishness" on images as opposed to texts allows American Jews to feel less dependent on mediators to furnish them with the kind of exposure to the texture of their past that will facilitate that process. Photographs, paintings, and drawings, whether or not they really are, feel more immediate and more readily available to an audience across an ocean, time, and cataclysm than do words.

All the chapters of this study focus on the term "salvage," in recognition of the salvage poetics at the heart of each author's selection of "artifacts" on which to base his or her text. The term "selvedge" in the title of the first chapter, obviously a play on "salvage," refers to the particular way in which Maurice Samuel worked his way into the text, as the voice of Sholem Aleichem, the pseudonym for Sholem Rabinowitz and the homodiegetic narrator of many of his works. In this chapter, we consider the role that narratology can play in the relatability of salvage poetic texts, and I posit that narratological divergences between Samuel's 1943 work on Sholem Aleichem and his 1947 work on Y. L. Peretz represent different kinds of "hybrid" texts. The Holocaust plays a significant role in the different way that Samuel comports himself as the first-person narrator in each text, given that *The World of Sholem Aleichem* came out before the full extent of the war was understood and *Prince of the Ghetto* after the Holocaust. In his treatment of Sholem Aleichem and the Y. L. Peretz texts, Samuel saw himself primarily as a translator. With this in mind, we consider, in this chapter, a postmodern discourse of translation conducted by scholars such as Kwame Anthony Appiah, Lydia Liu, Lawrence Venuti, and Gayatri Chakavorti Spivak that allows for cross-genre translations in a salvage poetic vein.

In chapter 2 of this study, "Salvage Inwardness: The Hasidic Tale in Abraham Joshua Heschel's *The Earth Is the Lord's*," we examine the role of the Hasidic tale as Heschel's chosen artifact in his construction of a salvage poetic. Examining his "depth theology" and the Yiddish concept of *innerlekhkeyt* or "inwardness" that Heschel gleaned from the Rebbe of Kotzk, we consider what Heschel felt he could, and could not, say in a work of folk ethnography written for an American Jewish audience.

Having taught Jewish studies in American universities for several decades, I have observed in the classroom that any time a student is shown a picture of an ultra-Orthodox Jew, they assume that Jew is Hasidic. This is the case among Jewish as well as non-Jewish students.

Why? Perhaps this can be attributed to the visibility of Lubavitch Chabad, a Hasidic movement that proselytizes other Jews all over the world, asking men to wear phylacteries and distributing Shabbat candles to women in public venues. Or perhaps this can be attributed to the size of the Hasidic communities in neighborhoods of New York such as Crown Heights and Borough Park. Furthermore, Hasidim in New York are highly active members of the business community and the retail community in certain arenas (like electronics and diamonds) and are therefore a distinct part of the street life not only in Brooklyn enclaves where they mostly keep to themselves but also in Manhattan where they interact with a wide variety of individuals.

Many works, scholarly and popular, have been written about Hasidim over the last several decades in America, responding to the American fascination with this community as well as fueling the American sense of familiarity with it. Samuel Heilman's *Defenders of the Faith* (1992) is probably the best-known American ethnography of this community.[49] Despite its professional origins, this book, interestingly, reproduces the generalized conflation of Orthodox Judaism with Hasidim, presenting itself as a view "inside ultra-Orthodox Jewry" but focusing exclusively on the Belz Hasidic community in Jerusalem. Other works by Janet Belcove-Shalin and Lynne Davidman have explored aspects of the Hasidic community in America from within the fields of anthropology and sociology, respectively.[50] A recent spate of creative writers, such as Leah Lax, Deborah Feldman, Shulem Deen, Chayah Deitsch, and Leah Vincent, among others, have published memoirs about escaping the Hasidic community, with the sociologist Hela Winston's book *Unchosen: The Hidden Lives of Hasidic Rebels* (2006) approaching the same subject from a sociological perspective.[51]

Public fascination with individuals who were insiders who became outsiders of their own accord is clearly relevant to our subject insofar as the recent popularity of these books and studies among publishing houses and audiences reflects the American desire to see into the world of Orthodox Jewry via Hasidic escapees. One could say that the contemporary fascination with Hasidim is the current variation on the interest in East European Jewry of a little more than half a century ago. Just as in *Life Is with People*, as we will see, New York informants rendered the inner world of East European Jewry accessible and safe, so too the words of Shulem Deen or Leah Vincent bridge the perceived gap between the inside and the outside.

Looking to other media, films about Hasidim have appeared for decades at nearly every annual Jewish film festival, including *Ushpizin* (2004), *A Price above Rubies* (1998), *A Stranger among Us* (1992), and *Kadosh* (1999). Chaim Potok's *The Chosen*, first published in 1967 and focused on a character destined to become a Hasidic rebbe in Brooklyn, New York, who opts out in favor of a secular degree in psychology, is probably the most popular American Jewish book ever written (at least all my students have read it without my prompting, far more than have read anything by Philip Roth, Saul Bellow, or Bernard Malamud before taking my American Jewish literature class). Lis Harris's journey into Crown Heights to write *Holy Days*, a book about Hasidim, which was published in several installments in *The New Yorker* in 1985 (I remember reading it with great excitement in high school), became a cause célèbre of intellectual journalism.[52] All this is to say that Hasidim have been the object of much American fascination for at least the last half century. Representations of Hasidim in popular media have become conflated with all Orthodox Jews and have come to constitute their own form of popular ethnography. Heschel's presentation of Hasidim in *The Earth Is the Lord's* was, I would argue, an important catalyst for this phenomenon.

Heschel's students have been associated with the neo-Hasidic religious movement, but no critics have discussed Heschel's participation in neo-Hasidism, as evidenced in his construction of *The Earth Is the Lord's*, from a formal literary perspective. It is important to remember that Hasidic literature has a fascinating multilingual and multimodal history, as many of the stories were communicated orally in Yiddish, then marked down by protégés and assistants, first in Hebrew and then translated back into Yiddish. Beginning, therefore, as an oral literature, Hasidic tales were transcribed into a written corpus to be read in a scholarly setting, as Hebrew was the language of scholarship. In time, these stories were deemed more suited to lay consumption and were therefore translated back into Yiddish. Without dwelling on the details of the entire Hasidic literary endeavor, suffice it to say here that the neo-Hasidic literary movement is quite separate from the spiritual and religious movement insofar as the religious movement is largely a product of American renewal, whereas the literary movement began in Eastern Europe with Y. L. Peretz and in Western Europe with M. Y. Berdischevsky. Both writers adopted, adapted, and disseminated Hasidic tales as part of a larger project aimed at preserving what were perceived to be indigenous Jewish literary folk forms and integrating those forms into a modern Jewish literary and cultural idiom.

As an exception to the clear-cut separation between neo-Hasidism as a spiritual movement and neo-Hasidism as a literary movement, Martin Buber is known to have fostered a synthesis of the two in German. While Buber's intentions were not entirely literary, his vehicle was nearly wholly so. As discussed earlier, he edited and adapted a host of Hasidic stories as part of his movement to bring assimilated Jews back into the Jewish spiritual fold, if not as practicing Orthodox, than as culturally confident and spiritually literate secularly educated Jews. Heschel's engagement with Hasidic tales followed his teacher, Buber, by similarly marrying the two elements—the literary and the spiritual—but for an American audience that, in the 1940s and 1950s, was configured dramatically differently than a German audience at the fin de siècle.

Chapter 3, "Salvage Literary Inference: The Inner World of the Shtetl in *Life Is with People*," introduces us to the only "professional ethnography" focused on in this study as a model of salvage poetics. Even though neither Elizabeth Herzog nor Mark Zborowski were ethnographers, their project was overseen by Margaret Mead, one of the best-known ethnographers of her generation, under the auspices of Columbia University's 1946 Research in Contemporary Culture Project, directed by Ruth Benedict until her untimely death in 1948. For students of Franz Boas (among whom Mead and Benedict figured prominently), whose work on Native American communities revolutionized the methods and practice of "salvage ethnography," works such as *Life Is with People* represented an important step away from the orthodoxies of fieldwork and exemplified the development of anthropological approaches to cultures at a distance and culture and personality, both of which nuanced notions of insiderness and inwardness in the study of others from an American perspective. Hence, throughout our discussion we will consider the impact of these three ethnographic schools of thought—salvage ethnography, culture at a distance, and culture and personality—in ethnographic thought and methodology as they affected the genesis of *Life Is with People*. Most critical, for our purposes, is the transformation of what was originally conceived as a professional ethnography into a folk one. *Life Is with People* is pivotal in how we understand the dynamics of developing a folk ethnography because it exemplifies an ethnographic project that grows out of its disciplinary parameters into the domain of popular audiences. In considering the contemporary field of anthropology that inspired *Life Is with People*, my hope is that we can better understand the interdisciplinary and trans-generic dynamics wherein popular audiences find ways to imagine cultural continuities across the abyss of historical cataclysm and geographic distance.

The centrality of *Life Is with People* to the American Jewish image of pre-Holocaust East European Jewish experience cannot be overestimated. While this work, as we have already seen, was not the first to attempt to represent culture in terms and categories that would be accessible and comprehensible to an American audience, it has proven to be the one with the longest staying power in the popular imagination. Maurice Samuel's *The World of Sholem Aleichem*, while essential to our understanding of salvage poetics because of its explicit streamlining of literary and ethnographic concerns, never quite got the public traction that Herzog and Zborowski's book received. Perhaps that is because *The World of Sholem Aleichem* was so closely focused on one writer, the eponymous Sholem Aleichem. As popular audiences drew away from the Yiddish fiction and author so popular among the immigrant generation, Samuel's strategic decision to link his pseudo-ethnographic overview to Sholem Aleichem proved less effective than he had intended.

Or perhaps Samuel's work did not remain in print and was not embraced nearly as loyally as was *Life Is with People* because it was harder for audiences to classify *The World of Sholem Aleichem* generically than it was for them to comprehend the place of *Life Is with People* within the popular discourse. While many anthropologists have rejected *Life Is with People* for what is perceived as a lack of rigor in its methods or a lack of accuracy in its representations, it remains the "most influential of popular renderings of East European Jewry in the English language."[53] It has stayed in the limelight, I would venture to say, because it marks a moment when anthropology became a popular medium and serves as a prime example of a work that, while vilified in anthropological circles, became valorized in popular circles. As Robert LeVine has discussed in an overview of the culture and personality movement, during the 1940s "the field [of anthropology] became highly visible, not only within anthropology and the social sciences but also among the educated public."[54]

The academic discipline of anthropology in America, therefore, during the period in which *Life Is with People* was published, took a simultaneous turn in two directions. On the one hand, practitioners of the culture and personality school moved away from the fieldwork imperatives that had been developing since the beginning of the century and into the arena of more conjectural and psychological approaches to culture in order to facilitate its study at a distance, even while other anthropologists entrenched themselves and insisted on the primacy of scientific and quantifiable methods, obtainable primarily through fieldwork but also through other means. On the other hand, because of the qualitative and humanist-oriented trends developing within the field, popular audiences were more interested and engaged in the studies being conducted. For audiences seeking a distinct cultural portrait that they could comprehend but still felt authentic and verifiable as a work of science, anthropology became a wonderful vehicle.

Thus the immediate post-Holocaust period corresponded to a transitional moment in ethnographic discourse that enabled works such as *Life Is with People* to deliver a clear and accessible depiction of East European Jewish experience just when it was most acutely needed. Because it was written within an anthropological context, *Life Is with People* was granted credence. It continued to maintain popular credibility even when the culture and personality school fell out of favor within the discipline in a process described by Robert LeVine, kicked off by unfavorable reviews of *The People of Great Russia* (1949).[55] This slippage between the academic and the popular marks the formal birth of popular or folk ethnographic approaches to East European Jewish culture in the postwar era.

In this chapter I argue that with the turn toward folk ethnography in works like *Life Is with People* there was also the opportunity to incorporate major cultural trends into the anthropological works themselves. Therefore, modernist literary trends become evident, though rather belatedly, in the narrative of *Life Is with People* as the authors sought ways to represent the shtetl as a subjective character with an "inner world." This literarization of the shtetl went beyond their reliance on their informants for literary allusions instead of actual memories of Eastern Europe. Rather, the very literary trends that undergirded modern Yiddish literature are evident in the construction of *Life Is with People*.

In chapter 4, "Salvage Montage: The Missing Piece in *A Treasury of Yiddish Stories, The Golden Tradition*, and *Image before My Eyes*," I examine three anthological works that attempt, each in its own way, to inject some realism into post-Holocaust folk ethnographies of pre-Holocaust East European Jewish life. I argue that the operant salvage poetic in these works is called "salvage montage" in deference to Georges Didi-Huberman's formulation of montage in relation to four Holocaust photographs taken by a member of the Sonderkommando in Auschwitz in August 1944.[56] In his defense of the display of those photographs in France despite critics' arguments that staging them betrays a tendency toward voyeurism and exploitation of Holocaust imagery, Didi-Huberman argues for the power of "images in spite of all." No representation of the Holocaust, be it a photograph or a memoir or a work of fiction or history or film, can ever purport to capture the "all" that was the Holocaust. But, he argues, to ban the display of works that capture even the smallest moment in the history of the genocide would be a form of collaboration with its perpetrators, who attempted not only to destroy a culture but also to wipe away any record of the process of destruction. In examining Eliezer Greenberg and Irving Howe's *A Treasury of Yiddish Stories* (1954), Lucy Dawidowicz's *The Golden Tradition* (1967), an anthology of essays by well-known East European Jews in the pre-Holocaust era, and Lucjan

Dobroszycki and Barbara Kirshenblatt-Gimblett's *Image before My Eyes* (1977), a history of photography in Poland, I consider, from the perspective of the montage, what is present and what is absent in anthologies of East European works compiled in three different decades after the Holocaust. Anthologies reflect the rather random process of selection and framing that takes place when bringing together works of the same genre but from different times and places and created by different individuals. Here we consider the benefits of acknowledging this arbitrariness to remember what is possible, and what is impossible, in the reconstruction of East European Jewish life through photographs, fiction, and essays for a post-Holocaust American audience.

Chapter 5, "Auto-Ethnographic Salvage: Roman Vishniac's *A Vanished World*," takes a close look at what can arguably be considered the foundational text for image books of East European Jewry, *Polish Jewry* (1947) alongside its later variation *A Vanished World* (1983). In reflecting on the narratives constituted by a series of captions preceding, accompanying, and following the photographs in this work, Vishniac's editor at Farrar, Straus and Giroux, Michael di Capua, says, "In the course of many hours working with Vishniac it began to seem that he had become a mythmaker of his past."[57] What are the stories that Vishniac wove in his captions to the photographs, and what is the ideological function of those stories within the context of salvage poetics? This chapter focuses on the intimations of "auto-ethnography" in Vishniac's attempt, through his captions, to weave himself into the photographs as a participant in the scenes he documented before the war. Throughout *A Vanished World*, Vishniac labors to demonstrate his status as an "insider" by narrating his photographs in surprisingly intimate ways, even though his family was one of very few Russian Jewish families with license to live and work in Moscow during the period when nearly all Jews in the Russian Empire were confined to the Pale of Settlement.

In the sixth and final chapter of this study, "Patronymic Salvage: Daughters in Search of Their Fathers," we consider the quest by two daughters for their father's name in image books and the way that family and ethnic albums can become hybrid salvage poetic works. In *They Called Me Mayer July* (2007), Barbara Kirshenblatt-Gimblett and her father, Mayer Kirshenblatt, coauthored an ethnography of the Polish town of Apt between the two world wars using the artifact of Kirshenblatt's memory and his paintings of Apt that are based on those memories. Memory is somewhat broadly construed here in that he also paints pictures of things he doesn't remember from his own experience, such as his own infancy and legends of the Jews of Poland alongside the Nazis' murder of his family. Like Vishniac, because he did not die in the war, having emigrated from Poland to Toronto in 1934, Kirshenblatt is able to use his own works as the artifacts of pre-Holocaust Jewish life that serve as the basis for his salvage poetic. Unlike any other artifacts that this study focuses on, however, Kirshenblatt's paintings were produced long after the war, in conjunction with interviews conducted by his daughter over the course of forty years.

Poyln (1999) features the photographs of Alter Kacyzne, murdered in Ukraine in 1941, gathered in one volume for the first time. His daughter, Sulamita Kacyzne Reale, asked YIVO to assemble this book out of Kacyzne's photographs held in its archive. Edited by Marek Web, a YIVO historian, the book articulates two simultaneous impulses: to memorialize and document Polish Jewry and to memorialize Alter Kacyzne. Like Vishniac's commission with the Joint Distribution Committee, Kacyzne, a Warsaw-based photographer, was commissioned to take the photographs in this book by two organizations, each for its own purposes: Hebrew Immigrant Aid Society (HIAS) wanted to document Jewish immigration to America from Warsaw in order to raise funds from American Jews, and *The Jewish Daily Forward* wanted the photos for their rotogravure weekend arts section to entertain Yiddish-speaking American Jews with images of the world they or their parents left behind not so long before. Given that the photographs in the book were conceived and originally viewed during the 1920s as documentary, viewing them after the war as a testament to a lost world was not so far afield. Like Kacyzne's photographs, other literary or photographic pre-Holocaust works that are already seeded with an awareness of their testimonial value, straddling an insider's and an outsider's perspective, are the most useful for redeployment within a salvage poetic frame.

Both Kirshenblatt and Kacyzne—Kirshenblatt in the ethnographic text accompanying his paintings, and Kacyzne in his poetic and quirky captions—emphasize names and naming in the communities they represent. It is with this focus on names and naming that I consider each of the image books analyzed in this chapter as they pertain both to the ethos of family albums, where individual members of both nuclear and extended families appear in photographs so that the album's viewers can identify them by name, as well as to what Jack Kugelmass has called "ethnic albums," or published photo books that come to be understood as representations of an ethnic community.

The Jewish interest in reconciling tradition and modernity long preceded the Holocaust. Since the eighteenth century many Jewish moderns have taken the path of least resistance, through assimilation and conversion. Others have attempted to take advantage of the best that non-Jewish culture has to offer while maintaining a commitment to Jewish continuity; under duress of war and anti-Jewish legislation, modern Jewish leaders have long worked to help their communities retain coherence through obeisance to tradition. Martin Buber and S. Ansky, with whom we began this discussion, were notable in their pre-Holocaust efforts to mobilize artifacts of traditional Jewish culture in recognition of the necessity to find ways to reconcile the freedoms of the Enlightenment with the cohesiveness and ethics of tradition. Through the literary work of translation, adaptation, and explanation in Buber's case, and the work of collection, recording, and analyzing in Ansky's, both individuals represent a pre-Holocaust model for the kind of salvage that is designed not simply for museums, but for the construction of an "authentically" Jewish future. Concerned with the renewal of the Jewish spirit, as was Buber, and with the maintenance of an "authentically" Jewish art, as was Ansky, both men anticipated the types of measures American Jewish scholars, writers, and artists would take in the post-Holocaust era when confronted with the end of European Jewry and the prospects for an American one. In what follows, we will explore the varieties of those poetics, as deployed in America after the Holocaust, as a model for Jewish continuity across geographical rifts and historical cataclysm. The fact that creators of the post-Holocaust works explored here have chosen to use pre-Holocaust artifacts already laden with a salvage consciousness testifies to the desire not only to salvage the past of Jewish culture after the greatest disaster in modern Jewish history, but to salvage the future as well. In the words of Lucy Dawidowicz, "East European Jewry was cruelly cut down. But vital elements of its culture survive. Perhaps we, heirs of that culture, can continue its tradition of conserving Jewish identity by fusing the old and the new."[58]

1

SALVAGE (SELVEDGE) TRANSLATION

Maurice Samuel's *The World of Sholem Aleichem* and *Prince of the Ghetto*

> The streets of Kasrielevky—let us be courteous and call them that—are as tortuous as a Talmudic argument. They are bent into question marks and folded into parentheses. They turn back upon themselves absentmindedly. They interrupt themselves as if to admit an anecdote.[1]

Kasrielevky, Sholem Aleichem's most famous fictional shtetl, is likened here to a text. It is a Talmudic argument, Maurice Samuel says in *The World of Sholem Aleichem*, filled with digressions, questions, and anecdotes. But this conceit of shtetl as text is more complex than it seems. The shtetl, as it has come to be popularly understood in America, is a simple place, running on Jewish time with the daily recitations of prayers, the weekly observance of the Sabbath, the monthly blessing on the new moon, and the annual observance of fasts and festivals. Even referring to the shtetl in the singular as "the shtetl" is a simplification of East European Jewish pre-Holocaust provincial life, because it was never only one place with one culture and one temperament.

Jewish experience in the provinces encompassed rich and poor; crafts-men and businessmen; businesswomen, housewives, and their indus-trious daughters; fathers and their precocious sons. But the Talmudic text to which the shtetl is likened here is anything but simple; it is a monster of a text, an impossibly convoluted treatise of many volumes with more questions than answers, which, for comprehension, requires mastery of at least two languages, a capacious memory for details, and a huge time commitment. Only very few people in the shtetl had access to the Talmud: men who had made it through the intellectual ranks of Jewish society and were furnished with the time and resources, pri-marily by wealthy in-laws, to turn Talmud study into a career. The majority of women didn't know Talmud, nor did the impoverished of either gender. And even the wealthy, by and large, knew it nominally, because, after all, if you were earning money, especially a lot of it, who had time to dedicate to full-time study? So by likening the shtetl to the Talmud, on the surface Samuel (in imitation of Sholem Aleichem's own idiom and style) is affectionately alluding to its not having had the privilege of being laid out by an urban planner. But a deeper read-ing of Samuel's conceit challenges the notion of the shtetl's simplic-ity, its straightforwardness, and its transparency. The shtetl is a place that only insiders can know—only those proficient in its culture, its languages, its assumptions, its desires. To familiarize outsiders with it is a nearly impossible undertaking. And therein lies Samuel's salvage poetic in *The World of Sholem Aleichem* (1943) and *Prince of the Ghetto* (1948). He presents his readers with a seemingly accessible, simplis-tic universe, but beneath the surface lies the urgency, the complexity, and the impossibility of real insight into a world destroyed.

Indeed, as has been widely acknowledged by scholars and cultural critics, the shtetl as it is known by American Jews is more textual than it is actual, more figurative than real. It has been created through the mediation of a variety of texts, be they fictional, cinematic, or pho-tographic. It is not too much of a stretch, then, to liken a shtetl, as Samuel does above, to a text. But what are the implications of liken-ing the streets of Kasrielevky to the Talmud, and how do they shed light on our investigation of salvage poetics? In this chapter, we will discuss the ways in which Maurice Samuel not only compares East

European Jewish pre-Holocaust shtetls to texts, but creates, in Barbara Kirshenblatt-Gimblett's terminology, "hybrid texts," or folk ethnographies of those shtetls on the basis of Yiddish fiction.[2] In his presentation of East European Jewish shtetl life, Samuel approaches the culture as one who must build a bridge between an ignoramus and a Talmud scholar. He must find a way to render a Talmudic text in terms that even someone ignorant of Hebrew and Aramaic, of Jewish liturgy and the Jewish calendar, can understand.

These texts, which are the first of the texts that we will examine together, were, in fact, the first written of the whole series. Furthermore, these books do not contain any images. Nevertheless, it is important to keep in mind that *The World of Sholem Aleichem* in particular had a tremendous impact on the staging of *Fiddler on the Roof* on Broadway. Many of Tevye's dialogues were adapted not from the Sholem Aleichem texts themselves or the Butwin translations that had been in circulation in the United States for about a decade. Rather, they were adapted from Maurice Samuel's rewriting/synopsis of the short stories. Therefore, as we begin tracing a trajectory here of the increasing dominance of images in hybrid works from 1943, with the publication of *The World of Sholem Aleichem*, to 2007, with the publication of *They Called Me Meyer July*, it is important to keep in mind that even a work like *The World of Sholem Aleichem* that contains no explicit visual image was utilized in works that were wholly visual, like *Fiddler on the Roof*.[3]

Of the many books in Samuel's corpus, *The World of Sholem Aleichem* and *Prince of the Ghetto* arguably acknowledged most directly the cataclysm that had befallen European Jewry and, by extension, world Jewry in the middle of the twentieth century. As such, analysis of these two books provides an excellent opportunity to discuss the impact of the Holocaust on the uses of literary texts in the creation of folk ethnographic works within the American Jewish community. At the heart of the undertaking is Samuel's understanding of how difficult it will be to portray the culture of East European Jewry to an American audience. He therefore chooses the vehicle he finds most conducive to different levels of explication: Yiddish vernacular literature in translation. Much beloved by many American Jewish immigrants during the great

migration of Jews from East Europe to the United States at the turn of
the twentieth century, this literature was no longer accessible, in Yiddish, to their children and grandchildren by the mid-1940s. Therefore,
Samuel drew on what had been a foolproof link between the Old World
and the New World for inhabitants of both places and sought to translate Yiddish literature. But he found, in the process, that translation of
that world required a kind of precision and complexity that exceeded
the normal bounds of translation. If you knew the shtetl, Sholem Aleichem made sense. If you didn't, it was like a Talmudic text.

In my teaching, I have found that Sholem Aleichem's Tevye stories are nearly impenetrable to my students because of their wealth of
intertextuality and their humor and pathos, which are largely based
on mistranslations, a mixing of registers, and a liturgical fluency.
The moving Yom Kippur prayers, recited as a reproof to a recalcitrant
horse in the first Tevye story, is beyond irreverent and hysterically
funny. But what if you do not know the Yom Kippur prayers? Most
people reading the text in Yiddish would. That, however, is not necessarily the case for someone reading it in English. Maurice Samuel,
confronted with an American audience in search of some access point
to a world in the process of being destroyed, sought a means to bridge
the gap. He did so as an ideologue, a teacher, a European-born Jew, an
English-speaking Jew, and as a writer.

Samuel adapted the voice of Sholem Aleichem to an American
audience in part by effecting a new layer of mediation in which his narrator takes on the vernacular voice of Sholem Aleichem, but with an
American twist. Of Tevye, for example, the narrator says, "Sometimes
he puts us in mind of a Job with a sense of humor and without the happy
ending, and sometimes of Charlie Chaplin."[4] In a description of Purim
gifts, or *sholechmones*, Samuel casts them in Christian terms: "How can
we prevent the gifts of Father's day and Mother's day and wedding day
and birthday and Christmas from degenerating into—well into mis-
siles instead of missives?"[5] In a quote whose allusion to Weehawken
is evocative of Philip Roth or Jerome Robbins, Samuel describes the
relationship between two little boys in a particularly famous Sholem
Aleichem story: "Two little boys born, as we would say, on opposite
sides of the tracks: Sholom Ber the son of a *nogid*, Berel the Red with

the lame foot, son of a nobody. It might have been anywhere and in any age in Teplik or Weehawken or ancient Babylon."[6] Finally, in a statement acknowledging his own literary education and reaching out to others with similar affiliations, he writes: "The nearest parallel to the intellectual transformation of the Russian Jewish youth in the later nineteenth century will be found among the scholars of the Italian Renaissance."[7]

Born in Romania in 1895, Samuel immigrated as a young child with his family to Manchester, England, where he was educated. In 1914 Samuel moved to New York, where he died in 1972. Between 1914 and 1972, however, Samuel became a lecturer, a writer, and a passionate promoter of Judaism, Yiddishism, and Zionism. His first and arguably most famous book, *You Gentiles*, was published in 1924. His last book, *In Praise of Yiddish*, came out in 1971. Samuel published over twenty works of nonfiction, six works of fiction, and twenty-two book-length translations from French, Hebrew, Yiddish, and German. A gifted linguist, Samuel translated at Versailles and at the reparations committee in Berlin and Vienna in 1919. That same year he went to Poland as a secretary on an American pogrom investigation committee. These experiences had a major impact on his career as a spokesman for Jews within both Jewish and non-Jewish contexts.[8]

Translation, to Samuel's mind, was the single most important vehicle for bringing East European Jewry to their American counterparts. We will explore the nuances of Samuel's approach to translation as complementary to his ethnographic aspirations, discussing through the crucible of Samuel's work on Sholem Aleichem and Y. L. Peretz how translation and ethnography worked together in the immediate post-Holocaust years in the United States.

Kwame Anthony Appiah has described the necessity, in a postmodern world, for the creation of what he calls "thick translations." Thick translations are "thick contextualizations," he says,

> a thick description of the context of literary production, a translation that draws on and creates that sort of understanding that meets the need to challenge ourselves and our students to go further, to undertake the harder project of a genuinely informed

respect for others. Until we face up to difference, we cannot see what price tolerance is demanding of us.[9]

Samuel's work marries Appiah's "thick translation" and Franz Boas's "salvage ethnography" to create what I would term a uniquely American Jewish, post-Holocaust "selvedge translation," a subset of "salvage poetics."

Appiah's "thick translation," based on the well-known ethnographic notion of "thick description," posits that the translator's role is not only to provide a semantic equivalency between languages, but to contextualize the cultures represented in those languages, to mark the distance between the cultures and to give each its due within each and every equivalency. "Salvage ethnography," generally associated with the pioneering work of Boas's American anthropological school, aims to capture and describe cultures nearing extinction. "Salvage poetics," a term I have coined in the context of early twentieth-century Hebrew and Yiddish literature, refers to the ways that ethnographic and literary concerns work together for purposes of cultural salvage. Finally, "selvedge translation" is a thick translation that presents its author auto-ethnographically, as a part of the culture represented in the text (even when he or she is not), in order to create an overlap in consciousness between the author and his audience. A "selvedge translation" uses a kind of auto-ethnographic consciousness, for purposes of salvaging a culture through the transmission of its texts from one language to another, and, in some cases, from one genre to another.

"Selvedge" literally refers to the edge of a piece of woven fabric finished to prevent raveling; this narrow strip at the edge is finished differently than the rest of the material, being intended to be cut off or covered by the seam when the fabric is assembled into a garment. In what I am calling here, for the first time, a "selvedge translation," the translator is working himself or herself into the fabric, finishing it with his or her own autobiographical intimations. The translator is not really engaging in "salvage" because in reality he or she is too far removed from the culture represented in the text to furnish actual artifacts of that culture or an intimate perspective into it. However, the translator is adding a new layer to the world represented in the original text—mediating it, engaging in a thick translation—and this creates a new kind of fabric, something external to the world being represented, in excess, but necessary for its preservation, as the outer margin of it, or as the stitching that keeps it from falling apart.

Mary Louise Pratt, in her work on travel writing, further defines auto-ethnography as part of her discussion of contact zones as "the space in which peoples geographically and historically separated come into contact with each other":[10]

> This term refers to . . . instances in which colonized subjects undertake to represent themselves in ways that engage with the colonizer's terms. If ethnographic texts are a means by which Europeans represent to themselves their (usually sub-jugated) others, autoethnographic texts are texts the others construct in response to or in dialogue with those metropolitan representations.[11]

Let us consider Samuel's works on Sholem Aleichem and Y. L. Peretz within the circle of these three ideas: a contact zone, auto-ethnography, and thick translation.

In *The Gentleman and the Jew* (1950), Samuel attempts to outline the differences between Jewish and non-Jewish thought and culture, beginning with non-Jewish literature.[12] He appears to be reaching out to non-Jews to make an argument for Jewish sophistication and legitimacy to counter what he perceives to be the non-Jewish sense of Jewish backwardness and provincialism. One could perhaps apply Pratt's definition of auto-ethnography to this work, as in it Samuel describes his own life as it relates to the reading and cultural practices he was taught during his upbringing in England; he is returning to his "origins" and explaining them to outsiders on their own terms. In his work on Sholem Aleichem, however, his audience is Jewish: "Sholem Aleichem is almost unknown to millions of Americans whose grandfathers made up his world. This is not simply a literary loss; it is a break—a very recent and disastrous one in the continuity of a group history."[13] In *The World of Sholem Aleichem*, Samuel is presenting Jews to other Jews. Whereas the contact zone in *The Gentleman and the Jew* is an English-speaking society that includes Jews and non-Jews, in

The World of Sholem Aleichem the contact zone is between East European Jewry and American Jewry. In *The Gentleman and the Jew*, the only requirement for Samuel to write auto-ethnographically is to be a Jew. But in *The World of Sholem Aleichem* he has to write of himself as an East European Jew; because he wants to introduce this culture to an audience that requires simultaneously an insider's and an outsider's perspective, he needs to make a strong argument for his own stake in and propriety over this culture. I would suggest that Samuel has developed a translation geared toward the salvaging of a culture in order to create an understanding of it for purposes of conciliation and commemoration, of identity building for Jews in America. He creates a selvedge translation, a thick translation with an auto-ethnographic backbone, in order to foster a stronger relationship between the culture within the text and the culture to which the text is being presented. Samuel, raised in England, is working himself into the fabric of East European Jewish life in *The World of Sholem Aleichem*, finishing it, or creating a selvedge, with his own autobiographical intimations. He is not really engaging in "salvage" because in reality he is too far removed from East European Jewish culture itself to "salvage" it. However, he is adding a new layer to the world he is representing—mediating it and pointing out its differences but naturalizing it into his own voice and experience to make it more sympathetic, more relatable. A selvedge translation like the one Samuel produces in *The World of Sholem Aleichem* creates a new kind of fabric: external to the world being represented, in excess, but necessary for its preservation as its outer margin or the stitching that keeps it from disintegrating forever.

In *Little Did I Know: Recollections and Reflections*, Maurice Samuel walks his reader through the chain of influences that led him to become the foremost American spokesperson for traditional Jewish culture in the decades spanning the interwar period and into the early 1970s:

> The closing circle of memory connects again with experiences long forgotten and reveals how much more they did for me than I was aware of for a time. The reading sessions were held irregularly, being dependent on the arrival of new material at

the bookseller's—periodicals and books, mostly from America. There were novels by Shomer, an immensely popular hack,
but also stories by the living classics, Sholom Aleichem, Yal
[Y. L.] Peretz, and Mendele Mocher Sforim. My father would hold
forth and we would listen, unmoving, enchanted, to whatever
had come to his hand, infantile trash or first-rate literature . . .
Many words and episodes connected with those readings made
permanent places for themselves in dormant memory cells, and
their emergence into consciousness depended on chance, above
all the chance that I would turn back to Jewish things.[14]

It was, according to Samuel, the modern Yiddish writers who brought
him back to Judaism, and perhaps that is why he works so hard to use
these writers to introduce Judaism to an American readership.

Generally speaking, *The World of Sholem Aleichem* is organized
around a handful of Sholem Aleichem stories, notably his Tevye
stories. However, Samuel does not preserve the stories whole cloth.
Rather, he shoots a commentary through them, using the stories as
backdrop for an introduction to the institutions, annual calendar, and
life cycle of a traditional Jewish provincial community. In order to better understand how Samuel deploys and mediates Sholem Aleichem's
stories in *The World of Sholem Aleichem*, what follows, briefly, is an
overview of the book's structure that will be the basis for comparing it
to Samuel's book on Y. L. Peretz, *Prince of the Ghetto*.

In *The World of Sholem Aleichem*'s introductory chapter, "Of Certain Grandfathers," Samuel discusses the importance of Sholem Aleichem's stories and sketches for understanding the world of so many
European Jewish "grandfathers" of Jewish Americans. He says:

We could write a Middletown of the Russian-Jewish Pale basing ourselves solely on the novels and stories and sketches of
Sholem Aleichem, and it would be as reliable a scientific document as any factual study: more so, indeed, for we should get,
in addition to the material of a straightforward social inquiry,
the intangible spirit which informs the material and gives it its
living significance.[15]

The Middletown studies he refers to were case studies of Muncie, Indiana, conducted by sociologists Robert Staughton Lynd and Helen Merrell Lynd. Their findings were detailed in *Middletown: A Study in Modern American Culture* (1929) and *Middletown in Transition: A Study in Cultural Conflicts* (1937). The 1929 book looked primarily at changes in a typical American city between 1890 and 1925. In their work on Middletown, the Lynds studied existing documents, statistics, old newspapers, interviews, and surveys. The stated goal of the study was to describe this small urban center as a unit consisting of "interwoven trends of behavior,"[16] and "to present a dynamic, functional study of the contemporary life of this specific American community in the light of trends of changing behaviour observable in it during the last thirty-five years."[17] Written in an entirely descriptive tone, the 1929 book treats the citizens of Middletown in much the same way as an anthropologist from an industrialized nation might describe a nonindustrial culture. Similarly, Samuel's presentation of the culture of the shtetl acknowledges its own textual bases and alludes to its own efficacy as a scientifically grounded resource; however, the textual bases Samuel uses to reconstruct the Pale are Yiddish fictional texts, not community ledgers, prayer books, or any other official or sacred document. His only resource was Yiddish literature.

After reviewing the importance of Sholem Aleichem's corpus, Samuel introduces us to Sholem Aleichem's most famous character, Tevye, in a chapter titled "Man in a Forest." Without any narrative framing, Samuel launches into a partial translation of the first story in the *Tevye the Milkman* story cycle (1894), in which Tevye is in the forest collecting wood and trying to say his afternoon prayers when his horse runs amuck and he is forced to scream and run during the usually silent and stationary Amidah prayer. This story in the original, as well as in Samuel's adaptation, introduces the readers to Tevye's simultaneously reverent and irreverent attitude toward Jewish tradition and prayer, as well as to his special, comedic relationship with God. Tevye is notorious for mistranslating and misquoting the sacred texts, but rarely does he speak to anyone better educated than himself who can correct him. The original readers—who were familiar with the intertextual references Tevye alludes to—see where Tevye has gone awry in his textual discourse, and therein lies the hilarity of the stories. Well aware that his American readership may not understand this inter-textual humor on which Sholem Aleichem bases the entire Tevye text, Samuel interjects explanatory material at certain critical moments to preserve that humor. When, for example, Tevye observes, "As the Holy Book says, man is dust and his foundations are of the dust; which, rightly interpreted, means that man is as weak as a fly and stron-ger than steel,"[18] Samuel frames this gloss of the Holy Book—which doesn't even approach the hilarity and poignancy of some of Tevye's mistranslations and misquotations in the original Tevye stories—with this explanatory interjection, "So, against the rising tide of despair, Tevye tries to spin the thread of rational discourse."[19] The key word here is "tries." As part of the same discussion, Samuel more explic-itly articulates the comic device at the heart of Sholem Aleichem's presentation of Tevye, something that an English-reading audience would be hard-pressed to identify in the absence of proficiency with "the Holy Books": "Should you begin to orate at him he will listen, despite an empty stomach, with the closest attention, and just when you think you are at your irresistible best he will interrupt you with a disastrous misquotation from the Holy Books."[20] Thus is the character of Tevye introduced to us. The next chapter, "Tevye the Dairyman," returns to that framing narrative voice, making a formal introduction retroactively:

> This is Tevye the dairyman you have just met—and why dairy-man you shall learn in the sequel—Tevye, the best-known and best-loved figure in the world of Sholem Aleichem. A little Jew wandering in a big, dark forest, symbol of a little people wander-ing in the big, dark jungle of history.[21]

While warning his readers "to approach [Tevye] with caution, curios-ity and liking, but not with the impulse to classify,"[22] he also encour-ages them to see him as an "ordinary, everyday Jew."[23] The tension between the particular and the general, between the "anecdotal" his-tory of a fictional character and the broader cultural description of a people, is laid out here in terms that anticipate the overall structure of the book. The book is meant to provide an overview of "ordinary" East European Jewish life, to limn the patterns and the commonalities of East European Jewish experience, as would a good ethnography. At the same time, it uses a Yiddish literary frame to entice a popular readership with the familiar affability that had come to be associated with Yiddish literature by mid-century in America. As argued by Erich Auerbach and his acolytes Stephen Greenblatt and Catherine Gallagher in their approach to New Historicism, literary anecdotes can provide a glimpse into historical vistas when carefully selected and appropriately framed.[24]

Echoed structurally by numerous photographic anthologies published in the postwar decades and by *Life Is with People*, the watershed American ethnography of East European Jews discussed further along in this study, *The World of Sholem Aleichem* is organized around the synagogue and the Sabbath, marriage, birth rituals (for boys, of course), death, and the holiday cycle. Neither a translation nor an ethnography, it is a cross between the two: a streamlined discussion of East European Jewish culture against the locale and the personae of a particular corpus of Yiddish fiction. The fiction grounds the descriptive elements of Samuel's ethnographic narration, localizes it, injects it with a degree of humor and personality, and enables Samuel to create a new narrative persona to replace the original one of Sholem Aleichem.

In Sholem Aleichem's original Yiddish tales, a homodiegetic narrator frames the stories by serving as interlocutor to the real storytellers, who may be passengers on a train, townspeople, or Reb Tevye himself. The narrator is an outside witness to the discourse of shtetl insiders, being called the Polish "Pan" instead of the Yiddish "Reb." Both mean "Mister," but "Pan" inspires confidence in his interlocutors as a cultural "outsider," inviting them to speak more descriptively about their own culture.[25] Sholem Aleichem, the narratorial persona, convinces the fictional characters to generate their stories for an outsider so that he can write about them, and, indeed, characters such as Tevye want to be written about. When Samuel in *The World of Sholem Aleichem* replaces Sholem Aleichem with himself as narrator, thereby framing the characters' stories and becoming their literary mediator, he does so quite deliberately within an American Jewish literary context, acting as the outsider who will give them a new literary life. But his framing becomes more complex than the original framing because it takes on an ethnographic mission as well as a literary one. While Samuel becomes a literary mediator, he also becomes a cultural mediator.

Characterizing his treatment of Sholem Aleichem and Peretz within the modern Yiddish literary canon, Samuel says, "These men must be interpreted. One must talk about them and around their people and its problems; one must retell their stories, one must hint and allude, interpolate, digress, find analogies."[26] The methodology that Samuel describes here applies equally well to both *The World of Sholem Aleichem* and *Prince of the Ghetto*. Indeed, he interprets the stories for us, retells them, hints, alludes, interpolates, digresses, finds analogies. Most important, in the case of both texts, Samuel states his purpose as being to introduce East European Jewish life, with gestures toward Sholem Aleichem and Peretz, respectively, as a means of illustrating his broader cultural points. Yet, although this methodological statement nicely encapsulates his approach to both literary corpora, the two books could not be more different. Many of their differences can be understood as an extension of the differences Samuel perceives between the two authors they represent.

In comparing Peretz to Sholem Aleichem, Samuel says: "He was, like Sholem Aleichem, a Jewish folk figure; on the other hand, and unlike Sholem Aleichem, he was the subtle, many-sided European intellectual."[27] This sense of Sholem Aleichem as artless in the face of Peretz's artfulness is further reinforced by Samuel's claim, which extends throughout *The World of Sholem Aleichem*, that Sholem Aleichem was not an artist but simply a cipher for the voices and culture of East European Jewry:

> The microcosmos of Sholem Aleichem is a true replica of the world. He was not a modern novelist with a special line; he did not set out to be refreshingly idyllic or sternly realistic. He did not even set out to be a Yiddish writer. In a letter which he wrote toward the end of his life to an old friend he tells how, late one

night, kept awake by business worries, he sat down at a desk and sought distraction by putting down on paper, in Yiddish, a fantasy of his own childhood. He did not invent. He merely recalled.[28]

At times, in his claims of Sholem Aleichem's lack of artistry, Samuel invokes classical images of mimesis, but with a twist: "Because he was the mirror of Kasrielevky, presenting the image of his own world to his own world, and to no one else, Sholem Aleichem had no thought of 'making a good impression: of practicing concealment or distortion.'"[29] And in a description of an encounter with Sholem Aleichem in New York City, just before the Yiddish author's death, Samuel insists:

> You would have taken him for a Hebrew teacher, a small town Rabbi, perhaps even for a wise old shopkeeper given to books and close observation of his customers; certainly an attractive, even a fascinating personality, full of years and suffering and accumulated comment on life, but not, in heaven's name, a literary genius.[30]

At several junctures in the text, Samuel emphasizes his perspective on Sholem Aleichem's writing voice as a speaking voice, representing the voices of ordinary people in a real world:

> He was not what we call a writer. He was a speaker. He chattered about his world. Or put it this way: he let his world flow through him, as through a funnel. He uses ordinary language; his stories, people, and townlets have the quality of anonymity; they are not thought up; they happen to be there, and Sholom Aleichem calls our attention to them, casually.[31]

In his most blatant (and perhaps most brazen) articulation of Sholem Aleichem's lack of artistry, Samuel compares him to other European writers and circumscribes his place in Yiddish letters:

> Many other writers have left us records of Russian-Jewish life, and some of them compare well with the best known in the Western world. None of them had this natural gift for complete self-identification with a people which makes Sholom

Aleichem unique. He wrote no great panoramic novels in the manner of a Balzac or a Tolstoy. He did not set out with the conscious and self-conscious purpose of putting it down for posterity. He wrote because of a simple communicative impulse, as men chat in a tavern or in a waiting crowd with their like. He never tried his hand at solemn passages and mighty themes, any more than people do in a casual, friendly conversation. But his language had an incomparable authenticity, and his humor—he is the greatest of Jewish humorists, and in the world's front rank—was that of a folk, not of an individual.[32]

In Samuel's estimation, the vernacular quality of Sholem Aleichem's language—which Samuel misidentifies as "authentic," "chatty," and "simple"—is what denudes Sholem Aleichem's texts of their artistry and renders them "folksy." Samuel seems to be arguing that Sholem Aleichem's fiction is not authored by an individual, but is the work of an entire people.

Are artistry and folksiness really incompatible? Indeed, Samuel's claims about Sholem Aleichem follow nearly a half century of upheaval in modern Jewish writing demanding that writers represent the "Jewish street" in works of fiction, writing about the real and not the ideal. The result was a revolution in Hebrew literary language and simultaneous appointment of Yiddish as a language of belles lettres for the first time. In the case of contemporary Hebrew writers, the only available language originated in sacred texts—biblical, rabbinic, and epistolary; consequently, the challenge of the Modern Hebrew revival was to break Hebrew free of its intertextual fetters and allow it to represent, as if mimetically (in a dynamic I have elsewhere termed "reverse mimesis"), a speaking culture.[33] In the case of Yiddish, the call to represent the "Jewish street" legitimated the use of Yiddish as a vernacular language within literary texts.

Whether or not Maurice Samuel really believed that Sholem Aleichem was artless, his approach to Sholem Aleichem, criticized by many in the years since the book's first publication, does reveal some of the subtle consequences of marrying ethnographic aspirations to literary analysis. Because Samuel wrote *The World of Sholem Aleichem* as a means for introducing the shtetl world to second- or third-generation American Jews, he decided that he could do so most effectively by focalizing that world through the work of a particular Yiddish writer. So why choose Sholem Aleichem as the "artifact" around which to build his hybrid text? Certainly, as mentioned earlier, Sholem Aleichem had very successfully built a bridge for earlier generations of immigrants. But also critical to Samuel's endeavor were the narratological aspects of Sholem Aleichem's work, which allowed his readers to feel as if they were listening in on a conversation, not reading a literary text. Sholem Aleichem is not the main character in his stories, but rather the narratorial persona who elicits discourse from people eager to speak with him: he is willing to listen, and he is enough of an outsider to be interested in the mundane, but enough of an insider to need no translation.

Maurice Samuel wanted to achieve the success that Sholem Aleichem had achieved in reaching the masses. In Samuel's case, it was the masses of American Jews who could no longer read Yiddish, yet who had a vested interest in familiarizing themselves with Jewish traditions as they had been practiced and lived in East Europe before the Holocaust. Just as Sholem Aleichem had struck gold in his vernacular framing, Samuel, who felt responsible for helping the American Jewish community to bridge the gap between the world they came from and the world they were trying to assimilate into, sensed that a friendly, accessible, nonantagonistic tone was in order.

In *The World of Sholem Aleichem*, Samuel morphs into Sholem Aleichem himself, excising the narratorial figure from the book's translations and synopses.[34] Samuel, for example, adopts the rhetoric of Sholem Aleichem himself in telling the story: "Get to the point, I hear someone say, and I should like to do it, but it is not easy, for we are moving in a world of talkers in which the preamble was usually the point; and it takes a little time to build up a decent anticlimax."[35] At other critical moments, Samuel inserts the idiom of the Jewish villagers featured in Sholem Aleichem's stories into his descriptions of that world, reminding us of his role as mediator and narrator through his active ventriloquism of fictional characters in the midst of his exposition: "The tumult of the marketplace is one of the wonders of the world. Paris, say the Kasrielevkites, is a dog by comparison."[36] This is a typical narratorial device of the classic Yiddish (and Hebrew) writers, who sought to create strong framing with homodiegetic narrators (like Sholem Aleichem or Mendele) in order to enhance the vernacular tone of their texts. Sometimes these narrators' voices blend with their characters' voices in order to remind their readership that the narrators and their speaking subjects were of the same milieu and moment. Gerard Genette calls this device "free indirect discourse," while Dorrit Cohn calls it "narrated monologue."[37] In either case, Samuel casts himself, through the very same devices deployed by Rabinowitz in his crafting of Sholem Aleichem's narrative voice, as a stand-in for Sholem Aleichem. To further reinforce this effect, at times Samuel situates himself within a lineage of transcribers following Sholem Aleichem, thereby finishing the job he started:

> A Jew with a citron of his own was widely envied. Moishe Yenkel, who lived in a townlet near Kasrielevky, waited ten years before he could buy one for himself; and a terrible tragedy happened. Leibel, his little son, was so fascinated by the precious and sacred fruit that he crept down from his bed in the night, took the *esrog* [citron] in his hand, and, seized by a frightful and blasphemous curiosity, bit off the head, thereby rendering the *esrog* unfit for ritual use. Sholem Aleichem thinks the incident worth recording, and I certainly think it worth mentioning.[38]

In a fascinating variation on Samuel's casting of himself in the guise of Sholem Aleichem, he describes, toward the end of *The World of Sholem Aleichem*, an encounter in New York's Lower East Side that quickly becomes an argument over who is to be considered the greatest living Hasidic rabbi of the 1940s in the United States:

> The competition became more furious, so that my friend Reb Leibel and I were forgotten in the midst of it . . . The files hummed in the dusty room, the tattered volumes of the Talmud looked down from the single bookcase with the cracked, unwashed glass. Where was I? In New York or in old Kasrielevky? In New York, I said to myself, because old Kasrielevky has been

> utterly destroyed, and all the places which harboured the saints
> have passed under the flaming harrow. This alone is left—this,
> and the record in Sholem Aleichem.[39]

Samuel loses track of where he is here, although he has never been in Kasrielevky—which not only no longer exists but never did exist because it is a fictional construct. But, Samuel claims, as the mediator of Sholem Aleichem's record he becomes, in part, a character in a Sholem Aleichem–esque drama, a bitter battle over the relatively trivial, a man in the know who essentially knows nothing.

In choosing to replace Sholem Aleichem with himself in his framing and presentation of Sholem Aleichem's stories, Samuel necessitates his minimization of the literary aspects of Sholem Aleichem's text. A literary purist might ask how he dare dismantle a work of art to that extent, inserting himself into it, rearranging it, altering its fundamental structure? But recall that he is using this text as a form of folk ethnography that he means to hand over to American Jewry as a vehicle for understanding their own history; hence it is important that he alter it in certain ways that make it more accessible: rendering it in English, contextualizing it historically and culturally, reframing it from the perspective of an English speaker who is a member of their own generation.

As an experienced translator and accomplished writer, Maurice Samuel also clearly understands the dangers of taking too many liberties with a literary text that he is rendering accessible to a foreign readership. Like Martin Buber in his acknowledgment of the kinds of violence—necessary violence in his opinion—that he wreaked on Hasidic tales by translating and adapting them for German readers in the 1930s, Samuel acknowledges in *Prince of the Ghetto* the problems inherent in performing the kinds of translations and adaptations he performs in his work on Yiddish writers. In this work he apologizes to those readers who may already be familiar with Peretz's corpus in the Yiddish original: "Here I will only say that between leaving Peretz unintelligible to outsiders (as would be the case if I translated him by brute force) and remodeling him into intelligibility at the risk of some evaporation, I have chosen the second course."[40]

Samuel has anticipated here the postmodern discourse of translation, which posits that any ethical translation draws attention to its
own tendencies toward assimilation of the original text into the cultural context of its target audience. Echoes and intimations of the original culture must remain in any translation. Lydia Liu has argued that

> the problem of translation has become increasingly central to
> critical reflections on modernity . . . We can no longer talk about
> translation as if it were a purely linguistic or literary matter; nor
> can we continue to acquiesce to the material consequence of
> what anthropologists have termed "cultural translation" prac-
> ticed for centuries by missionaries, ethnographers, travelers,
> and popular journalists.[41]

She adds that in the contemporary, postmodern academic climate,

> we are interested in the processes whereby translation has
> helped universalize the "modern" by rewriting and reinventing
> in the diverse languages and societies of the world during the
> shared and much embattled moments of globalization.[42]

Lawrence Venuti prescribes an approach to translation that is "minoritizing," in which a translator resists the assimilationist ethic that has
long characterized translation by signifying the linguistic and cultural difference of the languages in play. "Good translation," he says,
is minoritizing, releasing the "remainder" of the original language by
"cultivating a heterogenous discourse."[43] Tullio Maranhao and Bernard Streck argue that "translation domesticates alterity; it denies or
attempts to deny alterity by annihilating difference. But at the same
time it also has the capacity to liberate difference."[44] And, finally,
Gayatri Chakravorti Spivak claims that for her "translation is the most
intimate act of reading" and that she "surrenders to the texts when
[she] translates."[45] In other words, translating is a way of constituting
ourselves through recognition of the "other."

I would argue that by reframing Sholem Aleichem's works with
himself in the vernacular role of Sholem Aleichem, by treating a work
of Yiddish fiction as an artifact and presenting it to his American

Jewish readership in the form of an ethnographic text, Maurice Samuel is finding ways to preserve, if not the contours of the original text, the contours of its original conception and reception, and in so doing he is struggling to maintain the text's difference while increasing its accessibility. But in what way is Samuel attempting to preserve the contours of its original conception and reception if he is changing its genre, its narrator, and its language?

To understand what Samuel did, we need first to understand Sholem Aleichem's texts, which were revolutionary in their own time for their relatability. Conceived in the spirit of the Russian Skaz movement, his texts created a world of voices in which his contemporary Yiddish readership could hear their own. Until that point in Yiddish literary history, Yiddish literature tended to be designed for didactic, liturgical, or translational purposes.[46]

Samuel, however, was not drawing simply on the content of Sholem Aleichem's Yiddish stories to illuminate the East European Jewish world, but rather, in his presentation of Sholem Aleichem's unique vernacular style, was trying to create what Cynthia Ozick has called "a new Yiddish." In her controversial article "Toward a New Yiddish" (1983), Ozick argues that American Jewish literature must convey a "new Yiddish" in English—a Jewish idiom that defies the literary impulse toward assimilation into the American literary scene. Whereas she is highly critical of Norman Mailer, in whose work she discerns no distinctive Jewishness, she lauds Saul Bellow for creating a Russian Jewish idiom that is seamlessly translated into English yet maintains a certain distinctiveness that sets it apart from a standard American literary idiom.[47] We have already discussed the concept of a "new Yiddish" in the context of the transition of hybrid works throughout the twentieth century from largely textual to largely visual, arguing that American Jews' "new Yiddish" at the turn of the twentieth century was represented by a type of visual discourse that they could access without reliance on traditional forms of Jewish literacy. Here, in the middle of the twentieth century, "new Yiddish" in the works of Maurice Samuel can be seen in the politics of translation. Maurice Samuel's "new Yiddish" can be found in the way his English translations of Yiddish texts do not follow the standard linguistic protocols for translations, but rather preserve a history of intimacy, vernacularity, and folk ethnographic ambitions as he adapts them for an American audience.[48]

Ozick, in fact, had a special relationship with Maurice Samuel, having dedicated an essay to him in which she says,

> He set out like a climber negotiating a ledge; he hit on a point, sometimes an obstacle, sometimes a gratifying piece of good fortune . . . he was quick, he was fleet, he was dogged, he made connections. And still, when all this has been described, nothing has been described. What did he do? What was his job? His job was to address a generation and to explain.[49]

As a purveyor of "new Yiddish," by Ozick's assessment, Samuel strove to re-create a culture, to explain a moment and a place to a whole generation of American Jews who sought information about a world destroyed. In order to do so, he needed to draw on a series of texts that had done the very same thing in an earlier generation—spoken in the voice of a people about itself on the cusp of its demise.

I hesitate to argue that Sholem Aleichem wrote his texts with folk ethnographic ambitions, because I don't want to posit that salvage poetics can only express themselves in reprisals of texts with original salvage intentions. But what is important to recognize is that the particular literatures used by American Jewish adapters of Yiddish popular texts grew out of a moment in modern Jewish European history wherein Jews were moving en masse to big cities or to America. The younger generation was seeking knowledge outside of the Jewish literary canon, and modern youth groups and political movements were born even, and especially, among those who had stayed in provincial settings. Modern Yiddish (and Hebrew) literature grappled with modern Jewish experience, serving in large part as a locus for the complicated process of maintaining a cultural identity while adopting the norms and forms of modernity. What was Sholem Aleichem trying to accomplish in his depictions of gregarious, bumbling, striving Jews of East Europe: industrialists as well as *luftmenschen*, housewives as well as prostitutes? His fiction was both a commentary on and a continuation of Jewish life on the ground. It was not an idealization, not a prescription, but a reckoning. He wanted to show the Jews to themselves, their modernization as well as their traditionalism. In so doing, he created a perfect canvas for Samuel to paint his own portrait of American Jews reckoning with their own relationship to modernity. What were their prospects for preserving their tradition and still maintaining a foot in the New World?

In conjunction with and in contrast to Sholem Aleichem's particular vernacular presentation of the Jewish "street," Peretz's literary corpus, a bit more varied in genre and in style, maintained the pretext of belles lettres while allowing a popular glimpse into the underbelly of East European Jewish life—focusing on its classism, its poverty, its intellectualism at the expense of life-sustaining knowledge or capabilities. Peretz was a less forgiving writer than Sholem Aleichem. He didn't seem to have found East European Jewish foibles as engaging and amusing as did Sholem Aleichem. And thus he played a very different role than did Sholem Aleichem for a popular readership. Readers of Peretz appreciated him for his more conventional artistry than Sholem Aleichem provided, as well as for his honesty and his edge.

Peretz and Sholem Aleichem played different roles for American Jews. Even so, Samuel chooses to emphasize their similarities, not in style but in salvage mission, as he conceives it. Peretz, he maintains, is most useful to a second- or third-generation American-Jewish audience as a re-teller of Hasidic tales and less crucial as a critic of traditional culture. Whereas Samuel deemed Sholem Aleichem central to an American audience as the voice of East European Jewry, Peretz became his means of introducing modern East European religious literary norms to an American Jewish audience. Hasidic literature, cast earlier in the century by Buber as an indigenous modern Jewish East European folk form, became, in Samuel's hands, via Peretz, a means of reacquainting American Jewish with an "authentic" East European literary form of folk representation, uniquely modern but hagiographic and steeped in tradition. Samuel is explicit about why he chooses to represent only these texts in *Prince of the Ghetto*: "What Peretz did was to distill in his Chassidic and folk tales the spirit of east-European Jewry . . . [He was] entrusted with the timeless treasures of his people, the accumulated inheritance of many generations."[50]

In light of Peretz's literary choice to rework these earlier texts, Samuel writes about Peretz's presentation of himself in these works: "He was, in his stories, something of the maggid, or traditional preacher ... he loved and understood, with a depth which few have approached, the queer, futile, kabbalistic dreamers in the ancient out-of-the-way Talmudic academies."[51] Discussing his own objectives as an author and cultural critic, Samuel says, "I see myself as one of the maggidim, the wandering preachers of East European Jewry. My general objective is to help Jews acquire an interest in Jewish knowledge with the hope that they will transmit it to their children."[52]

A maggid would go from town to town sharing words of Torah and rabbinic legend, consoling the Jews in their exile and atoning in many cases for some misdemeanor of his own that destined him to an itinerant life, in exile from home and family; a maggid is a teller of tales who prioritizes the tale over his own physical sense of well-being and his own physical sense of welfare and being grounded in this world. Most important, a maggid is a re-teller of tales, someone who weaves earlier stories into his own as a means of linking the past with the present, of helping to make sense of the experience of exile through an articulation of stories of past exiles in the midst of the present one.

What are we to make of Samuel's parallel appellation of himself and Peretz as maggidim? Samuel claims to be a maggid in that he retells the stories of the Yiddish writers who came to define the experience of several generations of Jews, both in Europe and in the United States. But he acts as a maggid differently in his retelling of Peretz's stories and of Sholem Aleichem's stories. In Peretz's stories, Samuel views himself as a mediator for a literary corpus (Peretz's), which itself is mediating another set of texts (Hasidic stories). His work on Peretz in *Prince of the Ghetto* is primarily as a vehicle for a literary Jewish as well as a non-Jewish readership to understand that Jews have been artists, dreamers, and writers of fine literature throughout the modern period, from its earliest manifestation in the Hasidic movement and in its later one in modern Yiddish literature. In *The World of Sholem Aleichem*, on the other hand, the target audience is Jewish; Samuel's goal as stated in his introduction is to conduct a "pilgrimage among the cities and inhabitants of a world which only yesterday—as history goes—harboured the grandfathers and grandmothers of some millions of American citizens."[53]

The distinction between Samuel's identification with Peretz as a maggid and Sholem Aleichem as a pilgrim gets to the core of the differences between the two books. Although he explicitly calls himself a pilgrim like Sholem Aleichem, writing in his description of Sholem Aleichem's corpus, "It is all one long monologue, the recital of a pilgrimage,"[54] a pilgrim is someone who can walk through the streets and towns of a still extant world. A maggid, as Samuel identifies himself in *Prince of the Ghetto*, need not be in the world he describes. Indeed he can be centuries, or even millennia, from the world of his tales. And that is one of the fundamental reasons that, though only separated by five years, *The World of Sholem Aleichem* (1943) and *Prince of the Ghetto* (1948) are so dramatically different from one another in their approach to Yiddish literature as a basis for folk ethnographies of East European pre-Holocaust Jewish life within a post-Holocaust American context. In the earlier book Samuel addresses second- or third-generation American Jews who came from the Old Country in the years before the Holocaust. It was published in 1943, when East European Jewry was in the throes of its destruction by Hitler, but the extent of its fate was not yet well known in America. In fact, Jewish Europe had already undergone a wholesale destruction through the shifting borders of World War I and at least a century of encroaching Enlightenment, creeping from Western Europe to Eastern Europe, from the salons of Berlin to the study halls of Volozhin and Zhitomir. The story of Modern Hebrew and Yiddish literature, from the 1860s through the late 1930s, was the story of modernization, secularization, nationalization, politicization, and migration—from shtetl to big city, from Europe to the Americas and Palestine, from the houses of study to the universities (quotas permitting), from the homes of pious parents to the garrets of non-Jewish landladies. When in 1943 Samuel acknowledges in *The World of Sholem Aleichem* the decline of East European Jewish culture, he does so from the perspective of those Jews who left that world behind before the world was widely aware of the Einsatzgruppen or gas chambers. But by 1948, when *Prince of the Ghetto* was published, it was clear that a pilgrimage was no longer possible for his readers. They required a maggid. Of the plight of Polish Jewry, Samuel says:

> The Polish Jews who were the objects of Peretz's passionate and scrupulous concern have been wiped out by the modern world. Of the three and a quarter million, three million were done to death—gassed, machine-gunned, bombed, burned or buried alive. It did not matter at all whether they believed in the astronomy of Maimonides, derived from Ptolemy, or in Copernicus's; whether they were superstitious or scientific, antisocial reactionaries or social idealists. And nothing they could have done could have averted their fate! A whirlwind of human evil, altogether beyond their control and not to be evaded by any stratagem came upon them.[55]

Samuel emphasizes here the tragedy of Jewish intellectualism in the face of the Nazi Holocaust. *Prince of the Ghetto*, in its affirmation of Peretz's literariness, echoes this sentiment. In contrast to *The World of Sholem Aleichem*, which adopts the narratological style of Sholem Aleichem in its vernacular intimacy with the American reader, invoking Christmas trees and New Jersey suburbs, *Prince of the Ghetto* is geared toward a highly literate and highly literary readership. In his presentation of Peretz, Samuel attempts to demonstrate Jewish participation in literary discourse, not just during the period of Yiddish modernism that Peretz in large part defined, but during earlier periods that are preserved or "salvaged" in modern Yiddish literary texts. The register he employs throughout *Prince of the Ghetto* is best represented in the following passage, where he tries to give his readers a sense of the ecstatic culture of Hasidism:

> When Dante thunders against *accidie*, or heart heaviness, as a deadly sin, all he does is give us a sinking feeling at the stomach. Never was there gloomier exhortation to gaiety or a more depressing commendation of cheerfulness. Or, to take an altogether different instance, Spinoza's highly tenuous "intellectual love of God." There is something very real in the love of mathematical abstractions, and the simplest people have some

experience of it—witness the universal popularity of arithmetical puzzles. But this complete intellectual self-identification with the universe—at least as far as I can glimpse it in Spinoza—has little to do with the heart. "God intoxicated," Goethe called him.[56]

Moving from Dante to Spinoza to Goethe, and having alluded a few pages earlier to Proust, Samuel is targeting a highly literate audience for *Prince of the Ghetto*.

Because he is writing in English and granting access to an exclusively Jewish literary realm through his translation, Samuel is highly conscious of the risks he faces in a virulently anti-Semitic world. In discussing Peretz's more satiric writings, Samuel (who in the following text refers to the more satirical Peretz as P1 and the less so as P2) says,

> One advantage P1 enjoyed by virtue of the fact that he wrote in Yiddish for a closed audience: he was freed from the dilemma of the modern Jew who, writing about his people in the language of a gentile nation, must always bear in mind that his strictures are going to be read by the wrong people and may turn up in anti-Semitic pamphlets . . . One sometimes wonders whether the prophets would have been so outspoken if they had been prophetic enough to foresee that their denunciations of the Jewish people would be translated into every language in the world.[57]

Unlike Peretz, who, according to Samuel in the passage above, had the good fortune of writing for a "closed audience" in Yiddish, Samuel himself did not have that luxury, writing as he was in English. Speaking to his readers during a moment of universal self-castigation after the Second World War, the same year as the establishment of the State of Israel, Samuel is hopeful that an audience of "outsiders" may see the error of its ways. How could the nation that produced a fine literature, a literature to be discussed within the context of other fine literatures, be persecuted to the extent that it was in the Holocaust? Samuel's approach to Peretz's stories is respectful, maintaining their integrity. Even while presenting them whole cloth, he sometimes makes it unclear when the stories begin. Yet he always distinguishes between his voice as the narrator of *Prince of the Ghetto* and the narrators in the stories. Indeed, he chooses to reproduce stories that are intensely mediated, and self-conscious of their mediation, to draw attention to the fact that he, Samuel himself, is not stepping into the stories to mediate them as he did earlier in Sholem Aleichem's stories. A character in the well-known story "Between Two Mountains," for example, explicitly mediates a clash between the Hasidim of Biale and the Mitnagdim of Brisk. Shmayah, a student of the Rebbe of Biale (who, in his turn, was an errant student of the Rabbi of Brisk) and the narrator of the story, serves as the intermediary between these two rabbis when the Rabbi of Brisk's daughter is near death during childbirth in the city of Biale but her family refuses to allow the Rebbe of Biale to intercede with God on her behalf because of ideological differences. In introducing the tale (which he calls "Between Two Cliffs"), Peretz pointed out that "the man that tells the story is the one who is trapped between two cliffs."[58]

Throughout his studies of Sholem Aleichem and Peretz, Samuel employs a rhetoric of mediation, in which he discusses "insiders" and "outsiders" at varying levels. In *The World of Sholem Aleichem*, for example, Samuel discusses at great length the insiders of Old Kasrielevky and the outsiders of New Kasrielevky. Old Kasrielevky is the traditional, religious city, and New Kasrielevky is the city populated by Maskilim and secularized Jews, who, in the best of all possible worlds, work to educate their fellow townspeople and engage in political and nationalist organizing. In the worst of all possible worlds, they gamble, smoke on the Sabbath, and commit adultery as a matter of course. Nonetheless, old and new, inside and outside, as he defines them, are contained within the Jewish world.

In *Prince of the Ghetto*, however, he adds a new dimension to the mediation, presenting Peretz as an intermediary between the Jewish and non-Jewish worlds. As he begins an overview of Hasidism and explains the role of Peretz's stories in introducing the Hasidim to others, Samuel writes: "They could not explain themselves to others; their views and feelings had to be transmitted by emotional infection. Therefore it was inevitable that their foremost spokesman to the outside world should not have been one of them."[59] It is, in fact, unclear what Samuel means by "the outside world" because, particularly at the turn of the twentieth century, non-Jews presumably didn't read Yiddish, the language in which Peretz wrote. However, perhaps what Samuel means here is that Peretz's work of explaining Hasidism to the outside world through his adaptation of Hasidic tales within his own stories, is completed by the work of translators like Samuel himself.

Samuel sees himself as an outsider, akin to the way he describes Peretz. In his introduction to *Prince of the Ghetto*, Samuel writes the following:

> The man who has been alienated from his people and its ways during a number of formative years should enjoy a certain advantage when he has made his return: he should be able to see them from without and from within. He should be able to combine the appreciation of a stranger with the love of a kinsman, and, being of two worlds, he should—granted certain gifts—be well placed to act as interpreter between them . . . There is of course a corresponding disadvantage: he will never, in his position, become the unquestioning carrier of the tradition of his people. No matter how deeply he becomes implicated again in his folkways, he can never be the thing that he is explaining. His relationship to it will not be tacit, primal, and indivisible. He is touched with duality. His advantage is the advantage of an imperfection . . . If it is impossible for me to be a genuine insider because I have known what it is to be an outsider, I will at least put my reborn interest and affection at the service of permanent outsiders. If I cannot be a creator of Jewish values, I will try to be the interpreter of some of them . . . Now I, the returned stranger, must explain the world of this complex figure to other strangers.[60]

Why does Samuel feel that he has to justify his undertaking with Peretz by telling us that he has been alienated from his people, but that he has made a return? He acknowledges that he will never be the "unquestioning carrier of the tradition of his people," nor can he ever be "the thing that he is explaining." In this opening exposition on Peretz he calls himself a "returned stranger" and argues that he will never be a "genuine insider." He presents himself, however, not as a stranger, nor as an outsider, but qualifies his strangeness as that of a returnee, claiming insider status for himself even if not entirely genuine. To borrow his own rhetoric of "insider" and "outsider" from his introduction to Peretz, and to consider it in the context of his work on Sholem Aleichem, proves to be a fascinating exercise. Throughout that work Samuel presents the modernization of the shtetl in terms of "insiders" who constitute the traditionalist, Orthodox core of the provincial East European Jewish community versus "outsiders" who have left the world of the shtetl behind, if not geographically then ideologically. In other parlance, these "outsiders" would be called Maskilim or Enlighteners—those who sought to educate themselves in European languages and natural sciences and who migrated to big cities but inevitably returned to their hometowns to try to help shed the light of education and Europeanization on their more backward brethren.

This navigation of what it means to be simultaneously an insider and an outsider and what it means to mediate a literary text for different types of audiences determines, in the end, why *The World of Sholem Aleichem* presents us with one type of "hybrid" text and *Prince of the Ghetto* another. Although both focus on Yiddish literary texts as the basis for a more general extrapolation about Jewish culture and East European Jewish life, Samuel positions himself at the heart of the work on Sholem Aleichem as its narrator, while he doesn't insinuate himself into Peretz's text in the same way. In *Prince of the Ghetto*, Samuel relies on Peretz's own poetic of mediation to present the texts to his audience, whereas in *The World of Sholem Aleichem* Samuel presents himself as the mediating voice, in many instances replacing Sholem Aleichem. Why this difference? His audiences are different. He needs to insinuate himself into Sholem Aleichem's work because he needs to build a bridge between his popular audience and himself in order to educate them, orient them, and endear them to the literature and to the world represented therein. In the case of Peretz, he basically wants to orient a literary readership to the literariness of modern Jewish experience.

Another way to look at the difference between Samuel's approach in each of these texts is to consider them within the broader context of salvage poetics. Peretz, by rewriting and re-presenting Hasidic tales in his modernist corpus, was preserving a certain type of Jewish literature and the culture for which it served as an artifact. Peretz was already engaging in a salvage undertaking, which Samuel saw himself as transmitting through translation and light contextualization. In the case of Sholem Aleichem, however, the stories themselves, in their vernacular idiom, in their approachability and humor, were the stuff that required salvage, not its vehicle. Samuel must engage in the salvage of that work, so revolutionary in its moment, and indicative of an East European Jewish desire to be known on its own terms—in its daily routines and in its own voice. His reframing of those stories, his adoption of the vernacular norms that characterized and distinguished Sholem Aleichem's work within modern Yiddish letters, indicates Samuel's desire to reconstitute Sholem Aleichem's works for salvage purposes within an American Jewish context.

We have explored the differences between *The World of Sholem Aleichem* and *Prince of the Ghetto*, but it is also valuable to investigate their commonalities. Although in *Prince of the Ghetto* Samuel generally does not explicitly incorporate himself into the stories the way he does in *The World of Sholem Aleichem*, he is not entirely consistent in this. As we have already seen, Samuel simultaneously alludes to an audience that may or may not know Yiddish, an audience of both Jewish and non-Jewish "outsiders" in America. However, as the book opens, he adopts some of the narrative norms of *The World of Sholem Aleichem*, inserting himself into the book's first section as he translates and contextualizes Peretz's story "Mesiras Nefesh," or "Devotion unto Death." In his presentation of this story, he comes closer to "selvedge translation" in *Prince of the Ghetto* than anywhere else in the book. This is significant for a number of reasons. First, while I have tried hard to distinguish the styles and audiences for both of these books throughout this analysis, in his presentation of "Mesiras Nefesh" Samuel demonstrates affinities between them. Second, this same story is featured prominently in Irving Howe and Eliezer Greenberg's *A Treasury of Yiddish Stories* (under the title "Devotion without End"), which we will be discussing in the fourth chapter. Comparing Howe and Greenberg's and Samuel's translations of the same story helps us to understand that, though they differ in significant ways, Samuel's two major presentations of Yiddish fiction in *The World of Sholem Aleichem* and *Prince of the Ghetto* appear closer to one another when held up to other works that engage in variations of salvage poetics than when they are discussed only in relation to one another.

In his style of presenting and translating Peretz's "Mesiras Nefesh," Samuel demonstrates a tendency toward selvedge translation, even in a book where, as I have already asserted, he keeps himself mostly at arm's length. Samuel begins the story by naming its main characters—"Chiya, Chananya, and Miriam are the chief protagonists. Chiya we meet as a marvelous young man"[61]—and then dives right into the narrative without any separation of his voice from the story's narrative voice. This is reminiscent of his approach in *The World of Sholem Aleichem* wherein Samuel's voice becomes the voice of Sholem Aleichem. Furthermore, in comparing his translation to Howe and Greenberg's, we see that Samuel is more inclined toward streamlining Peretz's voice with his own, for the purpose of easing his readership into Peretz's original story. Samuel cuts out most of Peretz's intertextual allusions, in part due to his awareness that an English readership may not be able to identify those texts, hence they might not enhance the English version of the story in the way they would the Yiddish. On the other hand, Howe's and Greenberg's translation often preserves them. For example, in the following Howe and Greenberg preserve an allusion to Queen Esther and a quotation from the book of Proverbs is quoted directly:

> Miriam [Chiya's daughter] was like a gift from heaven, a child of loveliness. All of Safed basked in her beauty and goodness, saying, "Reb Chiya's daughter is radiant as the sun. She moves with the grace and charm of Queen Esther." But the ways of God are beyond understanding, and as King Solomon once said, "Whomever God loves, him does He chastise." Often the Almighty tests the pious by visiting many sorrows upon them to see how deep and strong is their faith. Be that as it may, the virtuous Sarah [Chiya's wife] suddenly fell sick.[62]

In Samuel's translation of the same passage, we read:

> Miriam grew in beauty and godliness and became a byword in
> the land. All of which was too good to last, even in a fairy tale.
> Suddenly, in the midst of one of his journeys, Reb Chiya received
> word that his saintly wife had been struck down by sickness.[63]

The allusiveness of the Howe-Greenberg translation is entirely omitted in the Samuel translation. While the diction of Samuel's translation is quite high, creating a biblical or formal effect, he avoids any
overt necessity for textual recognition or Jewish traditional book
learning. As Jeffrey Shandler has argued in his discussion of Yiddish in
America, rather than actually knowing Yiddish, many Americans have
a sense of Yiddish, and communicate in a Yiddish spirit as opposed
to a Yiddish vernacular.[64] A Yiddish post-vernacular, wherein Yiddish
functions less as a language than as a cultural association and/or a
mood, is the result.

 This suppression of Hebrew within the Yiddish, or the sacred language within the literary vernacular, is even more evident in the presentation, in both translations, of a letter Chiya writes to the head of
the Jewish community in Babylonia as he seeks out a husband for his
daughter Miriam. Howe and Greenberg's translation reads as follows:

> It was on this theme that he once wrote to the head of the Bab-
> ylonian yeshiva, a sage with whom he corresponded on all mat-
> ters holy and profane. He wrote in that flowery Hebrew which is
> only proper for such subjects, and as we transpose it here into
> profane Yiddish it must lose much of its sweetness.[65]

Samuel's translation of the same passage reads as follows: "He now
addressed himself to the incumbent in Babylon, and wrote to him,
in the flower and allusive phraseology proper to such a subject and
to such correspondents, the following letter."[66] Samuel's translation
does not allude to the Hebrew, which allows him to avoid acknowledging the translational endeavor altogether, further streamlining his
version for perusal by an audience not interested in baring the device
that brought the story to their door.

The original Yiddish version of this passage is particularly compelling because the narrator tells us that he will translate the letter into Yiddish, and, although he apologizes for doing so, he inserts Hebrew phrases in parentheses throughout, which suggests that the original text's Hebrew is essential to understanding what is being discussed:

> With help from Almighty God I have planted a beautiful garden (meaning: a yeshivah [ישיבה]), with all kinds of trees that grow all kinds of fruits (meaning: the students [תלמידים]) and because a particular fruit is growing plump and juicy (meaning: ready to be married off [ראוי לחופה]) I am looking for an appropriate person (a worthy groom [א שעהנעם מחותן]) and call to him to make a blessing over him (a marriage blessing [ברכת נישואין]).[67]

All the "translated" words and phrases, except for the fourth, א שעהנעם מחותן, are Hebrew words that have become part of the Yiddish language, incorporated from their Hebrew sacred sources within the domain of Jewish ritual observance and institutions. They are distinguishable, however, from Yiddish words of non-Hebraic origin in that they maintain their Hebrew, vowel-less spelling. Therefore, for a Hebrew-literate reader, these words are easily identifiable as both Hebrew and sacred, because it is only sacred Hebrew words that maintain their original Hebrew morphology in Yiddish.

By promising us a translation into Yiddish and then inserting Hebrew words into parentheses, Peretz is emphasizing the many layers of Yiddish language and culture. Despite its absurdity, the narrator feels the need to euphemize the Jewish institutions of matchmaking and marriage—which can easily be stated in a uniquely Jewish idiom, that is, a Hebrew-based Yiddish—while still alluding to the actual words used in the letter. His role as a translator is not only to render the florid Hebrew of the original letter into Yiddish, but to translate the Yiddish back into the Hebrew that strips the letter of its wholly metaphorical meaning. The complexities of this back and forth are lost in Samuel's translation because he chooses not to mention the narrator's role as translator from Hebrew to Yiddish. Certainly both translations (Howe and Greenberg's as well as Samuel's) lose the irony of the parenthetical

translations back into Hebrew-based Yiddish, but Samuel's is the far-
thest removed of the three from the ironies and humor of the letter
writer who chooses to obfuscate his message through metaphors and
who needs the letter's Yiddish translation to still provide Hebrew
language so that its readership will understand its message.

Maurice Samuel was well aware of the nature of Yiddish and the
role that Hebrew plays therein. In his final book, *The Meaning of Yiddish* (1971), Samuel devotes at least half the book to explicating the
linguistic components of Yiddish, with a thorough and erudite discussion of Hebrew's place in it. He says:

> The oldest words in Yiddish are taken directly from the Bible, the
> Talmud, the Midrash, and the various prayerbooks—daily and
> festival—the last two overlapping a great deal with the first two.
> These words, as we have seen, retain an evocative sacred or his-
> torical flavor, and even in completely secularized contexts lead
> the memory back to their origins.[68]

He continues his explication with a reflection on how this preservation of the Hebrew language within Yiddish serves a salvage purpose:

> It can hardly be doubted that this insulation of the Hebrew-
> Yiddish words from their Germanic and Slavic-Yiddish environ-
> ment had a cultural-spiritual purpose. The conscious motive may
> have been purely pietistic, a revulsion from the de-judaization
> of the Hebrew word. Certainly the effort was to keep Hebrew
> partly alive in the daily intercourse of the unlearned masses and
> just as certainly the successful resuscitation of Hebrew in Israel
> after two thousand years was thereby greatly facilitated. This
> far-flung "program," as it may justly be called, has no parallel
> in history.[69]

Samuel here articulates a view that the structure of Yiddish is designed
to salvage Hebrew. As we have discussed, his approach to Peretz's
work in general presupposes that it is already performing an act of
salvage by retelling Hasidic stories and folktales, and therefore Samuel need not recast it as a salvage work as much as he simply needs to

frame it anew for an English-reading audience. So too does Samuel omit any explicit framing of Peretz's ironic approach to the relationship between Hebrew and Yiddish as being either too nuanced and complex for an English readership, or already an act of salvage that needs no further introduction because this book was published just after the Holocaust when the need for cultural salvage was obvious.

The fact that this particular story finds its way both into Howe's anthology as well as Samuel's work draws attention to the story's themes as they might appeal to an American Jewish audience. Most important, the story is an amalgam of doubling. In it two matches are made, one successfully and one unsuccessfully; two widower fathers attempt to marry off their daughters to learned men, one successfully and one unsuccessfully; wealth is coupled in one instance with piety and in another with impiety. Most important is the doubling that characterizes the main protagonist of the story, Chananya, who, in line with a well-known Jewish folk motif, is stripped of his brilliant mastery of the Torah due to his excessive pride. After having shamed another scholar and deprived him of his bride, he forgets everything he knows and has to learn Judaism as would a child. This notion of knowing everything and nothing at the same time, this simultaneous gesture toward both knowledge and ignorance, making them opposite sides of the same coin, can be reassuring to a reader who knows very little about Jewish culture or literature. A story in which he who knows everything and he who knows nothing are not so distant from one another can be a very useful idea when presenting this text to an American gentile or especially an American Jewish audience. In an era where Jewish knowledge and literacy is waning, this may be an important populist message. Also, in a text where the author is adapting the work of another author in order to introduce him as representative of a foreign, yet highly personal and evocative culture, this doubling dynamic addresses the sense of the readership as possibly a group of "lost souls" who have only to have their eyes opened up to become "found" again.

Samuel, as have I argued, is interested in creating an image of the shtetl that puts an English-language readership at its ease. He is committed to helping them find themselves in these stories and to that end he re-creates their essence by inserting himself into them as an English-speaking Sholem Aleichem–type narrator speaking in a "new Yiddish." Howe, on the other hand, as I will argue further along, is addressing an audience whose own personal investment in the texts is not as important to him as is an embrace of this literature as worthy of global recognition and stylistic affirmation. It is true that Samuel is also aware of the highly literary appeal of Peretz and emphasizes that aspect of it. Even so, in his presentation of this particular story, he seems to pursue more of the approach he used in *The World of Sholem Aleichem*.

As we move into an analysis of Abraham Joshua Heschel's *The Earth Is the Lord's*, it behooves us to return for a moment to the beginning of our discussion of *The World of Sholem Aleichem* and *Prince of the Ghetto*. Why is it necessarily instructive to consider these works at the intersection of ethnographic and literary concerns and methods? If we believe that Samuel is engaging in selvedge translation in order to bring these Yiddish literary texts as close as possible to an American readership, then shouldn't we consider that anthropological models have been under highly critical scrutiny for the last half century at least as a means of othering, not building bridges? Ethnographers themselves have become acutely conscious of the colonial origins of modern anthropology. But because Samuel's text dabbles in folk ethnography while expanding its horizons through experiments in translation, he is able to move beyond the colonializing and/or othering tendencies of ethnographic texts in order to create a very special kind of thick translation, a selvedge translation that lays the foundation for Yiddish literature as folk ethnographic fodder in American Jewish post-Holocaust culture.

2

SALVAGE INWARDNESS

The Hasidic Tale in Abraham
Joshua Heschel's *The Earth Is the Lord's*

The little Jewish communities in Eastern Europe were like sacred texts opened before the eyes of God so close were their houses of worship to Mount Sinai.[1]

Koretz, Karlin, Bratslav, Lubavich, Ger, Lublin—hundreds of little towns were like holy books.[2]

Originally delivered as a eulogy of East European Jewry on January 7, 1945, at the nineteenth annual conference of the YIVO Institute, "The East European Era in Jewish History" by Abraham Joshua Heschel (1907–72) first appeared in print in Yiddish, in the March–April 1945 edition of *YIVO Bleter*. It appeared again in Yiddish the following year under the title "The East European Jew," published by Schocken. Also in 1946, an English translation of the original Yiddish text appeared in the first volume of the *YIVO Annual of Social Science*; this English version reappeared many times throughout the second half of the twentieth century, including, slightly abridged, as the preface to Roman Vishniac's 1947 *Polish Jews*. A longer version of the essay, and the one that serves as the basis for our analysis, alongside brief references to the original English translation published in the *YIVO Annual*, was first published by Henry Schuman in 1949 under the title *The Earth Is the Lord's: The Inner World of the Jew in Eastern Europe*, with woodcuts of scenes from shtetl life by Ilya Schor (1904–61).[3]

The visual aspects of *The Earth Is the Lord's*, alongside Vishniac's 1947 *Polish Jews* and Howe and Greenberg's 1954 *Treasury*, mark a critical example of the transition from text to image that I hope to document as American Jews during the immediate postwar period in America, having moved away from traditional Jewish literacy as well as from fluency in Yiddish, sought new ways to connect to an authentic "ethnic" East European Judaism. In his analysis of the relationship between image and text in American-Jewish constructions of authenticity, Ken Koltun-Fromm argues that "images and texts work together to construct powerful claims to authenticity, and to restrain lingering fears of inauthenticity."[4] Discussing Schor's contribution to Heschel's *The Sabbath* (1951), executed just one year after *The Earth Is the Lord's*, Koltun-Fromm says,

> Schor's engravings confront readers as visual markers of the ineffable. They evoke a world beyond technical culture and commerce and consider looking through to the beyond to be an authentic vision. Schor's images are persistently nostalgic of an East European Jewish heritage and move a viewer's gaze away from American civilization toward a more ethereal, Edenic past.[5]

In his reading of Schor's visual rendition of Heschel's presentation in *The Sabbath*, an anti-materialist theology in which the East European Jewish tradition is looked to as an alternative to the materialism of the quickly assimilating Jews of America, Koltun-Fromm observes, "Ilya Schor's engravings, appearing before each chapter in *The Sabbath*, capture this sense of a home beyond the American shores."[6] Structured similarly, the images in *The Earth Is the Lord's* also serve as an important commentary on the anti-assimilationist yet pro-modern ideologies implicit in Heschel's eulogy to East European Jewish culture and his appeal to spiritual authenticity for American Jews. While we will not focus exclusively on the visual aspects of *The Earth Is the*

Lord's, in this analysis we will discuss Schor's drawings as they pertain to our broader observation about the transition from textual to visual means of accessing an East European Jewish past for American Jews in the immediate post-Holocaust era, and the construction of a folk ethnography out of a marriage between the visual and the textual during those years.

Ilya Schor, born in Eastern Europe to a Hasidic family, like Heschel, and emigrating to the United States during World War II, also like Heschel, was considered by critics to offer in his art an unmediated, authentic version of East European Jewish life, based on personal experience and memory. His images of East European Jewish life and traditions in his work as a silversmith as well as an artist of Judaica, were considered "more real than dreams, more natural than what you see, more typical than what could be described."[7] As we will explore, these assertions of "typicality" and "naturalness," made by Stephen S. Kayser, an early curator at the Jewish Museum of New York, in reference to Schor's work, feed into Heschel's particular interest in *The Earth Is the Lord's* in animating the "inner world" of the Jews of Eastern Europe in a variety of different ways. The intricate drawings that precede each chapter of *The Earth Is the Lord's* play a crucial role in the salvage poetic of the book, a salvage poetic that appoints as its salvage artifact tales of the Hasidim. As Kayser further remarks in an introduction to a 1947 exhibition catalogue of Schor's paintings, on display at the short-lived "Gallery of Jewish Art":

> One thing in these pictures is not transitory; their substance. It has amalgamated all blood of the artistic forebears in order to bring out the indestructible strength of the little people appearing here. Within carved frames they live on to be your brethren. Welcome them as such.[8]

This exhortation to an audience of American Jews, echoing the rhetoric employed by Maurice Samuel in his opening to *The World of Sholem Aleichem*, speaks to Heschel's particular goal, one that we will trace throughout this discussion, to find a body of work that can speak to an American Jewish audience in search of a spiritual coherence that does

not threaten its status in a modern America. Alongside our discussion
of Heschel's rhetoric we will consider the particular contribution of
Schor's images to the salvage poetics implicit in *The Earth Is the Lord's*.

Heschel's "The East European Era in Jewish History," which preceded *The Earth Is the Lord's* with its accompanying illustrations,
though conceived as an oral eulogy, may be Heschel's most frequently
published work, according to Jeffrey Shandler. It is said to be the second of only three major Yiddish published works (his native tongue
was Yiddish), the first a book of poetry titled *The Ineffable Name of
God: Man* (1933) and the last a study of the Rebbe of Kotzk, *Kotzk
the Struggle for Integrity*, published posthumously in 1973. In a com-
memorative essay published after Heschel's death, the Yiddish edu-
cator and linguist Yudel Mark claimed that "The East European Era
in Jewish History" and its offshoots represent the heart of Heschel's
major philosophical works, *God in Search of Man* (1951) and *Man Is
Not Alone* (1956).[9]

In this chapter, we will look closely at different variations of
this eulogy-turned-panegyric in order to better understand how certain themes and strategies for transforming this text into a primary
source for American Jewish folk ethnography played themselves out.
We will consider the "insider" and "outsider" dynamics that we introduced in our discussion of Samuel's work as they pertain to the rhetoric
of an "inner world" in Heschel's 1949 title, as well as to the particulars
of Heschel's own biography and his standing in relation to his American audience. We will also look at how Heschel uses primary literary
texts, through retellings as well as allusions to bodies of work and
scholarly discourse, to construct a bridge between his American Jewish
audience and the pious Hasidic community he represents in *The Earth
Is the Lord's*. Heschel's effort at bridging will become the fulcrum of
our discussion as we try to understand how he explicates the centrality
of traditional Jewish scholarship to Jewish life in Eastern Europe. He
never quotes, however, from traditional Jewish scholarly texts or places
them into the mouths of his protagonists. Rather, he quotes mainly
from Hasidic tales and hagiographies.[10]

What does Heschel mean by the phrase "inner world" in the subtitle of his final published version of the original speech, *The Earth*

Is the Lord's? This notion of an "inner world" is essential to understanding the complex ways in which a living culture can best envision a dead culture, or a local culture imagine a distant one. Most important, an "inner" appellation can be understood as the articulation of a desire to access something seemingly inaccessible that is critical to self-understanding—while still acknowledging its generalized inaccessibility.

In this discussion, we will explore how Heschel's presentation of "inwardness" serves as something of a corrective for the binaries that other works we have explored or have yet to explore in this volume have established between "inner" and "outer" worlds, or between American and East European Jews. Different works strain in different ways to acknowledge the limitations of this binary construction of "inner" and its implied "outer" while still using this polarity to make their depiction of a destroyed world easily accessible. Maurice Samuel, as we have seen, attempted to merge his own voice with that of Sholem Aleichem, with mixed success, whereas in his later work on Peretz he kept a safer distance, reinforcing the idea that no matter how hard he tried, he would always remain an outsider to the worlds he was attempting to describe.

The "inner world" for Heschel is twofold: on the one hand, the texts of traditional Jewish scholarship constitute artifacts of the inner world of East European Jewry; on the other, Hasidim constitute the inner world not just of a localized Jewry, but indeed of the Jewish religion writ large. In tracing these two elements of Heschel's "inner world" as he calls it in the subtitle to *The Earth Is the Lord's*, I will continue our discussion of salvage poetics with a proposed conciliation of the series of binaries evident in the other texts we will look at. Because Heschel himself inhabited two worlds—that of Jewish tradition, and more specifically Hasidic Jewish tradition, in Eastern Europe and that of modern American Jewish progressive culture—he is best situated, among all the other authors and works we have examined, to propose a way to bridge the two.

Ilya Schor, too, seemed to be the most suitable artist for the project undertaken by Abraham Joshua Heschel in *The Earth Is the Lord's*. According to his daughter, the artist and scholar Mira Schor,

There was no else so qualified in his talents, his world view, and his closeness to some of the core spirit of Hasidism. Other Jewish artists of the period wouldn't have done as well: Mane Katz was too expressionistic, Chagall too much into his own style and mythology to think as intimately and philosophically about Judaism as Heschel. And no American could have the personal knowledge of a place and time. Ilya Schor's unique experiences as a child in a Hasidic family in Eastern Europe, as a teenager with a guild apprenticeship in pre-modern skills, and as a modernist artist in Warsaw, Paris, and New York made him the perfect and only illustrator for Heschel's text.[11]

In an unpublished lecture for a synagogue in Great Neck where he designed and executed an Ark, Schor discusses his Hasidic background: "I come from a small city in Poland and not only do I come from a small Jewish city but our little house stood in the most Jewish part of the city. My home was a fanatical Chassidic one." After leaving his Jewish upbringing behind, he describes his journey through Warsaw and Paris, studying art, saying that after all that, "when I sat down to make a cup, the cup that I made was a Kiddush cup. It came just like that, it was normal, spontaneous."[12] Schor's art, borne of a marriage of two worlds, in conjunction with Heschel's, served as the perfect bridge for American Jews to understand Heschel's portrait of East European Jewish culture in the postwar era.

Schor, conscious of a unique moment of openness within the American Jewish community toward the possibility of "Jewishness," points to the synagogue as a potential locus of Jewish artistic expression that could recapture some of the lost culture of Europe, but he laments what he considers a lack of interest or commitment on the part of the community. In another unpublished synagogue lecture, he says:

And let me say a few words what is going on right now, what happened in the Jewish world of art. In Russia the Jewish writers were killed by Stalin, the Jewish theaters closed. Six million Jews have been killed by Hitler, all the wooden synagogues burnt down, all the sources from where we took our imagination were filled with blood and then dried up. Two other great centers of Jews are now in the world, one in America and the other in Israel. What happened in America? A religious revival? Yes? But what about the arts? I would say and you can believe me, nothing happens. Yes, hundreds and perhaps thousands of synagogues are being built. Their style? Bauhaus Frank Lloyd Wright, the ultra ultra modern. The insides besides a few banal symbols cheaply executed or sometimes pieces of modern art without any Jewish meaning. We are only 16 years away from the great destruction of the Eastern Jews and it looks like it would be a thousand years ago.[13]

Thus, in contrast to what he was later to observe about the limitations of architecture and synagogue art as the locus of a reinvigoration of Jewish art after the war, the possibility of executing Jewish art in the pages of a book like Heschel's, it seems, provided Schor with an early opportunity to experiment with Jewish American interest in the artistic possibilities of revisiting the lost world. Illustration, in its combination of the textual and the visual, was to become the channel that architecture and synagogue art could not.

Around the same time that he illustrated *The Earth Is the Lord's*, between 1949 and 1953, Schor also illustrated Heschel's *The Sabbath* (1951) as well as an English translation of *Motel, Paysie the Chazan's Son* (1953).[14] Each of them, to quote Mira Schor, was "illustrated in a different register of representation and a slightly different hand," reflecting the level of experimentation he was engaged in during the immediate postwar period as he sought to renew Jewish artistic expression in America.[15]

To explore the complexities of bridging between East European and American Jewish culture by creating a uniquely, literarily inspired salvage poetic, we will look at *The Earth Is the Lord's*, one of Heschel's earliest works (in both Yiddish and English), in tandem with his final works (in both Yiddish and English) on the Rebbe of Kotzk. Through his presentation of the essentiality of traditional Jewish religious texts in forging Jewish community in Eastern Europe, attended by his illumination of the particular, modern, modernist, and literary Hasidic spirituality, we see Heschel articulating modernity for American Jews as an idea and a reality that can be understood in fundamentally Jewish terms but with a modern edge. In other words, Hasidism, to Heschel, represents modernity, and Hasidic tales are, as is Yiddish literature to the authors of *Life Is with People*, both Jewish and modern. Therefore, the portrait that he paints in *The Earth Is the Lord's* is of an inner world that is not out of reach or different from the experience of American Jews, but rather part of a modern continuum.

In her study of the popular arts of American Jewish ethnography, Barbara Kirshenblatt-Gimblett identifies *The Earth Is the Lord's: The Inner World of the Jew in Eastern Europe* as a critical harbinger for Mark Zborowski and Elizabeth Herzog's *Life Is with People*. Indeed, both works reduce East European Jewish life to almost entirely spiritualized sketches, ignoring geography, economics, and the bulk of modernity. Yet what is more important to Kirshenblatt-Gimblett in comparing the two books is that although *Life Is with People* was written as a formal ethnography, it borrowed liberally from the spirit and energy of Heschel's book. In its embrace of folk ethnographic terms and depictions, *The Earth Is the Lord's* served as a model for *Life Is with People*, perhaps inspiring Zborowski and Herzog to pursue a formal ethnographic project. Kirshenblatt-Gimblett says that "without ever using the term ethnography, the 1949 preface to *The Earth Is the Lord's* invokes this modality and transmutes it."[16] Consider, for instance, the following language from Heschel's preface to which she refers:

> The story about the life of the Jews in East Europe, which has come to an end in our days, is what I have tried to tell in this essay. I have not talked about their books, their art or institutions, but about their daily life, about their habits and customs, about their attitudes toward the basic things in life, about the scale of values, which directed their aspirations.... My task was, not to explain, but to see, to discern and to depict.[17]

Heschel's allusion here to the "daily life," "habits and customs," and "attitudes about the basic things in life," all of which he feels himself to have been tasked with seeing, discerning, and depicting, perhaps explains the ways in which Kirshenblatt-Gimblett identifies *The Earth Is the Lord's* as channeling an ethnographic modality. Even more important, however, is the way that *The Earth Is the Lord's*, despite its not having been written as a professional ethnography, or indeed *because* it was not written as such, took on the mantle of a folk ethnography, profoundly influencing even those professional ethnographies that were to follow it. Furthermore, the act of seeing the "daily life" of the Jews, described here by Heschel, beautifully echoes simultaneously the visual and ethnographic rhetoric used by Stephen S. Kayser in an assessment of Schor's art. There he says, "a vivid look into memory, and they appear: the little men with the great creed. Their prayers and their works, their ways and manners become alive in a few hasty strokes."[18] In a fascinating conceit of the theatricality that emphasizes the visual and the unmediated "everyday" quality of Schor's art, Kayser further remarks, "up goes the curtain of this little theater. How small a stage that is! The director, who is also a silver smith of minutest artistic forms, has the wings and all the characters at hand. At his will they appear. They do not act. They have no masks. Their roles and lives are one."[19] And in an overview of Schor's work, Dalia Tawil identifies these qualities as uniquely ethnographic: "He introduced the ethnographic image-symbols of Eastern European Jewry into the traditional forms of ceremonial objects of earlier periods and succeeded in evolving a completely Jewish ceremonial art."[20] Thus, as we proceed with our discussion of the perceived ethnographic qualities of Heschel's presentation, it is important to consider the visual aspects of that direction in his work as well, fostered not only by his rhetoric but by the choice of art to accompany his text and artist to execute it.

While Kirshenblatt-Gimblett identifies Heschel's ethnographic "modality" in his invocation of the collective and not the particular and in his use of language that leads the reader into the realm of the "cultural" as opposed to the historical, I will argue that Heschel invokes this modality most acutely through his deployment of the Hasidic tale throughout *The Earth Is the Lord's*. In his use of a variety of Hasidic tales he marks his text as "hybrid" in the sense that we have been tracing thus far throughout our study of salvage poetics. In *The Earth Is the Lord's*, Heschel appoints the Hasidic tale as the literary artifact on which he bases his depiction of East European Jewish pre-Holocaust experience both to render his account more accessible to a popular American-Jewish audience and to complicate and deepen the nearly totalizing way in which he presents Torah study and traditional scholarship as the cornerstone of the life he represents. Just as in *Life Is with People* the authors used a Yiddish literary framework to inject a modernist anthropological perspective as well as literary concerns with subjectivity into their ethnography, so too does Heschel in *The Earth Is the Lord's* choose the tales of the Hasidim as the literary corpus for maintaining a modern sensibility. In the salvage poetic at play here, which addresses an audience in dire need (according to Heschel) of spiritual direction through the prism of modernity, he uses stories couched in a religious movement that married modernity with piety and simultaneously valorized scholars while downplaying scholarship as the basis for a discussion of East European Jewish life. The Hasidic tales, therefore, provide the literary superstructure throughout Heschel's important work.

The Earth Is the Lord's, one of Heschel's earliest works published in America, is critical, as we will see, to his own philosophical oeuvre as well as to our understanding of the role of salvage poetics in the construction of a post-Holocaust American Jewish folk ethnography of pre-Holocaust East European Jewish life. To better understand this important 1949 book, we will also look at its 1946 precursor, "The Eastern European Era in Jewish History," with an eye toward some significant differences between the two, particularly in Heschel's deployment of Hasidic tales.

We will turn first to a tale that will serve as our first introduction to the role played by the Hasidic tale in Heschel's construction of a primary text of folk ethnography:

> Rabbi Zusya of Hanipol once started to study a volume of the Talmud. A day later his disciples noticed that he was still dwelling on the first page. They assumed that he must have encountered a difficult passage and was trying to solve it. But when a number of days passed and he was still immersed in the first page, they were astonished, but did not dare to query the master. Finally one of them gathered courage and asked him why he did not proceed to the next page. And Rabbi Zusya answered: "I feel so good here, why should I go elsewhere?"[21]

This story provides us with several variations on an "inner world." First of all, we glimpse the inner world of Hasidic life, with a Rebbe at its center, and his disciples, all male, around him. We learn that the Hasidim both championed and challenged the value of Talmud study, which gives the reader a sense of the Hasidic movement's history as a movement that was created to defamiliarize traditional notions of piety and its link to scholarship even while engaging in both. This story also gives us a glimpse into the "inner world" of Hasidic literature by embodying common elements, from the hagiography of a single named rabbi, to the anonymity of the collective consciousness, to the pithy statement resolving the felt conflict. Finally, we are witness to the inner world of Rabbi Zusya, a man capable of becoming permanently caught in a single text, with no desire to move beyond it.

Throughout *The Earth Is the Lord's*, Heschel creates a portrait of a people who, like Rabbi Zusya, stick to their *dalet amot* (in rabbinic parlance), or their tiny piece of the world. But they dig deeply into that piece of the world, finding comfort, meaning, and peace in spiritual depth but not intellectual breadth. Heschel's theology, called "depth theology," is implicit in the above tale. In his own words, depth theology "seeks to meet the person in moments in which the whole person is involved, in moments which are affected by all a person thinks, feels and acts. It draws upon that which happens to man in moments of confrontation with ultimate reality."[22] Depth theology, according to Heschel, is a method designed to help individuals evaluate "depth of faith." He asserts that "to apprehend the depth of religious faith we try to ascertain not so much what the person is able to express as that which he is unable to express, the insights that no language can declare."[23]

According to Heschel's biographer, Edward K. Kaplan, depth theology is "an integration of intuition and sacred history," which served throughout Heschel's career as the basis for his pluralistic and interfaith work.[24] Because depth theology enables individuals to trace the process of coming to faith and of using that faith to connect with others, it became the cornerstone for a Jewish theology of pluralism in which Jews of all types work together to find a common faith and also the basis for interfaith dialogue.

Commensurate, in visual terms, with the depth theology developed by Heschel, is the way in which Schor's paintings and sculptures embody a depth of craftsmanship (figures 2.1 and 2.2). According to Mira Schor, in her father's work

> every object is built up of or adorned with many details of religious and village life, each element is engraved, cut out of silver and gold or other metals, and soldered onto a surface that may also be engraved with Hebrew letters, floral patterns, or ornamental designs . . . Every piece has an unseen side that is often just as ornamented as the front so that no matter how beautiful and joyous the image, there is a sense of loss inherent to the construction of the work: some part of the representation is always just outside our field of vision—always lacking, despite the exhilaration of its existence.[25]

FIGURE 2.1. Ilya Schor, metalwork, front/back bracelet (1958). Used by permission of Mira Schor, 2018.

Mira Schor further comments on the cultural resonances of this kind of "depth" with reference to Hasidism:

> That the unseen is even more beautiful than the seen, yet in the more modest material of silver, is again a reflection of the Hasidic penchant for the mystical appeal of humility. The charm is in the individual detail, the musician or the dancer or the bird; the power is in the detailed nature of the execution and the transformation of a metal into lace.[26]

The darkness and complexity of Shor's drawings, and the wealth of ethnographic details behind all the human figures, mirrors the kind of "depth" discussed by Mira in her overview of her father's work.

This "depth" can be understood in light of ethnographic tableaux and narrative continuities, as well as in terms of the craftsmanship alluded to by Mira above. In Schor's image of the Simhat Torah

FIGURE 2.2. Ilya Schor, wood engraving. Illustration for chapter 4, "For the People," from Abraham Joshua Heschel, *The Earth Is the Lord's: The Inner World of the Jew in Eastern Europe* (New York: Farrar, Straus and Giroux, 1949), 39. Used by permission of Mira Schor, 2018.

celebration, for instance, featured on the cover of Heschel's book as well as preceding the second chapter "With All Thy Heart," we see a father leading his son to synagogue, but we also observe East European children's traditions of Simhat Torah: while men hold the Torah and dance with them, children hold flags topped with apples and candles. We also observe traditional Hasidic holiday dress: the men all wear *streimlach* or fur-ringed hats, while the children wear visored caps. The visual iconography of the shtetl is also represented in this picture, with a riot of wooden houses in the background of a multi-leveled wooden synagogue with exterior stairs and balconies. Finally, attention to the geography of the shtetl is paid through depiction of a bridge over a river. And, of course, there is a man leading a goat across the bridge and a water carrier in the far distance (figure 2.3).

Dalia Tawil contextualizes Schor's work within the world of modern Jewish literature from the turn of the twentieth century, acknowledging its role as the visual equivalent, as it were, of the types and scenes

FIGURE 2.3. Ilya Schor, wood engraving. Illustration for chapter 2, "With All Thy Heart," from Abraham Joshua Heschel, *The Earth Is the Lord's: The Inner World of the Jew in Eastern Europe* (New York: Farrar, Straus and Giroux, 1949), 18. Used by permission of Mira Schor, 2018.

popularized and "salvaged" within the works of Mendele Mokher Sforim, Sholem Aleichem, and even Chaim Nachman Bialik:

> As one looks at Schor's world one notices the same balance of hardship and humor that is so familiar to us from Jewish literature dealing with the life of the Jews of East Europe. Indeed, these images form what modern criticism regards as a language of sign symbols that visually complements the sign systems used by writers such as Mendele Moykher Sforim, Sholem Aleichem, Chaim Nachman Bialik, Zalman Shneour and others. Together, the literature and art works present the essence of the vanished Jewish shtetl.[27]

Thus the depth of detail, seen and unseen, in Schor's art is evident both in its presentation but also in the world of cultural associations it invokes, drawing on the tropes and types and salvage impulses of an entire generation of artists and writers. It dovetails as well with the quest for spiritual depth articulated in Heschel's rendition of Hasidic life in *The Earth Is the Lord's*.

Rabbi Zusya's immersion in the first page of the Talmudic tractate he is studying serves as a wonderful example of the kind of depth theology Heschel advocates. What the rabbi is doing is perhaps the theological equivalent of ethnographic "thick description." Rabbi Zusya is able to immerse himself in the Talmud not for its content, but as a container for his relationship with God, for his understanding of that relationship, and for his students' understanding of Zusya's understanding of his relationship with God. Rabbi Zusya, in order to find himself and God in dialogue with one another, does not feel compelled to go much further than deep down into the very beginning of the text, never moving beyond the first page, or possibly even the first word. He feels no compulsion to go further than the threshold of the text because that is where God wants to meet him.

The Hasidic tales that Heschel weaves throughout his portrait of East European Jews in *The Earth Is the Lord's* serve as Heschel's literary variation on his depth theology, which he believes will save American Jews from historical and spiritual oblivion—a theology of depth, not breadth; a theology of intuition and transcendence, not one of rationality and worldliness. *In The Earth Is the Lord's*, with the help of the Hasidic tales he incorporates, Heschel doesn't attempt to draw a complete portrait of a dead culture. Rather, he attempts to draw a culture that, to his mind, is still very much alive and kicking, a culture whose message is not one about the end of an era, but the beginning of a new one in America. For Heschel, the Hasidic tale provides a literary arc to his essay that enables its readers to imagine themselves within the scenes he presents of East European Jewish experience.

This literary arc, indeed, is echoed in the way that Schor's images present a simultaneously generic but also identifiably familiar cast of characters. Tom L. Freudenheim puts it aptly in his catalogue introduction to an exhibition of Schor's work, put on by the Jewish Museum in 1965: "He created characters from the past who continually run across his works like a cast of actors playing out a Sholem Aleichem story. Through these works we can almost relive the experiences of a period of Jewish life in East Europe: holidays, family celebrations, and all the joys which punctuate the existence of simple pious people." And as we move through the images alongside the text of Heschel's book, we see a marriage (figure 2.4), the birth of a child (figure 2.5), a child growing up on his mother's knee (figure 2.6), and a tallit-adorned father instructing his young son in how to put on phylacteries in synagogue (figure 2.7). These narrative continuities between the images, coupled with the wealth of allusions to Heschel's Hasidic tales creates a palimpsest (a favorite word of Ben Shahn's, as we will see, and also a favorite of Heschel's, who names a chapter in the 1949 book "A World of Palimpsests," in which he discusses the Jewish approach to history) of narratives of East European Jewry that gives us an access point to the comfortable terrain of plot and tale even while acknowledging the complexity, the depth, the unknowability, of a destroyed world.

Throughout his corpus, and quite acutely in the book and the essay we explore in this chapter, Heschel articulates, as he does in his definition of depth theology, the limitations of language to capture spiritual experience. Depth theology, as he says, attempts to understand "insights that no words can express." In *The Earth Is the Lord's* and his earlier essay, "The East European Era in Jewish History," Heschel appoints Hasidic tales as a counterpoint to the culture

FIGURE 2.4. Ilya Schor, wood engraving. Illustration for chapter 1, "The Sigh," from Abraham Joshua Heschel, *The Earth Is the Lord's: The Inner World of the Jew in Eastern Europe* (New York: Farrar, Straus and Giroux, 1949), 13. Used by permission of Mira Schor, 2018.

of Talmudic and Torah study that he presents as the cornerstone of traditional East European Jewish life. Hasidic tales, though textualized, are a modern variation of an oral tradition, and they represent a layer of discourse that approximates, within the cultural portrait presented by Heschel in *The Earth Is the Lord's*, the kind of coming to inner knowledge that is valorized and sought by depth theology.

Even the Talmud itself, which is considered the foundation of Jewish "oral law," is oral only insofar as it is the purported transcription of rabbinic oral discussions and interpretations of the Torah. Today, and in fact for over a millennium, the Talmud has been a canonized, codified text, qualifying as "oral" primarily in a historical sense. But the Hasidic tale, peppered throughout Heschel's discussion of the culture of study and piety in the East European pre-Holocaust Jewish

FIGURE 2.5. Ilya Schor, wood engraving. Illustration for chapter 5, "The Luxuries of Learning," from Abraham Joshua Heschel, *The Earth Is the Lord's: The Inner World of the Jew in Eastern Europe* (New York: Farrar, Strauss and Giroux, 1949), 45. Used by permission of Mira Schor, 2018.

community, in its terseness, represents the kind of stutter, or lack of language, that Heschel seeks to access in his depth theology. These tales say a lot in very few words, and yet resonate very strongly for Heschel as a means of communicating both the physical and the spiritual realities of East European Jewish society. More important, these tales represent Heschel's engagement with a familiar struggle, common to both theological and literary discourse. How does one represent in language human experience that exceeds the boundaries of the expressible? More specific to the issues we have been exploring throughout this study, how does one represent a culture that has been uprooted and largely decimated?

In attempting to sketch a portrait of pre-Holocaust East European culture while acknowledging the limitations of that endeavor in the aftermath of its destruction, Heschel taps into a modern Jewish literary form—the Hasidic tale—that addresses the kinds of limitations

FIGURE 2.6. Ilya Schor, wood engraving. Illustration for chapter 9, "The Devout Men of Ashkenaz," from Abraham Joshua Heschel, *The Earth Is the Lord's: The Inner World of the Jew in Eastern Europe* (New York: Farrar, Straus and Giroux, 1949), 65. Used by permission of Mira Schor, 2018.

in language and in spiritual understanding that he stumbles over in trying to represent East European Jewish life. Hasidic tales, while expressed in language, transcend language because of their pithy, allusive, and elusive style. For Heschel, the use of Hasidic tales in his portrait of East European Jewish culture is a literary intervention motivated by spiritual concerns; they provide a literary solution to the problem of the theologically ineffable. In our analysis, we will focus on these Hasidic tales as a literary solution to broader cultural formations, all part of the constellation of the "folk ethnographies" we have been tracing.

To flesh this out a bit more, let's return to the story of Rabbi Zusya. The Talmud is, by some accounts, the very thing that Hasidism broke away from: the perceived excess and spiritually bankrupt rabbinism and polemicism of traditional Jewish scholarly culture. And yet it is this very scholarly backbone with which Heschel so ardently balances his

FIGURE 2.7. Ilya Schor, wood engraving. Illustration for chapter 8, "The Deed Sings," from Abraham Joshua Heschel, *The Earth Is the Lord's: The Inner World of the Jew in Eastern Europe* (New York: Farrar, Straus and Giroux, 1949), 61. Used by permission of Mira Schor, 2018.

Hasidic tales throughout the text of *The Earth Is the Lord's*. In the book he attempts to construct an image of East European culture as comprising almost exclusively rabbinic study, even as the texts he quotes from, retells, and uses to color his portrait are Hasidic, not rabbinic. The Zusya text, in which Rabbi Zusya is studying Talmud, captures this paradox, creating an intriguing tension between the story Heschel explicitly tells (about Talmudic scholarship) and the story he implicitly tells (about Hasidic spirituality), between the exposition of the text (a story of an era of unremitting faith in traditional scholarship) and its literary construction (a stringing together of Hasidic tales).

This tension between a valorization of rabbinic scholarship and a fixation on the anti-rabbinic stream of Hasidic narratives is also apparent at the very beginning of Heschel's 1946 text (it appears significantly later in the 1949 text), where he asserts:

> No classical works were created in Eastern Europe. The *Gemara*
> and the *Mishneh Torah*, the *Zohar* and *Shulhan Aruch*, the Guide
> to the Perplexed and the *Ez Hayim* had their origin elsewhere.
> East European Jewry had no ambition to create final forms of
> expressions. Their works are so unique and so rooted in a world
> apart that they are less accessible to the modern man than the
> works of the Sephardic scholars. The Ashkenazic Jews are but
> little interested in creating literature; their works are notes that
> they have made in the cause of their teaching.[28]

While we may or may not agree with Heschel's statement that no Jewish canonical texts can be traced to Eastern Europe, this quotation
raises the question of what is the value of intellectual pursuits without the authorial impulse? What is the value of learning for teaching
but not for writing? In answer, Heschel says: "The storm of the soul
held under control becomes a mighty impetus of the intellect. The
inner restlessness finds expression in intellectual passion."[29] Learning
Torah is valorized, therefore, as a tool for understanding the self, for
giving "expression" to the "storm of the soul"; the intellect is only
useful when energized by the soul.[30] Herein we begin to see a resolution to the tension in Rabbi Zusya's tale: under the assumption that
Talmudic scholarship is devoted to the soothing of internal spiritual
unrest, then one can engage in it, as did Rabbi Zusya, not for its intellectual content, but for one's own spiritual development.

The key to bringing together the seemingly disparate elements of
Talmud Torah and spirituality in *The Earth Is the Lord's* is to penetrate
the "inner world" that Heschel identifies in the essay's subtitle. Understanding this world, Heschel suggests, is not accomplished through
the content of his exposition about the central place of Torah study to
East European Jewish identity, but via its illustration and illumination
by Hasidic texts. These texts, while celebrating Judaism and Torah, are
indeed a modern genre of Jewish literature, and they contain a complicated rhetoric of simultaneous embrace and repudiation of intensive
Torah study. As I hope to demonstrate in the course of this discussion,
this tension at the heart of Heschel's understanding of Hasidism itself
allows Heschel to forge a link to his American audience. At the same

time, these tales serve as a reminder of everything that can never be recaptured in East European Jewish experience.

For Abraham Joshua Heschel in *The Earth Is the Lord's*, the inner world is a state of mind, a kind of restlessness that can only be understood in the context of study and prayer, which to him is best exemplified by the figure of the Hasid. From its earliest articulation as a eulogy in 1945, *The Earth Is the Lord's* presented itself as a bridge between Hasidim and American Jews. On January 7, 1945, the American Jewish community had been aware at least to some extent that East European Jewry had been destroyed, having read reports of the Chelmno gassings on page six of *The New York Times* as early as July 1942.[31] YIVO itself, where the eulogy was delivered, had only five years earlier, in 1940, moved its permanent headquarters from Vilna to New York, in response to the Nazi advance in Eastern Europe.[32] Heschel's speech at YIVO evoked a perhaps unexpected response, which Deborah Dash Moore describes in her preface to *East European Jews between Two Worlds*: despite YIVO's identity as an avowedly secular Yiddish institution, after the delivery of Heschel's speech many in the audience stood up to say a spontaneous kaddish, or prayer for the dead.[33]

I recount this story because I believe the speech Heschel delivered that day did more than represent the demise of a culture and a community; it did more than evince religious feelings of grief, mythical or otherwise, among its secular audience. It represents as well the birth of a particular folk ethnographic idiom, borne of a unique salvage poetic. The description of an avowedly secular community reciting the prayer for the dead captures the spirit of a folk ethnographic sentiment, or, as I argued in the introduction, it captures the spirit of the popularization of traditional beliefs and customs in order to better understand the self on a communal level. In fact, the accompanying illustrations in the expanded version of that initial speech also reflect that transition from a more solidly grounded historical folk ethnographic sentiment to a more impressionistically or anecdotally grounded one, or the movement from textual proficiencies to a more visual dependency in the popular American imagination of pre-Holocaust East European Jewish life. Schor's illustrations operate as a parallel narrative to Heschel's, providing a visual window into the world of the Hasidic narratives Heschel works so hard to expand in this later version of the essay.

Reminiscent, perhaps, of the types of folk associations articulated in *The Earth Is the Lord's* through its development of the Hasidic tale as well as its visual illustrations of Hasidism made by Schor (or prescient, in consideration of the fact that YIVO's communal kaddish was recited before the book was published), the kaddish, in American culture, has become emblematic of cultural, not religious, Judaism. This is abundantly clear in the Roy Cohn death scene in Tony Kushner's *Angels in America* (1991) wherein Louis Ironson, a completely assimilated Jew, is pressed by Cohn's nurse (who has just stolen Cohn's AZT, an anti-AIDS drug impossible to obtain at the beginning of the crisis in the 1980s, when the play is set) to recite the prayer for the dead, and he somehow manages to say it flawlessly (with a little help from the ghost of Ethel Rosenberg, and a little confusion with kiddush and the Shema). The kaddish, Kushner submits to his audience, is no longer a religious ritual; it is an ethnic institution. The scene at YIVO, on the occasion of Heschel's eulogy for East European Jewry, similarly captures a moment in American Jewish consciousness that Heschel, for the duration of his illustrious career as a Jewish philosopher and political activist, was not only to address in his work but was to prescribe in *The Earth Is the Lord's*. Just as the kaddish, a prayer, became an icon for American Jewish identification, so too did Hasidic literature frame and render accessible a community which seemed untouchable but with which American Jews could readily identify if recast in "folk," as opposed to religious, terms.

Heschel uses Hasidism to build a bridge between East European and American Jewry, constructing a scaffolding for popular perceptions of East European Jewry and formulating a way "in" to the seemingly inaccessible, while acknowledging its ultimate inaccessibility. He is the first, I would posit, to present Hasidic Judaism to an American audience, not necessarily in his speech (as that was directed toward Jewish scholars and professionals), but certainly in the speech's later textual adaptations, where he significantly expands the discussion of Hasidism, presenting the Hasidic movement as nearly the sum total of traditional Judaism. He does so, knowing full well (having been born a Hasid and having lived as a Hasid until early adulthood) that Hasidism is just a sect of Orthodox Judaism that was, in fact, founded as a break from traditional practices and ideologies. For purposes of his presentation to American audiences, however, Hasidism represents to him a modern Jewish spiritual formation that American Jews can comprehend and perhaps identify with, from a secular perspective.

While neo-Hasidism has extended in our moment to the Jewish renewal movement, and Heschel certainly influenced its earliest manifestations, *The Earth Is the Lord's* presents us with an opportunity to better understand Heschel's literary undertaking as a neo-Hasidic writer, deploying Hasidic stories as the primary ingredients for his salvage poetics in the spirit of his teacher Martin Buber, but also the modern Hebrew and Yiddish writers. It is not coincidental that we began our exploration of salvage poetics with a discussion of Buber's foundational role in establishing the Hasidic tale as essential to helping modern secular Jews in Western Europe find a way back to tradition, even if not practice, and that we continue our exploration of salvage poetics with a discussion of how Heschel used Hasidic tales for a similar purpose in America.

My thinking about the Hasidic tale as quintessentially modern is not novel.[34] What I would suggest is an understanding of the role played by the Hasidic story in Heschel's essay that recognizes the implications missed by professional critics and laypeople alike who frequently read the essay as an homage to traditional scholarship and piety, a flattening out of the historical and communal complexities of East European Jews, and a whitewashing of the poverty and backwardness of that world. Although this reading has some truth, as his essay is too short and his language too poetic to be put to much historical use, his valorization of traditional Jewish scholarship and illustration with Hasidic tales tells a deeper story than what appears on the surface. Jeffrey Shandler has said:

> A more dispassionate reading of Heschel's essay reveals that the smoothing, soothing trope of harmonization is riddled with competing and contradictory lines of rhetoric, as the author strives

to straddle the gap between traditional culture and modernity, between faithful devotion and scientific scholarship.[35]

Heschel's attempt to illuminate the East European world for his audience is unlike that of other authors whose work we have explored because he was born into the East European world they so eagerly described and at the same time inhabited the modern Jewish world of progressive movements. The scion of a Hasidic family, Heschel didn't leave that world until he pursued a Jewish secular education at the gymnasium in Vilna as a teenager, and he earned a doctorate and liberal rabbinic ordination in Berlin before he was arrested and sent back to Poland in 1938. In 1940 he was "recruited" ("rescued" may be a more apt term) by the Hebrew Union College in Cincinnati, a Reform rabbinical school, along with a number of other East European Jewish scholars. In 1946, soon after delivering his East European speech at YIVO, he moved to the Jewish Theological Seminary in New York, where he remained until his death in 1972.[36] Most of his nuclear and extended family was killed in the Holocaust, and he never returned to Poland. Edward K. Kaplan captures the essence of Heschel's life story:

> Heschel's unique presence in the United States is a result of his having personally integrated the spiritual and intellectual treasures of three capitals of prewar Jewish Europe: Warsaw (his birthplace), Vilna ("the Jerusalem of Lithuania," where he received a diploma from the Yiddish-language *Real Gymnasium*), and Berlin (where he attended a liberal rabbinic school and a secular university).[37]

In describing Heschel's experiences between cultures and locales, Samuel Dressner and Kaplan present him as "the rebbe's son among secular revolutionaries," and they say that his "lifelong cultural alienation had begun" in Vilna.[38] This cultural alienation was to serve him well in finding a way to connect with American Jews while still maintaining a strong sense of himself as a pious, European Jewish scholar and teacher. He was able to bridge the gap between American secularism and traditional Jewish values with the help of Hasidic ideologies that promote "inwardness," a focus on the self and one's relationship to God as key to one's place in the communal order and the larger world. Alienation, indeed, Heschel seems to argue, can be a good thing if it promotes self-reflection and spiritual focus.

For Heschel, the Hasidim present an appealing access point to the "inner world" of Judaism because they practice a form of *innerlekhkeyt* or "inwardness." Thus, whereas Heschel's use of the term "inner world" seems to possess an "ethnographic modality," as articulated by Kirshenblatt-Gimblett, in fact for Heschel the "inner world" is as much a statement of spirituality as of culture. I will reflect on the synthesis of these two notions of inwardness, ethnographic and spiritual, as they play themselves out in *The Earth Is the Lord's*.

First and foremost, the secret of that inwardness is accessible only through engagement with Jewish texts. As Heschel articulates in all versions of his essay: "Study was a sort of longing, a pouring out of the heart before the Merciful Father, a sort of prayer, a communion and an ardent desire for a purified world. Inwardness has assumed super-real forms."[39]

Furthermore, he argues:

> Study was a technique of sublimating feeling and thought, dream and syllogism, of expressing pain in a question and joy in a solution found to a difficult problem in Maimonides. The tension of the spirit found an outlet in the contrivance of subtle, practically insolvable riddles, in yearnings and expectations, in the invention of new logical devices. The greatest joy was to find an answer to gnawing doubts.[40]

In *The Earth Is the Lord's*, Heschel famously refers to the Hasidic communities of Eastern Europe themselves as texts: "Koretz, Karlin, Bratslav, Lubavitch, Ger, Lublin—hundreds of towns are like holy books. Every place is a pattern, an aspect, a way in Jewishness."[41] Expanding on this idea, he says:

> The little Jewish communities in Eastern Europe were like sacred texts opened before the eyes of God so close were their houses of worship to Mount Sinai. In the humble wooden synagogues,

looking as if they were deliberately closing themselves off from the world, the Jews purified the souls that God had given them and perfected their likeness to God. There arose in them an infinite world of inwardness, a "Torah within the Heart," beside the written and oral Torah. . . . They often lacked outward brilliance, but they were full of hidden light.[42]

Personifying God and referring to his "eyes" as beholding the people of the shtetls named above, we are pulled once again into a visual rhetoric reinforced by Schor's illustrations. In a somewhat iconoclastic way, perhaps, the reader might be placed in the position of God looking at the subject of Heschel's exposition in the illustrations.

Continuing with this visual rhetoric, it is in the conflict between the lack of "outward brilliance" and the fullness, or recognition, of a "hidden light" that we see Heschel reaching out to his American audience in ways that revise their general attitude toward that world. His perspective turns upside down other efforts to capture the East European Jewish world that end up focusing largely on what it lacked. As Lucjan Dobroszycki and Barbara Kirshenblatt-Gimblett argue in her introduction to *Image before My Eyes*, the photographs taken by professional photographers such as Alter Kacyzne and Menachem Kipnis in Europe to be published in the rotogravure section of New York's *The Jewish Daily Forward* in the 1920s and 1930s enabled their American Jewish viewers primarily to appreciate how much better their American lives were than what they had left behind. As a result, the photo spreads of "Life in the Old Country" in the weekend arts section of the *Forward*—which largely portrayed people who looked desperately hungry, whose landscape was dismal and interior spaces claustrophobic—did more to reinforce faith in the New World than to inspire nostalgia or admiration. The illustrations by Schor, indeed, although finely detailed and dark in hue, are positively radiant through black-and-white contrast and in theme, as opposed to most of the *Forward*'s photographs. Indeed, it seems to me that Schor's images are the inked equivalent of Vishniac's black-and-white photographs, famous for their virtuosic play of light and shadow, many of which were published in America in *The Forward*, as we will discuss in chapter 5, and which were also exhibited for the first time two years before the publication of *The Earth Is the Lord's*. The "lack" in "outer brilliance" represented in these photographs was the very thing that Heschel attempts to redress in his essay and in the illustrations accompanying them:

> How do we appraise the historic value of an era? What standards do we use in measuring culture? It is customary in the modern world to appraise an epoch on the basis of its cultural progress, the quality of its books, the number of academies, the artistic accomplishments and the scientific discoveries made therein. We Jews, the first nation in the world that began not only to mark, but also to appraise and to judge, the generations, evaluate eras on the basis of different criteria, namely, how much refinement is there in the life of a people, how much spiritual substance in its workaday existence, i.e., how much metaphysics in its material aspect? To us culture is the style of life of a people. Our gauge of culture is the extent to which the people and not only individuals, live in accordance with the dictates of an eternal doctrine—the extent to which inwardness, mercy, beauty, and holiness are to be found in the daily life of a people.[43]

With its allusion to "culture," to "daily life," and most importantly to the "life of a people" (as in *Life Is with People*) this is certainly a critical locus for Heschel's ethnographic "modality," as well as for the representation of life-cycle events, domestic spaces, and synagogue culture in Schor's illustrations. Heschel, in seeking to distinguish between his own description of the East European historic era and other historical accounts, articulates his disinterest in the usual objective measures. Rather than reporting on numbers of books or cultural institutions, he is looking instead at elements that are essentially invisible: refinement, inwardness, mercy, beauty, and holiness. He wraps up his original essay with the following series of exhortations:

> In the spiritual confusion of the last hundred years, many of us overlooked the incomparable beauty of our old, poor homes. We compared our fathers and grandfathers, our scholars and rabbis, with Russian or German intellectuals. We preached in the name

of the twentieth century, measured the merits of Berditchev and Ger with the standards of Paris and Heidelberg. Dazzled by the lights of the metropolis, we lost at times the inner sight. The luminous visions that for so many generations shone in the little candles were extinguished for some of us.[44]

As Heschel seems to repudiate enlightenment, comparing the modern advancements of Jews both intellectually and geographically with a world left behind, he again casts his critique in visual terms. Our "old poor homes" had "incomparable beauty," though when compared to the merits of Paris and Heidelberg, of Germany and Russia, we lost the "inner sight," "the luminous visions that . . . shone in the little candles." As in my suggestion above that Schor's images provide Heschel's readers with the opportunity to look upon the Jews of Eastern Europe kindly and generously, as would God, perhaps in reference to the optimal "inner sight" presented here by Heschel, we are privy to an inner sight in reading this book, one that can only be provided by two "insiders"—Heschel and Schor.

This "inner sight" is reframed as a "hidden light" in the final statement of the 1946 essay:

A day will come in which the hidden light of the East European era will be revealed. This era was The Song of Songs ... of Jewish history in the last two thousand years. If the other eras were holy, this one is the holy of holies.[45]

Again, the particular character of East European Jewry is likened, in visual terms, to a "hidden light." He then further qualifies this era as the Song of Songs and the Holy of Holies, likening that which is hidden both to a canonic biblical book of poetry and to the sanctuary of ancient Judaism's holiest institution. Let's consider each of these allusions more deeply for a moment.

The Song of Songs, the biblical book, is a love story between a man and a woman, so erotic that it has been handily interpreted by the rabbis as an allegory for the love between God and the Jewish people in order to justify its racy presence in the Jewish biblical canon. Its traditional meaning is therefore invisible to the naked eye and can only

be understood as a Jewishly sanctioned text through the lens of interpretation. This interpretive lens, according to Heschel, is an essential
aspect of Jewish spirituality. In *The Earth Is the Lord's* (1949), Heschel
expands on this, saying:

> The words of the Torah, they believed, would not be grasped
> by means of literal interpretation. Nothing could be taken lit-
> erally, neither Scripture nor nature. No man, even if he lived
> a thousand years, would be able to fathom the mysteries of
> the world. Rabbi Nathan Spira of Cracow, the author of *The
> Revealer of the Deeply Hidden*, written in the seventeenth cen-
> tury, interprets in two hundred and fifty-two different ways the
> portion of the Pentateuch in which Moses pleads with God for
> permission to enter the Promised Land. . . . Everywhere they
> found cryptic meaning.[46]

The theme of entering the inaccessible—the promised land, for
Moses—is not coincidentally mentioned here, but is part of Heschel's
further development of his depth theology, his articulation of the
necessity to penetrate the "deeply hidden." To return, however, to
the closing statement of his 1945 lecture, published in the *YIVO Annual*
as quoted above, in 1946, the implications of hiddenness go further
than the interpretation of a text: "If the other eras were holy, this one
is the Holy of Holies." The Holy of Holies is only entered by the High
Priest one day a year, in a highly dangerous operation of repentance
from which many High Priests feared they would not emerge alive.
What are the implications of these metaphors for the "hidden light"
of the East European era? American Jews, it seems, must seek out
the hidden light in texts, in specific texts that require interpretation
and that attest to the deep love between the Jewish people and God.
Furthermore, they must find a way into the Holy of Holies—taking all
the risks that entails.

Heschel's audience, one could say, is in dire need of a reminder
that their limited view of East European Jewish experience, their
inability to see past the poverty or the criteria that conventional eval-
uative methods have imposed on their culture, sorely impacts their
own spiritual abilities, their own sense of self:

> Rich stores of potential energy, of intellectual resilience and
> emotional depth, gathered in the course of generations of a
> disciplined mode of life, are not contained in us. . . . We must
> retain the Jewishness of our fathers and grandfathers. Their law
> within the heart was not a matter of esthetics. Romantic por-
> traiture of Hasidism, nostalgia, and piety are merely ephemeral.
> They disappear with the first generation. Solidarity with the
> past must become an integral part of our existence.[47]

Heschel is suggesting that American Jews are not, in other words,
automatically in possession of their ancestors' legacy—their lives are
"not contained in us." Heschel calls for "solidarity" with a past that
exceeds the normal bonds of nostalgia. What constitutes this "solidarity"? Recognition and internalization of "rich stores of intellectual
energy, of intellectual resilience and of emotional depth." And the
Hasidim, he argues here, possessed those properties because they cultivated a "law within the heart."

In what is ostensibly an allusion to the eleventh-century Judeo
Arabic work *Hovot ha-Levavot*, or "Duties of the Heart," by the Spanish rabbi Bahyah Ben Yosef Ibn Pakuda, Heschel refers anachronisti-
cally to a particular type of Hasidic "inwardness" that American Jews
should aspire toward, a "law within the heart." *Hovot ha-Levavot*, a
treatise detailing ten ways to enhance one's spiritual life, is anchored,
as were many Spanish Jewish texts of the period, in mysticism and
hence is not a far cry from the ideology or the values of the Hasidic
community. However, the yoking of the culture of Hasidut with this
text through the phrase "law within the heart" evokes a marriage
of spiritual and intellectual values, with a simultaneous valorization of
both rabbinism (of which Jewish mysticism is a branch) and of Hasidic
repudiations of rabbinism.

The relationship between Jewish mysticism and the birth of the
Hasidic movement is well known and has been well documented
in the scholarly and religious literature. However, to explore more
deeply the role of Hasidism in Heschel's thinking about an "inner
world," we will consider the two different versions of the Heschel text
we have looked at—the 1946 English translation and transcription

of the original Yiddish speech in the first *YIVO Annual* and the 1949 publication of *The Earth Is the Lord's* side by side, with special attention to the preponderance and presence of Hasidic tales in each, as we seek to better understand the role of Hasidic tales in Heschel's construction of a salvage poetic.

The first six sections of the 1946 publication contextualize the culture of learning in Jewish Eastern Europe. Section 1 compares Sephardic and Ashkenazic culture in broad strokes, and section 2 lays the groundwork for Heschel's focus on spirituality and its connection to learning among East European Jews. Section 3 focuses on the "democratization of Talmudic study," introducing Rashi and the Tosafists as well as Maimonides's *Mishneh Torah* with a description of a child's first day in cheder. It is here that Heschel dwells on the nearly universal literacy of the Jewish population, focusing specifically on the male practice of learning Torah. He says:

> Poor Jews sit like intellectual magnates. They possess a wealth of ideas and of knowledge, culled from little known passages in the Talmud. One raises a question about a difficult passage in Maimonides; the other outdoes him in his answer, in the subtlety of his dialectic. The stomach is empty, the home overcrowded; but the heads are full of spiritual and cultural riches, and the Torah is free and ample.[48]

In the critical literature, passages like this evoke critiques that Heschel's essay is monochromatic and highly unrealistic. He doesn't really say enough, as one can see above, about the gendering of access to Torah and about the class structure of most Jewish communities in Eastern Europe: generally it was the privileged, the sons and sons-in-laws of wealthy merchants, who spent time learning Torah. To be sure, the community, reaching across class, supported some impoverished scholars, but this was because they were remarkable scholars, and they were few and far between. Also, while most Jewish males were able to study some Torah, the types of texts they could access diverged greatly, with serious Talmudic and legal study reserved for scholars who were cultivated from early childhood.

Section 4 continues to discuss the value of scholarship within the Jewish community by establishing similarities between modern scientists and "pious Ashkenazic scholars," asserting:

> To scientists, every trifle is significant, and its votaries inquire diligently into the most intricate properties of matter. The pious Ashkenazic scholars investigated with similar passion the laws that should govern the Jew's conduct. The devotion and honesty invested in their work have their parallel in scientific research.[49]

Here Heschel invests himself in convincing a scientifically aware population that the study of Torah is just as rigorous as science. Heschel's YIVO audience, comprising primarily historians, linguists, and sociologists, was presumably skeptical about whether the living power of Torah study might be relevant to Jewish continuity in the present, although they might have appreciated it as a historical or cultural artifact.

Section 5 focuses on the alleged harbingers of modern Hasidim, the twelfth- and thirteenth-century *Hasidei Ashkenaz,* or the Pious Men of Ashkenaz:

> The times are bad for the Jews; they are persecuted and hunted on all sides. Massacres are a daily occurrence; Jews are led to the slaughter like sheep; but all this is accepted willingly in submission to the Divine Will. With superhuman fervor they sacrifice themselves for their faith. The Pious Men of Ashkenaz attach great importance to the daily conduct of Prominent Jews.[50]

The importance of *Hasidei Ashkenaz* and their lasting effect on Judaism has been widely debated, and in fact the only major text to come out of this movement was *Sefer ha-Hasidim* (The Book of the Pious) by Judah Ben Samuel of Regensberg (1150–1217). Heschel's devoting an entire section of his lecture to such a minor movement can be understood as a means of building context for his emphasis on the modern variation on the early "Hasidim" in the essay's seventh section.

In section 6, Heschel continues his buildup to the modern Hasidim by discussing the mystical teachings of Rabbi Isaac Luria (1534–72) and the seventeenth-century *Zohar*. He encapsulates the aim of Jewish mysticism, saying: "The sense of man's life lies in his perfecting the world. He has to distinguish, gather, and redeem the sparks of Holiness scattered throughout the darkness of the world."[51] With this background, we arrive at the beginning of section 7, the essay's climax, which is also the first section to include a Hasidic tale.[52] This is in contrast to the expanded 1949 version of the essay, where the first Hasidic tale appears prior to the formal introduction of Hasidim. Thus in the early essay we do not encounter Hasidic tales until the seventh section, which introduces Hasidism, whereas in the later expansion, we encounter Hasidic tales before we encounter Hasidism itself. This important discrepancy demonstrates how Hasidic tales, for Heschel, become useful in his later work beyond their value in portraying the Hasidic community. In the transition from the 1946 essay to the 1949 essay, we see the essay growing into a polished literary work for which Hasidic tales become formally essential and not just supplementary to his description of Hasidim.

Let's look closely for a moment at the first tale introduced in the 1946 essay, as compared to the first one in the later version, which addresses the culture of Torah study, bringing together somewhat conflicting impulses within Hasidic ideology. The first story in the 1946 essay, however, is strictly engaged with matters of the physical versus the spiritual body:

> The story is told of a melamed [children's teacher] making a wintertime pilgrimage afoot to his Rebbe. The town's rich man passed by in a sumptuous coach, drawn by four horses. Seeing the melamed, he asked him into the coach. The melamed consented, and was soon snugly tucked away in a corner, covered with heavy warm blankets. The rich man then offered him some brandy, cake, even some roast goose. Suddenly the melamed turned to the rich man, saying: "Pray: tell me, what is your worldly joy, your *olam ha-zeh*?" The rich man was astonished: "Don't you see the luxurious coach and the expensive foods? Are they not enough of this worldly joy?" "No," replied the melamed, "these are your otherworldly joys, the acme of your joys, your *olam ha-ba*, but what is your *olam ha-zeh*?"[53]

In this story we encounter a major theme of Hasidic literature: the simplest people are in a position to make the profoundest discoveries, to teach their superiors—intellectually, as well as socially—about the finer nuances of the spirit. Here the melamed, who occupies the lowest rung of traditional Jewish society, teaching children for a pittance, hints to the town's rich man (the *gvir*) that he is squandering his life in the world to come by living in the lap of luxury in the present. In this same section, this story is followed by another tale:

> The story is told of a scholar who once came to a "Rebbe." "What have you done all your life?" inquired the "Rebbe." "I have gone through the Talmud three times," replied the scholar. "But what of the Talmud has gone through you?" countered the "Rebbe."[54]

Here we see a repudiation of Talmud study in the absence of spirit, another classic Hasidic motif. This provides an interesting counterpoint to the 1949 version's story about Reb Zusya, who remains immersed in a single page of Talmud, thus undermining of the notion of Talmudic breadth in favor of depth.

Significantly, both of the above tales also appear in the 1949 essay, but in an expanded form, as does the story we will touch on soon. From the very beginning and presumably in the essay's earliest, oral form (as the 1946 version is said to be a direct transcription and translation), Heschel incorporated certain Hasidic tales at certain critical junctures. As the essay grew, the frequency of these tales increased, and what had been a charming detour in the earlier essay became a building block of the later one.

Returning to our review of the earlier essay, we see that the final Hasidic story appears in section 8, immediately following our introduction to Hasidim in section 7. Here we see the initial version of Heschel's early claim in the later essay about how no scholarly literature of any worth was created in Eastern Europe. This tale involves the Baal Shem Tov, the founder of the Hasidic movement:

> The story is told that once the Baal Shem with his disciples came to Berdichev to see the famous R. Liber. The latter was not at home, for it was the day of the fair, and he had gone to the market.

> Arriving at the market place, they saw R. Liber conversing with a peasant. Do you know with whom R. Liber is speaking? The master queried. "It is Elijah," he said, and beholding the amazement of the disciples, he added: "It is not R. Liber that is privileged to have a revelation of Elijah, but Elijah that is privileged to have a revelation of R. Liber."[55]

With this tale, we revisit the notion of inwardness. What could make R. Liber a figure of such veneration, even in relation to Elijah the Prophet? In this scenario we witness the undoing of the popular Jewish understanding that spiritual depth decreases as generations get farther from Mount Sinai. Indeed, in an idea explored in more detail in a section of the later essay, the Hasidim posit that in each generation there are at least thirty-six righteous men on whose behalf God sustains the world. While this idea originates in the Talmud, it was first popularized by the Jewish mystics and then by the Hasidim. The possibility of a single person garnering the respect and admiration of Elijah the Prophet originates, it would seem, in the notion of the thirty-six righteous men. A natural extension of this idea is that since we don't know who those righteous are at any given time, anybody has the potential to qualify. In other words, anyone, at any given time, might achieve, or even exceed, the spiritual status of Elijah the Prophet.

The path to achieving such high spiritual status is through inwardness, the human potential to inhabit the self so completely that a person transcends the self. In depth theology this means, as Shai Held puts it, that "Heschel's work is animated by a passion for self-transcendence, for moving beyond an exclusive focus on the ego and its needs and desires." Clarifying this assertion, Held writes:

> The unique barbarism of modern times, Heschel argues, stems from self-assertion utterly without bounds, from callousness to the call of God and the reality of other selves. The only hope for humanity lies, consequently, in a rediscovery of wonder and a renewed openness to demands that come from outside of us.[56]

This "rediscovery" of wonder can only be achieved through a deep understanding of the self, through engagement with one's own way of seeing the world and a tweaking of that vision to encourage and accommodate wonder. Transcendence of the self is therefore coupled with the significance of the self. Once we become open to our own possibilities, then we can recognize God's need for us. According to Held, "the sentence that appears in Heschel's writings more frequently than any other is a simple one: 'God is in need of man.'"[57] In Heschel's own words:

> There is only one way to define Jewish religion. It is the awareness of God's interest in man, the awareness of a covenant, of a responsibility that lies on him as well as on us. Our task is to concur with this interest.[58]

The paradox of deeply understanding the self so that one can achieve transcendence as the basis of religious experience and social responsibility is not by any means unique to Heschel. Søren Kierkegaard called the kind of inward-looking practice that promotes ethical integrity "indirection."[59] More important, the Kotzker Rebbe (Menachem Mendel Morgenstern of Kotzk, 1787–1859) called this *innerlekhkeyt,* or "inwardness." We will revisit the Kotzker Rebbe's notion of *innerlekhkeyt* as it pertains to Heschel's notion of the "inner world of the Jew in Eastern Europe" as we turn now, more fully, toward *The Earth Is the Lord's*—the 1949 expansion of the 1945 speech and the 1946 essay—in order to investigate the deployment of Hasidic tales therein.

The first Hasidic tale in *The Earth Is the Lord's* (1949) appears before the first mention of Hasidim. That tale, about Rabbi Zusya of Hanipol (Meshulam Zusha of Hanipol, 1718–1800), does not appear at all in the 1946 essay. The tale is part of section 5 of *The Earth Is the Lord's*, in a discussion about the value of Torah study, and the tale implicitly critiques the dangers of attempting to focus on breadth instead of depth. Another tale is also cited in *The Earth Is the Lord's*, before we are introduced to the Hasidim as well; it appears in section 7, "A World of Palimpsests," which grapples with the layers upon layers of meaning invested in everything in the world of the traditional East European Jew, at the center of which resides a faith in God: "To them, history was only an intimation. Things were like palimpsests, Heaven the tangent at the circle of all experience."[60] In a discussion of how these palimpsests affect the "itinerary of one's life," Heschel tells a story about Rabbi Israel Baal Shem (Israel ben Eliezer, 1698–1760), the founder of modern Hasidism:

> Once, it is told, Rabbi Israel Baal Shem, the founder of the Hasidic movement, looked despondent and sick at heart. When his disciples asked him for the cause, he told them: There was a man who was very wicked. After he died, there was no way of saving him. But God had mercy upon his soul, and it was decreed that it should be incarnated in a frog and lie near a spring in a distant land, and should his son ever come to that place and drink of the water of the spring after saying the blessing over the water, the soul would be redeemed. But the son was very poor and had neither the means nor the opportunity to travel to distant places, so God caused that he should become the butler of a rich man who once became ill and the doctors declared that he would be cured if he went to a certain spa. The rich man went there and took his butler with him. Once while taking a walk together, the butler became unbearably thirsty—he almost died of thirst. (His thirst was so great because he was near the spring where the soul of his father was lying.) When he began to search for water, he found a spring. In his great thirst he forgot to say the prayer, the blessing over the water, and the soul remained unredeemed. . . . The Holy One, blessed be He, concluded the Baal Shem, did so much to make the redemption possible, yet all was in vain. Who knows what will be the end of its way?[61]

The point of this story is manifold. God has his hand in everything; all the manipulations that had to take place so that the sinful man's son would drink water out of a particular stream were managed directly by God; God wants the best even for sinners and will do anything to change their destiny, even turning them into frogs. For our purposes, this story is important because in Heschel's book it is our first introduction to the Baal Shem Tov, even before we are introduced to the movement he founded. For the "scientific audience" listening to the oral version of Heschel's first essay, this would have been an unusual introduction to the Baal Shem Tov, for obvious reasons.

A man turning into a frog? Redemption depending on a blessing? A blessing depending on a chance sojourn in a resort town? This tale, while rather unremarkable to those familiar with the genre (I heard a similar story at age ten in a camp cafeteria that was supposed to inspire the children to say the blessings over water each time they took a drink), could be rather alienating to the uninitiated, who might wonder what kind of culture invests frogs with that degree of sacred power. Clearly Heschel is using the story to illustrate the extent to which East European Jews of an earlier generation would go to affirm God's immanence in the world. Our lives are a "palimpsest" of intentions and destinies, overseen by a power greater than ourselves who leaves no stone (or frog) unturned. The story leaves one significant, rational question unanswered: How did the Baal Shem Tov know about this arrangement? This story exhibits no formal concern with veracity, and Heschel makes no attempt to frame it in order to justify its lack of realism or of point of view. He bares the device of his story's lack of credibility in order to illustrate the depth of the layered and inscrutable "palimpsest" that Heschel is creating in this section. In contrast to the rhetoric of veracity that characterizes the frames of classic Yiddish fiction, something we will consider in greater depth when we analyze *Life Is with People* in the next chapter, what we see in the Hasidic tales used by Heschel to enliven his portrait is very different. To Heschel, the power of the stories he tells does not reside in their realism; rather, they are an effective tool for allowing an American audience to understand the irrepressible spirituality, the irrational faith, that characterized the East European Jewish community as he saw it. For him, it is not important to hear the voices of individuals in the community he represents, as it is for Zborowski and Herzog. Rather, it is the encounters with the ineffable, with the voices of the spirits, and Hasidic stories that were written to represent those encounters are a perfect vehicle. Schor's illustration for this chapter is one of the strangest illustrations in the book, echoing this theme of the irrational and anti-realist. In it, not-quite-human figures wearing prayer shawls are ensconced in a tree beneath which is standing a man. The palimpsest he is illustrating here seems to be one in which the human being is always surrounded by spirits that he can neither see nor recognize, but they are as omnipresent, and as mysterious, as anything can be.

When we are finally formally introduced to the Baal Shem Tov in the 1949 publication, we find an intriguing similarity with the 1946 essay that reflects Heschel's movement between Hasidism and the movement's essential figures as he seeks to capture the essence of the East European Jew. The 1946 essay introduces the Hasidic movement in section 7 with the following line: "Then came the Hasidim and brought down heaven upon the earth."[62] Using similar language in section 11 of *The Earth Is the Lord's*, after a significantly expanded introduction of *Hasidei Ashkenaz* and the Kabbalah, Heschel writes: "Then came Rabbi Israel Baal Shem, in the eighteenth century, and brought heaven down to earth."[63]

The distinction between the similar language in the two versions of Heschel's work follows the more general movement of Hasidic tales between hagiographies and anonymous vignettes. The examples we have already seen of each—Rabbi Zusya in the first tale and a generic melamed in another—beautifully evoke the dynamic movement between the particular and the general that we will trace in our overview of American ethnographic movements in chapter 3; this occurred most acutely in the culture and personality school, where Mead and Sapir, in different ways, attempted to theorize a way to draw broad cultural conclusions from attention to individual experience. Modern Jewish literatures, notably Hebrew and Yiddish work at the turn of the twentieth century, also grappled with the possibilities and limitations of the "universal particular." Because these literatures were born at a moment of profound political foment with nationalism on the rise, the story of individuals leaving the confines of traditional society came to be understood as the story of a generation. Stories that did not fit certain conventional narratological and narrative patterns did not meet the criteria of the "universal," and were deemed to be either insignificant or too particularistic. Such stories, including those written in Hebrew that took place in the shtetl, stories written from the perspective of women, and stories that did not trounce the religious experience were deemed "charming," "nostalgic," and even "ethnographic," but never universally or, at the very least, nationally representative.

The Hasidic tale, as presented by Heschel, strives as well to operate on at least two different levels. On the one hand, he uses them to emphasize the importance of the Hasidim to East European Jewish life. On the other hand, he uses them to transmit a spiritual message born of the historical tale he is telling—the values articulated in these stories can be internalized by all Jews for a better understanding of the self, God, the Jewish community, and humanity as a whole. The contrast between Heschel's decision in the 1946 essay to introduce the Hasidim without first mentioning the Baal Shem Tov and his later decision in the 1949 work to introduce the Baal Shem Tov before the Hasidic movement as a whole reveals an interesting movement away from generality and toward specificity.

Throughout *The Earth Is the Lord's* we encounter Hasidic tales. In its fifteen sections (expanded from ten in the earlier work) appear eight Hasidic tales (expanded from the original three).[64] Of the additional five in the 1949 book, four follow the pattern of hagiography, naming specific rabbis, and only one, "Thirty-Six Zaddikim," which we read in section 13, does not:

> Koretz, Karlin, Bratslav, Lubavich, Ger, Lublin—hundreds of little towns were like holy books. Each place was a pattern, an aspect, a way of Jewishness. When a Jew mentioned the name of a town like Miedzybosh or Berditshev, it was as though he mentioned a divine mystery. Supernatural splendor emanated from ordinary acts. "Why do you go to see the rebbe?" someone asked an eminent rabbi who, although his time was precious, would trudge for days to visit his master on the Sabbath. "To stand near him and watch him lace his shoes," he answered.[65]

This story about an anonymous rabbi and his anonymous rebbe (Hasidic leader) is incorporated into one of the most famous passages in Heschel's essay. In it, he lists a series of famous Hasidic sects and the towns they came from, with the exception of Lublin, which isn't a small town at all, but the largest city in Poland east of the Vistula River. The "little" towns, he says, were like holy books, presenting a metaphor that reproduces itself throughout the essay in various allusions to the Jews as texts, and to the locales as texts, for example, "The little Jewish communities in East Europe were like sacred texts opened before the eyes of God so close were their houses of worship to Mount Sinai."[66] This passage also serves as a microcosm of the entire essay, which emphasizes scholarship and a love for books as the key to the spirituality and the psychology of the religious Jewish community Heschel describes. At the same time, this brief, anonymous Hasidic tale articulates a very different message: the Rabbi (himself a well-known personage) goes to his rebbe not to learn with him or from him, but to watch him tie his shoes. Is there a discrepancy here between the valorization of the text and the disregard for scholarship in the face of this holy persona?

A glimpse at the final Hasidic tale in *The Earth Is the Lord's* might help us to answer that question:

> In the spiritual dimension, self-renunciation counts more than achievement of scholarship. Rabbi Isaac Meir Alter of Ger, the outstanding Talmudic scholar in Poland of his day, came to his master, Rabbi Mendel of Kotzk, and asked him to read the manuscript of a work he had written. It was a commentary on *Hoshen Mishpat*, the Jewish civil code. A few weeks later, the rabbi of Kotzk sent for the author. "I have studied your manuscript," he said. "It is a work of genius. When published, the classical commentaries, which have been studied for generations, will become obsolete. I am only grieved at the thought of the displeasure which this will cause to the souls of the saintly commentators." It was a winter evening. Fire was burning in the stove. Rabbi Isaac Meir took the manuscript from the table and threw it into the flames.[67]

Isaac Meir Rothenberg Alter (1799–1866), the founder of the Ger Hasidic dynasty, may or may not have destroyed a manuscript at the behest of the Rabbi of Kotzk, but he did publish many other books on the Talmud. The crucial part of this tale, however, resides in its placement in *The Earth Is the Lord's* as the last Hasidic story, and the conclusion of the three sections devoted to a discussion of Hasidim. Even as he invokes one of the most famous Hasidic Talmudic scholars of all times, Heschel tells us that he burned his most important manuscript in deference to the memory (and the scholarship) of his ancestors and predecessors. The Kotzker Rebbe's role in this affair (be it fictional or not) is also crucial.

In his final book, *A Passion for Truth* (1973), which is an abbreviation and expansion of his final book in Yiddish, *Kotzk: The Struggle for Integrity* (1973), Heschel discusses his own conflicted relationship with the Kotzker Rebbe. He says:

> The earliest fascination I can recall is associated with the Baal Shem, whose parables disclosed some of the first insights I gained as a child. He remained a model too sublime to follow yet too overwhelming to ignore. It was in my ninth year that the presence of Reb Menahem Mendl of Kotzk, known as the Kotzker, entered my life. Since then he has remained a steady companion and a haunting challenge. Although he often stunted me, he also urged me to confront perplexities that I might have preferred to evade. Years late I realized that, in being guided by both the Baal Shem Tov and the Kotzker, I had allowed two forces to carry on a struggle within me. One was occasionally mightier than the other. But who was to prevail, which was to be my guide? Both spoke convincingly, and each proved right on one level yet questionable on another. In a very strange way I found my soul at home with the Baal Shem but driven by the Kotzker. Was it good to live with one's heart torn between the joy of Mezbizh and the anxiety of Kotzk? To live both in awe and consternation, in fervor and horror, with my conscience on mercy and my eyes on Auschwitz, wavering between exaltation and dismay? Was this a life a man would choose to live? I had no choice: my heart was in Mezbizh, my mind in Kotzk.[68]

Who was the Kotzker Rebbe? Born in 1787 in Bilgoraj near Lublin in a non-Hasidic family, the Kotzker Rebbe was attracted to the Hasidic movement in his youth. First he became a disciple of Reb Yaakov Yitzhak of Lublin, the Seer, then of Reb Yaakov Yitzhak of Pshyshke, and finally of Reb Simha Bunam. He was named Bunam's successor and lived first in Tomashov and then in Kotzk. He died in 1859 at the age of seventy-two.[69]

The Hasidism of Kotzk was dominated by intense individualism, with little attention paid to the community.[70] Kotzkers intellectualized

Hasidism. Reflection and analysis took precedence over emotion and imagination. According to Heschel, "rather than devote time to the mysteries of the worlds on high, one was to learn what to do about the confusion in his own soul. In Kotzk fantastical or mystical realities were transmuted into human experience."[71] As described earlier, struggle to understand the confusion in one's soul had to precede the next phase of struggle, which was to get as close to God as possible:

> A major phase of the struggle was to disentangle oneself from enslavement to the self. The inexhaustible intransigence of self-interest bore the poison that destroyed individuality and freedom. For the Kotzker, one became an authentic Jew only when he moved out of the prison of self-interest, responding with abandon to Heaven's call. He who remained deaf to it was devoid of faith and lived a farce, for to have faith meant to forget the self, to be exclusively intent on God.[72]

Heschel argues that Hasidism in general, and the Kotzker's ideology in particular, marks a major shift in Judaism, from the object to the subject, from actions to the focus on an "I," who was created in the image of God and can become a partner to God, indispensable to him, if that "I" is properly freed of his or her self-interest. Thus, according to Heschel, the Kotzker was a tortured forbidding man because of his emphasis on "inwardness." In discussing common elements in the philosophies of the Kotzker and Søren Kierkegaard, he says:

> The Kotzker was concerned with the problem of truth as it pertains to self-knowledge. The problem is acute because nothing is easier than to deceive oneself. As the mind grows sophisticated self-deception advances. The inner life becomes a wild, inextricable maze. Who can trust his own motivations? his honesty? Who can be sure whether he is worshipping his own ego or an idol while ostensibly adoring God?[73]

The Baal Shem Tov encouraged his followers to approach Jewish texts and Jewish sages with an eye toward the individuals behind the ideas, with a respect for the spiritual accomplishments of the whole person, and not just the intellect. In so doing, he founded a movement that valued humanity over scholarship, scholars over texts, and feelings and relationships over the nuances of language or the complexities of knowledge. It took several generations for the Kotzker's approach to come to the fore, but the continuity between the Baal Shem and Kotzker is clear. If individual experience matters in one's relationship with God, then individual consciousness must be carefully manipulated in order to maximize that relationship. Heschel is one of the only Jewish philosophers, however, to articulate this continuity, which he does by dwelling in his writings on the fact that he holds both within his soul. As we saw above, however, he sees their coexistence within his philosophy and his consciousness as something of a dialectic, and a painful one at that. Jewish philosopher Arthur Green tells us:

> Heschel was the scion of several of the great Hasidic families of Europe. Raised to continue in the family tradition, it was at first assumed that young Heschel, who was a Talmudic as well as a spiritual prodigy, would be a great figure within the Hasidic world. On his mother's side, he was most closely related to his uncle, the Novominsker Rebbe, whose court had moved to Warsaw where Heschel was raised, and on his father's side to the Kopyczienicer branch, who were centered in Vienna, but also to the Czortkow and Husiatyn branches of the Ruzhin family, the descendants of the Maggid of Miedzyrzec. These were all Ukrainian and eastern Polish dynasties. Members of Heschel's family were culturally immigrants to Warsaw, where Hasidic Jewry was dominated by Kotzk and Ger, to which he had no family connection. As a Hasidic youth in Warsaw, he was, however, taught in the Ger schools and had a personal tutor who was a devoted Kotsker Hasid. Hence the very different worlds that Heschel late in his life referred to as Miedzybozh and Kotsk came to dwell together in his soul.[74]

Framing his discussion of Hasidism in *The Earth Is the Lord's* between the Baal Shem Tov and the Kotzker, Heschel anticipates, early in his career, the lifelong struggle that he would experience as he attempted to theorize a new Hasidic theology, uniquely designed for Americans. His 1945 talk and its 1949 adaptation became the blueprints for his effort to achieve that goal by balancing his portrait of Torah study as the larger frame for his portrait of East European Jewish culture with Hasidic tales that punctuate his text and continually mediate and qualify the scholarly model.

Many of the impulses we have been tracing throughout our bigger discussion are evident in Heschel's essay: the desire to invite Americans into a world they are indebted to culturally but alienated from religiously and culturally; to communicate the inaccessibility of a destroyed world even while giving the impression of accessibility; and to streamline a complex culture while leaving scars of that complexity behind, alerting an audience to their inadequacy at really apprehending what has been placed before them. In *The Earth Is the Lord's*, this fascinating interplay between the spiritual portrait Heschel attempts to limn and his intellectual message, between the metaphorically overdetermined depiction of East European Jewish culture as a culture of scholars and the "heart"-centered world of Hasidic tales, reflects a larger conundrum: Can Heschel really reach American Jews?

Heschel's linguistic choices at the end of his life can help us to illuminate some of his thinking around American Jews' ability or inability to comprehend the messages he is trying to communicate about Hasidim, spirituality, and the American Jewish scene. In an essay on Heschel's final work, *Kotzk: A Struggle for Eternity*, Annette Aronowicz proposes some possible explanations for why he wrote it in Yiddish. (As Shandler points out, after leaving Europe, Heschel's Yiddish publications were few and far between.)[75] Aronowicz suggests that for Heschel, maintaining "the continuity of the Jewish tradition requires a leap out of the world of American and Israeli culture. Yiddish would signal a gap between the Western secular world and the East European one."[76]

Echoing the rhetoric of Dawidowicz, as we will see, in her memoir about her year in Vilna just before the outbreak of World War II and Vishniac's claim to have been one of the last to witness the lives of East European Jews before they were murdered, Heschel writes near the end of his introduction to *Kotzk*, "I am the last of a generation, perhaps the last Jew from Warsaw whose soul lives in Mezbizh and whose mind lives in Kotsk"[77]—a line that does not appear in the book's English version. In exploring why this is so, we should consider Shandler's argument in his essay on Yiddish signification in Heschel's work that Heschel can say certain things in Yiddish that he cannot say in English. Indeed, according to Morris Faierstein, Heschel only felt comfortable writing about the Holocaust in Yiddish.[78]

Furthermore, in English he may not have wanted to declare himself the "end of a line," because his American project was about continuity. He fought to make Judaism ethically and spiritually relevant to modern Jews throughout his career, and he insisted that even American Jews without the language skills to access the primary texts could find a way into that culture: through social activism, through prayer, and through study that, in the spirit of depth theology, described above, took the whole person and the depth of the culture into account. So how could he say that he was the last of a line of people who believed in the "I" of the Kotzker as well as the "thou" of the Baal Shem?

There is a hopelessness, and a haplessness, underlying salvage poetics. Can a text really save a culture? Heschel's incorporation of Hasidic tales into The Earth Is the Lord's is, it seems to me, his figural Yiddish, the remnant of the Yiddish and oral original that he so quickly transcribed and translated. It is in these Hasidic stories that Heschel feels comfortable articulating, albeit obliquely, the tensions he feels between fantasy and reality in American apprehension of their East European ancestors. It is the dialectic between the Baal Shem Tov and the Kotzker Rebbe, between the champion of inclusiveness and the champion of exclusiveness, that ultimately takes center stage in The Earth Is the Lord's. The text's climax grows out of Heschel's desire to represent Hasidism in all its beautiful and fruitful contradictions: as a repudiation of scholarship and an embrace of scholars, as a repudiation of ritual and the bulwark of observance. At the heart of his presentation of these contradictions are the two figures who occupied Heschel's spirit for so many years—the happy rabbi (the Baal Shem Tov) who prayed in the fields and embraced the traces of God in every living creature, and the severe rabbi (the Kotzker Rebbe) who lived in seclusion for the last twenty years of his life and burned every word he ever wrote. Nothing was good enough for the Kotzker; no one possessed the kind of self-awareness that could enable a practice of a self-abnegation that would allow his ideals to be realized.

Heschel's *The Earth Is the Lord's* anticipates a failure akin to that of the Kotzker Rebbe. Who among his American audience could possibly achieve the kind of "inwardness" and spiritual well-roundedness prescribed in *The Earth Is the Lord's*? Its Hasidic tales are orally resonant, an extension of the original oral speech, pithy and striking in their content, but ultimately they undermine the essay's broader theme: in their very orality they allow the text to pretend that it is accessible and its ideals attainable, but at the same time their conflict with those very ideals is encoded within them.

In the concluding section of *The Earth Is the Lord's*, "The Untold Story," Heschel reflects on the Jewish Enlightenment and the place of the modern Jew within Jewish tradition. But at the same time some critical pieces of the story are missing. In the exquisite woodcut by Ilya Schor that illustrates the chapter, five Jews—a scribe, a ritual slaughterer, a rabbi, a workingman, and a musician—are inserted into an ornate backdrop. The figures included remind us that the story of women is untold, in the book's illustrations and its text. Another untold story might be the one that was just unfolding in 1949 when *The Earth Is the Lord's* was first published: the story of what the Jews in America would do with their knowledge of the Holocaust, how it would affect their relationship with their East European past, and how they would forge their identity on its crucible. Heschel, along with Vishniac, Samuel, Howe and Dawidowicz, and Zborowski and Herzog, all write their salvage poetic texts in the hope of accommodating American Jews, no matter who they are, what languages they read, and what Jewish practices they are familiar with. The need to do this became urgent in the aftermath of the Holocaust. Heschel, a living embodiment of the possibilities inherent in the building of bridges between cultures and of the obligation, having survived the catastrophe, to forge a connection between the living and the dead, felt this need acutely.

Though he wrote very little about the Holocaust itself, Heschel did actively address it on a number of different occasions. In an essay on Heschel's response to the Holocaust, Morris Faierstein tells us:

In the immediate postwar period, Hasidism appeared to be dead. The great center of Hasidic life in Eastern Europe, the vast majority of Hasidic leaders and their followers, had been destroyed in the Holocaust. The revival of Hasidic life in America was wishful thinking. In the wake of this catastrophe, Heschel, in association with the YIVO Institute, hoped to preserve the few remnants of Hasidic manuscripts and other documents that somehow survived the destruction. In addition, people who had direct experience of Hasidic life in Europe were asked to record their memories, the stories they had heard, and any other information they had in order to preserve the memory of Hasidism. The revival of Hasidic life in America that is a part of the contemporary American Jewish landscape did not become a reality until the 1960s and could not have been foreseen in the 1940s and 1950s.[79]

Faierstein goes on to tell us that between 1949 and 1965 Heschel published five articles on the Baal Shem Tov, some in Yiddish and some in English, all to serve as preliminary studies for a major biography of the Baal Shem Tov. He never completed this project, and in the 1960s he turned to the Rebbe of Kotzk, completing two major works on him, one in English and one in Yiddish, both published posthumously—the last works he ever wrote.

Further explaining the link between Heschel's commitment to explicating Hasidism for Americans and his commitment to rendering Jewish spirituality accessible to American Jews, Heschel reflected on his identity after the Holocaust in a 1965 lecture at the Union Theological Seminary in New York:

> I am a brand plucked from the fire, in which my people was burned to death. I am a brand plucked from the fire of an altar to Satan on which millions of human lives were exterminated to evil's greater glory... [On this altar] so much else was consumed: the divine image of so many human beings, many people's faith in the God of justice and compassion, and much of the secret and power of attachment.[80]

Continuing, Heschel articulated his mission for American Jews in light of his identity as a singular remnant of the destroyed East European

Jewish world, as "shar[ing] the certainty of Israel that the Bible contains that which God wants us to know and hearken to; how to attain a collective sense for the presence of God in the biblical words." He considered American Jews to be in the throes of what he called a "second Holocaust," stricken with a plague of "spiritual absenteeism."[81]

For Heschel in the late 1940s, the Hasidic tales in the various published versions of his YIVO lectures did more than tell a story about a lost world. They conveyed the possibility of rejuvenation for a population of Jews who, to his mind, may have survived the Holocaust physically intact, but not spiritually. His description of a "culture" in *The Earth Is the Lord's* is one of literacy and inwardness that worked symbiotically to connect the Jewish people of Eastern Europe with God. For Heschel, the incorporation of the Hasidic tale into *The Earth Is the Lord's* was a first step toward salvaging Hasidism for American Jewish posterity, but also toward saving American Jewry.

With Heschel's help, Hasidism became not only an object of American Jewish fascination, but also, through its stories, a window into the possibilities inherent in telling tales where salvage and spiritual aspirations intersected. Although the stories in *The Earth Is the Lord's* did preserve a literary corpus to some extent, they also sought to transmit a culture—not for posterity, but for renewal in the present day. The possibility of success was, in the twilight years just after the war, shadowed by the grief of loss. The transformation of the essay from a spoken eulogy to an illustrated book also casts a shadow insofar as Heschel was among the first to acknowledge the necessity for American Jewry of a visual means of grappling with the legacy of the past and its lessons for the present and the future. The introduction of Ilya Schor's woodcuts in the latest version of the essay, with their accompanying critical discourse of iconicity and ethnographic transparency, mark the beginning of the transformation of American salvage poetics from the textual to the visual, one which would continue in full force with the 1947 publication of Roman Vishniac's *Polish Jews*, with its abundance of images and its minimalistic captioning.

The sense of hopelessness permeating American Jewry in the late 1940s was the source of the tensions we have been tracing between the anti-scholarly ethos of most of the stories and the scholarly exposition

Heschel provides. This same tension was reflected in Heschel's own psyche, with his spirit torn between the Baal Shem Tov and the Kotzker, between the spirit of generosity and the spirit of self-flagellation. Having left unfinished his project of writing a history of the Baal Shem Tov, his career and writing ended with the Kotzker, and we can assume that his own journey was reflected in the subtle irony implicit in the marriage he creates between Hasidic tales and a description of unadulterated scholarship in *The Earth Is the Lord's*, which reflects two contradictory stories.

The Earth Is the Lord's operates on two levels: the Hasidic tales prescribe a spiritual future, with an exposition of bookishness among East European Jews describing their past. Where that past and that future were to come together was at the heart of Heschel's salvage project. Like the other neo-Hasidic writers, he sought an indigenous Jewish literary form for the scripting of a new Jewish idiom, both literary and spiritual. His hybrid text, *The Earth Is the Lord's*, which marries the literary and the ethnographic, presented a new type of Hasidism for an American Jewish audience. While Heschel knew that this neo-Hasidism would never reproduce the depth or hope of the community he had lost, his goal was to provide a model for modern renewal on American ground.

3

SALVAGE LITERARY INFERENCE

The Inner World of the Shtetl in *Life Is with People*

> It would be impossible to list all the Yiddish and Hebrew literary and autobiographical works that have contributed as background to this study.[1]

> Literary sources have been subsidiary to material obtained from informants but have been of indispensable help in getting both confirmation and perspective.[2]

Abraham Joshua Heschel, in *The Earth Is the Lord's*, illuminated an inner world for East European Jewry through tales of the Hasidim, creating an image that would be palatable for an American audience in search of its ethnic roots in spiritual terms. The inner world that we will explore in this chapter also depends on literary representations in the construction of an ethnic portrait. In her critical introduction to the 1995 edition of Elizabeth Herzog and Mark Zborowski's *Life Is with People: The Culture of the Shtetl* (originally published in 1952), Barbara Kirshenblatt-Gimblett sums up the book as follows: "The task, now a sacred duty, was to recover the inner life of East European Jewry, its values and the distinctive culture they animated."[3] What I hope to do in this chapter is to understand how this notion of an "inner world," when refracted through *Life Is with People*, illuminates a broader disciplinary context for salvage poetics in American post-Holocaust representations of pre-Holocaust life. The shtetl's "inner world," I hope to demonstrate, is formulated in *Life Is with People* in literary terms, on the basis primarily of what individuals in the shtetl may have read, and what informants not from the shtetl may have read about them. I call this dynamic, wherein the authors of the book rely on allusions to literary sources—not intertextual allusions, but inferential ones—based on their own general impressions gleaned from literary sources alongside those of their informants, "salvage literary inference." Through the lens of salvage literary inference, in this analysis of *Life Is with People*, I will consider "inwardness" as an extension of the major discourses—literary modernism and ethnography—that the authors struggle to engage as they find a place for themselves within their portraits of East European Jewish life.

A metaphor of the "inner world" described in *Life Is with People* can be found in the book's description of traditional Jewish Sabbath laws as practiced in the "shtetl." On the Sabbath one is forbidden from carrying objects from the private to the public domain and vice versa, but if the public domain is rendered private, carrying can take place. In describing the carrying of private possessions from the private domain into the public domain on the Sabbath, the text discusses the legal fiction of an *eyruv*, or a "fence," that allows for such an activity:

> If a fence has been constructed around a group of houses, the area enclosed may be regarded as one's home and objects may be carried in it. The fence, *eyruv*, is a cord or a wire, stretched around the shtetl, under the supervision of the rabbi, who concludes the ritual by declaring that "this is no longer a public domain, but the domain of an individual." There is always the danger, however, that—despite the weekly inspection—the "fence" may be broken at some point, in which case carrying would no longer be permissible.[4]

Through the construction of an *eyruv*, or a particular sort of fence, the "inner" world of the private individual is extended to include the external, public world of the community. This newly enlarged private domain is continuous and singular—the Jewish individual is not carrying from one private domain to another, but has extended his or her own private domain to include that of many others. Hence, the way to carry objects from one domain to another is to turn the public domain into a private one, not to turn a private one into a public one. It is the private domain, the individual experience, that takes precedence here, defining mobility and laying the legal parameters for what it means to possess an object and attempt to take it out into the world. According to Jewish law, with the help of an *eyruv*, the world becomes merely an extension of the private domain on the Sabbath.

This private domain transposed onto an "inner world" represents several important facets of *Life Is with People*. As reflected in the title and according to the book's authors, traditional East European Jewish life was a communal existence, a life lived with people, not a life lived alone. The value of collectivity as a religious and social value is woven throughout *Life Is with People*:

> To sin publicly is a crime, but to insist on privacy if you are not sinning is a serious misdemeanor. Again, the lives of the *shayneh layt* [the upper class] must be open to all. One of the worst things you can say of a man is, "he keeps it for himself," or "he hides it from others," whether it is money or wisdom, clothing or news.[5]

This concern about the higher class rendering itself transparent to the prying eyes of its neighbors is generalized elsewhere in the following statement: "Locked doors, isolation, avoidance of community control, arouse suspicion. 'You know, so and so locks his doors' is a comment which implies that so and so has something to hide."[6] "It is proverbial," the authors remind us, that "'there are no secrets in the shtetl,' and the shtetl itself jokes about the need of everyone to know."[7] And yet there is some discomfort with the idea that there is no individuality, no sense of the private in the community under discussion. Therefore, the notion within traditional Judaism of extending private space in order to subsume and encompass public space, as demonstrated in the *eyruv* formulation, butts against the idea that communal identity, collective consciousness, is always the better route.

Tension between the private and the public, between the inner world and the outer world, as it were, comes to a head in *Life Is with People* in the following statement:

> Within this community where each person is linked and identified with the group and all its members, the individual is never lost. He is merged but not submerged. In the shtetl crowd each person has his own face and his own voice. Nearly everyone in the shtetl was a separate character—a type all for himself. Each one has a name, a nickname, a specialty or at least a distinctive trait. One is a student, the other a specialist in military strategy because years ago he was a soldier in the Russian army. The cantor is an authority on music, but he may be challenged by a tailor who considers himself a better expert, *meyvn*. The shtetl accepts everyone's specialty and everyone feels free to challenge the connoisseurship of anyone else. It is a good day for the congregation when three or four experts begin a hot discussion in the shul, during the interval between the afternoon and evening prayers. Everyone can join in and offer a few clever words. No one admits defeat, everyone is right even if the others do not agree. Faces are red, hands fly in excited gestures—if they are not busy twisting somebody's button or lapel—all talk together, each wanting to outshout his opponent. Suddenly the *shames* [the sexton] hits the table with the palm of his hand and the argument is over—it is time to pray.[8]

In this passage we see one of the most important salvage poetic devices in the text, a device that flags the text's literary aspirations not simply as a stylistic necessity, but as a point of reference. Thus is born the notion of "salvage literary inference," wherein the authors of *Life Is with People* rely on literary texts and literary norms in order to explicate East European Jewish culture. The overwhelmingly literary inspiration for the study conducted in *Life Is with People* is evident in the above passage, where the literary notion of "types" animates a scene that gives the reader a sense of Jewish discourse, Jewish time, and community. The "types" are presumably reproduced in all shtetlach and animate all interactions as well as the spirit of the community.

In a remarkable moment, the possibility of individuality despite the study's communal orientation is recuperated in the language of early twentieth-century literary criticism.[9] Shtetl Jews, in the above passage, can claim some individuality as "types": a student, a soldier, a cantor, a tailor. But by generalizing those individuals as types, the sense of individuality, inwardness, and subjectivity granted Jewish people in the "shtetl" is immediately retracted; because they are "types," these individuals only operate in tandem with others just like them.

The impulse toward generalization from anecdotal, or individualized, information is, perhaps, key to the link between literary and ethnographic discourses in *Life Is with People*. Zborowski and Herzog explicitly articulate the influence of literary sources for *Life Is with People* and their own literary aspirations in the book's introduction:

> It would be impossible to list all the Yiddish and Hebrew literary and autobiographical works that have contributed as background to this study. The works of such writers as Sholem Aleichem, Mendele Moykher Sforim, Y. L. Peretz, Sholem Asch and others have probably contributed more than the academic discussions. It is feasible only to acknowledge in general terms a debt to all the many writers, living and dead, whose names are not mentioned here.[10]

Indeed, in an oft-quoted 1952 review of the book by Moshe Decter in *Commentary*, he says, "With all due respect to Ruth Benedict, Margaret Mead and the authors of *Life Is with People*, it can be safely asserted that the greatest anthropologist of the shtetl was the Yiddish novelist and writer Mendele Mokher Sforim."[11]

After having asserted the overwhelming significance of the works of well-known Yiddish literary authors, the authors then qualify their statement:

> Literary sources have been subsidiary to material obtained from informants but have been of indispensable help in getting both confirmation and perspective—that is, in checking the existence, the dimensions and the incidence of the patterns and features described by the informants.[12]

Implicit in both the authors' original statement and their subsequent qualification is the clear and immeasurable impact of Yiddish literature on *Life Is with People* and, in turn, on cinema and popular ethnographic perceptions. Even though Sholem Aleichem and Mendele Moykher Sforim, among others, are mentioned in passing as "supplementary" to the interview sources, I would argue that they are, in fact, the authorizing spirit of the undertaking. What the authors of *Life Is with People* are doing is inferring cultural details through their, or others', readings of Yiddish literary texts. The ramifications of salvage literary inference can be felt throughout the book.

The classics of Yiddish literature make several appearances in the study, but nowhere more explicitly than in our introduction to women's culture in traditional East European Jewish society. The chapter titled "The Woman's Share" presents the institution of the book peddler as the source of women's literary engagements. After an introduction to the *Tzena U'rena*,[13] the seventeenth-century Yiddish weekly digest of the Torah portion set alongside well-known rabbinic midrashim, the *Bovo Bukh*,[14] Yiddish stories adapted from an Italian epic in the sixteenth century, and the *Tkhines*, women's petitionary prayers authored by a wide variety of religious and popular writers beginning in the seventeenth century, the reader is told that all these books are made available to women by the local book peddler, or *moykher sforim*:

> These are only one part of the books brought in by the book peddler, *moykher sforim*, on his way from shtetl to shtetl. As he approaches the marketplace with his skinny, dejected nag and tumble-down cart loaded with books and ritual wares, the girls come running, shoving and crowding to get first chance as he cries, "Books for women and sacred books for men." The "books" are in Yiddish and the sacred books: in Hebrew.[15]

Just after we encounter the institution of the book peddler, we meet the corresponding literary persona:

> One of the well-known Yiddish authors of the 19th century, Mendele Mokher Sforim, took his pseudonym from the book peddler. Like Sholem Aleichem, he wrote Yiddish under a pen

name in order to preserve his status among intellectuals, while writing under his real name in Hebrew for serious magazines and newspapers, addressed to a male audience. Despite the precaution, these men were proud of their mission in writing with a purpose, a *takhlis*, though perhaps the chief function it performed was beyond the original aim. For it was these novels that first brought knowledge of the shtetl into the modern West. Sholem Aleichem's epitaph, which he himself wrote and which can be seen on his grave in New York, sums up his own purpose and the social cleavage that gave it significance: Here lies a Jew, a simple one, He wrote in Yiddish for women and for the *prosteh* [simple] folk he was a humorist, a writer.[16]

This, our first introduction to Yiddish literature in the book's exposition, is presented as the reification of the abstract book peddler who brings books to women and *prosteh* (uneducated) men. The institutions of the "shtetl" are to be understood, therefore, according to this exposition, as embodiments of the Yiddish literature that, for so many of the study's informants, constituted Jewish literature; neither the Bible nor the Talmud nor the prayer book figured as literarily significant for them and in fact are not discussed in any committed way anywhere in the study. Only Mendele and Sholem Aleichem warrant a full-page discussion. The reason for this is stated quite succinctly in the above quote: "It was these novels that first brought knowledge of the shtetl into the modern West."

Like Maurice Samuel, Zborowski and Herzog seem to be writing their own variation, albeit an ethnographic one, on Sholem Aleichem's and Mendele's Yiddish novels. As they introduce the abstracted institution of the book peddler, before introducing Mendele himself, it is hard not to notice the literary, descriptive flourishes in their description: "his skinny, dejected nag and tumble-down cart loaded with books and ritual wares," and "the girls come running, shoving and crowding to get first chance." This lead-up resonates with the description of the literary book peddler and may even be an unattributed quotation from him. This is where "salvage literary inference" comes in. Cultural details are inferred from literary impressions, not from any explicit allusion to these literary texts. But moments like this, in which the introduction of a cultural institution is followed by a description of literary figures, signal the origins of many inferences the text makes.

Many of the works we are looking at share this feature of repurposing fiction for popular ethnographic apprehension. Samuel, as we have discussed, wants to rewrite Sholem Aleichem, to channel him. And here, though their ethnography is based on interviews with individuals, Zborowski and Herzog intimate that Western knowledge of the East European Jewish experience actually resides in Yiddish literature.

What we have here, in this elaboration on Yiddish literature, is a unique attempt to provide us with an "insider" perspective on East European Jewish culture through its literature. But Zborowski and Herzog do not represent the traditional Jewish literature—the Bible, the Talmud, the liturgy, the responsa, or the codes that dominated traditional Jewish praxis and intellectual discourse for over a millennium. Rather, it is the modern Yiddish literature, produced at the turn of the twentieth century that they rely upon. While the portrait of East European Jewish life created in *Life Is with People* by a team of anthropologists and their assistants is often accurate, and is particularly interesting in light of the way that they cobbled it together from informant interviews and group discussions, it is missing any serious engagement with the traditional and religious Jewish texts, such as liturgy and rabbinic literature, that determine Jewish theology and practice. In Heschel's *The Earth is The Lord's*, we observed that while obeisance is paid to traditional religious literature as the cornerstone of East European Jewish ethnic experience, the only texts developed, explored, and incorporated into the essay are Hasidic texts. While Heschel chose one body of texts over another in deference to his audience, one gets a sense in *Life Is with People* that the authors chose Yiddish literature over traditional religious texts in deference not only to their audience, but to themselves as well. What brought them to the shtetl to begin with? Was it the Torah or the Talmud? No. Presumably it was translations of Yiddish literature. In light of Jonathan Boyarin's observations that the issue of textuality is essential to the study of literate cultures and that anthropologists have, by and large, eschewed studying such cultures in service to the disciplinary ideal of fieldwork and in situ observation,[17] in a culture as textually oriented as Judaism it is a serious misapprehension to avoid any engagement with traditional, religious Jewish texts as they inform Jewish life, even in dialogue with the reports of their informants. For these researchers, the world of traditional Jewish textuality seems to be a world bereft of the "inner" spirit of the people. Since their informants seem to have been largely ignorant of those texts, they were excluded as a resource.

The "inner world" of the East European Jew, therefore, as depicted in *Life Is with People*, is not the world of traditional Jewish literacy. This is in direct contrast to the inner world portrayed by Abraham Joshua Heschel in much of his *The Earth Is the Lord's: The Inner World of the Jew in East Europe*, which we explored in chapter 2. To authentically enter the "private domain" of the traditional Jew, it seems to me, one must enter the world of Jewish scholarship and prayer, at least to a significant degree, as these elements of Jewish textuality play a significant role in the discourse and praxis of that culture.

It is not that traditional religious texts are not alluded to. On the contrary, texts are alluded to throughout the book, giving us a sense of what the authors of the study consider "insider" information, and what they dismiss as such. One moment that is particularly illuminating in capturing what is and is not important to the authors when it comes to reporting on literary commitments takes place in the description of the children's cheder. The cheder is the school that the boys attend, usually at their teacher's house, to learn first the Hebrew alphabet, then basic prayers, then the Pentateuch, and finally graduating to rabbinic literature when they have demonstrated proficiency with the foundational texts and if their parents can afford to let them stay in school. The text reads:

> During the hour that the *melamed dardaki* [the teacher of young children] goes to minyan, he leaves the children of the cheder behind in the twilight. What do they do for that hour? Above all this is the hour for stories. Crowding together against the winter cold and the fear of the wonders they are describing, they tell each other tales in which themes carried over from pagan myths jostle with folklore rooted in the Talmud. In the *melamed*'s absence the strict program of Hebrew erudition is broken into by a medley that mingles biblical miracles with the spirits and

demons shared by all the folk, Jews and peasants alike. The boys
tell each other in turn about the spirits who throng the *shul*
[synagogue] after midnight, and the tricks they play on anyone
who has to sleep there, so that a beggar would rather sleep on
the floor of the humblest house than enjoy the hone of a bench
in the shul. They tell about the devils who haunt the woods at
night, the *sheydim*, and how some of them even get into the
shtetl streets when it is very dark. They tell about the dybbuk
who enters the soul of a person so that he becomes possessed
and speaks with a voice not his own, uttering blasphemies that
would be far from his true mind. They tell of Lilith, Adam's first
wife, who steals children; and of children kidnapped from their
parents by gypsies or by wicked men who deliver them into
army service. Children of Hassidim will repeat tales their father
brings from the rebbe's court about the miracles wrought by
wonderman.[18]

A key sentence in the above passage gives us a sense of what the
authors view as "insider" information; it tells us that the children take
a break from their intensive Hebrew instruction during their teacher's
brief absence in order to share tales with one another that are also
shared by peasants. This passage represents one of the most detailed
accounts in *Life Is with People* of the kinds of tales shared among people in the shtetl, albeit children in this case: stories about dybbuks
and Lilith and *sheydim* (demons) and devils. In this description, we
observe an attempt to convince the reader that the stories at the heart
of these children's consciousness are actually universal stories—"tales
in which themes carried over from pagan myths jostle with folklore
rooted in the Talmud" and which are "shared by all the folk, Jews and
peasants alike"—not stories that are particularly Jewishly grounded.
What are we to learn from this about the place of Jewish literature in
the consciousness of the Jews being described? Not much, apparently.
Not only are the details of the learned exchanges in the teacher's presence entirely omitted, but the passage expands significantly on the
folklore the students share with the local non-Jewish peasants.

The authors of *Life Is with People* are trying not to alienate their
readership by delving too much into the depths of the culture of study

they are describing, avoiding the reality that children traditionally begin the book of Leviticus at age five despite its focus on Temple rituals and sacrifices. The only thing deemed worthy of detailed description in this excerpt appears to be local folk literature, the texts shared by the Jews and the surrounding culture. Given that this ethnography does not engage with a specific locale and historical moment and is instead, in its quest for Jewish "core culture" only engaged with the presentation of Jewish tradition as it is observed by Jews the world over, this literary detour into local folktales seems highly out of keeping with the rest of the text.

The scene in the above passage is one of intimacy among the boys of the cheder, outside the prying surveillance of their teacher. The "inner world," therefore, that we become privy to is a folk world of storytelling that deviates significantly from the world of traditional Jewish study that the boys are engaged in day in and day out from toddlerhood through, for many, early adulthood and beyond. Interestingly, at the inception of modern Hebrew and Yiddish literature in the late nineteenth century, largely in the forms of memoir and bildungsroman, the cheder story is central. The most frequently told narrative is one of childish intrigue and rabbinic cruelty, wherein the spirited and intelligent youngster is beaten into submission by an unintelligent and impoverished teacher (if he were more intelligent, he would be teaching older students; if he were less impoverished, he wouldn't need to teach at all). The birth of the modern Hebrew and Yiddish writer, then, is marked by a trope of cheder stories whose point is to describe the oppression of traditional textual engagement and the breaking away from that culture in favor of other literary endeavors. The story told in *Life Is with People* seems to be a variation on that trope, with the folk literature serving as the substance of the literary detour, instead of European belles lettres, which in the memoiristic literature most often serves as the alternative literary pursuit. Introducing an oral literature rather than a written literature at this juncture, while still maintaining allegiance to the cheder trope of the Yiddish and Hebrew memoiristic literature that marked the birth of a modern secular literary consciousness, demonstrates a fascinating allegiance to both elements at once—ethnography and modern Jewish literature.

When the authors do address traditional Jewish texts, their approach is limited at best. When they do mention the traditional textual curriculum, they do not animate it or infuse it with the kind of literary language we observed in the cheder passage. The authors of the study do not entirely avoid a description of the traditional world of texts that Jewish boys study from the age of three. But the authors use of salvage literary inference lies not in the description of textual institutions, but rather in passages like the two cited above introducing the book peddler and the scene of the cheder at twilight, where the authors take on a literary voice, and we get a sense of the role in which they cast themselves. Note, for example, the stylistic differences between the above passages and the following descriptions of the three levels of cheder—the elementary, the *khumesh* (Pentateuch), and the *gemoreh* (Talmud) cheders: "In this first and most elementary cheder, the pupils learn the elements of reading, and the prayers. Within a few months a child has mastered ivreh, the mechanics of reading, as differentiated from ivreh tyutsh, reading with translation."[19] The introduction to the *khumesh* cheder reads as follows: "The *khumesh* boy does not begin his study of the Pentateuch with the first book Genesis, and its delightful stories, but with Leviticus, the dull and difficult theory of sacrifices."[20] Finally, the *gemoreh* cheder is described in the following way:

> The *gemoreh cheder* is devoted chiefly to study of the Talmud, which covers an infinite variety of aspects and problems, ancient and contemporary, religious and secular. Talmudic studies consist of continuous discussion, commentary and interpretation with the help of innumerable commentators and interpreters. With equal concentration the child of eight or nine must study the holiday ritual in the Temple of Solomon, the ethics of man-to-man dealings, the laws of divorce, or the rules governing connubial behavior during menstruation.[21]

In the above presentations, there is no setting of scene, no light or darkness, no sense of the physical environment. There is no investment in giving the reader any insight into the content or the style of the books invoked. It seems, then, that the cheder scene, with its digression into the territory of the Yiddish and Hebrew memoiristic literature wherein the absence of the authority figure, or the rebbe, invites a kind of literary meditation on alternatives to traditional textuality, and the Mendele scene, where the mention of the great Yiddish literary figure invites a detour into a literary style that could have been taken from his own works, reflects an engagement with the themes and style of Yiddish secular literature. It is more than the themes and the literariness of that literature, however, that inspires the authors of *Life Is with People* to adopt its tone, ambience, and voice.

Conceived at the birth of European modernism, and identified by many readers and critics as modernist in its concerns and often its style, Modern Yiddish literature, interestingly, offers the authors of *Life Is with People* an opportunity to introduce their readers to a modernist engagement with subjectivity and interiority, or—to return to our earlier parlance—an "inner world." The way that the narrative becomes specific and animated in its discussion of more literary texts while excluding traditional Jewish ones reflects a modernist narratorial commitment to modern Yiddish literary sources—one in which the narrator gives us a glimpse of his or her own meta-textual concerns and preoccupations.

In a text that valorizes collectivity, maintaining that "life is with people," but also identifies Yiddish literature as the first Jewish literary attempt to communicate Jewish individuality and subjectivity and uses it as a significant ethnographic resource, the authors are hard-pressed to hold onto both at once: collectivity and subjectivity. This reflects Richard Handler's observation in his study of modernism and anthropology that one of modernism's major tensions is "between a quest for self-expression and the desire to recover a viable tradition."[22] The implications of this struggle can be seen in the modernist rhetoric of both T. S. Eliot and James Joyce in their quests for tradition in *The Wasteland* and *Ulysses*, respectively. At the same time, both works are renowned for the individuality of their voices and their commitment to subjective consciousness and stylization of interiority. In this book the movement between the abstract book peddler and the pseudonymous author, Mendele the Book Peddler, emphasizes the dynamic wherein the ethnographer uses literary allusion to recuperate the subjectivity and individuality of his or her subject. Because the generalized book peddler is compressed into the literary book peddler, even if we don't glimpse an actual individual book peddler in the shtetl, literary allusion is used to move us in that direction.

Another "character" that facilitates an awareness of the "inner" world of East European Jewry as an articulation, in part, of the individual personalities that constitute the collective, is the "shtetl" itself, the small town around which the entire book is organized and which becomes a literary presence. Barbara Kirshenblatt-Gimblett, in her introduction to *Life Is with People*, beautifully spells out the process whereby the entire East European Jewish culture was honed to a singular "shtetl":

> First, they posited the shtetl as a cultural island and identified it with the entire East European Jewish culture area. They then proceeded in the mode of salvage ethnography to reconstruct by means of interviews what could no longer be observed. Finally, they wrote about that world as if they had done fieldwork in a living community.[23]

She argues, in conclusion, that appointing the shtetl as the study's subject "became a textual way to achieve coherence, totality, and authority in the representing of East European Jewish culture."[24]

Although Kirshenblatt-Gimblett describes the need to delimit the book's subject to a particular geographic area, in keeping with anthropological norms of that moment, she asserts that "in identifying Jewish life in Eastern Europe with a timeless shtetl, this celebration of a lost world was more literary than historical in character."[25] Indeed the idea of a "shtetl" as emblematic of East European Jewish culture as a whole grew out of the ubiquity of the nineteenth-century shtetl as a subject in Yiddish literature. Barbara Kirshenblatt-Gimblett argues throughout the introduction, therefore, that the term "shtetl" should have been kept a literary term in *Life Is with People*, not turned into an ethnographic one.

In an effort to acknowledge Kirshenblatt-Gimblett's important insight but to expand on it, this discussion seeks a literary way to understand the ethnographic undertaking, to bring together the ethnographic and literary discourses. The authors of *Life Is with People*, I contend, find a way to animate the shtetl as one would a literary character in order to announce the literary origins of their notion of the shtetl. This, perhaps, is their way of taking responsibility for their reliance on a literary trope as the justification for their ethnographic project. In other words, this book is inspired by a literary concept—the quest for subjectivity and individuality within the explicitly collective vision. *Life Is with People* is first and foremost an expansion of a literary trope, and at times it relies on literary conventions in order to make itself accessible and engaging. The shtetl in *Life Is with People* functions similarly to what I argued in chapter 1 about the literary figure of Sholem Aleichem in Samuel's book—both literary figures enable the author to build a bridge between an American-Jewish readership and East European Jewish culture.

Discussing the ramifications of using literary models to construct the shtetl as the subject of an ethnographic inquiry, Kirshenblatt-Gimblett observes:

> Consistent with its literary models, *Life Is with People* produced a composite portrait of a virtual town, not an empirical description of an actual one. The goal was to delineate the general patterns of East European Jewish culture, rather than inventory its customs, in order to illuminate how cultural practices shape personality.[26]

She concludes that "by the end of the book, the shtetl has become a protagonist in its own right" and that "the shtetl is represented in anthropomorphic terms, so fully animated had it become for the authors."[27]

While I agree with Kirshenblatt-Gimblett's observation that the shtetl becomes a character in its own right, I would like to correct her apprehension that this only happens in the last chapter of the book, "How the Shtetl Sees the World." Indeed, it is not only at the book's end that the shtetl "becomes a protagonist in its own right," but it speaks in its own voice from the very beginning and throughout the book as an autonomous character, with its own agency—particularly through the authors' investing it with voiced subjectivity. Let's consider this "voice" to better understand how the authors develop the shtetl into an animated protagonist, and the implications of this animation for our understanding of *Life Is with People*'s literary inspiration as well as its salvage poetic properties.

In an overview of the history of the Jews and their ability to withstand the ravages of time and trauma, the book asserts: "According to the shtetl, the children of Israel have survived solely because of the covenant made with God in accepting his law."[28] And in a continuation of this statement: "It is the covenant with God, says the shtetl, that has enabled a weak and homeless people to survive the great empires of Egypt and Babylon, Greece and Rome, Byzantium and Islam and has caused their sacred books to enter into the Holy writ of half the world." I include both statements here even though they overlap in content, because they build rhetorically on one another, moving from a simple statement of theology that any shtetl inhabitant could have made to one demanding the knowledge and scope of a scholar. The authors are able to beg the bigger question of who precisely is making these observations by attributing a voice to the shtetl, through framing words like "according to" and "says."

In a later discussion on the divine significance of Torah study, another statement of theological scope, minus historical perspective, attributes agency to the shtetl: "The importance, the prestige, the glamour attached to study flow from Mount Sinai. Here, according to the shtetl, were forged the values by which the people live and the social structure through which those values are expressed."[29] In fact, the ahistoricism implicit herein is far more typical of what a traditionally educated Jew might assert. In a summary articulation of this phenomenon of ahistorical apprehension of Jewish theological imperatives, the text reads: "The shtetl endows the far end of its continuum with attributes of the near. The past is conceived in the image of the present, and the foreign is envisaged as a reflection of the familiar."[30] Here, the authors use the verb "endows," apparently wanting to continue to attribute these rather complex insights to the shtetl itself, and not to themselves; but they choose not to use a simple word reflecting personal agency or communication, like "said" or "according to."

There is a struggle throughout this text, as in many modernist Jewish texts, to negotiate the agency of a narrator vis-à-vis his or her subject. In *Life Is with People*, as we track the "voice" of the shtetl and the different types of agency attributed to it, we can also detect some anxiety on the authors' part about inserting their own voices into the text. At times, as we have already observed, they take on not just the tone of literary authors, with descriptive, colorful, and even poetic language, but that of specific literary authors, as was the case with the Mendele passages. At other times, they retain a purely objective voice, as they did in the three cheder passages describing the study of traditional texts. The moments when the authors feel compelled to attribute the text's voice to their subject itself create an effect of subjectivity but also a strange disembodiment because the subject is conceived as collective. In instances where they directly quote informants, we get a better glimpse of the struggle being enacted between the anthropologists and their subject. For example, the third chapter, "No Bread, No Torah," is the first to quote directly from informants on a regular basis. In a discussion of Jewish financial heroes, Rothschild, Brodsky, and Baron de Hirsch, an informant says:

> Brodsky was a millionaire . . . the richest Jew in Russia. . . . When the Russian government closed the yeshiva, we appealed to Brodsky and he bribed the authorities to reopen it. This happened very often. Once, I recall, he was in the town and he came to say goodbye to the head of the yeshiva. He wanted to give him money. But the head of the yeshiva said that he had enough money to live on and besides, for teaching you don't take money. But there are poor students who need help. So, Brodsky immediately gave the order that from that day on, every student should receive ten ruble a week. Can you imagine, ten ruble a week? It's a fortune—enough for a whole family to live on. Brodsky was a good person. Imagine, he gave ten ruble a week to those boys—ten ruble. A nice tsdokeh![31]

The transition away from this direct quotation reads as follows:

> Those money heroes are popular personalities in shtetl daydreaming. In the short hour between afternoon and evening

prayer service at the shul, the hungry and ragged will count and recount the treasures of the Jewish millionaires, will discuss their financial operations, and will formulate their advice about the best way to handle all that wealth. Brodsky and Rothschild are not remote, semi-mythical personalities. They belong to the shtetl. The undernourished luftmentsh or the footsore peddler trudging along with his bony horse knows that his chances of becoming a Rothschild or a Brodsky are slight, and that dumplings in a dream are not dumplings but a dream. Nevertheless, with his traditional hopefulness, his *betokhen* [faith], he dreams about what he would do if by some miraculous luck, mazel, he would win a fortune with the eighth of a lottery ticket he bought instead of patches for his shoes. The contents of his dream in themselves point up the meaning of money for the shtetl: he would buy a seat on the Eastern Wall of the synagogue; he would build a new hospital and get rid of Reb Khayim as president of the Talmud Torah Association.[32]

Here, the authors go so far as to pepper their language with idioms that create the effect of free indirect discourse: "dumplings in a dream are not dumplings but a dream." In this way they appear to use the voices of the informants as jumping-off points for their own storytelling, for their own validation as storytellers.

Anthropologists have long engaged in literary writing, even fictionalizing their field reports and adopting the novel form to communicate their findings.[33] This incorporation of the literary realm is one source of the postmodern self-consciousness in anthropological theory that postulates the need for literary self-awareness in the production of anthropological texts. But what is going on in *Life Is with People*, I would argue, goes beyond the adoption of literary norms in the presentation of ethnographic findings. Through salvage literary inference, the book is written in dialogue with Yiddish literature in a way that folds the voices and the norms of that literature into itself, partly in order to acknowledge their own and their informants' reliance on these texts in their report on East European Jewish culture, but also because of the broader context of representational norms embedded in modern Jewish literatures at the turn of the twentieth century.

Modern Jewish literary models were explicitly concerned about narrative authority within the context of the imperative to represent the Jewish world "as it is" for the first time in over a millennium. Early in the twentieth century, "as it is" was generally understood by Hebrew critics and writers as a form of realism and naturalism, wherein literature was pressed to move away from the realm of the epic myth or the ideological manifesto, both of which dominated Hebrew letters in the nineteenth century.[34] With the advent of modernism, however, "as it is" became a code phrase for interiority—for the psychological experience of the modern Jew. The authors of *Life Is with People* also struggle to find access to that inner world as they attempt to represent the "inner world" of East European Jewish society, while still demonstrating their ethnographic findings in an authoritative way. The push and pull, between perspectives, between the purportedly subjective account of the culture and anthropological objectivity, between the voices of informants and the voices of a narrator who enters the consciousness of the informant, is fairly typical of both the modern Yiddish classics and the Hebrew revival, which had been popularized about half a century earlier. Mendele, for example, writes extensive prefaces to most of his Yiddish works, framing his stories in order to justify their genesis as a speech act or a "vernacular" event, in keeping with the idea of Yiddish as the vernacular language and the need to make that vernacularity one of its literary distinctions when Yiddish began to be used within a literary context. For his part, Sholem Aleichem is not just a narrator, but an interlocutor in his stories, adding a layer of storytelling in which his protagonists entrust their stories to him, and he in turn writes them down, explicitly tracking the story's progress from oral to written for his readers. Yosef Haim Brenner frequently presents his Hebrew stories as "found texts" and mediates them for his readers in a highly self-conscious and meta-textual manner, as if he seeks literary precursors while still maintaining the reader's awareness of the present experience of generating a text. Dvora Baron, about whom I have written extensively, engaged in what I have termed "tugs of war" over issues of narrative authority as a woman writing in Hebrew at a moment when a secular Hebrew writer had to have demonstrated proficiency in the language of religious texts, texts that were largely unavailable to girls and women in a highly gender-segregated culture. Because the modernization of Jewish society corresponded with the deployment of both Yiddish and Hebrew as modern literary languages, the writers, who often wrote in both languages simultaneously, had to demonstrate their commitment to modernity even while using languages that had been largely reserved for religious instruction. One literary technique they used to overcome some of these inherent contradictions was to employ elaborate framing mechanisms where they drew attention to their narrative challenges.

The challenges faced by the authors of *Life Is with People* were not just narrative. They were methodological as well, within the contemporary discourses of ethnographic studies. *Life Is with People* was published as a showpiece for the culture at a distance method that had in the previous decade become a popular way to grapple anthropologically with cultures that had been rendered inaccessible by the iron curtain. Committed to an "insider perspective" on cultures that were inaccessible, culture at a distance prescribed a group exploration, through careful selection of native or near-native informants of the culture in question and advocated a process of consensual deductions within a working group assigned to grapple with the information gleaned from those informants. Also in the years immediately prior to the publication of *Life Is with People*, the culture and personality school sought to find another way into the "inner lives" of its communities, by turning its attention to the relationship between individual psychology and society. Applying psychoanalytic methods to the study of culture, the culture and personality school of ethnographic scholarship argued that the best way to understand individual psychology within the context of a community is to view the community as constitutive of the individual personality. The culture and personality movement sought to bridge the perceived gap between sociology and psychology through the intervention of cultural anthropology, eschewing biological explanations for individual variations in the human population, in favor of cultural ones.

Both culture at a distance and culture and personality had been largely dismissed within professional anthropological circles as not "scientific" shortly before the publication of *Life Is with People*. Nevertheless, the destruction of East European Jewish culture at the same time that these approaches were falling out of favor presented an example, in extremis, of how these ethnographic approaches could be utilized in situations when all other options seemed inadequate. Those trying to explicate the culture of East European Jewry in the early 1950s were best served, it seemed at the time, by a method that could rely on informants who had emigrated to the United States before the war, or who were born to parents who had done so in previous generations. Similarly, how else could one explain the cultural patterns of a people that seemed so "other" in America than to frame it as a "pattern of culture," as articulated by Ruth Benedict in her famous manifesto on the culture and personality school?[35] Thus, in seeking out a textual model in literary modernism, an ethnographic method in culture at a distance, and a justification in culture and personality for the "otherness" of Jews in America in the years after the Holocaust, *Life Is with People* presented its own variation on contested ethnographic methodologies through its deployment of salvage literary inference.

Barbara Kirshenblatt-Gimblett has written extensively about the history of *Life Is with People*, highlighting its importance as "the first major anthropological study of East European Jewish culture in the English language."[36] I will simply touch on the highlights of its publication. The initial motivation for the research embodied in *Life Is with People* was the 1946 Columbia University Research in Contemporary Culture Project, which, as described above, was primarily an experiment in studying culture at a distance. In a 1953 manual detailing the method, titled *The Study of Culture at a Distance*, Margaret Mead and Rhoda Métraux describe it as follows:

> This manual is concerned with methods that have been developed during the last decade for analyzing the cultural regularities in the characters of individuals who are members of societies, which are inaccessible to direct observation. This inaccessibility may be spatial because a state of active warfare exists—as was the case with Japan and Germany in the early 1940s; or it may be—as is now the case of the Soviet Union and Communist China—due to barriers to travel and research. Or the inaccessibility may be temporal since the society we wish to study may no longer exist. It may have been physically destroyed and the

survivors scattered, as is the case with the East European Jewish
small towns; it may have been altered by drastic revolutionary
changes, as is the case in Indonesia and Thailand. We then face
a situation in which we have access on the one hand to many
living and articulate individuals whose character was formed in
the inaccessible society and on the other hand to large amounts
of other sorts of material—books, newspapers, periodicals, films,
works of popular and fine art, diaries, letters—the sort of materials with which the social historian has learned to deal without
the benefit of interviews with living persons. By combining the
methods of the historian with those of the anthropologist, who
is accustomed to work without any documented time perspective, we have developed this new approach.[37]

We have here a description of a truly fascinating combination of circumstances. In the aftermath of World War II, the military tasked
Columbia University anthropologists to study cultures that had fallen
under the influence of the soviet sphere. The geographic objects of
this study, as described above, were inaccessible due to political
restrictions on travel, as well as cultural extinction. However, there
were informants galore, outside of their geographic domains, eager
and willing to be interviewed about their homelands, their home cultures, or the "worlds" they had left behind either in their own generation or in prior ones. Resources for the anthropologists involved in
this study were not restricted by any means to local, New York informants. Mead and Métraux describe "other materials" that came in
handy, such as books, letters, fine arts, and films, for example. Finally,
what we see in this methodological description is a rather puzzling
statement about how its practitioners are accustomed to working
"without any documented time perspective." While they describe
the methodology of culture at a distance as a combination of historical and anthropological methodologies, they immediately articulate
a resistance to anchoring their study in a particular time or place.
Rather, they are invested in studying what they call "core culture."
The anti-historical ramifications of this study of "core culture," as
they define it, can be understood when they say, in their introduction
to *Life Is with People,*

> Because the core culture is the subject of study, no effort has been made to cover all the shades and levels of acculturation as expressed during the twentieth century in such developments as secularized schools, modifications of dress, political and labor activities and generally increased participation in the life of the larger society.[38]

As we have observed throughout this study thus far, and will observe, particularly in our presentation of Lucy Dawidowicz's *The Golden Tradition* as a repudiation of this phenomenon, the image of East European Jewish culture as completely divorced from other cultures, as well as from modernity, is fairly typical of many of its postwar representations. In culture at a distance, the quest for a "core culture" through the methodology of stripping anthropological observations from any kind of "time perspective," may be at the heart of the popular ignorance of modernity's impact on traditional East European Jewish ways of life for at least more than half a century before the Holocaust. The foundational position of *Life Is with People* within the culture of Jewish American folk ethnographies illuminates that tendency to ignore modernity within the East European Jewish pre-Holocaust sphere, and perhaps that tendency can even be attributed to it.

In light of the broader concerns we have explored throughout this study about how different media were used to build bridges between American Jews and their East European Jewish forebears, this method of stripping East European Jewish culture of its particular temporality and historicity ensures a high degree of familiarity and accessibility for its readership. Because American Jews in New York were the informants, the fiction they read (i.e., Sholem Aleichem, Mendele Mokher Sforim, Y. L. Peretz, Sholem Asch), the films they watched, the art they viewed, the memoirs they consumed, all contributed to the portrait constructed in *Life Is with People*. This world, in other words, was familiar and personal; it was not rooted in any manifestly alien time or place because the time was indeterminate ("without any documented time perspective") and the place far away ("at a distance"). The whole method underlying the project, in fact, as we have already seen, was conceived as an antidote to "inaccessibility." What could be more accessible than gathering information from informants in New York City who shared many of the same cultural memories, literary interests, culinary associations, and ritual observances (or lapses) as their audience? *Life Is with People* was an ethnography of New York Jewish impressions or memories of East European Jewish culture, cobbled together out of interviews by a team of anthropologists and their assistants with first-, second-, and even third-generation "informants."

Clearly, as Mead and Métraux assert, it would have been impossible to do an in situ study of East European Jewish culture in the early 1950s. To clearly render the necessity of this method, particularly in the case of East European Jewry, the authors of *The Study of Culture at a Distance* say,

> This method is applicable when it is essential, either for exigent political reasons or in order to obtain a background for some other piece of work, to know something about a period or a culture that is not accessible but from which there are still living representatives who can be interviewed.[39]

The very exigency that animates this method also inspires its success among American Jews in the postwar era. On the one hand, so many left behind were dead. On the other hand, so many who had emigrated to the United States in the decades, or even the moments, before the war were very much alive. There was a need, it seems, to assert the testimony of the living as a way of acknowledging those who died. Valorizing this testimony as a definitive source on a culture nearly extinguished allows the living to stand in for the dead, making the dead, perhaps, live on. In other words, the testimony of the living enlivened the dead, relieving some of the guilt, and some of the horror, of having escaped that fate.

A culture may be represented in many ways in the aftermath of its cataclysmic destruction—in literature, photography, painting, and anthologies, to name just a few media. In this chapter, however, we have observed laypeople making an effort to do so in a formal ethnography, sanctioned by the academic community and based on testimony of the community most aware of the losses entailed, and thereby presenting a fascinating paradox and an important basis for our development of the concept of salvage poetics. In presenting East European Jewry to American Jews in their own image, the authors of *Life Is with People* created a classic *of* American Jewry, not just *for* American Jewry. Kirshenblatt-Gimblett sums this up by stating, "Anthropology has always been, to some degree, an applied science, and *Life Is with People* shows the discipline applying itself to the situation of American Jews in the immediate post-war period."[40] Therefore, *Life Is with People*, according to Kirshenblatt-Gimblett, doesn't provide as much insight into East European Jewry before the Holocaust as it does into American Jewry after it.

In *Life Is with People*, where methods of culture at a distance and culture and personality were deployed in tandem in order to produce a salvage ethnography, the authors were compelled to present a text that animated their subject psychologically even while acknowledging the challenges inherent in researching a community in absentia or even psychologizing that community. The dynamics of coming close and yet maintaining a distance, of infusing the text with moments of free indirect discourse in order to give voice to their subject while still insisting on the authors' authority as scientists, is not simply an anthropological phenomenon. It is a literary phenomenon highly reminiscent of the challenges surrounding the birth of a modern Jewish literary idiom. Just as Hebrew and Yiddish writers were pressed to speak for the Jewish collective but at the same time to illuminate individual consciousness as a way of acknowledging modernity among the members of that collective, just as modernism sought to articulate the presence of a tradition at the heart of modernist sensibilities, so too did the writers of *Life Is with People* seek to articulate a collective, traditional experience in the voice of a modern subjectivity.

In their preface, the authors talk about how some informants, listening to other informant interviews, were concerned that their peers were using their knowledge of literature in order to answer their interviewers' questions, and not drawing from their own experience:

> All quotations from informants are given verbatim, without change of tense or grammatical construction. We felt that the

culture could speak most clearly through their own unedited words. Apparently, many of the informants sensed the nature of the interviewing. One of them protested when a fellow informant tried to introduce secondary sources: "You are telling her what you read in books and what you heard. Books she can read herself, she doesn't have to ask you. She wants to know what I saw . . . so let me tell it my way."[41]

This concern about other informants relying on texts and other resources is fascinatingly in evidence throughout the text on the researchers' part as well. As we have seen, they sum up the informants' testimonies in a literary style, using them to give flavor to the text, but blending their own voices with those of their informants, blurring the lines between the discourses. Merging their consciousness with their informants' through the use of free indirect discourse, to my mind, reveals what seems to be a level of self-consciousness on the part of the authors with regard to their relationship to literary texts as well as to resources other than informant testimonies. While the culture at a distance methodology does stipulate, as we have seen, that the portrait of a culture gleaned at a distance take into account all kinds of peripheral resources, including literary ones, it seems that explicit, articulated confidence is placed in the strength of testimonies; there is some hesitation to acknowledge the impact of literary texts on the style of their ethnography.

There are three levels of narrative in *Life Is with People* and understanding the interrelationship between these discursive styles sheds light on the relationship between stylistic choices and consciousness of salvage literary inference. The first layer of discourse is direct quotation of informants. The second is in free indirect discourse, wherein the narrative takes on the voice of an informant, either directly after a quotation or independently of one. Finally, there is a level fashioned to sound like scientific, objective observation.

Although we have touched on all three levels of narrative in our preceding discussion, it may be worthwhile at this juncture to take a closer look at a moment of free indirect discourse independent of direct quotation by informants. Why? Because when the authors take on the voice of informants, without the justification of an immediate quotation preceding it, what we see is a demonstration of their comfort level with fictionalizing their exposition. The liberties they take at these junctures with the voices of East European Jews are at the core of the "inner world" they seek to represent. At the same time, as we have seen, there is some struggle with authorizing that "inner world," authenticating it and tracing it back to the anthropologists instead of the informants. At the heart of this quandary lays the position of the informants vis-à-vis the anthropologists. In *Life Is with People*, because all the interviews take place in New York in the 1950s, the informants themselves are already a step removed from the subject of the ethnography, and their accounts a form of mediation. If the subject was Orthodox Judaism as practiced in Eastern Europe, then perhaps the informants could provide that information directly to the anthropological team. But because the stated subject is the culture of the shtetl, the fact that the informants are in New York and not in the shtetl itself puts them at a remove from the ethnographic subject. In passages like the following description of a wedding procession, the authors cut right to the chase, allowing us into the minds of what they perceive to be the typical shtetl dweller, but bypassing the informants' testimony and forfeiting social science's objectivity:

> As the procession passes, all the town folk who are not in it look and comment from the street: what a beautiful *khossen* [groom]; how pale he is! You know he is a famous yeshiva student. Yes, they say her father bought him with a sackful of gold—ten thousand rubles, it is said. Still his caftan is a queer cut, isn't it? And his earlocks, they look like corkscrews—those galitsianers! The bride also will be admired for her beauty and her beautiful dress, though with all his money her father might have gotten her a better one. She looks nice but they say she really has trouble with her liver. And all the in-laws, how blown up with pride.[42]

In this passage, which could well have been lifted from a Sholem Aleichem text, we are witnessing a kind of spite, social competition, national pride (in the gripe against the *galitsianers*[43]), and unkindness. It captures the voice of a housewife, or a merchant, someone without as much money as the bride and with less learning than the groom. This is another example of the "type" scene we viewed earlier, wherein the individuals in the shtetl are animated against the backdrop of its collectivity through a description of the different personality types that typically populated it. Yet this passage in essence takes us one step further in its descent into the individual consciousness. Whereas in the earlier "type" passage we really end up right back where we started because the "types" strip individuals of their individuality, here we really have entered the individual consciousness through the borrowing of idiomatic language, evident in phrases such as "and his earlocks, they look like corkscrews—those galitsianers" or "they say she really has trouble with her liver." While the idiomatically inflected voices used here distinguish these "types" from the earlier ones we observed, nevertheless, in the absence of names, in the absence of any physical description of the speakers (remember, they are seeing but they are not seen) we are still in the realm of the "typical." We are hearing the voices, but not seeing the figures. We are given access to subjectivity without a subject.

Life Is with People is structured in such a way as to force the authority of an intermediary onto it. In this text, the acts of ventriloquism, where the narrators speak in the voices of their subjects, as in a literary text written in a style of free indirect discourse or narrated monologue, seem to demonstrate an overriding concern that the mediating voice, in this case the voices of the ethnographers, has the final word. And their voice is most evident, perhaps, at those moments of free indirect discourse when we get closest to the possibility of an interior subjectivity for individuals in the shtetl, but are unable to identify those individuals. Perhaps this is to remind us that there is no such thing as a direct quote in a study such as this one where every individual scenario is reviewed and debated by committee and/or couched in general terms.

This effort to noticeably mediate even while granting individual subjectivity to protagonists is also evident in narrative fiction, particularly that of Jewish writers at the turn of the twentieth century. For them the position of the narrator vis-à-vis the culture represented in the text is rather fraught, because, as I have argued, the act of writing about the shtetl or the Old Country was, in and of itself, a form of breaking away from it. The need to document it is, in part, a confession of sorts, of the author's role in deconstructing it via his or her abandonment of it.

The subtle shifts throughout *Life Is with People* between the individual voices of imagined characters, the voices of informants, and the voice of the narrators are matched by the interesting shifts between individual and collective consciousness. Granting individual consciousness to the collective shtetl is accomplished not only through giving it agency via active verbs, as observed above, but also by coupling the term "shtetl" with other nouns that modify it in a variety of ways, for example, "shtetl folk" and "shtetl picture." Both, interestingly, tap into discourses that are implicit in the broader context of the popular American Jewish ethnography of pre-Holocaust East European Jewish life that *Life Is with People* helped establish.

The "folk" are invoked in a discussion of how inhabitants of the same shtetl tend to gravitate toward one another when they look across a broader array of East European Jews, creating a network of compatriots. This is one way of navigating the fact that the shtetl has been appointed the singular, homogeneous term for all of East European Jewry in *Life Is with People*. Here the term "shtetl" refers to the local community as well as a broader national community:

> Despite local pride and prejudice, the region or country is also felt as a wider community. The people who apply derisory nicknames to inhabitants of a neighboring shtetl will feel a sense of kinship with them as compared to outlanders and will join them in the cultivation of unflattering regional stereotypes. A "Litvak," a "Galitsianer," a Hungarian, a Ukrainian is "outlandish" everywhere but in his own province. The long caftan and the fur hat of the Hungarian Jew are at odds with the custom of Lithuania, and the man who wears them will be viewed askance. In Poland the shorter coat will offend and its wearer will be given the scornful appellation "*Der Daytsh*," the German.[44]

Reminiscent of Margaret Mead's essay, "We Are all Third Generation," what is argued here seems to be that "we are all shtetl folk."[45] In her essay, Mead argues that America comports itself as a nation of third-generation immigrants, who seek out people from their hometowns and become attached to others for no reason other than a common geographical origin. In the above selection we see an attempt to link Mead's idea of Americanness to that of the shtetl, with an articulation of the "shtetl folk" as akin to Americans in their quest for "landsmen" or historical neighbors. The idea of a folk is further defined in *Life Is with People* with the statement: "The shtetl folk feel themselves united not only by bonds of blood, belief, and usage, but also by their common burden and reward."[46] The commonality within the shtetl is emphasized by the authors through the addition of the word "folk," and the desire for commonality is attributed to the shtetl's inhabitants themselves. They bring themselves close to one another through both their geographic origins and their religious commitments. Clearly, within the discourse of anthropology, as we already observed in our analysis of the cheder passage, the notion of a "folk," or at least a folk literature as exemplified in the pagan tales shared in cheder when the rebbe stepped out for evening services, is crucial to generalizing the Jewish particular. Folk literatures are understood to be extratextual in many cases, a literature generated in voice, passed from generation to generation, representing individual voices in their variations, but also communal history in the abundance of those variations. By calling East European Jewry "shtetl folk," the authors of *Life Is with People* simultaneously humanize the shtetl, and reinforce its communal implications.

Robert K. Redfield, in a 1947 essay titled "The Folk Society," theorizes a method for comparing societies and generalizing from them by designating ideal folk societies as bases of comparison: "This type is ideal, a mental construction. No known society precisely corresponds with it, but the societies which have been the chief interest of the anthropologist most closely approximate it."[47] He concludes that "the folk society is an isolated society. Probably there is no real society whose members are in complete ignorance of the existence of people other than themselves," but this folk society is useful to the scientist as a comparison to urban societies. "In short, we move from folk society to folk society, asking ourselves what it is about them that makes them like each other and different from the modern city." How do the "shtetl folk" compare to this model of the "folk society"? The folk society is an ideal society imagined for purposes of cultural comparison. And the shtetl folk? Perhaps one could argue, in the same vein, that it is an ideal society, imagined as such for purposes of comparison to the American Jewish community. What we are seeing in *Life Is with People* is the creation of a collective mythologized image of a culture in order to mobilize self-reflection on the part of American Jews. The idea was that by using the assumptions of anthropology, such as the creation of a "folk society" in order to better understand "modern" or "urban" societies, American Jews would be better able to critique their own culture.

The "shtetl picture" is presented at the end of the book, in the chapter referred to by Kirshenblatt-Gimblett as the place where the shtetl takes on a life of its own:

> Within the shtetl, however, the picture of the Jew contains both good and bad and presents them simultaneously. The Jew, even in abstraction is "*nur a mentsh*" [just human] having in him the "good impulse" and the "bad impulse."[48]

The Picture of Dorian Gray comes to mind with this presentation of the *yetser hora* and the *yetser ha-tov* (the evil and the good inclination) as being part of a "picture." But more important is that the shtetl itself constitutes a picture, one that can be "seen" by outsiders, but can also see others, as articulated in the chapter title "As the Shtetl Sees the World." Indeed, throughout this discussion, we are finely attuned to the role that visual culture, and particularly photography, plays not only in apprehension of East European pre-Holocaust life, but more generally in the context of the creation of a popular ethnography. Johannes Fabian argues in *Time and the Other* that the visuality of ethnographic studies insists on denying the "coevalness to its other," or the "foreign" culture therein described, thus consigning ethnographic studies to a form of colonialism. Seeing the ethnographic subject visually forces its otherness to the fore, insisting on its prior identity, on its having existed before the moment in which the photograph was taken and later observed by the viewer. The words "shtetl picture" therefore assign a kind of otherness to the shtetl that is, to some extent, balanced by the agency implicit in the idea that the shtetl is capable of seeing others as well.

Both of these ideas, "shtetl folk" and "shtetl picture," reflect the dynamic tension wherein the authors struggle both to implicate themselves in the construction of an "inner world" for the shtetl by infusing their narrative with literary touches such as free indirect discourse and to disengage themselves by relying on direct quotations and expanding upon them. This quest for a way to depict an "inner world" is echoed by their struggle between depiction of a collective and of individuals, between consciousness of a folk as both a collective figuration and a humanizing one, and, finally, between the realism of relying on a picture and the subjugation that implies.

The authors' struggle for authority and voice, for inwardness and narrative control, is typical of the modernist struggle to strategize modes of subjectivity. This speaks directly to the issue raised by Barbara Kirshenblatt-Gimblett in her discussion of the primacy of the shtetl as a focal point of subjectivity within *Life Is with People*. The presentation of the shtetl as a thinking, feeling, speaking subject is fundamentally a literary representation, conceived in dialogue not only with the Jewish literary texts that preceded it and influenced it, but also with a broader literary moment: modernism. The authors are writing an ethnography based not only on what Kirshenblatt-Gimblett terms literary texts, for example, Abraham Joshua Heschel's *The Earth Is the Lord's* and Bella Chagall's *Burning Lights*, but also on Yiddish literary texts and on the great modernist texts of earlier decades, such as James Joyce's *Ulysses* and Henry Roth's *Call It Sleep*, that represented the experience of minority populations within urban settings. How, within the modernist moment, can you draw a portrait of a culture without allowing it to speak, without allowing its subjectivity to emerge? The shtetl doesn't just take on a life of its own in the book's final chapter, but exhibits one throughout the text; and the strategies for animating that life speak to the book's fundamentally literary character and its debt not only to Yiddish literary texts but to the modernist literary moment.

The marriage of literary modernism and ethnographic writing was evident in the community of ethnographers who produced *Life Is with People*. Richard Handler notes in an essay on Ruth Benedict, who directed the Columbia University Research in Contemporary Culture Project that spawned *Life Is with People*, that many anthropologists of the period viewed themselves as artists as well as scientists.[49] Mead herself was a published poet. Handler also notes that Boasian anthropologists engaged in an ongoing debate over how to establish an anthropological theory that could account both for tradition and considerations of "culture" as a collective formation, and for the power of the individual in constituting a culture. Edward Sapir, for example, focused on the individual as a crucial locus of cultural action and refused to reify culture, whereas Ruth Benedict, particularly in her famous work *Patterns of Culture* (1934), emphasized cultural integration and the determination of individuals by culture. Handler points out that "when Ruth Benedict came to anthropology, the Boasian school was beginning a transition from the study of the distribution of isolated culture traits to the study of cultural wholes and the processes whereby traits are assembled to form such wholes."[50] In a 1938 essay on his anthropologist's "credo," Boas asserts:

> It must be admitted that too great an emphasis on individualism would weaken the power of the community. However, the ethical principles of the in-group when clearly recognized will prevent individualism from outgrowing its legitimate limits and becoming intolerable egotism.[51]

At the same time, with the rise of Nazi Germany, he acknowledges that "in our communities individuals cannot act according to their own whims without interfering with the freedom of others. It is, however, intolerable that the state should force a person to actions that are against his intellectual or spiritual principles."[52]

Ruth Benedict, in her discussion of the individual and the community, basically argues that there is no such thing as an individual without a community, sidestepping the issue of an anthropological methodology for distinguishing the voice of an individual from that of the community. She does not acknowledge, the way Boas does, that advancements in communities are catalyzed by wayward individuals, exceptional people with visions that do not conform to the collective. In *Patterns of Culture*, she says:

> The life-history of the individual is first and foremost an accommodation to the patterns and standards traditionally handed down in his community....From the moment of his birth the customs into which he is born shape his experience and behaviour. By the time he can talk, he is the little creature of his culture, and by the time he is grown and able to take part in its activities, its habits are his habits, its beliefs his beliefs, its impossibilities his impossibilities. Every child that is born into his group will share them with him, and no child born into one on the opposite side of the globe can ever achieve the thousandth part. There is no social problem it is more incumbent upon us to understand than this of the role of custom. Until we are intelligent as to its laws and varieties, the main complicating facts of human life must remain unintelligible.[53]

Therefore, to understand the experience of individuals, one need only understand cultural systems. This is best achieved through what has been called by Handler a "comparative hermeneutics of culture."[54] This comparative method, as we saw in the case of a "folk society," encourages schematization and generalization, the creation of ideal "types" such as a folk society and the alignment of different cultural systems with one another.

In its invocation of subjectivity despite the overwhelming pull toward a collective, what we see in *Life Is with People* is, perhaps, a glimpse into the moment during which ethnographers were writing with a modernist consciousness. Modernism's quest for both tradition and individuality is the very issue at hand for American Jews who sought an ethnic tradition that would help them make sense of their future in America. As in Edward Sapir's call for an approach to culture and personality that would impose some sense of the particular and the personal despite the overwhelming collective impulse of Mead's approach, in *Life Is with People* we are witness to what might be called "salvaging cultural subjectivity," or the preservation of the possibility of individual voices while attempting to understand a culture. In our formulation of salvage literary inference as the underlying salvage poetic in *Life Is with People*, we can see an attempt, through the fashioning of subjective literary voices, to resolve the felt tension between the collective and the individual in popular portraits of the shtetl.

4

SALVAGE MONTAGE

The Missing Piece in *A Treasury of Yiddish Stories,*
The Golden Tradition, and *Image before My Eyes*

In compiling our anthologies we were not merely exercising personal tastes, we were undertaking an act of critical salvage.[1]

Presentations on East European Jewry have often been nostalgic and have dwelled upon the themes of Jewish piety and isolation, poverty, and persecution. They have also treated the East European Jewish community as historically, geographically, and culturally undifferentiated.[2]

East European Jewry was not, as the sentimentalists see it, forever frozen in utter piety and utter poverty.[3]

Irving Howe and Eliezer Greenberg's *A Treasury of Yiddish Stories* (1954), Lucy Dawidowicz's *The Golden Tradition* (1966), and Lucjan Dobroszycki and Barbara Kirshenblatt-Gimblett's *Image before My Eyes* (1977) directly channel the folk ethnographic spirit of the pre-Holocaust period while attempting to avoid the pitfalls of post-Holocaust undertakings that they perceived as doing violence to both the memory and history of a complex, multidimensional culture. All three works exemplify variations of "salvage montage," a combination of salvage poetics with montage poetics, which seeks to salvage a culture destroyed in the Holocaust through a postwar repurposing of prewar texts and photographs using the generative, multivalent techniques of montage. Considered in terms of their reliance on images, as we have been tracing throughout this study, one would arrange them with Dawidowicz's work first, Howe and Greenberg's second, and Kirshenblatt-Gimblett's and Dobroszycki's third, as Dawidowicz uses no visual images, Howe and Greenberg incorporate images by Ben Shahn (1898–1969) very sparingly, and Dobroszycki and Kirshenblatt-Gimblett's book is dedicated primarily to the history of photography of Polish Jewry before the Second World War. Howe and Greenberg's book in particular, alongside Abraham Joshua Heschel's *The Earth Is the Lord's*, published just a few years earlier, as we discussed in chapter 2, marks a transitional moment in American Jewish salvage poetics during the immediate post-Holocaust period, a moment during which it became apparent that verbal texts, literary or other, were no longer adequate "artifacts" for the construction of a post-Holocaust American folk ethnography of pre-Holocaust East European Jewish life. Rather, Howe and Greenberg's book, with its smattering of images by Shahn echoed a discourse established by Heschel in which texts were bolstered, supplemented, and punctuated by carefully chosen artistic images in order to create a greater opportunity for audience access among American Jews who were no longer fluent in Yiddish or in Jewish culture and literature in general. As we discuss salvage montage here, we will consider the role of these transitional hybrid texts, texts with a modicum of visual supplementation, as a means of testing the waters for a more aggressive shift into images for the purpose of constructing a folk ethnography of pre-Holocaust East European Jewish life during the post-Holocaust period in America.

The term "montage" has generally been theorized in cinematic discourse, where it refers to the "splicing together [of] sections of film resulting in a series of shots that presents an idea or group of ideas";[4] in film, montage is meant to produce the kind of allusive image that reveals a truth through the interpretive demands it places on its viewers. Using a "deconstructive aesthetic," or signifying through indirection, the "truth" revealed by montage has "little to do with what we can actually see."[5] Rather, it strives "to reproduce the very nature of perception itself, which is synthetic, simultaneous, and multilayered."[6] Montage enables its viewers to engage in a "new way of seeing" and a "new way of perceiving culture."[7] The necessity to perceive East European pre-Holocaust culture afresh, as identified in the anthologies under discussion, leads us to the notion that in a post-Holocaust world these anthologies can function as montage. These montage works press their readers to reconsider preconceptions about pre-Holocaust East European Jewish life and to explore more deeply the varieties of culture in the destroyed world as well as the variegated voice or perspective that its aesthetic artifacts represent. In the reconstitution of an American Jewish ethnicity, these montage works serve as a critical model for the variety of experiences and models implicit in a fully fleshed out ethnic identification.

Most important, the term "salvage montage" coined for this essay draws on the notion of "montage" introduced by Georges Didi-Huberman.[8] In *Images in Spite of All*, he explores the outcry that ensued in the wake of an essay he published on the historical and philosophical value of four photographs taken in August 1944 by members of the Sonderkommando, a special team of prisoners at Auschwitz-Birkenau who were selected by the Germans and "forced on pain of death to lead, often using deception, arriving Jews to the gas chambers, empty the gas chambers, shave the corpses and pull their teeth before they stacked the bodies on pyres in trenches for cremation, all the while knowing their own days were numbered."[9] The Sonderkommando was systematically gassed after a certain amount of time working the gas chambers so as to ensure that the secret work of the gas chambers not be revealed. The photographs, taken at great personal risk with a smuggled camera and a snippet of film, depicted Sonderkommando members incinerating hundreds of thousands of bodies in pits outside the gas chambers and naked women standing in line waiting to enter the gas chambers.

Critics of Didi-Huberman's analysis of these photographs accuse him of claiming to capture the entire "truth" behind the Holocaust in these isolated images, of thinking that these photographs somehow transmit it "all." But Didi-Huberman, drawing on the concept of "montage," argues that he presents these photographs "in spite of all," that they serve as just a piece of the "all" that was the Holocaust. To repress these photographs or silence them would be to negate the enormous risk undertaken by members of the Sonderkommando in secretly documenting its work on the eve of their own death. The photographs in question, Didi-Huberman argues, function in tandem with the many written testimonies that Sonderkommando members buried on the periphery of the gas chambers. These notes and journals, found after the war, taken alongside oral testimonies and the four Sonderkommando photographs, serve together, in Didi-Huberman's terms, as a type of "montage" that is conscious of its own lacunae, of its own lack of comprehensiveness. Each disparate yet complementary element of this montage of the crematoria at Auschwitz serves to deepen the sense of what went on there as well as the sense of the impossibility of representing "all" of what went on there.

While his critics call it impudent to try to "imagine" the war with the help of these isolated photographs, Didi-Huberman suggests an inherent link between imagination and montage: "imagination is a montage of various forms placed in correspondence with one another."[10] He further affirms that considering these materials as part of a montage "is a question of putting the multiple in motion, isolating nothing, showing the hiatuses and the analogies, the indeterminations and over-determinations."[11] Alluding to Walter Benjamin's *Arcades Project*, Didi-Huberman points to the strengths and limitation of montage, which, he concludes,

> is valuable only when it doesn't hasten to conclude or to close: it is valuable when it opens up our apprehension of history and makes it more complex, not when it falsely schematizes; when it gives us access to the singularities of time, and hence to its essential multiplicity.[12]

To return to our postwar American context, what does it take for American audiences to "imagine" the world of East European Jewry before the war? What do they risk in doing so? In his discussion of how the concept of montage helps him to repudiate his critics, Didi-Huberman says:

Yet, why a montage? We use the term "montage" for two reasons. First, because the simple "shred of film" extracted from
Birkenau by the members of the Sonderkommando presented
not one but four images, each distributed according to a temporal discontinuity: two sequences, from one end to the other,
showing two distinct moments of the same process of extermination. Second, because the readability of these images—and
thus their potential role in providing knowledge of the process
in question—can only be constructed by making them resonate
with, and showing their difference from, other sources, other
images, and other testimonies.... It is a question of putting the
multiple in motion, isolating nothing.[13]

Because anthologies collect works already published elsewhere,
they serve to heighten our sense of their contents as a montage of
various reception histories and publication contexts. Anthologies
strive toward comprehensiveness, even while emphasizing in subtle
and sometimes not so subtle ways their many gaps. As Didi-Huberman
argues in the case of the Sonderkommando images, it is impossible to
reconstruct the "all" of the East European Jewish life that was destroyed
because of the very fact that it was not only destroyed but also that its
destruction mediates every attempt to comprehend what came before
its destruction. In exploring the three anthologies *A Treasury of Yiddish
Stories*, *The Golden Tradition*, and *Image before My Eyes*, I use the term
"montage" in my formulation of "salvage montage" in order to try to
characterize the dynamics underlying their efficacy in a salvage context. These works—each in its own way because each focuses on a different medium and was crafted from different generic and disciplinary
perspectives in different postwar moments—approach with a critical
eye the "sentimentalism" they perceive in other post-Holocaust American representations of pre-Holocaust East European Jewish life. Each
anthology to be discussed here attempts to unravel the monolith of
American Jewish assumptions that pre-Holocaust East European Jewish culture was singular, religious, and distinctly monochromatic.

As I continue to synthesize the visual and the textual as essential
media for understanding the dynamics of salvage poetics, it is important to note that Didi-Huberman's notion of montage grapples with

visual discourse in a way that continuously alerts us to the dialogue between visual and textual discourses. In this chapter we are looking at a book of photographs as well as its film adaptation (*Image before My Eyes*) alongside a lightly illustrated collection of short fiction (*A Treasury of Yiddish Stories*) and another collection of biographical and autobiographical writings with no illustrations at all (*The Golden Tradition*).

Refuting those critics who claim that it is better to withhold photographs of violence from the public eye in order to avoid their being disseminated for purposes of voyeurism or pornography, Didi-Huberman insists that doing so would be collaborating with what he calls the "Nazi machinery of dis-imagination"[14] and the "Nazi obliteration of the archives."[15] Setting these photographs apart, claiming that they are too sacred and too vulnerable to be viewed by the public, Didi-Huberman argues, constitutes a kind of sacralization that indeed extends the Nazi violence through the imposition of a kind of sacred silence. Sacralization goes hand in hand with denigration, Didi-Huberman reminds us, shedding some light on the urgency with which our anthologists seek to desacralize East European Jewish life. "To speak of Auschwitz in terms of the unsayable," he says, "is not to bring oneself closer to Auschwitz. On the contrary it is to relegate Auschwitz to a region that Giorgio Agamben has very well defined in terms of mystical adoration."[16] This "mystical adoration" of pre-Holocaust East European Jewry is precisely what Dawidowicz, Greenberg, Howe, Kirshenblatt-Gimblett, and Dobroszycki are trying to counteract in their anthological works of salvage montage. Post-Holocaust Americans are suffering from a variation of the "dis-imagination" mentioned above; the edited works under discussion draw on an archive of writings and photographs that preceded the horror, that turn into artifacts of a lost world, thus providing an antidote to the obliteration of the archives hoped for by the Nazis, and countering the machinery of dis-imagination that accompanied that obliteration.

Arlette Farge, a theorist of the archive, points to the archive's "essential lacunary nature." "The archive is not a stock from which we draw for pleasure," she says, in Didi-Huberman's summary of her work, "it is constantly a lack . . . developed with repeated cross-checkings and by montage with other archives."[17] When considered in this light, our anthologies function as a type of archive in their own right. They omit far more than they include, functioning as part of a broader montage, and of that they are highly self-conscious. That self-conscious awareness of their missing pieces is the focus of this discussion; in each of the three anthologies presented here at least one significant element is missing, and that element is an essential part of the popular discourse on pre-Holocaust East European Jewish life. In the case of the Howe and Greenberg anthology, it is an articulation of the fact that the original Yiddish literary texts they collected are themselves highly critical of the monolithic, sentimentalized view of the shtetl that many Jews, even in modernity in Eastern Europe before the war, had adopted. Howe and Greenberg argue that the source of the sentimentalism is much of the literature itself, without being attentive to the fact that the reception history of the fiction they anthologize plays a much larger role in that process of misprision than the literature itself. However, the literature they select, the particular stories in the anthology, demonstrates this to be otherwise. In other words, the stories in the anthology decry the framing provided by Howe and Greenberg, articulating a rather unsentimental and unsavory approach to the popularized, monolithically pious shtetl despite their protestations to the contrary. Clearly Howe and Greenberg select these stories for that very purpose, but they find it difficult, in their framing of the stories, to divorce themselves from the idea that it is the stories themselves that promote that sentimental vision. Why? Because in becoming anthologists and translators they themselves represent a significant mechanism in the mediation of these stories, promoting a particular type of presentation and a particular type of reception. Therefore, what is missing here is an explicit awareness of the mechanisms of mediation and subsequent reception responsible for rendering these stories sentimental. In eschewing awareness of a whole layer of mediation, Howe and Greenberg rely on many of the truisms and assumptions that readers of this work in translation, unaware of the power of mediation on the construction, reception, and representative efficacy of these works, rely upon. Indeed, I would argue that their insertion of Shahn's drawings, since they are largely impressionistic, with a focus on the human figure to the exclusion of any context, but representative of that context in their iconicity (figure 4.1), furthers the tension between the sentimental and the real that they express in their volume. Shahn, born in Eastern Europe and trained as both an artist and photographer, even serving as a member of the FSA (Farm Security Administration) photographic corps during the 1930s, struggled in his work to articulate in drawing what he was able to articulate in photography, namely, the general in the particular, the state of a culture in the visage of the single person. His contribution to Howe and Greenberg's anthology, as we will explore, heightens a sense of the abstract sentimental shtetl, while being grounded in a career that

FIGURE 4.1. Drawing from *A Treasury of Yiddish Stories* (1954). © 2019 Estate of Ben Shahn/Licensed by VAGA at Artists Right Society.

worked against that. The missing piece in this anthology, therefore, is an awareness of its own sentimentalizing impulses, brought to bear by the stories chosen in contrast to their framing, but also by the drawings accompanying the stories.

In the case of Dawidowicz's anthology, what is missing is a nuanced sense of the Jewish community as comprised in modernity not entirely of secular Jews. Religious orthodoxy is largely ignored in the selected essays and Dawidowicz's framing of them in *The Golden Tradition*. Thus, in trying to demonstrate that the world of pre-Holocaust East European Jewry was far more than a world of "piety," she avoids the presence of piety in a world that was to a large extent characterized by it. And finally, in Dobroszycki and Kirshenblatt-Gimblett's anthology, the Holocaust is palpably missing. But here too, as in the other anthologies, this omission, deliberate as it is, causes the anthology to self-consciously declare its presence in a variety of underhanded ways that we will trace.

Montage as a concept captures the dynamics and goals of these three different anthologies, because it is a juxtaposition, and sometimes a clash, of different elements and its effectiveness is generated largely through the constructions of its audience; the narrative unfolding is not told but rather hinted at and its larger emotional impact is ineffable. While the collections do not engage in the intricacies of montage as they have been described and analyzed within a cinematic, or even a literary, context, montage is a good descriptor for the structure and goals of these works in that each addresses the overly simplistic and monochromatic cultural construct that many American Jews associated with East European Jewry. These works try to debunk that construct or to fill it out by unifying different pieces of a larger puzzle. The gestalt presented by each anthology unfolds gradually, and the reader must bring his or her own distinct impressions and biases to bear. Ultimately the montage in these anthologies and the reader's response to it function to desacralize East European Jewish culture, to transform it from stasis to dynamism, from simplicity to complexity, and from old to new. The back and forth implicit in the selection and juxtaposition of these stories, essays, and photographs, contextualized by elaborate and deeply ambivalent introductions, constitutes the effect of montage. This montage, I believe, functions on the level of each work individually as well as across all the works taken together, both in their common goal of reinforcing the complexity and variety of pre-Holocaust East European Jewish experience and in some of their common strategies.

In each of these works we find a dialectic between the need to diffuse the monolithic sense of pre-Holocaust East European Jewry among an American readership by creating distinctly salvage montage responses to it and the inevitability of each work's reliance on some of those very same assumptions they are trying so hard to dispel. Perhaps this can be traced to the identity of each of the authors, as either North American–born Jewish children of immigrants or, in the cases of Dobroszycki, Greenberg, and Shahn, immigrants to the United States themselves. Dobroszycki, a Polish-born historian who survived the Lodz ghetto as well as a series of concentration camps, emigrated to the United States in 1970; he served as a historical consultant to YIVO for many years prior to and following his immigration.[18] The Russian-born Greenberg was a Yiddish critic and poet who emigrated to the United States in 1913,[19] and Shahn, born in Lithuania, came to the United States at the age of eight in 1906. The marriage of popular expectation of nostalgic depictions of East Europe among American Jews and a sense of didactic obligation among the writers and editors discussed here creates a powerful disjuncture between the articulated goals of each volume and their own implicit preconceptions. Because each of the three books features artifacts of pre-Holocaust East European Jewish experience in a different medium and each editor or set of editors approaches the subject matter from a different discipline, the types of presentations, intentions, and disjunctures vary.

It is important to consider whether the types of salvage montage these editors construct is already a response to the very inconsistencies that they themselves perceive as inevitable in their presentations of pre-Holocaust East European Jewish culture. While each attempts to present a "world in motion,"[20] a rapidly modernizing world, a dynamic, urban, secularizing, politicized, engaged world, that in no way fits the stereotype of the singular, religious, impoverished community that had come to define, with the help of the other books in this analysis, pre-Holocaust East European Jewry, they also rely, in part, on those very same assumptions and stereotypes they attempt to debunk. The montage form of each collection animates a deconstructive process wherein the stereotypes and misapprehensions coexist with artifacts in the form of essays, photographs, and fiction that refute them.

A good starting point for tracing the kind of montage poetics our anthologizers have put into place to offset some of the implicit stereotyping and misapprehension that they persist in communicating is to consider Howe and Greenberg's selection of stories in *A Treasury of Yiddish Stories* in relation to claims made in the book's introduction and in Howe's other writings. In *A Margin of Hope*, Howe's intellectual memoir, for instance, he describes his generation of thinkers, writers, and scholars as path breakers. They were children of Jewish immigrants who were not only willing to acknowledge their background but also were turning to it as a source of inspiration for their intellectual work:

> This was probably the first time in American cultural history that a self-confident group of intellectuals did not acknowledge the authority of Christian tradition. A whole range of non-Christian references was now reaching at least some American literary people, terms like Hasidism, place names like Chelm, proper names like Sholem Aleichem. *Partisan Review* printed some, if not enough, criticism of Yiddish writers—Isaac Rosenfeld on Peretz and me on Sholem Aleichem; the magazine was just starting to confront its anomalous position as the voice of emancipated Jews who nevertheless refused to deny their Jewishness.[21]

What is fascinating about this statement is the collection of terms, names, and places to which Howe refers in order to illustrate his *Partisan Review* peers' engagement with the world of their "fathers." Chelm was known in the Jewish literary imagination as a city of fools. Indeed, when the Yiddish press in Europe published stories of Chelm, its native inhabitants (because it was also a real place) claimed they couldn't find matches for their daughters because the city was coming to be known as a city of fools and no one would take their daughters seriously.[22] Howe's identification of Chelm here as one of three nodes

of recognition for American-Jewish literati—Chelm, Hasidism, and
Sholem Aleichem—may suggest that he is familiar only with the Chelm
of myth. Even more surprising is when Howe refers to Sholem Aleichem
as a "proper name" without acknowledging the fact that it is a pseudonym for Sholem Rabinowitz, taken from a Hebrew and Yiddish greet-
ing best translated as "How do you do?" The allusion to Hasidism, as we
have already discussed, also reflects the movement, begun earlier in the
century in Germany by Martin Buber, to reclaim Hasidism as a source
of Jewish spirituality and authenticity in a rapidly assimilating western
European milieu. All three elements that served, in Howe's words, as
"non-Christian references" are basic, mediated, accessible representations of Judaism for a wholly ignorant, albeit Jewish audience. The identification of *Partisan Review* writers, among whom he included himself,
with these particular "places" and "proper names," says more about
what they didn't know than what they did. The tension between their
own tendency toward simplification and nostalgia and their desire to
break that stereotype is nicely spelled out here, not in an expository
manner, but through the series of allusions Howe employs. This is
not to say that Howe himself was ignorant of anything but the most
accessible cultural icons, or even of the background to the three iconic
terms he alludes to in the above statement. Rather, he chose to identify
his peers and readership with these most basic of allusions in order to
emphasize the limited parameters of the discourse in his generation.

In the introduction to *A Treasury*, Howe and Greenberg pinpoint
their mission in selecting and translating Yiddish stories for a popular
American audience:

> It is a literature virtually unknown to Americans. The reasons for
> this neglect are many: translations that are often inadequate,
> because done by devoted non-literary people, or are twisted
> into sentimentality, because done by translators whose attitude
> toward Yiddish is one of familiar condescension.[23]

Howe and Greenberg's collection of new translations, therefore, are
meant to be a response to the kind of sentimentality, the kind of "soft-
ness," that preceded them. Greenberg and Howe position not just the

introduction but the translations themselves as a means of recontextualizing these stories. Then, after a lengthy description of East European Jewish culture as a literary culture, a culture of sanctity and otherworldliness that strongly resembles Abraham Joshua Heschel's description in *The Earth Is the Lord's*, they write: "We recognize the danger of romanticizing the Jewish world, of assuming that it was all of one piece and forgetting that much of it was ignorant, provincial, superstitious, and sometimes even corrupt."[24] Surprisingly, however, Howe and Greenberg view the romanticization of the Jewish world of Eastern Europe in the literature itself, and neither in its framing or reception in the postwar era, nor strictly in the ways its literature was translated, as they claimed earlier:

> One of the immediate motive forces behind the appearance of the new Yiddish literature in the 19th century, especially behind the world of its founding father, Mendele, was the desire to stir the blood of a society that had gone sluggish, to cleanse a people that had suffered too long from the effects of isolation, poverty and violence. Once the foundations of this society began to crumble, an impulse arose among the Yiddish writers—most notably in the later stories of Peretz—to romanticize the very world that Mendele had so bitterly attacked. And once this world had been destroyed in the gas chambers, the romantic impulse became irresistible; it acquired a new and almost holy authenticity; for how could the Yiddish writers separate the sanctification of their martyrs from the celebration of the world that had given rise to them?[25]

Howe and Greenberg's work as translators and editors therefore must respond, according to this statement, not just to misconceptions among their audience, but to something inherent in the literature itself, something that forces its readers to misunderstand and miscategorize the East European Jewish world reflected in this literature.

Howe and Greenberg don't recognize, however, their own participation in that particular interpretation of the literature. In the introduction to *A Treasury*, for example, they refer to "the shtetl" as a unitary creature with anthropomorphic agency, something we have seen in our discussion of *Life Is with People*: "Some rabbis, to be sure,

were ready to receive the new learning of the West, but by and large
the shtetl felt that any large infiltration of Western thought would be
its undoing; and it was right."[26] Their representation of "the shtetl"
here as an undifferentiated body, with its own attitudes and feelings,
is not at a far remove from viewing the world of East European Jewry
in general as a strangely undifferentiated culture.

The drawings by Shahn selected by Greenberg and Howe to illustrate the book participate in this interesting lack of differentiation and
nuance. Echoes, and in some cases, reproductions of the very same
drawings included in two collections of Sholem Aleichem's stories in
English, published in 1946 (*The Old Country*, translated by Julius and
Francis Butwin) and 1949 (*Tevye's Daughters*, translated by Francis
Butwin), the Shahn drawings that accompany Howe and Greenberg's
anthology tend to be stark, focused on a human figure in isolation,
decontextualized, with an intense gaze. Reminiscent of Vishniac's
focus on the human face, which we will discuss in the next chapter,
with the drama of the photographs emerging from their play of light
and darkness, Shahn, in his engagement with East European Jewry for
the Sholem Aleichem anthologies as well as Howe and Greenberg's
seems to be drawing from an already extant visual discourse that
brings the works directly into the realm of the comfortably sentimentalized, emphasizing the religious, impoverished male.

Each section of the anthology ("The Fathers," "Portrait of A
World," "Jewish Children," "Breakup," and "New Worlds") is preceded
by a drawing (with the exception of the last section, titled "Folktales")
of a single figure, or at most two figures standing in close proximity
to one another (a man and a woman in "Portrait of a World"). In each
of the images, the dynamism resides primarily in the gaze and in the
hands of the figure at its center (figures 4.2 and 4.3). The figures of
the goat and the violin in the hands of the male, bearded Jewish figure in traditional dress represent a Chagall-esque concession to what
Dalia Tawil has called the "ethnographic image-symbols of Eastern
European Jewry."[27] As we document the transition from a textual to a
visual folk ethnography, these images, very sparingly placed throughout the volume, serve as an excellent reminder of how this shift took
place not only in medium but also in complexity. It seems that the

FIGURE 4.2. Drawing from *A Treasury of Yiddish Stories* (1954). © 2019 Estate of Ben Shahn/ Licensed by VAGA at Artists Right Society.

need for visual stimulus was based on a need for a simpler mode of access and a simplifying message as well. While Shahn is by no means a "simplistic" artist, the starkness of these drawings, in contrast to his later drawings on Jewish themes that he made during the last decade of his life (figures 4.4 and 4.5), emphasizes the movement, in hybrid works and folk ethnographies conceived with salvage intentions, toward the streamlined and the sentimental.

This overly simplistic view of the culture described in the literature Greenberg and Howe select, translate, and disseminate in *A Treasury* is also evident in their depiction of class struggle, or lack thereof, in the stories. In their introduction to *A Treasury*, Howe and Greenberg, despite the fact that Howe was a committed democratic socialist

FIGURE 4.3. Drawing from *A Treasury of Yiddish Stories* (1954).
© 2019 Estate of Ben Shahn/Licensed by VAGA at Artists Right Society.

all his life, fail to identify the class conflicts embedded in much of Yiddish literature, partly, I would argue, because of their blindness to its depiction of the nuanced social structure of East European provincial life. This leads to some intriguing critical machinations on their part, as they try to make sense of this literature for a popular American audience. In what follows, they argue for sharp differences in the formation of social class in city and small town:

> Socially this world had not yet split into sharply defined classes. Though some Jews settled in the larger cities, such as Warsaw and Lodz, where they hardened into a proletariat and middle class, most of them continued to live in the shtetl. One could

FIGURE 4.4. "Allegory" (1948). © 2019 Estate of Ben Shahn/Licensed by VAGA at Artists Right Society.

hardly speak of rival classes in the shtetl, since few Jews owned any massive means of production and fewer still sold their labor power.[28]

A consciousness of social class permeates much of Yiddish literature, in my reading of it. Most of the communities described in the stories are divided into the haves and the have-nots. The business class eats well, dresses well, and educates their children (sending their daughters off to finishing schools in other cities where they read secular literature and often convert to Christianity). The working class, on the other hand, lives from hand to mouth and suffers. The scholars are either the poorest of the poor, bartering their wives' Sabbath money for charitable causes and living in the house of study and waiting for handouts from the community, or, miraculously, the richest of the rich, having married a rich man's daughter and living off his generosity for as long as humanly possible. Can it be possible for a reader

FIGURE 4.5. "Where wast Thou? God's Answer to Job" (1964). © 2019 Estate of Ben Shahn/Licensed by VAGA at Artists Right Society.

to claim that this literature does not demonstrate an awareness of social class?

Howe and Greenberg's denial of the class-consciousness in the volume's Yiddish stories, leads them to strenuously, and sometimes tenuously, configure the world of East European Jewry in ways that render it devoid of the real class struggles it articulated:

Only if the pressures of the external world had suddenly been removed would the suppressed economic conflicts within the shtetl have reached full expression. As it was, the shtetl nestled in the crevices of a backward agricultural economy, where Jews, seldom allowed to own land, lived by trading, artisanship, and their wits. There were however rigid castes, based partly on economic position and partly on religious status—that is learning. Those who romanticize the shtetl seldom remember, or remember to report, that it was customary for the artisans to be shunted off into separate synagogues and that within the synagogue itself the social hierarchy was precisely reflected by the seating arrangement. The shtetl did not strictly speaking have social classes but it was still far from being a democratic community.[29]

Arguing here that it was externally imposed economic pressures that kept the Jewish community from paying close attention to its class distinctions, Howe and Greenberg conclude that "this condition of permanent precariousness gave the East European Jews a conscious sense of being at a distance from history."[30] Thus, Yiddish literature itself, according to Howe, promotes nostalgia and sentimentality. He deflects all blame from readers, critics, and audiences, claiming that the literature itself is ahistorical and class blind.

What Howe and Greenberg argue in their introduction, however, is not borne out in the stories they themselves select. The form of the anthology, the montage that Howe and Greenberg put together, forces them to accomplish what they meant to accomplish—even though their introduction, in its insistence on streamlining and oversimplifying the social structures that the stories reflect, doesn't really further that cause. Several stories in A Treasury in fact deconstruct the shtetl rather than constructing it as a nuclear, autonomous, idyllic site for all East European Jews.

In Sholem Aleichem's "Dreyfus in Kasrilevke," the uninvited appearance of a newspaper in town during the Dreyfus affair yanks the inhabitants of a fictional shtetl into the maelstrom of modern Jewish history.[31] In response, they rail not only against the news of the accusations levied against Dreyfus but also against the incursion of the news itself, which destroys the peace of their beautiful, blissful isolation. As the story ends, they turn against the paper rather than the perpetrators of the crimes it reports, asserting their rejection of the power of a piece of paper to wreak havoc on their world. The story, written on paper, deconstructs itself, referring to real historic events yet profoundly denying the efficacy of the paper in transmitting them. The fictional shtetl of Kasrilevke, which exists only on paper, has negated its own existence by challenging the very existence of paper as a medium for verbal and historical transmission.

The shtetl is more explicitly emptied out as a signifier in a story by Y. L. Peretz called "The Dead Town," in which a town, unnamed, is invisible to the surrounding gentiles and even to the surrounding Jews.[32] The "dead town" is known only to its inhabitants. The homodiegetic narrator, trying to ascertain what kind of metaphorical meaning a "dead town" possesses, tries out different possible scenarios: A poor town? A small town? A town of ghosts? No, says the narrator's unnamed and undeveloped interlocutor, this is a "town like every other town,"[33] with living inhabitants, a synagogue, and even a hospital and a hotel (or at least there once was a hotel, and even if the hospital is small, it is still a place for sick people). This dead town turns out to be a town where its inhabitants have lost their zest for life: "For even if a feather were placed under the nose of a living man, do you think he would bother to remove it? Or to brush aside a troublesome fly?"[34] And because there is no impulse toward life in that town, the dead return to live in it:

> And if sometimes it happens, as it did among us, that a corpse creeps out of his grave, he does not even begin to remember that he has already recited the last confession, gasped his final breath, and died. As soon as the potsherds fall from his eyes, he goes straight to the House of Study or to the ritual bath or home for the summer. And everything is again the way it was.[35]

As in many of Peretz's stories, this one requires a suspension of the norms that govern the reading of many of the book's tales. Instead of being charmed or galvanized or shocked, the reader is left simply confused. Is this a town of the dead or a town of the living? Does this town exist in this world or in the world to come?

Immediately following "The Dead Town" is Peretz's "Neilah in Gehennah," which takes us to the heavenly tribunal of a hated citizen of the town of LaHDaM, the acronym for *lo hoyu dvorim me-olam*, meaning, in Hebrew, borrowed as a Yiddish idiom, "these things never were."[36] The devil himself has never heard of this town because none of its citizens are ever sent to hell. Why? Because there is a cantor in the town whose voice is so sweet, whose prayers are so poignant, particularly on Yom Kippur, the Day of Atonement, that the dead of LaHDaM are automatically admitted to heaven. In a Jobian gesture Satan takes away the voice of the cantor, who immediately commits suicide and goes to hell (because suicide is forbidden), where he chants the closing prayer for Yom Kippur there and thereby releases all those imprisoned in its cauldrons. Thus hell empties out. In time, the story closes, hell fills up again, "and although additional suburbs were built, it still remains crowded."[37] Hell, in this story, therefore has more of a real existence than does the shtetl.

"These things never were" is a code word in Yiddish for "pure fiction." And these three stories at the anthology's heart, which were carefully selected from the literary corpora of well-known Yiddish writers, serve in fact as a reminder that the portraits of the shtetl presented in them are pure fiction. The shtetlach they represent exist only for their own inhabitants, in a historical vacuum, and they are invisible to the powers on high (and down low).

In Avrom Reisen's "The Poor Community," another shtetl is stripped of everything with which shtetlach have become associated in the aftermath of the Holocaust.[38] Having spent all their communal money to pay a visiting cantor on a regular Sabbath, the town's inhabitants don't have the sufficient funds for a cantor and Torah reader on the High Holidays. In order to pray, they must leave their town and join a minyan in the neighboring town:

> On the morning of the first day of Rosh Hashonoh, when the townspeople on their way to Sosnovtchine passed their old dilapidated synagogue, standing there with cloudy eyes, woebegone and orphaned, their hearts felt sore and tight, and silently, without words, only with their eyes, they begged its forgiveness.[39]

The impossibility of prayer, of spiritual expression in a town without money belies the common discourse found in Heschel's *The Earth Is the Lord's* and many other popularly read descriptions of East European Jewish life. By the reckoning of many of these sources, prayer is the only thing East European Jews could do well, even without fiscal resources. But here poverty leads to the emptying out of their symbolic locus: the shtetl without money is a shtetl with an empty synagogue, a shtetl without prayer.

This montage of empty, dead, evacuated shtetlach can be understood as a post-Holocaust phenomenon—a form of back-shadowing, in Michael André Bernstein's formulation, wherein Jewish experience in Europe before the Holocaust is viewed through a lens of inevitability.[40] In other words, one might argue about these stories, as Barthes does about his photographs, that they serve as a specter of their own death.[41] But do they? I would assert that the images of shtetlach captured in *A Treasury* serve as a kind of photographic negative reminding us of the artifice underlying the stories' production and their insertion into the anthology, but not necessarily a projection of death. These evacuated shtetlach, these cities of the dead, emptied out of prayer, these cities named LaHDaM for *lo hoyu dvorim me-olam*, remind us that perhaps the singular, luminous shtetl identified in *Life Is with People*, *The Earth Is the Lord's*, *The World of Sholem Aleichem*, or even *Fiddler on the Roof* as the locus of East European Jewish life, as the voice and face of East European Jews, simply does not exist.[42]

Howe and Greenberg's claim about the lack of historicity in the modern Yiddish literature of East European Jewry, even though the stories themselves do not bear it out, is clearly at odds with Dawidowicz's mission to rehistoricize that culture for a popular audience. Whereas Howe views the stories themselves as lacking in historical perspective, for Dawidowicz the problem is that the reception of East European Jewish texts lacks historical perspective. In fact, she argues that ahistorical post-Holocaust perceptions of pre-Holocaust East European Jewry follow a long line of such perceptions, her major battle being against "forgetfulness and selective distortion," according to Neal Kozody's introduction to Dawidowicz's 1982 essay collection, *What Is the Use of Jewish History?*[43] The tool she used to fight such misperceptions was the popularization of Jewish history, and in her introduction to this essay collection, Dawidowicz makes some important and incisive observations about the relationship of Jews throughout their own history to narratives of that history—as a backdrop to the type of "mythologies" that she sees growing up around American Jewish perceptions of pre-Holocaust East European Jewish life:

> Though the Jews have always been history conscious, living with the dual perspective of catastrophe and deliverance in forward moving time, they have, paradoxically, seldom been history oriented. That is to say: in Jewish consciousness throughout the ages, the specific events of Jewish history have often been transformed into transcendent myths of history. . . . The great historic myths that were fashioned out of historical reality and integrated into the living traditions of Judaism and of the Jewish people are the products of a process of selection whose criterion may have been the usefulness of their remembrance in serving a national Jewish purpose.[44]

Dawidowicz's critique of how Jews have related the history of pre-Holocaust East European Jewry centers on her concern over the imposition of a historic myth on the actual history. She does acknowledge the cultural advantages evident in the rabbis' use of history to create a national sense of the past and to forge the parameters of Jewish culture in the present as one of constructive remembrance: "It was they who molded Jewish historic consciousness out of the events of the past, appropriating history in the service of Jewish survival and of the survival of Judaism."[45] Nevertheless she seems not to want to let this happen in the case of East European Jewish history. Why not? Because if it becomes mythic too soon, the magnitude of the calamity will fade away; the memory of the individuals she personally knew who died in the Holocaust, those with whom she spent 1938 in Vilna, will not be preserved.

Indeed, the Holocaust is considered by many within the Yiddish-speaking, ultra-Orthodox community to be the "third destruction," in line with the destructions of the two Temples in Jerusalem. Dawidowicz wants to prevent the story of a world destroyed during the modern period from following the same path as those of ancient times, or the cultures lost in those destructions:

> The Temple's destruction convulsed the course of Jewish history, and the tremors of that catastrophe agitated the subsequent centuries. Yet, how extraordinary it is that except for Josephus, whom the Jews considered a traitor, no coherent Jewish account was ever produced to describe and explain the events leading up to and encompassing the destruction of the Second Temple. . . . The rabbis turned their backs on history at this juncture.[46]

Dawidowicz is committed, through her historical work, to teaching a history that not only tells the story of East European Jews, but at the same time serves a community in need of a governing mythology that offers a coping mechanism: an acknowledgment of the destruction's magnitude without falling prey to "sentimentalism," as she puts it. In part, what Dawidowicz is documenting is not the absence of history, but a desire for myth that, at certain historical junctures, simply obscures history.

On closer scrutiny, however, Dawidowicz herself articulates a mission of reengaging with the realities of East European pre-Holocaust Jewish life in the face of widespread mythologization that is not fully borne out in the execution of her project. Although Dawidowicz sets out explicit goals regarding her desire to free representations of pre-Holocaust East European Jewish life of the overwhelming onus of "piety and poverty," she herself puts in place impediments as she attempts to fulfill them. Just as Didi-Huberman acknowledges the self-conscious gaps that necessarily populate any attempt to represent an incomprehensible world, and he champions the montage form as a way of taking those gaps into account, so too does Dawidowicz employ a montage, in the form of an anthology of nonfiction, to acknowledge the shortcomings of her own attempt to redress the misrepresentations of East European Jewish culture even in her own corrective.

In composing *The Golden Tradition*, Dawidowicz anthologized both autobiography and biography:

The autobiographies I sought were those of men, in William James' words, "whose genius was so adapted to the receptivities of the moment or whose accidental position of authority was so critical that they became ferments, initiators of movement, setters of precedent or fashion." But because the material was not always available, I have tried to repair the gaps with memoirs about them.[47]

She then describes her rationale for this approach:

The historical review that follows is an attempt to put these memoirs in the perspective of their time and place and to describe some relevant social, political, and economic currents that affected our memoirists. I have tried to show the tension between assimilatory tendencies and survivalist values among East European Jews, and I have cited the autobiographies as illustrative documents.[48]

On her motivation for bringing together the particular selections she has chosen, she writes:

I was guided also by the desire to show the diversity of Jews and their culture, the centripetal and centrifugal forces that moved them, and the variety they brought to Jewish thought and life. East European Jewry was not, as the sentimentalists see it, forever frozen in utter piety and utter poverty.[49]

In the above statement, Dawidowicz coins the oft-cited phrase attributing to "the sentimentalists" exclusive views of East European Jewry living in "utter piety" and "utter poverty." She then proceeds to draw an extensive picture of the "transformation" of East European society that began during the late nineteenth century in response to the forces of modernity and the influence of the Jewish Enlightenment, which had taken root in Western Europe about a century earlier. The important theme that she traces throughout her historical overview and in the essays she selects to flesh it out with the voices of its actors is one not only of change but also of salvage. She attempts to document how

East European Jews, seeking change, also sought to preserve their Jewish identity, whether by choosing alternatives to religion or by modifying religious observance so as to make it compatible with modernity. Dawidowicz's notion of return despite a commitment to modernization, this need to assert the continuing hold of tradition despite the winds of change, in fact, serves as an example of mythologizing and sentimentalizing history itself:

> East European Jews turned and returned. Though they had not abandoned Judaism or Jews, they had fought against the obscurantism of traditional Judaism and become freethinkers. Some had advocated assimilation, others had devoted themselves to the radical movement. Their return was toward a more intense form of Jewish identity and a passionate reaffirmation of their ties with the Jewish community and its fate. Every Jewish movement, no matter how secular, offered the possibility of such return.[50]

Like Maurice Samuel's assertion that Jewish Americans should familiarize themselves with their East European forebears because who they are has everything to do with where they come from, Lucy Dawidowicz, in her essay collection *On Equal Terms: Jewish Identity in America*, explains that East European Jewry's American descendants connect most with their forebears' eagerness to assimilate modern values while still maintaining their Jewish identity:

> While working on that book, I realized that we American Jews are not only the descendants of East European Jews but indeed their inheritors, even if we do not fit the stereotype of tradition, Talmud, and piety. We may be Americanized, Anglicized, acculturated, secularized, modernized, yet we are their children and grandchildren, flesh of their flesh. And we are in fact truer than one might think to the wisdom they transmitted on how to cope with modernity.[51]

In reflecting on this continuity between the generations, across the geographic divide and over the temporal abyss of the Holocaust, she returns to the stereotypes that most Jews in America attribute to their East European ancestors:

> Tradition, Talmud, piety—these are both the stereotype and the reality. Tradition, Talmud, piety are the heritage that East European Jewry passed on to the Jews of America and in Israel. But they are only part of the reality of East European Jewish life and culture, and only part of the heritage bequeathed to us. There was also another reality and another heritage—the experience of Jewish modernity as it worked itself out in Eastern Europe and as it was transmitted to subsequent generations.[52]

While Dawidowicz acknowledges in the above passage that tradition, Talmud, and piety are both the stereotype and the reality, we see very little of this religious world represented in *The Golden Tradition*. Her goal, in the book, is to assert that the pre-Holocaust East European Jewish world was constituted by far more than the world of traditional Jewish study and religious practice. In doing so, she manages to represent that world as nearly devoid of its religious component. What is apparent in this montage, therefore, is the deliberate omission of those aspects of pre-Holocaust East European Jewish life that were religious. While it is true that not all East European Jews before the Holocaust were religious, it is certainly not true that most people were not. Nevertheless, Dawidowicz's attempts to recuperate modernity in post-Holocaust representations of that world overwhelm the anthology, creating something of an imbalance and perpetuating some of the shortfalls that she is trying to address: this was not a one-sided existence, be it in the direction of piety and poverty as in the works she attempts to redress, or of modernity and secularism, as she herself appears to argue. Only two of *The Golden Tradition*'s sections—"Early Hasidism," which is the first one, and "The World of Tradition"—focus on the traditional world of East European Jewry. The others look more at modernization in Eastern Europe: "The Haskalah," "The Quest for Education," "Scholars and Philosophers," "Literary Men," "The Arts," "Marginals," "In the Zionist Movement," "In the Revolutionary Movements," and "In Political Life."

Yet even the two sections focused on the apparently traditional have a modernist aspect. Hasidism, while often conflated with Jewish Orthodoxy and traditionalism, was in fact a movement that developed in opposition to traditional Judaism during the eighteenth century. The reason for its inclusion in Dawidowicz's volume is the unique literature it developed, a hagiography of Hasidic rabbis that was valorized, as we have discussed, during the first few decades of the twentieth century, when sources of Jewish culture were sought as models for secular Jewish aesthetic expression. This hagiography inspired the neo-Hasidic literary movement spearheaded by Y. L. Peretz, as exhaustively described by Maurice Samuel in his adaptation and contextualization of Peretz's work. Perhaps more famously, as explored in our introduction, Martin Buber, through his translation of Hasidic anecdotes and hagiographies into German, inspired a generation of young, assimilated German Jews to revisit their religious origins, if not in practice then as an important facet of their forsaken culture. This use of Hasidic tales as a bridge to modern American Jews was also apparent in our discussion of Heschel's use of Hasidic stories in his representation of traditional East European Jewish life. That the Hasidic movement, associated with Orthodoxy, had a published literature that resonated with modern writers and thinkers is probably the most important reason that Dawidowicz begins her collection there.

"The World of Tradition," the only other section of the book dedicated to traditional Jewish society, provides sketches and reflections of major figures in the Orthodox world of East European Jewry: Israel Salanter, the founder of the Musar movement; Sarah Shneirer, the founder of the Bais Yaakov schools for girls; the Gerer Rebbe and the Rebbes of Belz and Sadeger; and a few others. Again, her inclusion of these figures presupposes that the texts written about them would have been accessible to a secular readership. *The Golden Tradition* is a book about modernity and its impact on tradition. It is not a book about tradition. That may be due, in part, to the way she constructed the book—as a series of essays written for a modern audience. More important, however, is that all the essays were autobiographical or biographical, self-conscious genres that were a symptom of modernity, particularly within the Jewish community.[53]

How could Dawidowicz have composed the book differently so as to present a more comprehensive and perhaps more accurate view of pre-Holocaust East European Jewry, as she intended to do? She could perhaps have included some ethnographic essays, such as those written by Hirsz Abramowicz, to round out the volume.[54] Because she relied exclusively on genres that imply modern notions of literariness, which at the time of the publication of *The Golden Tradition* did not include ethnographies, she was able only to represent a narrow swath of the East European Jewish world, that which was self-reflective and literarily self-conscious. Although this certainly fills in a gap among popular readers who are accustomed to the Tevye version of Jewish life before the Holocaust, it does not provide a much more well-rounded variation on East European Jewish life.

Why does Dawidowicz take *The Golden Tradition* exclusively in the direction of modernity? The book is dedicated to Zelig and Riva Kalmanovich, the couple who served as her surrogate parents during her year in Vilna studying at the YIVO Institute (established in 1925) and were killed in Estonia in 1943. She left, upon their urging, just before the outbreak of World War II, taking the last ship from Copenhagen to Boston.[55] In her autobiographical writings on the experience, she says:

> Vilna exists now only in history, only in memory. One of the last people to have seen Vilna, I have been haunted by the compelling Jewish obligation to remember. . . . I felt it was my duty to resurrect it, if I could, by recreating the life in that world capital of the realm of Yiddish, as I had known it in the last year of its authentic life.[56]

Dawidowicz views herself not as one of the last *surviving* people to see Vilna, but as one of the very last people to see Vilna *at all*. Vilna by this reckoning is not to be understood as a Lithuanian city, but as a Jewish world destroyed in the war. She considers herself the last to see it because she was among the last to see it untouched by war. The war not only destroyed its Jewish inhabitants, but it destroyed the culture that made Vilna hers during the year she spent there.

Called by Napoleon "The Jerusalem of Lithuania" and featured prominently in the photographic histories of pre-Holocaust East European Jewry—because of its picturesque Jewish quarter, which housed several of the most illustrious Jewish libraries in the world, and it being the seat of the Vilna Gaon, the foremost Talmudic interpreter of the modern age as well as the leader of the anti-Hasidic movement—Vilna was for centuries the center of Jewish learning in Eastern Europe. Its level of rabbinic intellectualism was echoed and even equaled in its secular Jewish intellectualism. It was in Vilna that the Jewish socialist movement, the Bund, was born, and it was there that YIVO, which was to become the central institution of East European Jewish archival and scholarly research, was established.[57] Dawidowicz was sent to YIVO by a teacher, Jacob Shatzky,[58] a Polish Jewish historian who—after she had a disappointing start in a master's program in English literature at Columbia University—encouraged her to try her hand at Jewish history in YIVO's Aspirantur program, which was established in 1934 and terminated in 1940 with YIVO's move to New York; the program was among the first to train scholars of Jewish studies.[59] 1938, the year that Dawidowicz spent in Vilna, was the most formative year of her life and her career, both for professional reasons and in terms of her commitment to teaching about pre-Holocaust East European Jewish life as well as the history of the Holocaust itself. Of her time there, she says:

> To be sure, I saw it with American eyes, but these were not just curious eyes looking for exotica in an alien world. At twenty-three I already belonged to two worlds, having been educated in two cultures. Still half in love with Keats and English poetry, I was being drawn inexorably, during those terrible years of the 1930s, into the turbulent vortex of Jewish life. I was moved by Jewish sorrows, gripped by the drama of Jewish experience. I went to Vilna not as a tourist but as a Jew, to search out the continuities of Jewish history, the connections between my world and that which my parents had left behind.[60]

In *The Golden Tradition*, Dawidowicz sought to place herself directly into the narrative of East European modernization prior to the Holocaust, much like Roman Vishniac, who grew up in a privileged Moscow household and experienced neither the privations nor the discrimination against Jews that occurred in the provincial segments of the Pale of Settlement (which in fact came to be associated with most of his photographic oeuvre), yet labored excessively to create threads of affiliation, native identification, and auto-ethnographic empathy with the subjects of his photographs, as we will see in the next chapter. And just as Maurice Samuel, born in Romania but raised and educated in England, sought to blend his voice with Sholem Aleichem's in *The World of Sholem Aleichem* in order to elaborate a narrative of personal return, so too does Dawidowicz seek to tell a narrative of return to a place she never really inhabited.

In reflecting on her project and the role that her 1938 journey to Vilna to study at the newly minted YIVO institution under the tutelage of its founders and ideologues played in her life's work of recuperating the image of East European Jewry from the clutches of popular sentimentalism, she says:

> History written from the inside, from the perspective of the participant or the participant observer, conveys an immediacy that cannot always be captured when history is written from documents alone. That kind of immediacy I tried to introduce in my first book—*The Golden Tradition: Jewish Life and Thought in Eastern Europe*. It consists of autobiographies, memoirs, and letters of some sixty persons, as well as reminiscences about them.[61]

Because she was in Vilna for a year, Dawidowicz sees her work as that of a participant observer, as it were, someone writing simultaneously from the inside and the outside.

"Return" for Dawidowicz has both religious and cultural connotations, serving as an acknowledgment of what she realizes may have been missing in *The Golden Tradition*'s unremitting focus on secularity. Throughout her writings Dawidowicz extols the figure of Nathan Birnbaum, a secular Zionist organizer who founded the first Jewish nationalist movement, *Kadima*, as a student at the University of Vienna in 1883.[62] Then on a lecture tour in Poland and Russia, he became "enamored of God" (to quote Bernard Malamud).[63] His "return" to Judaism does not comport with the idea of a cultural return common within modern Jewish experience of the turn of the twentieth century. Nevertheless, Dawidowicz's fascination with Birnbaum captures not only her theme of modern East European Jews finding strategies for preserving Jewish tradition despite their commitment to modernity, but also her own increasing attraction to traditional Orthodox Judaism.

In an essay on her experience later in life of going week after week to sit on the women's side of a synagogue in Queens, New York, Dawidowicz acknowledges her own return to traditional modes of Jewish observance despite not having been raised in a religious home.[64] Indeed her first synagogue experience took place in Vilna, and because she found it singularly alienating she refused to go back that year.[65] In light of her own deep-seated commitment to representing Vilna, the Jerusalem of Lithuania, as her own city, the city she fled because of the Holocaust, the city that she was one of the last to see, Dawidowicz's careful resistance to portraying East European pre-Holocaust Jewry as a world where religious Jews still constituted the majority of the population is striking. Dawidowicz does acknowledge that her view of Vilna may have been somewhat limited:

> Now in retrospect, I think my sentimental vision of Vilna blurred my perception of its social realities. I looked at Jewish Vilna as a living relic of the past rather than as a society in the process of change, however slow that change.[66]

What role did Dawidowicz's conflicted sense of her vision of Vilna play in the construction of *The Golden Tradition*? Throughout *The Golden Tradition* Dawidowicz focuses on well-known and lesser-known people who tell stories of return. I will explore a few of these narratives of "return" in light of her articulated goal of providing a more realistic, modern, and nuanced portrait of the world of East European Jews before the Holocaust and thus recuperating the religious aspects of the culture that she so assiduously attempts to repress.

Dawidowicz features essays by S. Ansky and Chaim Zhitlowsky, important figures in the Jewish ethnographic and Yiddish nationalist movements respectively, each of whom exemplifies for her the notion of "return." She quotes Ansky speaking on the twenty-fifth anniversary of his literary debut about his return to his people after sixteen years working against political oppression:

> Twenty-five years ago when I first began writing, my striving was to work on behalf of the oppressed, the laboring masses, and it seemed to me then—and that was my error—that I would not find them among Jews. I thought it was impossible to hold oneself aloof from politics and, again, I did not find any political currents among Jews. Bearing within me an eternal yearning toward Jewry, I nevertheless turned in all directions and went to labor on behalf of another people. My life was broken, severed, ruptured. Many years of my life passed on this frontier, on the border between both worlds. Therefore, I beg you, on this twenty-fifth year of summing up my literary work, to eliminate sixteen years.[67]

Ansky's idea of eliminating the years of his life when he was engaged in activities that he either subsequently renounced or in hindsight did not perceive to be of a piece with his lifework is particularly fascinating in light of Dawidowicz's own renunciation of the religious, parochial, and provincial elements of East European Jewish life in *The Golden Tradition*. Only those writings that acknowledge the impact of modernity on tradition make their way into the volume. But in her inclusion of this long Ansky quote describing the nature of the dynamic interchange between modernity and tradition, Dawidowicz seems to be moving toward an acknowledgment of the sovereignty of tradition despite modernity. Indeed, perhaps what she is approximating here is reminiscent of Glazer's "Jewishness"—an ethnic Judaism that need not depend entirely on religious identification. One can return to the tradition from an ethnic standpoint, without committing to the religious aspects of the culture.

In a different yet resonant vein, her excerpting of an essay of Zhitlowsky's emphasizes the struggle to find an articulation of a Jewish ethnic tradition despite the overwhelming force of modernity. Zhitlowsky's piece discusses his alienation and that of his generation from the traditional Jewish communities depicted in isolated Yiddish works influenced by the Haskalah:

> Many of that generation, having shed their tears over Nekrasov's poetry, made a binding covenant of tears with the Russian people. Why not with the Jewish people? Pondering the assimilatory effect that Russian literature with its Turgenevs and Nekrasovs had on us, I find it was because we had no such Jewish literature. That was before Sholem Aleichem and Peretz: there were only individual works in Yiddish that had not yet converged in one stream of literary development. These individual works presented descriptions of Jewish life that could not evoke love or even feeble sympathy for their Jewish characters and situations. They described a world decrepit and moldy, rotting away and fouling the air with its stench of corpses. Those literary works were the product of the Haskalah, with a totally negative attitude toward prevailing Judaism and to all the institutions it had shaped. It was enough to compare descriptions of childhood in Yiddish literature with those in Russian literature, and you could understand the differences between our lives and theirs.[68]

For him and his fellows, "return," finding a way to work on behalf of Jews, required the development of a coherent Yiddish literature that could endear Jews to themselves. Thus with the birth of modern Yiddish literature, these alienated Jews were suddenly able to identify as Jews without committing themselves to Orthodoxy and to work for Jewish causes even if quite far removed from that religious milieu. In other words, Yiddish literature furnished them with an ethnic mouthpiece. He concludes his reflection in the following way:

> Later, when I had again become Jewishly conscious, I realized that had we had a progressive cultural Jewish environment in Yiddish and a Yiddish literature which would have depicted Jewish life as the Russian or Polish literatures depicted theirs—then our radical youth would not have made such an assimilationist break.[69]

As in her documentation of the "returns" of Ansky and Zhitlowsky through the medium of Yiddish culture and literature, Dawidowicz documents the "return" of Abraham Liessen from Marxism to the Jewish Bund, as he followed the Marxist prescription that its practitioners and ideologues consider the concrete social conditions surrounding them and realized that his were Jewish. Even more extreme was the case of Vladimir Medem, baptized at birth, who started the Bund. She calls his story a "unique personal history of coming back to the Jews."[70]

One of the most fascinating accounts of "return" invoked by Dawidowicz in *The Golden Tradition* is the one told by Sophie Günzberg (one of only three women featured in the book). Her father, Baron David Günzberg, the son of the man who bankrolled Ansky's ethnographic expedition and one of a small number of uniquely wealthy industrialist Jewish families in Russia at the turn of the twentieth century, inhabited a socioeconomic position similar to Vishniac's. Sophie Günzberg recounts in her reflection on her father:

> We used to spend at least two months a year in our estate in Podolia. The estate was large, including our house, a huge garden, the caretaker's house and garden. . . . About 18 kilometers from our estate there was a Jewish town called Khashtchevat. The authorities were not particularly hostile to this town but did not allow it to expand beyond set boundaries. Its inhabitants, being faithful observers of the commandment to be fruitful and multiply, soon found themselves in a grave situation. Two or three times a year, our parents would visit this town sometimes taking us along. . . . Since we, the children, were Günzburgs whose duty it was to assist the Jews of Russia, we were taken to this town at an early age to see how its unfortunate population lived. In Petersburg we were taught to listen to those whose hearts were encumbered and to help them, not merely with money.[71]

While this "return" on the part of the Günzbergs can be viewed as an expression of their sense of charity, the fact that the children were brought back to the same village several times each year in order to see how the "other half lived" and to reinforce their sense of compassion implies its own kind of return to origins. This "return," reminiscent of Vishniac's "return" to the Jews of Carpathian Ruthenia from his own privileged vantage point in Moscow, took place along a geographic axis, and not just a spiritual or communal one, as described by Ansky and Zhitlowsky.

How does this type of return fit into Dawidowicz's broader vision of return, as expressed throughout *The Golden Tradition*? For Dawidowicz, whose very physical survival can be attributed to the fact that she traveled to Vilna on the eve of World War II on an American passport and was able to leave on the last boat back to Boston, there is no possibility of a return to the Vilna she knew for one fleeting year. Although Max Weinreich left at the same time and, with Dawidowicz's help, among others, was able to rebuild YIVO in New York, the vast majority of the students and teachers with whom she studied and cavorted in 1938 were murdered over the course of the following six years.[72]

As Dawidowicz grapples not only with her geographic distance from the world that so absorbed her for a year of her life, but also with her intellectual, cultural, and spiritual distance from it, she addresses the absence of a substantial religious presence in *The Golden Tradition* through the volume's narrative of return. While the stated goal of the book is to reconcile the modernity of East European Jewish culture with the anodyne visions of it promoted in the popular literature of the moment, Dawidowicz's stronger impulse, it seems, is to reflect on the role of tradition in that world as both a corrective to its rampant modernity and as a reminder, to herself, of what she is missing from her limited point of view. As a student of YIVO for one year, she knew one aspect of Jewish life—the modern, the progressive, the Yiddishist, the self-reflective. *The Golden Tradition*, primarily articulating that vision, leaves room, through its lacunae and its variety of voices, for a subtle theme of return that addresses Dawidowicz's own sense of inadequacy, her own need to go back to a place that, like Sophie Günzberg, she never really left behind because she never actually inhabited it in any real way.

In counterpoint to Dawidowicz's vision of Vilna as presented in *The Golden Tradition*, Irving Howe, in his autobiography, describes the poet Isaac Rosenfeld as a young man: "It was not hard to imagine him in a Vilna yeshiva, elucidating points of Talmud. . . . Visiting Isaac, I would beg him to do his Yiddish version of Prufrock."[73] What for Howe seems an easy marriage of inclinations—the Jerusalem of Lithuania with T.S Eliot, the Vilna of old with the Vilna of new—is not so easy for Dawidowicz to openly acknowledge in her book. And yet the place, faith, and tradition that she could not feature explicitly is there in myriad ways, through the book's montage construction—primarily through the narrative of return through which she acknowledges the missing piece in her selection of texts. Religious Judaism is not directly acknowledged as a major part of modern East European Jewish experience in *The Golden Tradition*, but it is implied in her focus on texts that attempt, consistently and emphatically, to reconcile tradition and modernity, to document "returns" of many different varieties but mostly to the Jewish fold through whatever means necessary: charity, Yiddish literature, and the like. The element of montage articulated here is one that acknowledges the necessity of lacunae, of blind spots, and tries its hardest, in self-conscious ways, to recuperate what is missing without entirely succeeding.

Whereas the story of Jewish Orthodoxy is missing from Dawidowicz's anthology, it is the Holocaust that is absent from *Image before My Eyes*. Like the other two anthologies treated in this chapter, *Image before My Eyes* frames itself as an attempt to modify the public's perception of pre-Holocaust East European Jewry. Presented as a photographic history of East European Jewry from 1864 until the outbreak of World War II in 1939, the authors acknowledge the limitations of the photograph:

> Though the camera does not lie, the photograph is neither value free nor does it provide more than a de-situated fragment, accidently preserved through time, of a larger picture. As John Szarkowski has remarked, "to quote out of context is the essence of the photographer's craft." One important way of compensating for the fragmentary character of the single photograph is to place it in the frame of reference provided by a large collection of related images and to gloss it on the basis of the materials conventionally used by the historian and the ethnographer. This is what we have attempted to do in this photographic history of Jewish life in Poland.[74]

The goal of the book's editors, therefore, is to make use of an archive of photographs on Polish Jewish history and to de-fragmentize those photographs—to fill in the gaps left by their medium as well as by their collective presentation as disparate parts of a whole. Reminiscent of the role photographs play in the construction of cultural montages, as raised in Didi-Huberman's discussion of the Sonderkommando photographs, these photographs too are perceived by Dobroszycki and Kirshenblatt-Gimblett to be an essential part of a montage-like corrective to misapprehensions of East European pre-Holocaust Jewish life. However, this corrective can only work, according to Dobroszycki and Kirshenblatt-Gimblett, when framed by an account that puts them into context.

The stated goal of the book's 1980 film version is to "dig a tunnel through the Holocaust" in order to construct a realistic rendition of pre-Holocaust East European Jewry, unsullied by the overwhelming shadow that tends to obscure the world destroyed in it.[75] In book form, however, *Image before My Eyes* omits more than it includes, and occludes more than it illuminates, due in part to its nearly total omission of the Holocaust.

To provide a final example of salvage montage in service of rounding out, or rendering more realistic, portraits of pre-Holocaust East European Jewish culture in the post-Holocaust decades without presuming to fill in all the blanks or giving a complete picture, we will focus on the book version of *Image before My Eyes*, with brief allusions to the film. Whereas in the case of *A Treasury* we observed how Yiddish literary depictions of the shtetl deconstructed Howe and Greenberg's own somewhat simplistic view of pre-Holocaust East European Jewish life (which was reinforced by Shahn's drawings), despite their attestations to the contrary, and in *The Golden Tradition* we explicated the narrative of return that allowed Dawidowicz to reclaim Jewish tradition from the detritus of streamlined depictions of the shtetl, what I hope to trace in *Image before My Eyes* is the presence of the Holocaust in a volume that insistently avoids it.

Why is this important? Telling a history of Polish Jewry without an acknowledgment of the Holocaust is like telling a history of pre-Holocaust East European Jewry without an acknowledgment of Jewish Orthodoxy. Arguably, knowledge of the Holocaust is what brings Jewish American readers to this book, so it is worthwhile to question whether a photographic history of East European Jewish life in the pre-Holocaust period can avoid at least some reflection on the Holocaust narrative and the role it played in overdetermining certain aspects of the world destroyed.

This brings to mind the famous discussion in Barthes's *Camera Lucida* of the way that photographs tell their own future. In his discussion of Alexander Gardner's photograph of Lewis Payne, Barthes says:

> In 1865 young Lewis Payne tried to assassinate Secretary of State W. H. Seward. Alexander Gardner photographed him in his cell, where he was waiting to be hanged. The photograph is handsome, as is the boy: that is the studium. But the punctum is: he is going to die. I read at the same time: This will be and this has been; I observe with horror an anterior future of which death is the stake. By giving me the absolute past of the pose, the photograph tells me death in the future.[76]

To clarify the terminology Barthes uses here, the "studium" is the social context for a photograph, something in it that most viewers recognize simply by virtue of what they already know about the photograph's subject. The "punctum" is a unique "prick" that takes place in viewing the photograph: that moment of recognition between the viewer and the photograph's subject in which the viewer realizes why the photographer took the photograph in the first place, what the photograph portends, or even what the photograph is irrevocably and palpably missing for all eternity. In the Lewis Payne photograph, Roland Barthes can't help but see not only that the photograph's subject is awaiting his death, but also that when he is viewing the photograph, about a century later, the subject is already dead. The punctum of the photograph, for Barthes, is its "anterior future."

Indeed, essential to my notion of salvage poetics is the idea that in attempts to reconstruct the world that was destroyed, the reception of pre-Holocaust works through the prism of the Holocaust is unavoidable. Post-Holocaust audiences of course cannot change the content or form of the works they use as part of their arsenal of artifacts for reconstructing lost worlds. However, their selection of some works and not others, their preference for some media and not others as they construct a folk ethnographic approximation of pre-Holocaust East European Jewish life, is based on both their projected expectations and the form and subject matter at hand.

Viewing all of Jewish history through the lens of destruction can lead to some interesting understandings of that history, and viewing East European Jewish culture through the lens of the Holocaust is no exception. However, in the case of *Image before My Eyes*, a disjuncture between the historical and ethnographic narratives in the volume forces its readers to seek out a consistent through line. The ethnographic narrative is revealed in the three hundred photographs selected out of the ten thousand in the Polish Jewry collection at YIVO. A separate ethnographic historical frame is couched in the narrative outlining major institutions and moments in East European Jewish life that in a general sense is reflected in the photographs. The photographs are not constitutive of Polish Jewish history, but confirm the historical narrative through illustrative examples of the dominant narrative presented in the historical text. At the same time, the photographs stand on their own, independent of the historical narrative, which does not address any of the photographs in particular. Applying Barthes's photographic terminology, the studium of the volume is articulated in the historical narrative, but the punctum is in the photographs themselves—just as ethnographic anecdotes "prick" their audiences with concrete examples of broader phenomena, and those broader phenomena are deduced from an assemblage and an assimilation of those anecdotes.

One might argue, following Barthes, that for many readers the punctum of the volume as a whole, its "prick" when you take the photographs and the historical essay together, is the Holocaust itself. Readers seek the Holocaust in every frame, trying to understand the future of its subjects and to see hints of it in the past. Although the volume's editors state that their determination to avoid the Holocaust is its organizing principle, nevertheless the Holocaust sneaks into the book in various ways that contrast with its dominant poetic. The montage formed between the photographs and the text, and even between the different photographs in relation to one another, leaves room for articulating this underlying punctum for its audience; the book itself hesitates to foreground the Holocaust, but the Holocaust itself is unavoidable in perusing a book like this.

In *Picture Theory*, W. J. T. Mitchell discusses "composite forms" in which texts and images are brought together in a variety of ways.[77] He points to an "image/text" problem in Western culture: an expectation that when images and texts are juxtaposed, the image will either illustrate the text or the text will narrate the image. He asks whether circumstances exist in which the two media, situated side by side, need not necessarily be in dialogue with one another. Mitchell analyzes a variety of "photographic essays," which, he writes, "foreground the dialectic of exchange and resistance between photography and language, the things that make it possible and sometimes impossible to read the pictures or to see the text illustrated in them."[78] In his reading of James Agee and Walker Evans's *Let Us Now Praise Famous Men*, Mitchell points to Agee's claim in the book's introduction that "the photographs are not illustrative. They and the text are coequal, mutually independent, and fully collaborative."[79] Mitchell elaborates by saying, "The co-equality of photos and texts is, in one sense, a direct consequence of their independence, each medium being given a 'book' of its own, each equally free of admixture with the other—Evans providing photos without text, Agee a text without photos."[80] Summing up his reading of *Let Us Now Praise Famous Men*, Mitchell says that Agee and Evans's collaboration is "governed by a rhetoric of resistance rather than one of exchange and cooperation."[81] The book—written during the Great Depression and commissioned for *Fortune Magazine* in the spirit of, but not in collaboration with, the Farm Security Administration's project of rural rehabilitation—featured the lives of sharecroppers in the dust bowl. The separation between photo and text therein, Mitchell concludes, "is, in effect, a sabotaging of an effective surveillance and propaganda apparatus, one which creates easily manipulatable images and narratives to support political agendas."[82]

In *Image before My Eyes*, though the editors claim to be using the photographs to anchor the surrounding text, to be telling the history of Polish Jewry as it arises out of the photographs selected from YIVO's Polish collection, there is a significant disjuncture between the photographs and the texts, or, in Mitchell's terms, a kind of resistance rather than cooperation. The way the two media are juxtaposed detracts from the power of the photographs; instead of the text being separated from the photographs, it is woven throughout, forcing the reader, in order to finish reading a paragraph, to turn the page without looking at the pictures. The reader can go back, but it doesn't always happen. Furthermore, the photographs and the text are often only loosely related; a chapter on communal institutions, for example, features photographs of executive boards of community kehillot (Jewish self-governing bodies), Zionist leaders laying wreaths on the tomb of the unknown soldier on Polish Independence Day, and the funeral of Rabbi Elias Haim Meisel in Lodz. This last caption states, "Rabbi Meisel, a great philanthropist, built a factory for handweavers who were unemployed as a result of the mechanization of the textile industry" (figure 4.6).[83] The surrounding text discusses the relationship between

FIGURE 4.6. "The funeral of Rabbi Elias Haim Meisel (1821–1912) in Łódź, a great philanthropist, built a factory for handweavers who were unemployed as a result of the mechanization of the textile industry. Studio: American Photographer." From the Archives of the YIVO Institute for Jewish Research, New York.

the Polish government and kehillot. Following this text is a series of photographs: a woman who founded a free-loan society in Vilna (figure 4.7), boys being measured for new clothes purchased for them by the kehillah of Szereszow, a Jewish sports club in Bialystok, emergency ambulances parked in front of a first-aid association in Bialystok, and elderly people in a garden at Vilna's home for the aged. All these are examples of communal institutions, but none of them are discussed in the surrounding text. Additionally, none of them are

FIGURE 4.7. "Dvora Esther Gelfer (1817–1907)." From the Archives of the YIVO Institute for Jewish Research, New York.

in direct dialogue with one another, with the exception of those that seem to represent the same community geographically (i.e., Bialystok or Vilna), although the institutions represented in each frame are distinct and unrelated. The subject of each photograph has its own fascinating history and raises a slew of questions for the reader, which cannot be asked or answered in the brief surrounding text. This is fine, of course; narrative details about every single image would warrant a very different kind of book. But the dynamic created by the wealth of images and the paucity of narrative surrounding them is one of allusion and indirection as opposed to illustration and information.

Also of interest is that in some instances the audience is apparently meant to recognize certain images—without any special comment from the editors. For example, toward the end of the book is a picture of YIVO's founders, including Kalmanowicz, the man who hosted Dawidowicz in Vilna upon her arrival in 1938 and served as her surrogate father throughout the year (figure 4.8).[84] Although for

FIGURE 4.8. From the Archives of the YIVO Institute for Jewish Research, New York.

someone (like me) who has just finished reading Dawidowicz's auto-biography this is a tremendous discovery, the text surrounding it makes no special note of YIVO or its founders. Earlier on, a picture of a Towarzystwo Ochrony Zdrowia or Society for the Safeguarding of Health (TOZ) camp features Marc and Bella Chagall,[85] but Chagall's involvement in Polish-Jewish institutions is not remarked upon in the text. His presence is noted only in the caption (figure 4.9).

The most important disjuncture in the book is the absence of any explicit discussion of the Holocaust in the narrative, although at several unexpected points the fate of the photograph's subjects during the Holocaust is mentioned in captions. A Vishniac photograph of Rabbi Leybl Eisenberg, the town rabbi of Lask, appears just before the image of Rabbi Elias Haim Meisel's funeral, both under the category of Jewish communal organizations. The caption under Eisenberg's photograph concludes: "He died in the Chelmno death camp in 1942" (figure 4.10).[86]

In only one place does the historical narrative surrounding the photographs explicitly discuss the Holocaust. In a section on synagogues in part 2 ("The Persistence of the Past"), we are introduced to Szymon Zajczyk, "one of the foremost specialists in the history of synagogues and Jewish sculpture in Poland." After some details about his education and his output as a photographer and a historian, the text reads:

> During the German occupation, in 1940, Zajczyk and his family were confined in the Warsaw ghetto. With the help of his former professor, Stanislaw Herbst, they later escaped to the "Aryan side," where, in hiding, Zajczyk continued to write. On June 4, 1943, he was discovered and killed.[87]

There is no photograph of Zajczyk, nor are any of the pictures of wooden synagogues that precede this gloss attributed to him.

Part 3 of the volume, "Camera as Chronicler," concludes (in the middle of the book) with a photograph of "German soldiers en route to Poland in September 1939. The slogan emblazoned on the train reads 'we're going to Poland to beat up the Jews'" (figure 4.11).[88]

FIGURE 4.10. Roman Vishniac, *Rabbi Leibel Eisenberg (reading) and his shames [synagogue caretaker]*, Lask, ca. 1935–38. © Mara Vishniac Kohn, courtesy International Center of Photography.

The temporal end point of the album, therefore, is actually at the album's center—an example of the war popping up in unexpected and unframed places, despite the authors' deliberate avoidance of too much engagement with it. This disturbing photograph is followed immediately by part 4, "Creating a Modern Existence," which jars the reader by returning to the beginnings of urbanization of Polish Jewry during the nineteenth century.

Image before My Eyes is driven by the YIVO Archive and what it contains: even the archive's captions accompany the photographs

FIGURE 4.11. From the Archives of the YIVO Institute for Jewish Research, New York.

in the volume. If the destiny of the photographic subject was known (as was apparently the case for Rabbi Leybl Eisenberg), then that appears alongside the photograph.[89] But the majority of the subjects' destinies are unknown and unarticulated. Similarly, the photographs' relationship to the historical text is remarkably loose, with the expectation that the reader will make sense of the images in an associative and generalized manner. What we have in this volume are bits and pieces of a photographic archive and a narrator telling us how they fit, generally, into the bigger picture of Polish Jewish life. Because the text does not address the photographs specifically, the reader is left with a visual impression, but without a clear sense of time or place or specifics.

Like Dawidowicz's volume, *Image before My Eyes* emphasizes the modernity, urbanity, and culture of Polish Jewry in the pre-Holocaust period. The fourth and final part of the book traces the modern communal and cultural institutions in Poland that served the Jews and helped them to move away from the strictures of religious orthodoxy. The book ends with photographs of the Yiddish theater and cinema, which the 1980 film, directed by Josh Waletzky and Jerome Badanes, takes as its major theme. The film is punctuated throughout with the voice of a subject, Lilian Klempner, who sings the tunes from classic Yiddish cinema and theater as a kind of equivalent to the narrative backdrop we find in the book. Furthermore, the voices of informants in the film address specific photographs (of themselves or of their communities) that flash onto the screen, serving as something of a corrective to the disjointedness of image and text in the book.

The film, therefore, offers a very clear correlation between image and text—image as it appears in photographs, film stills, and home movies; and text, as it can be heard from the voices of Polish-born Jewish informants. The voice and image of Sophia Dubnow Ehrlich, daughter of the famous historian Simon Dubnow and wife of Bund activist Victor Ehrlich, accompanies many of the pictures, as does the voice and image of Dina Abramowicz, YIVO librarian and daughter of Hirsz Abramowicz, the historian and ethnographer of Jewish Vilna and its environs. Roman Eisner, brother of Gustave Eisner, a travel agent who "filmed the Jewish streets" in Eastern Europe when he accompanied clients on visits back to their hometowns, narrates his brother's films as well as photographs of himself as a young man. Most moving, perhaps, is the testimony of Chienna Kosowsky, who narrates a home movie in which she appears as a young girl on the streets of the shtetl she hails from.

Although the term "montage" is derived from cinematic discourse, *Image before My Eyes* as a film does not have the montage effect described in the books we have analyzed because it creates too streamlined a product. In it, the voices of survivors match up with images of life in Eastern Europe. In the book, there are several simultaneous narratives: the narrative of the YIVO photographic archive whose images had not previously been used to tell a well-rounded story about Polish Jewry when the volume was conceived; the textual narrative of Polish Jewish history that accompanies these images in the book, but doesn't flesh them out; and the narrative of the Holocaust underlying the conception and execution of the book. This missing narrative is the one that brings American readers to the book and unifies the book, in its anterior future, as its subjects disappear into the horizon of the war to come.

Moshe Vorobeichic-Raviv in *The Ghetto Lane of Vilna* (1931) published a series of montage photographs in which pious Jews are set into strangely disembodied backgrounds, laid, like a palimpsest, over scenes of Vilna (figure 4.12).[90] Carol Zemel argues that these images articulate a confrontation between tradition and modernity. She says,

> The picture's air of timelessness is interrupted not, however, by the photographer's intruding presence, but by the photograph's modernist montaged style, which shatters the cohesion of the image and flash forwards the Jewish elder into history as a small pale apparitional echo at the lower left.[91]

This visual montage suggests a model for salvage montage. It is the future and past embedded in these images of the present, the sense of transition and transformation always to be found in these images, that lays the foundation for their future application within a salvage poetic framework or a folk ethnographic reinvention in a post-cataclysmic age. At the same time, the anthological format of each of the books we discussed allows for a kind of dialectic. The expected is presented, but the unexpected emerges as well, because of the nature of the montage form. This synthesis of the unexpected and the expected—images of shtetlach interspersed with stories of the anti-shtetl, secular modernity always pulling toward tradition, and Polish-Jewish history viewed against the specter of the upcoming Holocaust—presents opportunities to recognize and interpret both the strengths and the limitations of presentations and perceptions of pre-Holocaust East European Jewish life in a post-Holocaust world.

36. Awaiting Customers

.36 הַצְּפִיָּה לְקוֹנֶה

FIGURE 4.12. © Moshe Vorobeichic-Raviv #36, *The Ghetto Lane in Vilna* (1931), by permission of Yossi Raviv.

5

AUTO-ETHNOGRAPHIC SALVAGE

Roman Vishniac's *A Vanished World*[1]

Sometimes I think I prefer the storyteller in him to the photographer.[2]

Cameras, in short, were clocks for seeing.[3]

Among the most iconic photographs of East European Jewish life taken in the pre-Holocaust period is the image of a bearded elderly man with his hand to his head (figure 5.1). His large, bony nose divides his face in half, with one side shaded and one side illuminated. He wears a hat and looks directly out at the viewer. Printed in 1947 on the second-to-last page of Roman Vishniac's *Polish Jews*, with the caption, "OLD MAN [Carpathian Ruthenia],"[4] this photograph is followed by the final image in the book, that of a gravestone on which are carved the words, "Here is buried a wise, scholarly, innocent, righteous, God-fearing man, who studied the words of the Torah day and night. He was a righteous innocent, Rabbi Barukh Yaakov son of the distinguished Avraham Shlomo, may his name be for a blessing" (figure 5.2).[5] Above these words is an image of an open bookcase, framed by the date of Rabbi Barukh Yaakov's death: "the 13th of Av 5589 [12 August 1829]."[6] Certainly, the gravestone is not to be understood as a monument to

FIGURE 5.1. Roman Vishniac, *An elder of the village, Vysni Apsa, Carpathian Ruthenia*, ca. 1938. © Mara Vishniac Kohn, courtesy International Center of Photography.

the man pictured on the page before him. But the implication is that this is the marker befitting a man of his ilk after he dies a dignified and timely death.

The same image of the old man appears in Vishniac's later book, *A Vanished World* (1983), both on the cover of and as the third photograph, where it is presented by two captions. Beneath the photograph itself, we read: "An elder of the village. Vrchini (Upper) Apsa, Carpathian Ruthenia, 1938."[7] The second caption, which appears in a "commentary on the photographs" between the book's preface and the photographs themselves, says:

> It was 1938, but warmth and light were provided in the dwellings of the village of Upper Apsa by burning branches and logs. I remember so well the firelight illuminating the hands and face of this village elder, whose advice was sought by members of his community. How wise and comforting a man he seemed to be.[8]

FIGURE 5.2. Roman Vishniac, *In the old Jewish cemetery of Lublin*, ca. 1935–38. © Mara Vishniac Kohn, courtesy International Center of Photography.

In the progression of these three captions through the two volumes, we begin with a generic categorization of the image, identified only as an old man in Carpathian Ruthenia, with the additional implication, provided by the photograph following it, of mortality and dignity. The sequence of the two photographs in *Polish Jews*, therefore, offers an implied commentary that words do not provide. This remarkable economy of verbal language and reliance on a visual narrative for emotional and historical content in *Polish Jews* disappears thirty-six years later in *A Vanished World*. There, the caption directly beneath the same photograph of the "old man" identifies its subject as an elder of the village, specifying as well his location within Carpathian Ruthenia and the year the photograph was taken. In the third caption, appearing in the "commentary on the photographs" at the back of *A Vanished World*, Vishniac, it seems, wants to ethnographically contextualize the most distinctive aesthetic feature of the photograph: the play of light and darkness on the old man's face. Though Vishniac's deliberate uses of light in many of his photographs is typical of documentary photography, in this caption Vishniac does not discuss the photograph's lighting as anything but a natural part of the environment, a function of the way homes were heated and lit in the village of Upper Apsa in Carpathian Ruthenia, 1938. The final statement in this caption introduces Vishniac's own sense of alienation from the scene he photographs. The word "seemed" indicates that although he wants to render judgment on the photograph's subject, describing him as "how wise and comforting a man," he cannot do so definitively and must qualify his observation. What we read here in this final caption is both ethnographically charged and highly personal.

This constellation of captions and implications for the same image highlights several crucial aspects of Roman Vishniac's iconic photographs of East European Jews taken on commission for the American Joint Distribution Committee (JDC) from 1935 to 1938, to help raise consciousness in America and Western Europe of the impoverishment of East European Jews during the interwar period. First, Vishniac's photographs have had a rich and evocative afterlife, appearing again and again in exhibits, books, and other publications, from their first staging as an exhibit at the JDC offices in 1938 until the present moment;[9] their social context differs in each publication and presentation, first appearing during the war, and finally, reflecting a prewar world destroyed, for an audience without firsthand experience of that world. Second, over the course of the half century in which Vishniac published these photos, they told an increasingly more complex, reflexive tale, moving from social documentary to auto-ethnography as their captions became simultaneously more personal and more ethnographically ramified. Before the war, as evident in the composition of the photographs themselves as well as the goals of his commission by the JDC, Vishniac tells a story of Jewish poverty and the need for relief and immigration. He also tells the story of the German Jewish valorization of East European Jewish experience and the need to reclaim Jewish traditions, exemplified by God-fearing Jews as part of a process of combatting Jewish assimilation. Finally, in his dominant choice of subjects, he tells the story of the role performed by the Jewish male visage within modern European visual economies of ethnicity. After the war, Vishniac tells a story about himself, about the Holocaust, and about pre-Holocaust East European Jewish culture.

Maya Benton has said, "That one set of photographs could be interpreted and employed in so many ways is a testament to the power and influence of Vishniac's images."[10] Jeffrey Shandler has affirmed, "From these different presentations an understanding of Vishniac's work as visualizing a lost culture emerged."[11] Benton's use of the term "interpreted" and Shandler's of "emergence" are important to consider here as we begin a discussion of the unique auto-ethnographic tonalities in Vishniac's successive presentations of his work in the decades since the initial commissioning of his photographs of East European Jews. Vishniac's own framing and reframing of these photographs in numerous publications and exhibitions all serve as interpretations of one another and also explain the emergence of a uniquely reflexive, culturally descriptive voice.

This chapter explores the development of an auto-ethnographic voice in Vishniac's iconic *A Vanished World* (1983) against the backdrop of its harbinger, *Polish Jews* (1947). While many of the photographs in *A Vanished World* have appeared elsewhere, most notably in Raphael Abramovitch's *The Vanished World* (1947) and in an unpublished monograph *A Pictorial Visit to the Jewish Children in Poland* (1938), as well as in the Yiddish press (appearing first in *The Jewish Daily Forward* on September 25, 1938),[12] I have chosen to focus primarily on *Polish Jews* and *A Vanished World* because they are in a unique dialogue with one another, and contain many of the same photographs from Vishniac's JDC commission. From a narrative perspective, the earlier book is exceedingly spare, with minimalist captions, as we have already seen, and the later book contains a layering of maximalist captions, wherein Vishniac inserts himself into the images as something of a native informant. In the nearly forty-year interval between the publication of the two books, through an increasingly rich and complex body of captions, Vishniac provides a fascinating example of salvage poetics arising out of pre-Holocaust works in a post-Holocaust era.[13] Vishniac's JDC photographs, taken for documentary purposes before the war, became in the postwar era, with the help of Vishniac's increasingly auto-ethnographic rhetoric, a primary source for folk ethnographic reconstructions of pre-Holocaust East European Jewish life. James Buzard defines auto-ethnography as "a form of self-narrative that places the self within a social context."[14] Indeed Roman Vishniac, in his presentation of iconic photographs of pre-Holocaust East European Jews in the post-Holocaust era, is increasingly invested in presenting himself as a means of channeling a lost culture.

Tracing the development of the captions across the two publications and focusing specifically on the captions in *A Vanished World* from a literary perspective provides a fascinating insight into the ways in which Vishniac sought to construct a particular kind of narrative in America in the decades after the Holocaust. His increased emphasis on verbal storytelling to supplement the photographs and the personal nature of many of these stories reveal Vishniac's consciousness of the importance of telling the story of a lost culture through the story of a living self, bringing together a salvage impulse with an autobiographical one, or what I have called here "an auto-ethnographic impulse."

While just over 300 nonscience photographs (as he worked as a science photographer for many years) taken by Vishniac were published in his lifetime, many thousands more have come to light in recent years through the work of Maya Benton and her colleagues at the International Center of Photography, in collaboration with the Photography Archives at the United States Holocaust Memorial Museum in Washington, DC, under the guidance of Judith Cohen.[15] An exhibit, "Roman Vishniac Rediscovered" staged from January to May of 2013, and on tour until 2023, provides a broader context for his oeuvre.[16] While Vishniac's work has long been associated primarily with the images of Jews in Carpathian Ruthenia and elsewhere in Eastern Europe, with an emphasis on impoverished farmers, scholars, and laborers, mostly male, taken for the JDC, "Roman Vishniac Rediscovered" opens a window to a far more varied photographic career than has heretofore been acknowledged. Vishniac, for example, according to Bernadette Van Woerkom, took a series of photographs in the late 1930s, again for the JDC, of Jewish students from Germany and Austria living in an agrarian youth training camp in the Dutch Polder as part of the European Halutz movement. Between 1934 and 1941, the camp trained 684 student refugees in agriculture and traditional crafts that would enable them to immigrate to Palestine and elsewhere.[17]

In addition to that cache of photographs, a significant number of Vishniac's photographs are situated in Berlin, where he in fact developed his particular approach to portraiture, made his reputation as a photographer, and established a studio. Several of those photographs appear in *A Vanished World*, but only insofar as they pertain to the rise of Nazism.[18] In the exhibit catalogue for "Roman Vishniac Rediscovered," David Shneer and Ute Eskildsen both explore Vishniac's photographic activity in Berlin before the war.[19] Also in the catalogue we learn from Atina Grossman, Avinoam Patt, Daniella Doron, and Steven Hoelscher that alongside landscape photographs of a decimated Berlin, in a series of photographs commissioned by the United Jewish Appeal and the JDC in 1947, Vishniac documented the immediate postwar experiences of refugees in displaced persons camps in Germany and France in photographs to be used in postwar publicity to raise money for resettlement and emigration efforts.[20] Being postwar, these photographs did not find their way into either of Vishniac's iconic anthologies.

Vishniac's photographs of Jewish and Chinese communities in New York, alongside his photographs of burlesque clubs there, round out his corpus to include far more than the prewar photographs taken on commission for the JDC on the eve of World War II.[21] Furthermore, his photomicroscopic images, enlarged, colorized images viewed through microscopes, received attention primarily within the scientific community. In 1971 an exhibit at the Jewish Museum in New York featured these images alongside his 1935–38 JDC images.[22] Notably, during Vishniac's lifetime, in all the stagings of his JDC photographs, however, the JDC commission was not mentioned.

Because the Jewish Museum publication (produced in conjunction with the Fund for Concerned Photography, a precursor of the imprint of the International Center for Photography) *The Concerns of Roman Vishniac* contains narrations by Vishniac that serve as a model for the narrations that would find their way into his 1983 *A Vanished World*, and because he juxtaposes his iconic East European prewar photographs with his photomicroscopy in *The Concerns of Roman Vishniac*, in the course of this discussion we will touch upon this publication briefly.

I have narrated the broader scope of Vishniac's photographic activities here because I agree with Maya Benton, who has argued that it is crucial to recognize that Vishniac's iconic prewar JDC photographs were only a small part of a larger whole.[23] For purposes of our discussion, understanding that Vishniac's photographic vision extended beyond the pre-Holocaust East European corpus of photographs is essential to our analysis of his own role in making them iconic; Vishniac's narration of the photographs—his framing and reframing, presenting, representing, and repurposing of these photographs, to the exclusion of any other photographs he took at the same time or within the same general period—is crucial to the role they play in the popular American post-Holocaust imagination of pre-Holocaust East European Jewish life.

My approach to Vishniac in this chapter is neither to discuss the breadth and variety of his images nor to examine his life and career, but rather to focus on one particular publication, *A Vanished World* (1983), against the backdrop of its harbinger, *Polish Jews* (1947), because of the particular ways in which Vishniac contextualized, framed, captioned, and narrated the later book. This chapter is an exploration of the dynamic development of a salvage poetic in the conjunction of

Vishniac's photographs with his verbal framing of them. A narrative grows out of Vishniac's major publication, *A Vanished World*, that provides an extremely valuable insight into the peculiar and compelling nature of salvage poetics.

Salvage poetics, as we already know, represent the marriage of salvage impulses and poetic form; in a post-cataclysmic era, the documentary features of that pre-cataclysmic work come to dominate its presentation but with a shifting emphasis. While we know that that the JDC photographs were commissioned for documentary purposes, the particular documentary mission of these photographs shifted from raising consciousness of a pressing economic need among East European Jews in the pre-Holocaust period to representation of "a vanished world" after the Holocaust. This took place not only because of the war's intervention but also with the help of the uniquely auto-ethnographic narrative that develops in conjunction with Vishniac's successive presentations of these photographs, culminating in *A Vanished World*.

In this exploration of Vishniac's photographic anthologies, we will consider a special aspect of salvage poetics that is unique to his corpus as it developed over time. Unlike other well-known photographers from the pre-Holocaust era such as Alter Kacyzne (1885–1941) (to be discussed in chapter 6) and Menachem Kipnis (1878–1942), Vishniac survived the war and was able to recast his photographs in response to the needs of a post-Holocaust American audience.[24] In doing so, he places himself into the photographs, first as a participant observer and finally as a native informant, claiming the world represented in the photographs as his own. As in all the examples to be presented throughout this study, salvage poetics depend on the presence of "artifacts" and the construction of an explanatory and culturally descriptive frame around them. Here Vishniac's frame for his photographic "artifacts," or the pictures he took from 1935 to 1938 for the JDC, is an auto-ethnographic one.

Why think of this as the development of an "auto-ethnographic" voice? Because Vishniac's captions increasingly frame his story as autobiography and ethnography simultaneously, moving toward a rhetoric of "the study, representation, or knowledge of a culture by one of its members."[25] Clearly, Vishniac was not a professional ethnographer, nor is the use of the term "auto-ethnography" in the context of this discussion of salvage poetics meant to imply that Vishniac was actually telling his own story as a member of the "vanished world" he photographed before the war. Vishniac's casting of these images within the penumbra of his own desire to identify with their subjects appeals to an American Jewish audience because many Jewish Americans in the post-Holocaust era sought to see themselves in a world where they had never lived but with which they strongly identified.

Roman Vishniac's progressive captioning and reframing of his pre-Holocaust portraits within the post-Holocaust period, beginning in 1947 and continuing on for the next forty years, reflects an increasing sense of his own role as "just one witness." The well-known historian Carlo Ginzburg says that although "just one witness" disqualifies a testimony according to Jewish law (which requires two witnesses), it must, in the context of the Holocaust, suffice.[26] But to what is he witness, and how is his testimony received? Of interest here is the way in which these photographs, taken in the pre-Holocaust period, become altered in the post-Holocaust era by Vishniac's conflicted sense of his identity as someone who was both a Holocaust survivor, and not, both an East European Jew, and not.

Having been detained in France in 1939 under unknown circumstances, but released one month later, Vishniac, his first wife, Luta, and his two children, Wolf and Mara (who had temporarily sought refuge in Sweden), met in Lisbon and set sail for New York in December 1940.[27] Although Elie Wiesel predicts in his foreword to *A Vanished World* that Vishniac will write about his experience in war-torn Europe—"Someday he will tell us how he fooled the Gestapo. And the informers. And death"[28]—Vishniac never does. Nonetheless his captions and the auto-ethnographic narrative that he crafts out of his iconic photographs mark an impulse to tell not only the story of the murdered subjects of his photographs but also of his own experience as witness to a "vanished world."

Despite the fact that the intensely personal tenor of many of his later captions would indicate otherwise, Roman Vishniac's photographs are commonly used as generic illustrations for traditional

Jewish life. In a 2010 monograph on the visual culture of Chabad, for example, Maya Balakirsky Katz begins her discussion of "The Hasidic Image" with an allusion to Vishniac's *A Vanished World*. "Perhaps more than any other images purporting to represent prewar Jewish life," she says, "photographer Roman Vishniac's work for Jewish relief organizations in the 1930s, published under the telling title *A Vanished World*, supplied American audiences with their quintessential images of Eastern European Hasidim."[29] In countless films, photo-anthologies, and introductions, Vishniac's photographs have served as a quick and easy gateway into the world of pre-Holocaust East European Jewish life. Yet the story that Vishniac's books tell is a very different one—about his own position as an assimilated Russian Jew exiled to Berlin after the Russian Revolution.

Roman Vishniac's father, Solomon, one of the few Jews given the right to live and work in Moscow, became one of Russia's leading manufacturers of umbrellas. The consequent luxury and ease that characterized Vishniac's early life as a Jewish boy growing up in an assimilated family in Moscow was a far cry from the life of most Jews in Russia. Yet because most Jews were not permitted to live or work in Moscow—the only place where, by most accounts, a decent living could be had—Solomon Vishniac ended up sheltering many students in flight from the law, who were seeking to matriculate at Russian universities despite restrictive admissions quotas on Jews. Vishniac, in a 1955 interview with *The New Yorker*, recalls them in the following way, "They had a special kind of face, those people, a special kind of whisper, and a special kind of footstep. They were like hunted animals— a terrible thing to be. I can never forget them."[30]

As a Russian Jewish émigré between the two world wars, Vishniac can be counted among the multitudes of East European Jews flooding into Germany, and particularly Berlin, during that period.[31] Germany, sharing a border with Eastern Europe, experienced during the nineteenth century a dramatic rise in East European Jewish immigration as Jews flooded west.[32] East European Jews, bordering Germany and constantly infiltrating her space and consciousness, became the living reminder to German Jewry of the traditional Jewish culture it had recently rejected. The East European Jew was the bad memory of

German Jewry come alive and an ever-present threat to assimilationist aspirations.[33] Jacob Fromer, in his introduction to Solomon Maimon's autobiography, described the Jewish ghetto in Berlin as a kind of anthropological curiosity: "Whoever desires to experience an ethnological sensation need not venture to the far corners of the world. For that, a day's journey from Berlin will suffice. One need only cross the Russian border to find an almost unknown human type full of mystery and wonder."[34] Of a divided mind regarding East European Jews, many German Jews attributed German anti-Semitism to the presence of these largely destitute, "unenlightened" East European Jews in their midst. At the same time, as attested in Fromer's statement, East European Jews became the objects of anthropological interest as well as objects of pity and charity for the more privileged German Jewish population. A handful of German Jewish writers, most famously Karl Emil Franzos (1848–1904), mediated the image of the East European Jew for a German-reading audience through works such as *Aus Halb-Asien* (1876). With the help of such books, "a thoroughly acculturated German Jewry had created the stereotype of the Eastern Jew as its mirror opposite."[35] According to Steven Aschheim in his study of the relationship between German Jews and their East European counterparts,

> between 1905 and 1914 alone, approximately 700,000 East European Jews passed through Germany to embark at Hamburg or Bremen or other West European ports bound for the United States. Although statistics are not complete, we know that a large proportion of the total of 2,750,000 East European Jewish immigrants who left Europe for overseas lands between 1880 and 1914 passed through Germany.[36]

German Jews were quite generous in their offer of aid to the immigrant masses, but mostly, it is conjectured by historians and cultural critics alike, in order to facilitate their departure from German soil.[37]

The "anthropological" fascination with East European Jews that grew out of this German Jewish context translated itself, during the interwar and the Weimar years, into a movement that has been called the "cult of the *Ostjude*." This movement has generally been character-ized as a fetishization and essentialization of the East European Jew and East European Jewish experience by a generation of German Jewish youth who had been born into German Jewish *bildung*, or "culture," with all its attendant legacies and privileges. The mostly assimilated and spiritually disaffected generation of the "cult" was largely secure finan-cially, but despite their embrace of the German values of *bildung*, which they had come to represent and to embody for non-Jewish Germans, anti-Semitism was on the rise.[38] An articulation of the urgency with which East European Jewry became a cultural focus, and the financial and cultural investment placed therein, Berlin's Judische Volksheim (Jew-ish Folkhome), a club devoted to the education of East European Jewish youth and a celebration of their native culture, was established in 1916.[39] Occasional, and in some cases not so occasional, visitors to the Volk-sheim included Martin Buber, S. Y. Agnon, Franz Kafka, and Chaim Arlo-zoroff, all key Zionist leaders, writers, and public intellectuals.[40]

A glimpse into S. Y. Agnon's (1887–1970) place as a symbol and voice of East European Jewry in Berlin of the second decade of the twentieth century gives us some insight into the place Vishniac may have imagined for himself in the 1930s as a Russian-born Jew trans-planted to Western Europe and commissioned to photograph East European Jews. In 1907 Agnon, the well-known Galician-born Hebrew writer, had settled in the port city of Jaffa in Palestine, where he pub-lished his signature story, "Agunot," in 1908. But in 1912, with the encouragement of his mentor and friend Arthur Ruppin to broaden his literary, cultural, and linguistic horizons as an up-and-coming young writer, Agnon moved to Germany, where he established his reputation as the foremost Hebrew writer of his generation.[41] Agnon spent four of his twelve years in Germany in Berlin, a crucial gathering place of Hebrew writers during the interwar years—M. Y. Berdichevsky made his home there and, temporarily, Chaim Nachman Bialik. Reflect-ing on the role Agnon played in the cult of the *Ostjude* during those years, Gershom Scholem, the German-born world-renowned expert on Jewish mysticism who participated actively in the valorization of East European Jewish life during the interwar period in Berlin, wrote: "For us every Eastern Jew was a carrier of all the mysteries of Jewish existence, but the young Agnon appeared to us as one of its most perfect incarnations."[42]

While living in Berlin, Vishniac's experience was likely quite different than Agnon's, although less so in hindsight. David Shneer has argued that "as a natural scientist, Vishniac likely did not socialize with Max Weinreich, a founder of YIVO; U. Z. Grinberg, rising star of Yiddish and Hebrew poetry; or the other founders of these émigré Jewish cultural institutions."[43] Indeed, given Vishniac's presence among a large group of privileged "refugees" from Russia living in the Wilmersdorf community on the edge of Charlottenburg (affectionately called Charlottengrad in recognition of its Slavic settlers), I would be hard-pressed to argue that Vishniac was identifiable in any significant way with the "Eastern Jews" who were the focus of the cult of the *Ostjuden*. After his arrival in America, however, when the events of the Holocaust were coming to light and he was able to reflect back on the documentary value of the photographs beyond their contribution to the JDC's work on behalf of East European Jewish refugees, Vishniac did come to identify himself as an East European Jew. His preface to *A Vanished World* provides us with an articulation of this:

> From earliest childhood, my main interest was my ancestors. My grandfather Wolf and my parents told me about the activities of my forefathers following the establishment of the Pale of settlement by the pseudo-liberal tsarina, Catherine II. They told me of the restrictions against Jews, and how Nicholas I forced the conscription of Jewish boys with the intention of converting them to Christianity. My great grandparents "bought" these child soldiers from the Russian officers for the weekends and taught them how to remain Jews. By doing so, my great grandparents were risking persecution and exile to Siberia, but they persisted. My own activities began when I was eighteen, early in the First World War. The Jews of the Pale who resided in the battle zone were declared German spies and were forcibly transported to the Russian interior in cattle cars, without food or water, and without any provision for housing once they arrived.... This was but a prelude to what was to come two decades later. I was living in Germany in the thirties, and I knew that Hitler had made it his

mission to exterminate all Jews, especially the children and the women who could bear children in the future. I was unable to save my people, only their memory.[44]

In this statement Vishniac narrates his place as a Russian, the descendent of pious Jews, a witness to the destruction of Jews in World War I, and a prophet of future destruction in World War II.[45] The preface is accompanied by a portrait of his grandfather, Wolf Vishniac (1836–1908), sporting a long, white beard and traditional rabbinic garb—a square black yarmulke and a gabardine.

But it is not just Vishniac's personal history that is articulated in the captions and their surrounding narratives in *A Vanished World*. Indeed, close scrutiny suggests they encapsulate the history of the representation of East European Jews in Western contexts. The composition of Vishniac's photographs themselves, and the nature of the texts he wrote to accompany them, may have been in dialogue with Arnold Zweig and Hermann Struck's *The Face of East European Jewry* (1920), an earlier book that grew directly out of the German Jewish fascination with East European Jewry and came to emblematize, in visual terms, the cult of the *Ostjude*.[46] *The Face of East European Jewry* was the result of a collaboration between Zweig, a young German Jewish writer, and Struck, a Zionist artist responsible for the most famous extant portrait of Theodor Herzl, an image that has come to be known as "the countenance of the movement."[47] Zweig first encountered East European Jewry in 1917 when stationed as a soldier outside of Kovno in the wartime press division at Ober-Ost, where he was able to observe, up close for the first time, "East European Jews personally."[48] In addition to his portraits of the Zionist leadership, Struck had published the cover illustration of the 1916 *Ostjudische Erzahler* (East European Jewish Storytellers), a collection of classic modern Yiddish fiction and poetry in German translation. Anticipating the future collaboration of the two men, Zweig in 1918 reviewed Struck's first volume of etchings of East European Jews. Although the two men created *The Face of East European Jewry* largely as an illustration of Struck's etchings, the faces he depicted were the guiding spirit behind Zweig's heartfelt account of the character and the plight, as the case may be, of both the individual East European Jew and his community. With the publication of *The Face of East European Jewry* in 1920, the radical glorification of the *Ostjude* reached its height.[49] This was the same year that Roman Vishniac arrived in Berlin.[50]

The iconography of the face of the East European Jew was a German Jewish phenomenon, inspired in part by Martin Buber's wildly popular depictions of Hasidic rabbis in his adaptations and translation of Hasidic tales throughout the first several decades of the twentieth century. The photographic art of portraiture had become popular in Germany as well, with notable examples by artists such as August Sander, who undertook a monumental project of typologizing human beings in photographs in order "to reflect the universally human." In the mid-1920s, Sander conceived his work *People of the 20th Century* in forty-five portfolios, which were intended to contain 500 to 600 photographs.[51] *Antiltz der Zeit* (Faces of the Age) was published in 1929, an echo of Zweig and Struck's *Das Ostjudishe Antlitz*, the German title of their *Face of East European Jewry*. This focus on physiognomy, or a series of human "types," as representative of an age, undoubtedly influenced Zweig's unique fascination with East European Jewish faces and inspired his statement, in *The Face of East European Jewry*: "Is the Jew of the East perhaps really an old man at the end of a long life, unable to be rejuvenated or to be born again, standing before his imperceptible death?"[52] In his diary in 1920 Isaac Babel similarly reflected on the face of a bearded scholarly old man as a synecdoche, or a code, for the world of East European Jewry: "Their faces: This is the ghetto, and we are an ancient people, exhausted but we still have some strength left. . . . They are like portraits, elongated, silent, long-bearded."[53] The whole first chapter of *The Face of East European Jewry* is populated by, and indeed written to accompany, a variety of images of these faces (figures 5.3., 5.4, and 5.5).[54]

Roman Vishniac, arriving in Berlin in 1920, had more in common with the native German Jewish population, from the standpoint of his education and level of assimilation, than with the East European Jewish masses that many of the German Jews reviled. At the height of a general fascination with typological portraiture, he seems to have adopted, aesthetically, a German photographic sensitivity to human

FIGURE 5.3 Hermann Struck, Old Man I, from Arnold Zweig, *The Face of East European Jewry*, edited, translated, and with an introduction by Noah Isenberg (Berkeley: University of California Press, 2004).

FIGURE 5.4 Hermann Struck, Old Man II, from Arnold Zweig, *The Face of East European Jewry*, edited, translated, and with an introduction by Noah Isenberg (Berkeley: University of California Press, 2004).

FIGURE 5.5 Hermann Struck, Old Man III, from Arnold Zweig, *The Face of East European Jewry*, edited, translated, and with an introduction by Noah Isenberg (Berkeley: University of California Press, 2004).

physiognomy as representative of something much greater than the individual countenance. Indeed, in much of his unpublished work, newly exhibited within the last few years at the International Center of Photography, we see the influence of this kind of photographic aesthetic particularly in his Berlin street photography. At the height of German Jewish attempts to fight assimilation he realized, perhaps, that as an East European Jew himself he had a certain kind of intimate access to the very population that was being, at that very moment, so highly valorized. His photographs were the photographic equivalent, perhaps, of Struck's drawings (compare figure 5.6 and figure 5.7).[55] But even more interesting is that the juncture of physiognomic, typologizing portraits and praise for their photographic subjects introduced by Struck and Zweig in *The Face of East European Jewry* seems to have been adopted over time by Vishniac in subsequent publications and republications of his 1930s photographs of East European Jews.

Not only did Vishniac ultimately echo the style of Struck and Zweig's portrait essay and turn it into a photographic essay by infusing

FIGURE 5.6 Hermann Struck, *Old Man IV*, from Arnold Zweig, *The Face of East European Jewry*, edited, translated, and with an introduction by Noah Isenberg (Berkeley: University of California Press, 2004).

FIGURE 5.7 Roman Vishniac, [Man standing in the entrance of Samuel Rubin's mixed goods store, Teresva], 1935–38. © Mara Vishniac Kohn, courtesy International Center of Photography.

his photographs with words, but he also enhanced the element of valorization in Struck and Zweig's project. As German Jews exploring their Jewish heritage through the figure of the East European Jew, Struck and Zweig idealized the Jew through language and image. Vishniac participated in this discourse as a photographer recently arrived from Eastern Europe himself. Influenced by the general German Jewish ethos surrounding East European Jews as part of the cult of the *Ostjude*, his poetics were grounded in an acknowledgment of the simultaneous "otherness" and "desirability" of the world of East European Jewry.

The JDC commission to document that world in something of an anthropological light, therefore, can be seen at the very inception of those images in the 1930s—not strictly because of their impending demise, as Vishniac later indicates in his account of the project after the Holocaust. Rather, he was inspired and motivated in part by his own experience as an East European Jew with a Western European Jewish sensibility, in dialogue with Western Jews seeking out the East buried deep within themselves. As in a typical salvage poetic configuration, what we see here is the creation of an archive of salvage artifacts—the documentary photographs commissioned by the JDC to represent a world already in decline before the war for fundraising purposes in the United States and Western Europe—that were to be mobilized and repurposed in the post-Holocaust era as part of a movement to salvage and memorialize the destroyed world of East European Jewry.[56] The auto-ethnographic salvage that I document here in Vishniac's rhetoric and in his reframing of this particular set of JDC photographs articulates an important moment in the formation of a salvage poetic: the balancing of documentary with anthropological impulses by placing the self into the frames. Vishniac claims these subjects as intrinsic to his own history as an act of salvage. He recognizes the faces of his own ancestors in his photographic subjects as a means of bridging a series of gaps—between the Old World and the New World, the pre- and post-Holocaust eras, the East and the West. The implications in these photographs, as presented in his framing of them, bring them closer to his audience, thereby increasing their exigency and their impact.

In one of the first reviews of *Polish Jews*, we see a hint of the delicate balance between the ethnographic and the personal that Vishniac may have felt he had to confront. In 1947 in *The New Yorker* under "general" books, Edmund Wilson writes:

> An album of photographs, taken a year before the war in Europe, of Orthodox Jews living, working, going to school, and worshipping in the ghettos of Poland, Ruthenia, and Lithuania.[57] The book is a pitiful record of a people and of a centuries-old way of life now irrevocably gone. The photographs are beautiful; they are un-posed and many of them are reminiscent of the paintings by the Dutch and Flemish masters of the seventeenth century.[58]

Similarly framed by a brief introduction in its frontispiece, *Polish Jews* is presented in the following way:

> In [1935–]1938 on the eve of the Second World War, Roman Vishniac traveled from the Baltic Sea to the Carpathian Mountains photographing the Jewish communities of Eastern Europe. The Jews of Eastern Europe—we call them "Polish Jews" in our title, for reasons of cultural (not physical) geography—were at that time only a year distant from catastrophe. The collection

of photographs that Roman Vishniac brought back constitute the last pictorial record of the life and character of these people. From this wealth of material, thirty-one photographs were selected for this book, not merely because of their aesthetic value, but because they make up together one great portrait of a life abjectly poor in its material condition, and in its spiritual condition, exaltedly religious.[59]

In the book itself, Vishniac is featured as the photographer of these doomed people. In *The New Yorker* review, however, his name is not even mentioned. The photos are treated almost entirely from an ethnographic and aesthetic perspective, situating them at the juncture of witness to a lost world and seventeenth-century portraiture. This erasure of the photographer and absolute focus on the photographs' ethnographic value can be read in strict counterpoint to the intensely personal framing of these photographs, as presented in layers of captions accompanying them in subsequent publications.[60]

In 1971 Vishniac was one of several photographers featured in a series called *The Concerned Photographer* and coedited by Cornell Capa and Michael Edelson. The purpose of the series was to serve as an "antidote to the accepted bland notion equating the objectivity of a photographic image with dispassionate neutrality."[61] In introductory remarks, Cornell Capa articulates his vision for *The Concerned Photographer* as a forum for humanism in photography. Vishniac's familiar selection of JDC photographs are interspersed with examples from his photomicroscopy, a photographic technique using polarized light, developed by Vishniac in order to capture the beauty of microorganisms in their minutest details without disturbing them or their natural habitat. A photo representing the surface of his own skin is magnified 200 times (figure 5.8), and a photograph of anthrax bacillus is magnified 2,250 times.[62] Facing the anthrax bacillus is a familiar photo of a grandfather and granddaughter engaged in conversation, which is included in both *Polish Jews* and *A Vanished World* (figure 5.9).[63] Preceding the image of the skin is a famous image of a little girl stuck in bed all winter for lack of shoes, with the flowers her father painted for her to look at on the wall behind her (figure 5.10).

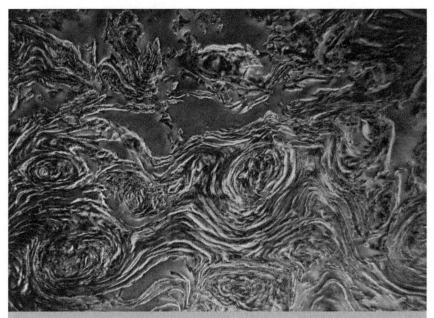

FIGURE 5.8 Roman Vishniac, [Cross section of skin from Roman Vishniac's Thumb]. © Mara Vishniac Kohn, courtesy International Center of Photography.

The juxtaposition of Vishniac's photomicroscopy with his images of East European Jews is summed up in the editorial comments made by Michael Edelson as follows:

> This is the relationship of . . . Roman Vishniac and the many worlds around him: the big ones and the small ones; the pretty ones and the ugly ones; the obvious ones and the deeply hidden ones that only a camera and a lens can uncover for they are invisible to the naked mind and eye of man.[64]

In an earlier statement, Cornell Capa remarks that Vishniac "searches for and finds the essence of the world and man who inhabits it."[65] The common discourse among Edelson, Capa, and Vishniac himself as each one reflects on Vishniac's career is that he seeks out the hidden, and through his photographs he renders visible the invisible, be it microorganisms or human beings. The fact that a magnification of his own skin appears beside his East European subjects may, not

FIGURE 5.9 Roman Vishniac, *Grandfather and granddaughter, Warsaw*, ca. 1935–38. © Mara Vishniac Kohn, courtesy International Center of Photography.

too subtly, return us to our contention that Vishniac's photographic work with East European Jewry before the war was, to a large extent, an exploration of his own East European origins within a West European exile. He was, in other words, exploring what he presents as his own history, identifying himself with the subjects of his photographs even while maintaining a comfortable distance from them.

Elie Wiesel's foreword to *A Vanished World* maps out the complicated dance that defines the auto-ethnographic salvage poetic evident in Vishniac's work. A close friend of Vishniac, Wiesel reads the man behind the pictures into each and every one of Vishniac's photographs, saying of him, "It is always the man who is revealed in

FIGURE 5.10 Roman Vishniac, [Sara, sitting in a basement dwelling, with stenciled flowers above Her head, Warsaw], ca. 1935–37. © Mara Vishniac Kohn, courtesy International Center of Photography.

his work."[66] And it is the man behind the pictures, telling the story in each picture, who, through the narrative, comes to be a figure within. In an engaging rhetorical move Wiesel positions himself as a child and Vishniac as a photographer coming through his town, "Dear Roman Vishniac, where did we first meet? Somewhere in the Carpathians, a timid Jewish boy waved you away for it was dangerous for an outsider to venture along the brink of the abyss: was that me? Was that you?"[67] What does Wiesel mean when he says that he could imagine himself waving Vishniac away because it was dangerous to venture along the brink of the abyss? Is he somehow waving the photographer away from the world of Jews, which is soon to be destroyed, as if Vishniac himself is immune to destruction, despite being a Jew? Here Wiesel pulls Vishniac into his own company as an artisan of words—"sometimes I think I prefer the storyteller in him to the photographer"—insisting that Vishniac's photographs are the equivalent of storytelling, but at the same time he is pushing Vishniac out of his circle, denying him a role as a subject of the photographs, by insisting that such a man should steer clear of the "abyss," whatever that abyss may be.

Just as he reads Vishniac into each picture while denying him the right to be read in, Wiesel reads Vishniac's complex relationship to the Holocaust into each picture:

> A supreme witness, Vishniac evokes with sorrow and with love this picturesque and fascinating Jewish world he has seen engulfed by fire and darkness. . . . He loves them because the world they live in did not, and because death has already marked them for its own—death and oblivion as well.[68]

This statement turns out to be a prime moment of simultaneous inclusion and exclusion as well. Wiesel casts Vishniac as a prophet of the Holocaust who steers clear of it: "Someday he will tell us about the looted sanctuaries, the wreckage of prayer, the desolation he had foreseen, had seen before taking it with him in his camera to entrust to us for safekeeping."[69] Wiesel sees the Holocaust in every picture not because Vishniac took pictures of the Holocaust, but because he responds to Vishniac's articulation of his own awareness of the impending event. While we know that Vishniac was commissioned to take the photographs by the JDC for documentary purposes and was not moved to do so independently through some kind of prophetic inspiration, this dialogue between Wiesel and Vishniac opens up for us a key mechanism of salvage poetics. Because the JDC commission already acknowledged the decline of that world during the interwar period, after its cataclysmic demise in the Holocaust that acknowledgment grew in dimension, becoming a kind of prophecy. In *Night*, in fact, Wiesel employs a rhetoric of prophecy in the character of Madame Shechter, who "saw" the flames of Auschwitz, who "anticipated" the genocide before arriving at the concentration camp on the train.[70] Vishniac's prophecy, borne of the same impulse of hindsight, based on the original intention of his JDC commission, is not so contrived within the context of salvage poetics, wherein engagement with future calamity is embedded in the effort to salvage a lost past. Even so, Wiesel calls on Vishniac to enter, as it were, the concentrationary universe—the universe of the Holocaust with its alternative reality, its alternative sense of morality and time, even while pushing him out. Wiesel insists on Vishniac not yet having depicted the event itself as a way of qualifying what it is that Vishniac actually was able to capture. "Who can resist the lure of the past?" he asks.[71] But it is really the future that Wiesel honors Vishniac for—the future of the photographic subjects as victims-to-be that somehow Vishniac anticipated and thus motivated him to take the photographs.

Skating between binary oppositions—the past of the present, the future of the past, language and image, insider and outsider, Wiesel extols Vishniac's intimate encounter with the world lost in the Holocaust. But Wiesel, not so subtly, insists that we recognize the incommensurability of that loss. Vishniac has not captured the Holocaust, and he is not a writer, and he is not a Jew from the Carpathian Mountains. Wiesel issues a call to battle, which determines the direction of this volume. He demands a justification, an affiliation from Vishniac. In his complicated web of captions and myths and words, Vishniac figuratively rises to that call.

Taken metaphorically as a response to Wiesel's challenge to him, throughout *A Vanished World*, Vishniac refigures himself as a participant observer. The ethnographic conceit works well here because, as a photographer, Vishniac is necessarily on the outside looking in, but as an East European Jew having spent nineteen years in Germany at the height of the cult of the *Ostjude* he is accustomed as well to emblematizing the desirable "outsider," the East European Jew so close to the heart of the spiritually bereft, assimilated German Jew, and yet so culturally far away. In truth, as we have discussed, Vishniac was a far cry from the type of the *Ostjude* prevalent in Germany during the interwar period. And yet, throughout his commentary on the photographs in *A Vanished World*, he continuously presents himself as one of his subjects, through intimate encounters with them narrated in his captions. The salvage poetic that Vishniac crafts in *A Vanished World* is a poetic of both being there and not being there, of observing a world from its margins, and yet making pronouncements about that world's essential character, like an ethnographer or a "participant observer."

Image 20 of *A Vanished World* gives us a background on Jewish Poland prior to the war and begins a thread on Vishniac's place within the photographed landscape: "an economic boycott of Poland's three and a half million Jews occurred in the late 1930s."[72] The worried couple featured in this photograph were apparently victims of this boycott (figure 5.11). Vishniac explains how he knows this: "After I took this picture of the obviously worried couple, I followed them, introduced myself . . . and inquired about their problem . . . (why was I there, at that moment?)"[73] This parenthetical reflection—"why was I there, at that moment?"—serves as an interesting introduction to the role he will cast himself in throughout this commentary. In his commentary on images 27 and 28, both of porters, Vishniac talks about how the boycott forced many Jews into that occupation: "Even though their task was menial and their life hard, they never forgot their traditions and their heritage" (figures 5.12 and 5.13).[74] In his large leap from his own desire to grasp the contemporary experience of the Jewish porters to his assertion about their loyalty to Jewish tradition, Vishniac flirts with his role as participant observer in taking these photographs: someone familiar with their religious beliefs and their practices and not just an outsider viewing what appears to be their economic distress. Again emphasizing his personal connection to a photograph,

FIGURE 5.11 Roman Vishniac, *Jewish couple, Warsaw*, ca. 1935–38. © Mara Vishniac Kohn, courtesy International Center of Photography.

Vishniac in a later comment describes an intimate glimpse into the sleeping quarters of twenty-six families living in a basement apartment: "I learned about the heroic endurance of my brethren."[75] With the porter, identified by Vishniac in his captions as Nat Gutman, Vishniac presents himself more as a native informant than a participant observer. In image 29 we see the meager porter's meal of dry bread that Gutman and his wife "shared" with Vishniac (figures 5.14, 5.15, and 5.16). A rhetoric of participation, of sharing, of commiseration creates an impression of participant observation and auto-ethnography. This is further enhanced by a narrative of return that is fostered in later presentations of Vishniac's work, documenting his postwar return to Europe.

After the war, in 1947, Vishniac returned to Europe on a final JDC commission along with a United Jewish Appeal (UJA) commission and a *Forward* commission in order to document the lives of Jewish refugees and Jews in displaced persons camps. In captions written

FIGURE 5.12 Roman Vishniac, *A member of an artel of Jewish Porters, Warsaw*, ca. 1935–38. © Mara Vishniac Kohn, courtesy International Center of Photography.

posthumously by employees of the ICP archive, these images are presented as part of a narrative of return. While he himself did not author these captions, nor did he publish these photographs during his lifetime, the narrative of return presented here is a natural extension of the narrative of return implied in the photographic collections he himself created. While what empowered Vishniac to take these pictures in the first place was his status as an outsider with the means and mobility to document the life of a people stymied by poverty and politics, he becomes an insider "returning" to the place where the

FIGURE 5.13 Roman Vishniac, *Licenses for members of the artel of Jewish porters, Warsaw*, ca. 1935–38. © Mara Vishniac Kohn, courtesy International Center of Photography.

photographs were taken, an "in situ" native informant. His act of having photographed them positions him, after the war, as one of them—a survivor plucked from their ranks. What are the implications of this dynamic change in his status? Vishniac struggles to represent this world from every perspective: that of an insider, that of an outsider, that of someone who was there with them when they had not yet been murdered, and that of someone who survived the killing machine in order to tell the tale of their death.

In the introductory blurb to the commentary that precedes the photographs in *A Vanished World*, Vishniac casts himself in a very

FIGURE 5.15 Roman Vishniac, *The meager meal of a porter's family, Warsaw*, ca. 1935–38. © Mara Vishniac Kohn, courtesy International Center of Photography.

FIGURE 5.16 Roman Vishniac, *Porter Nat Gutman, Warsaw*, ca. 1935–38. © Mara Vishniac Kohn, courtesy International Center of Photography.

special light vis-à-vis his subjects. "Why did I do it?" he asks. He answers by asserting that the narrative he is about to write is a more essential testament to his photographic subjects than the photographs themselves. Because the people in the photographs no longer exist, it is only his narrative on the photographs that will make the photographs meaningful: "If I am to breathe life into the pictures that follow, it is by providing you, the reader, with my thoughts about them. The pictures depict people and places that no longer exist, yet in my memory they do exist."[76] One of the most interesting aspects of this rhetoric is that Vishniac doesn't seem to believe that his photographs are sufficiently representative of the "vanished world" they are connected with. Only he can make them representative, in language. This is in direct contrast to the way that the photographs themselves carry the narrative forward in *Polish Jews*, which shares so many of the same images (albeit a much smaller selection) as *A Vanished World*, but preceded it by nearly forty years.

Since the very birth of the medium of photography, its claims to realism have been undermined. Walter Benjamin famously discusses the "optical unconscious" in which, despite the proliferation of images "in the age of mechanical reproduction," that which is captured by the camera in the moment of the shutter's click is never to be reproduced by the acting subject of the photograph and never to have been witnessed before.[77] The camera immortalizes the fleeting, not the permanent, captures at times an expression or a gesture unrecognizable even to the subject himself or herself, or to the photographer beholding the subject. On a historical level, that optical unconscious can create a glimpse of merely a moment, not an era, or a shadow, but certainly not a "world." Over the course of the last century, Benjamin and countless other theorists of photography have articulated that while photography was conceived as a precise alternative to the approximate art of painting, over time photographs have come to be viewed in quite a different light. Photographs, because of their aspirations toward the real, are, in fact, far more suspect, far more deceptive than media that do not pretend to channel the actual.

According to Victor Burgin, "photography is invaded by language ... we rarely see a photograph in use which is not accompanied by language."[78] W. J. T. Mitchell invokes James Agee's statement in the introduction to *Let Us Now Praise Famous Men* (quoted in the previous chapter), documenting the lives of impoverished tenant farmers during the Great Depression: "the photographs are not illustrative. They and the text are coequal, mutually independent and fully collaborative."[79] According to Mitchell, in contrast to the "sort of rhetorical reinforcement and repetition" evident in more conventional photo essays, *Let Us Now Praise Famous Men* "resists" a clear-cut "rhetorical relation" between photo and text. Contemporary literary texts, most notably W. G. Sebald's *Austerlitz* (2001) or Ronit Matalon's *The One Facing Us* (1995), serve as novelistic variations on the simultaneous independence and symbiosis of photo and text described by Mitchell in his reading of *Let Us Now Praise Famous Men*.[80] The works display a unique synergy created by the coupling of an image and a text, often at odds with one another, or at the very least in a dialectical or a dialogic relationship.

Do the auto-ethnographic captions Vishniac writes go so far as to work against the images in the photographs themselves? To my mind, Vishniac's account of his own participation in the moments he captures on film only enhances them. Vishniac is trying to draw an auto-ethnographic portrait, a portrait of a culture through a portrait of himself. With the help of photographs and a succession of accompanying texts, Vishniac successfully mobilizes the particular salvage poetic features of the photographs he took for the JDC before the Holocaust in order to foster the creation of a popular ethnography of pre-Holocaust East European Jewish life among American post-Holocaust audiences.

The fact that Vishniac's extensive captions were largely written in the postwar period raises the very important specter of a time lag in our apprehension of salvage poetics. Jean Muhr and John Berger discuss, at some length, the way in which "photographs have been taken out of a continuity. If the event is a public event, this continuity is history; if it is personal, the continuity which has been broken is a life story."[81] Furthermore, they assert that

> a photograph arrests the flow of time in which the event photographed once existed. All photographs are of the past, yet in them an instant of the past is arrested so that, unlike a lived past, it can never lead to the present. Every photograph presents us with two messages: a message concerning the event photographed and another concerning a shock of discontinuity.[82]

In other words, it is important to acknowledge, in our salvage poetic reading of Vishniac, that we consider a single historical event (the Holocaust) as a crucial factor in the deployment of salvage poetics—the event that translates the original documentary impulse into a folk ethnographic consciousness. Yet it is also critical to remember that the photograph, as argued above by Berger and Muhr, removes the subject from a historical continuum. Perhaps the photograph is the one medium that transcends the very historical event that motivates it and defines it. The photograph, taken before the event of the Holocaust with or without a consciousness of the impending event, is only contextualized in terms of the Holocaust by the narratives surrounding it. Thus the photograph exists outside the flow of time and is only placed into time by the language contextualizing it. For purposes of understanding Vishniac's project of framing and reframing, layering and re-layering texts around his photographs over a period of about forty years, it is important that we maintain a sense of the privilege afforded him by the very medium of the photograph, to pluck it out of real time and impose on it his own particular sense of the real.

In *What Do Pictures Want?*, W. J. T. Mitchell discusses how people have historically believed that images possess a kind of magical vitality, a kind of mythical "vagueness" that governs our sense of their role in our lives. The example he gives of this vitality is that very few people believe that a photograph of their mother is actually their mother.[83] Nevertheless very few people would be willing to deface a photograph of their mother or poke out the eyes of their mother in a photograph. Drawing on Barthes's theory of the "punctum" and the "studium," in which the studium is the rational, the linear, the historicizable aspect of a photograph, whereas the punctum is the "wound" left by the photograph—the aspect of the photograph that contains the photograph's vital center and that communicates its magical and mythical vital essence to some of its viewers—Mitchell proposes that we consider the "desire" of photographs and try to understand what they "want" from their viewers.[84] Answering this question, Mitchell asserts, forces us to acknowledge the continuing potency of the notion that photographs are somehow magical or vitalistic.

The photograph constitutes, as Berger and Muhr articulate, "a resistance to history, an opposition to history" by virtue of it being "more traumatic than most memories or mementos because it seems to confirm, prophetically, the later discontinuity created by absence or death." Indeed the powers to prophesy and to instill trauma, the power to confirm absence or fill in discontinuities, are all implicit in the kinds of narrative license Vishniac took in his presentation of his 1930s photographs of East European Jews. In the particular narratives told by pre-Holocaust photographs in a post-Holocaust world, I would argue that magic is the dominant force, turning documentary photos into auto-ethnographic ones that illuminate an entire era for popular audiences.

This magic is not irrational. Rather, it is cultural. Roman Vishniac, a Russian Jew, found himself in Berlin in the 1930s, having left a few years after the Russian Revolution and following his wealthy industrialist Jewish family, who escaped during the upheaval. He was commissioned to take photographs by the Joint Distribution Committee as part of a campaign to raise consciousness about Jewish poverty in Eastern Europe during the interwar period and to solicit donations to aid in their immigration to the United States. In dialogue with works such as Arnold Zweig and Hermann Struck's *The Face of East European Jewry* as well as August Sander's *Faces of the Age*, he sought, from the very beginning of his photographic undertaking, to address a fascination with and typologization of East European Jewish faces through photography. In the aftermath of the Holocaust, Vishniac's project became less documentary and more auto-ethnographic in so far as he sought to insert himself, through his narratives, into the photographs that came increasingly to identify the world of European Jews over the next several decades. The simultaneous forces of assimilation and dissimilation, of the valorization and demonization characteristic of German responses to East European Jewish immigration during the period between the two world wars, all find their way into the continuing story of Vishniac's personal journey through the landscapes and lives he photographed in the years immediately before the Holocaust. Vishniac's captions and narratives, when considered in an increasingly auto-ethnographic light, illuminate a critical stage in the creation of a folk ethnography of pre-Holocaust East European Jewish life in the post-Holocaust period. They tell the story of a particular brand of salvage poetics, rooted in documentary, cultivated in a rejection of Jewish assimilation, and coming to full fruition in a post-cataclysmic moment that sought an easily accessible panorama of a "vanished world" in the construction of a new, American-Jewish, post-Holocaust ethnic reality.

6

PATRONYMIC SALVAGE

Daughters in Search of Their Fathers

> I was named after my great-grandfather Mayer Makhl Gut-makher. Everybody in town had a nickname. Mine was Mayer *tamez*, Mayer July, because July was the hottest month of the year. Mayer *tamez* means Crazy Mayer. People get excited when it is hot, and I was an excitable kid. I was always on the go. I was very smart and very hyperactive. Of course, they wouldn't call me Mayer *tamez* to my face. They were afraid to do that. There were a bunch of Mayers. So to tell them apart, each had a nickname. Which Mayer do you want? Mayer *tamez*? Mayer *treyger*, Mayer the Porter? Or Mayer *droybe*, Mayer the Goose Carcass?[1]

In the first paragraph of *They Called Me Mayer July: Painted Memories of a Jewish Childhood in Poland before the Holocaust* (2007), a visual and verbal account of Mayer Kirshenblatt's life in Apt, Poland, between the world wars, he explains his given name, his nickname, and the nicknames of all the other Mayers in his town. He seems to be saying that not being masters of our own names is what makes us a member of a family and a community; we are named by others who in that act of naming help us to define not only our identities but their own as well. How you name others is, perhaps, even more important an indication of who you are, than what you are named, because as someone who names others you are an agent, whereas when you are named, you may or may not live up to the expectations established in the name given to you.

Names and naming also appeared briefly in chapter 2 of this study of salvage poetics as we considered the different types of characters appearing in the Hasidic tales Heschel used in *The Earth Is the Lord's*. Some stories were rendered with anonymous subjects or "types," while others functioned as hagiographies, detailing the wonders of particular rabbis' teachings or lives. In this exploration of two daughters' search for their fathers in collections of those fathers' visual art, we will expand this distinction between the named and the unnamed in order to wrap up our discussion of salvage poetics. Our exploration in this chapter of the father's name, or the father's nickname, as the case may be, will shed light on our earlier discussions regarding the nature of the arti- facts used in hybrid texts to represent and explain pre-Holocaust East European Jewish life in the post-Holocaust era, the interplay between being an insider and an outsider that is so essential to representing a lost culture, and finally the relationship between ethnographic and aesthetic discourses on pre-Holocaust East European Jewish life during the post-Holocaust era in America. We will be focusing on two image books—*They Called Me Mayer July*, whose images are paintings, and *Poyln: Jewish Life in the Old Country*, which uses photographs—that operate simultaneously as "family albums" and as "ethnic albums." These books emphasize both the individual and familial identity of the artist whose work constitutes the aesthetic "artifact" at the album's center and the ethnic community represented in the album's subject matter.

Why do I read each of these albums as constituting both a family and an ethnic album? On the one hand, they are inspired, coauthored, or edited by the artists' daughters, and they both grapple, in different but complementary ways with issues around naming their fathers. Yet, even as they identify their own fathers in and around the images in the albums, each daughter acknowledges the inevitable anonymity per- taining to visual subjects captured just before a cataclysmic event and observed by strangers after it—not every person in every image can be named, as they can in a family album. But within the genre of post-Holocaust image books used to focalize the American Jewish sense of community and history, these photo albums occupy a familiar, ethnic place despite the anonymity of some images.

As our exploration of salvage poetics draws to a close, we will focus in this chapter on the two books that inspired this project to a large extent: the first book a collection of paintings made by Mayer Kirshenblatt in the 1990s, and the second a collection of photos taken by Alter Kacyzne in Poland throughout the 1920s.

In *They Called Me Mayer July*, the images of paintings are accompanied by ethnographic essays that Kirshenblatt wrote in collaboration with his daughter Barbara Kirshenblatt-Gimblett in what has been called, by Barbara Myerhoff, a "third voice." This voice is created, in Myerhoff's words, "when two points of view are engaged in examining one life."[2] Neither wholly the informant's nor the anthropologist's, but a combination of the two, the "third voice" attempts to articulate the experience of the telling as part of the portrait being drawn.

Kacyzne took the photographs in *Poyln: Jewish Life in the Old Country* (1999) for two American institutions, the Hebrew Immigrant Aid Society (HIAS) and *The Jewish Daily Forward*. An aspiring writer and the proprietor of a renowned photography studio in Warsaw, Kacyzne was killed in the Jewish cemetery of Tarnopol, Ukraine, on July 7, 1941, along with five thousand Tarnopol Jews as he fled Lvov; his last moments were witnessed by a survivor of the massacre, the poet Nakhman Blitz, and documented by him in an article he published in *Dos Naye Lebn* in 1945.[3] Kacyzne's wife, Hannah, was killed in Belzec, and his only survivor was his daughter, Sulamita Kacyzne-Reale.[4] *Poyln*, which was edited by YIVO historian Marek Web, was published with Sulamita's encouragement, as cited by Web in his acknowledgments:

> Sulamita Kacyzne-Reale, Alter Kacyzne's daughter, spared no time or effort to keep YIVO's interest in the project alive. Just as she worked tirelessly to preserve and publish her father's literary output, Mrs. Kacyzne-Reale never ceased encouraging YIVO to make his photographic masterworks available in a single

volume. Thus the appearance of this book in print is largely the result of her efforts on behalf of Alter Kacyzne and his creative legacy, although, sadly, she passed away a few months prior to publication and so did not see the fruit of her labors.[5]

Kacyzne's photographic images are omnipresent in the literature of East European photo books that have flourished between 1945 to the present, perhaps even more so than Vishniac's. They also appear in the backdrop to films about the region and the interwar era, and, attributed or unattributed, on countless websites.[6] One even appears on the cover of the film adaptation of *Image before My Eyes*, which we discussed briefly in chapter 4. By Web's account, YIVO ultimately decided to put his photographs together in a single volume due to Kacyzne's daughter's persistence.

The artifacts at the heart of the salvage endeavors represented in this chapter, the photographs in one book and paintings in the other, differ in their vintage: the photographs were produced before the Holocaust, while the paintings were produced long after. But in *They Called Me Mayer July* the paintings are presented as the product of Mayer Kirshenblatt's memories of pre-Holocaust Apt, as the book's subtitle, "Painted Memories of a Jewish Childhood in Poland before the Holocaust," suggests. Therefore, we will consider the "artifacts" that form the basis of *They Called Me Mayer July* to be both the pre-Holocaust memories that inspired Kirshenblatt's paintings and the ethnographic narrative that he and his daughter developed in their collaboration. The paintings and the ethnographic narrative surrounding them in this book are the frame, similar to the other salvage framings that we have observed throughout this study. Considering memories as artifacts may be a bit of a stretch, but they are rendered concrete—by this process of basing his paintings on them, which is central to the ethnographic project his daughter oversees—and therefore compatible with the other artifacts we have discussed throughout this study.

Both *They Called Me Mayer July* and *Poyln* use their selected "artifacts" to create combined ethnic and familial albums. Mayer Kirshenblatt's fixation on and fascination with nicknames is a product of his memories of the Old Country, which his daughter, editor, and catalyst for the project, Barbara Kirshenblatt-Gimblett, mobilizes to create simultaneously an ethnic and a familial account of both her father's early life and the pre-Holocaust culture of Apt. Names and naming as a means of transforming an ethnic into a familial album also play a significant role in our understanding of *Poyln: Jewish Life in the Old Country*. Sulamita Kacyzne-Reale has to make do with the only photographs that survived the war—those her father sent to HIAS and *The Forward*—in creating *Poyln*, even though her father was among the best-known photographers in Jewish Warsaw and undoubtedly took many prewar pictures of his small, young family. *Poyln*, then, seems to be Sulamita Kacyzne-Reale's best effort to come up with a family album. Her father may not be the subject of the photographs that serve as salvage artifacts, but his was the eye behind the viewfinder and the aspirational literary voice behind the captions. At the same time, Web, the book's editor, frames it as a study of geography and language, catapulting it into the realm of the ethnic album. Therefore, we will read this book simultaneously as an attempt to re-create the voice and vision of the man Alter Kacyzne, so violently murdered along with the culture of pre-Holocaust East European Jewry, and an attempt to represent the culture itself, through his photographs.

From its very choice of title (*Poyln* is the Yiddish inflection of Poland), Web frames the book as a glimpse into Yiddishland—the supra-territorial and meta-historical construct unified by the Yiddish language.[7] The book begins with a statement about the Yiddish language:

> In Alter Kacyzne's lifetime, Poland was home to 3.1 million Jews, almost all of whom spoke Yiddish. Indeed, in a 1931 census 80 percent of Polish Jews declared Yiddish their mother tongue. And to them Poland was Poyln, Warsaw was Varshe, Krakow was Kroke; the picturesque town of Kazimierz on the river Vistula was Kuzmir oyf der Vaysl; and the little hamlet Zczieciol—for no apparent reason—was known as Zhetl. One story has it that when a Viennese Jew asked a Galician Jew the name of the city their train was passing through, the Galitsiyaner said, "The Gentiles say Rzeszow, but the whole world calls it Rayshe."[8]

Like the *Galitsiyaner* in the above vignette, *Poyln*, in Web's framing of it, seeks to present a portrait, through Kacyzne's photographs, of a single world, united by the Yiddish language. Sulamita's quest for her father's vision and voice throughout *Poyln* is counterbalanced by YIVO's quest for a portrait of *Poyln*. Rather than seeing the two in conflict, however, when considering the volume in terms of the salvage poetics that can help transform a family album into an ethnic album and vice versa, we can see the two forces working symbiotically.

In a discussion of Hasidic photo books published in the second half of the twentieth century, Jack Kugelmass suggests that ethnic photo books are a key ingredient of auto- or folk ethnography, created by laypeople who seek to better understand themselves in relation to a collective past.[9] In analyzing *They Called Me Mayer July* alongside *Poyln*, I offer an expansion of the photo-book genre that Kugelmass presents, and suggest that we consider not just photographs but also paintings in light of the kind of folk ethnography practiced by American Jews. In this discussion, I will categorize both book types as "image books."

John Szarkowski has argued that "the central act of photography is the act of choosing and eliminating, it forces a concentration on the picture's edge, the line that separates 'in' from 'out' and on the shapes created by it."[10] How an image book is framed, therefore, is essential to its status as a family or an ethnic album, or a hybrid of the two. Szarkowski's observation about what "separates 'in' from 'out'" should now be a familiar aspect of salvage poetics, as we have observed the lengths to which different authors will go in order to assert their sense of ownership over, or alienation from, the artifacts they are framing, as they attempt to produce a portrait of East European Jewry in the aftermath of its destruction.

Emphasizing his status as an outsider rather than an insider, Mayer Kirshenblatt goes out of his way to remind us that he is actually outside of the world he paints and narrates. At key moments in *They Called Me Mayer July* he reminds us that what he is painting is from the perspective of a child: "The places I remember exist no more. They are only in my head, and if I die they will disappear with me. I paint these scenes as I remember them as a little boy looking through the window."[11] Kirshenblatt is telling us here not only of the temporal distance between him and his painted memories, but also of the distance that cataclysm has imposed between him and the landscape of those memories. There is no way to confirm the places or scenes that populate his memory, and subsequently his paintings, because they were destroyed in World War II. Indeed, both he and his daughter describe returning to Apt only to find that the buildings of his childhood, notably his grandmother's house, are no longer there. Most interesting, however, is his metaphorical observation that he is looking through a window at the scenes he depicts, thereby articulating the fact that he feels, quite explicitly, like an outsider looking in.

Kirshenblatt is very clear about what he does and does not know as a result of having left Apt before the war, in 1934. But although he did experience as a child many of the things he remembers, the fact of his pre-Holocaust emigration from Apt distances him and makes him feel like a child looking through a window. In the book's introduction, he valorizes his status as someone who did not live through the war, because it enables him to look beyond the war and remember the destroyed world as it had existed before:

> In the steam room at the gym or in a corner of the health club, I'd get together with my buddies. Most of the people there are Holocaust survivors. Within five or ten minutes of any conversation, whether the topic was politics, women, this or that, we would be back in the concentration camps, on the march, in the railroad cars, in the bush with the partisans. It was as if there was no life before the war, so overshadowed had their memories become by the pain they suffered. I lost many members of my family in the Holocaust, but God spared me from living through that horror myself. He also blessed me with a wonderful memory.[12]

Kirshenblatt's sense of being an outsider is fostered by his distance from the world he describes, both in terms of his experiences as a non–Holocaust survivor and the temporal distance between his immigration and the present moment in which he produces his paintings.

On the other hand, throughout *Poyln*, Alter Kacyzne's sense of being an outsider grows out of the contrast between his identity as an aspiring writer and secular Jew working and living in a major metropolitan setting and the provincial communities he visited and documented. Commissioned by HIAS in 1921 and the *Forward* in 1925, Kacyzne, originally from Vilna, traveled throughout Poland taking pictures of subjects that "may be of interest to the reader in America."[13] Based in Warsaw, where he had a photography studio, and a member of the secular Jewish literary intelligentsia, with close ties to S. Ansky and Y. L. Peretz,[14] Kacyzne was an outsider to the scenes of piety and poverty (in Dawidowicz's terms) for which his photographs were most famous. While he did not shy away from major metropolitan areas, most of the photographs that have survived (because they were sent to New York) focus on scholars, workers, and the impoverished. These were, presumably, the images that the readers of *The Jewish Daily Forward* wanted to see, as they reminded them of why they had immigrated or gave them a sense of their own relative well-being in America.[15] The HIAS photographs were of a similar ilk; commissioned to document the emigration process to America and thereby to garner financial support from American Jews, they exuded poverty.[16]

While he made a successful career of photography, both in his studio and as a correspondent, Alter Kacyzne's great love was writing. Many of his works, fictional and journalistic, were published in Europe, but very few in the United States. He was eager to send feature articles and vignettes to accompany his photographs to Abe Cahan for publication in the *Forward*, but Cahan was not interested. And even though Kacyzne beseeched Cahan to appoint him as the *Forward*'s Soviet Union correspondent, Cahan sent I. J. Singer, Isaac Bashevis's older brother and a well-known Yiddish writer himself. Kacyzne had to settle for clever captions as his channel for literary expression in the *Forward*, and in many instances, even these were altered for publication, to make them more vernacular or "chatty," as Web calls it, and less poetic.[17]

Kacyzne's sense of alienation from his subjects can be felt in an excerpt from correspondence he wrote to Cahan when challenged to explain a request for reimbursement of a travel expense:

> If you think being tossed about along these broken old Polish back roads is such a great pleasure, you're much mistaken. I do

this because I have to look for more material. If I just sat around in Warsaw I'd have no new stuff for you. You seem to be asking me how I get around. Well if I send you photographs from Galicia or Volhynia, it's because I'm there on a lecture tour—I do also happen to be a writer, Comrade Cahan.[18]

It is at this intersection of his being a writer and an inhabitant of Warsaw that we find the crux of Kacyzne's status as an outsider vis-à-vis his subjects. As we discussed in the context of Samuel's adaptations of Peretz and Sholem Aleichem, the modern Jewish writer's task, in the first half of the twentieth century, was to provide access to the traditional Jewish world, but from something of a distance. That distance, that sense of being both an insider and an outsider simultaneously, created the auto-ethnographic effect we have identified: the return of the native son as an observer and an analyst, but no longer a full participant in that world. Kacyzne, as a writer and a photographer, found himself in the same position. Through his viewfinder, Kacyzne is situated between the interests of an American Jewish audience and the impoverished European Jewish populace that American readers were eager to see. Less interesting to them were the intelligentsia, the secular Jews of Europe, the city dwellers, and the business community. Kacyzne found himself in the difficult position of trying to establish a place for himself within the Yiddish literary intelligentsia of Warsaw, while both his writing and his photographs focused on a population he was diligently trying to distance himself from.

Just as Mayer Kirshenblatt introduces himself via his alter ego through his nickname, Mayer *tamez*, Alter Kacyzne's photographic corpus and accompanying captions introduce us to his literary alter ego. In a photograph titled "Starting the Day" in section 2 of *Poyln*, we encounter a scene captured by Kacyzne in 1925 in Tshorkev, Tarnopol province (figure 6.1): In the center of the photo three men sit on packing crates in front of a display window, where foodstuffs and household goods are artfully arranged. To the right of the display window is a metal door, shut. Two of the men, with long white beards and identical black hats, coats, and shoes, are in conversation; one holds a book (not a sacred book, but presumably some kind of journal) in

FIGURE 6.1 Alter Kacyzne (1885–1941), *Tshortkev (Czortków Tarnopol Province)*, 1925, "Tshortkever Jews taking a holiday on Sunday when stores are closed by law." From the Archives of the YIVO Institute for Jewish Research, New York.

his lap, and his face is turned toward his interlocutor who is holding a cane out to his right. A third man, with a shorter and better-trimmed beard, sits slightly above and just behind them. He is more tidily dressed, with the addition of a necktie and a well-fitted long black coat. He leans his elbow on a cane with his cheek on his hand, his mouth slightly open, his face directly facing the camera. To the left of the display window are two posters side by side, one in Polish and one in Yiddish, advertising a literary lecture, in Polish, by "A. Kacizne," and in Yiddish, by "Alter Kacyzne." The lecture's title (on the Yiddish poster) is "Literature: A National Treasure." Kacyzne's caption for the photograph reads: "Tshortkever Jews taking a holiday on Sunday, when stores are closed by law." In this caption he does not allude to the fact that he is the subject of the posters. Web, however, adds a note, in brackets, beneath Kacyzne's caption: "[On the wall is a poster announcing a lecture by A. Kacyzne on the subject, 'Literature—A National Treasure.']"[19]

Kacyzne, a major figure in the modern, secular Yiddish literary community of the interwar period has placed himself into this photograph in that guise. Given his statement in the letter Cahan cited above that he was on a lecture tour while taking photographs for the *Forward*, has he taken this picture to demonstrate to Cahan that he is also a literary figure and not just a photographer? Or perhaps he inserts his name on a poster advertising a literary lecture as a way of signing the photograph for his American viewers, as a writer, knowing that Cahan is reluctant to let him actually write for them.

For a viewer unaware of the photographer's identity, the poster in the background would serve as simply that: background. Perhaps a viewer who could read Yiddish or Polish would be able to deduce something about the town because it hosts literary lectures. But someone unable to decipher either language would simply see two pious, and one slightly less pious, idling older men. As in many of Kacyzne's photographs, the human figure who is spatially front and center is not the image's focal point. Rather, it is often some figure looking around from behind or to the side who draws the viewer's eye. In this image, it is the well-groomed man with the shorter beard sitting slightly behind the other two men. In contrast to the other men in the photograph, in his more modern mien and his more engaged and more solitary presence, he balances the Kacyzne posters on the other side of the image, emphasizing the poster's, and by extension, Kacyzne's centrality to them.

One can imagine that for Sulamita Kacyzne-Reale, her father can be found in each and every one of the volume's image. His is the authorizing eye behind each photo, and it is his viewpoint that attests his existence: What did Kacyzne consider worthy of photographing in his journeys through Poland? How did his particular sensibility as an artist and photographer dictate how Americans viewed East European Jewry for nearly a century? Even more important, perhaps, is whether viewers of these images after the Holocaust considered the photographer's own fate as essential to these images.

Jack Kugelmass has argued:

> Certain types of commercially created photo albums may play a
> role for large collectivities such as ethnic groups much like the
> role played by family albums for extended families. They cele-
> brate group unity in the face of widespread dislocation, they pro-
> voke group memory and they may even contribute to a collective
> dialogue on the nature of group patrimony and the perceived
> problem of cultural attenuation and social fragmentation.[20]

In his discussion of coffee-table photo books, which he views as one of
three important elements of American Jewish folk ethnography (the
other two being tourism and stand-up comedy or humorous writing,
as alluded to in the introduction to this study), Kugelmass echoes discussions of photography by Susan Sontag and Pierre Bourdieau, who
argue that family photographs serve as a means to endow ruptured
social units with a sense of coherence and meaning. They point to the
contemporaneous advent of photography in the nineteenth century
and of industrialization in the West, with its accompanying break-
down of extended-family units.[21] Annette Kuhn theorizes that family albums often become expositions on nuclear families by focusing
on individuals in the bosom of their parents and siblings from birth
through adulthood, while Marianne Hirsch, in her well-known work
on post-memory among the children of Holocaust survivors, has discussed the role of family albums in the creation of a sense of extended
families.[22] For Hirsch, photographs of strangers in her own family
album attest to the family that she once had, but was destroyed in the
war; for her, family albums feature family members who may or may
not be alive but with whom family ties have been severed.[23] In light
of this, it is only one step from "extended-family albums" to communal family albums, because so many extended-family albums contain
photographs of people unknown to the viewer but who, through their
very presence in the album, hold a position of value in forging the
viewer's personal identity. The post-memory that grows out of family
albums, the sense of the self within the broader context of historical
events as they pertain to the individual who didn't experience those

events directly, is precisely where we begin to see the final type of salvage poetic we discuss in this chapter. With their images of known and unknown family members, family albums testify to the place of individuals within a broader collective of belonging. As Barthes has argued, photographs provide "evidential force,"[24] and Sontag has stated that "as photographs give people an imaginary possession of a past that is unreal, they also help people to take possession of space in which they are insecure."[25] I propose here that books like *They Called Me Mayer July* and *Poyln* can serve for American Jews as family and ethnic albums that enable them to consolidate their identities as Jews in the post-Holocaust era. In part this is because these books marry nuclear- and extended-family albums, facilitating a further leap from extended-family album to ethnic album. For purposes of this discussion, I will draw on Kuhn's notion of "memory work" based on family albums that extends the parameters of the family into the broader culture, and Kugelmass's observation that ethnic albums can serve a critical role in the creation of American Jewish folk culture.

The photographs and images in these two books weave a web of interconnections: familial, cultural, historical, personal, and collective. Through the challenge of locating the particular man (Kacyzne) within the broader culture, and the broader culture within the particular man (Kirshenblatt), we experience, writ large, the various impetuses of salvage poetics: first, to appoint aesthetic works as cultural artifacts; second, to identify in fiction, photography, and painting the kind of anecdotal evidence that can be used to both generalize and to specify as a form of cultural "thick description." Third, to tell a story with both a studium and a punctum, the culturally general and the individually specific, the descriptive and the emotive.[26]

I propose that the memory work of American Jews is not based on photographs of them or people they know, but photographs of Jews in the pre-Holocaust period who somehow constitute a part of who they, post-Holocaust American Jews, are—individually as well as collectively. In the absence of other evidence, in the absence of continuity, in the absence of language, how have American Jews reconstructed the past that is so integral to their present? These albums that exist at the border of the familial and the ethnic consolidate a sense of collective identity by presenting a communal family that demonstrates national continuity—despite assimilation and modernization and despite the material, linguistic, and human losses entailed by the Holocaust.

Key to the transformation of ethnic albums into family albums in both *They Called Me Mayer July* and *Poyln* is the very palpable discourse of names in each. In *They Called Me Meyer July*, as alluded to earlier, Mayer Kirshenblatt describes time and again the types of nicknames given to members of his community of origin, reflecting how those nicknames affected their recipients' lives. For example, Malka, the young girl who fell into a soldier's latrine on the outskirts of the town during World War I earned the nickname "Malkaleh Shit" and had a very hard time finding a mate (figure 6.2). Or take the case of Harshl Kishke:

> Harshl Kishke's real name was Harshal Orlan. Kishke is the Yiddish word for intestine or gut and refers also to a delicacy, stuffed derma, which is made by filling a cow's intestine with flour, fat, and spices and roasting it. Why they called him Harshl the Stuffed Intestine, I have no idea.[27]

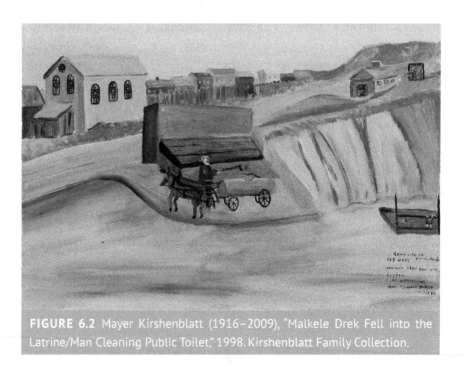

FIGURE 6.2 Mayer Kirshenblatt (1916–2009), "Malkele Drek Fell into the Latrine/Man Cleaning Public Toilet," 1998. Kirshenblatt Family Collection.

Kirshenblatt doesn't know why Harshl was named for stuffed derma, but he knows his name and his nickname.

In another instance, he explains the Hebrew etymology of a Yiddish-inflected name in his description of Yarmye Zajfman, the hotelkeeper in Apt: "On the southern outskirts of town was Yarmye's Hotel, named for its owner, Yarmye Zajfman—Yarmye is the Yiddish version of Yirmeyahu, the Hebrew name for the biblical prophet Jeremiah."[28] Again and again Kirshenblatt returns not only to the details of the names of the people in his hometown, but he maps out the importance of nicknames as a significant part of each and every individual's identity, locally but also nationally and even historically. Take the case of the legendary Ester, girlfriend of the Polish Kazmierz Wielki, or King Kazmierz the Great (1310–1370). According to Kirshenblatt:

> Her name was Ester, but she was known affectionately as Esterka in Polish and Esterke in Yiddish. She was sort of parallel to Ester of Purim fame. She was also, it was said, instrumental in the king's inviting Jews to Poland to promote commerce. That would have been about seven hundred years ago. King Kazmierz was said to have entertained Ester under a great oak tree.[29]

Accompanying this account is a painting of Ester (or Esterka or Esterke) with the king under the great oak tree (figure 6.3). In providing both this legendary figure's given name as well as its Polish and Yiddish translations, we see that Kirshenblatt's book is written and illustrated in the voice of a native son of two nations: the Jewish and the Polish. Providing nicknames for even ancient legendary figures such as Ester, who played a significant role in the history of both the Polish and Jewish nations, clearly conflates the ethnic with the familial.

If we compare *Poyln*'s photographs, drawn from the YIVO Archives, to the original pages of the *Forward*, where many were published, we see that the *Forward* did not translate the Yiddish captions exactly into English, with a significant difference lying in each language's approach to naming the photographs' subjects. Marek Web, in his introduction to *Poyln*, points out the fact that in the 1999 publication of Kacyzne's photographs, his original Yiddish captions (translated into English) are

FIGURE 6.3. Mayer Kirshenblatt (1916–2009), "King Kazimierz the Great Entertaining His Jewish Girlfriend Esterka," May 1997. Kirshenblatt Family Collection.

recuperated.[30] But if we consider several of the spreads in which many of Kacyzne's photographs were originally published in *The Forward*, we can't help but notice, in comparing the Yiddish captions (presumably Kacyzne's) with their English "translations," that the English assiduously avoids naming the photographs' subjects while the Yiddish consistently names them. Take, for example, a photograph that appeared on June 6, 1926. The English caption reads: "Sticking to his last: An old shoemaker of Radom Poland who has been on the job for 55 years." In Yiddish, we read: "He's been hammering this way since 1871—Moshe Mendel Fishman—one of the oldest cobblers in Radom Poland."[31] Or, on December 19, 1926, in a full-page spread titled "Types and Scenes from Jewish Life," we see an image captioned, in English, "the daughters of a Jewish Baker," and in Yiddish, "Sarah the baker's daughters."[32]

Why did the editor deem it appropriate to remove the subjects' names from the English captions, while keeping them in the Yiddish?

Perhaps his decision to use English captions represented his realization that readers of the English edition were one step further removed from the Old Country than the Yiddish readers of the special weekend arts section. Their sense of identifiable or named "family" was therefore diminished. Moshe Mendel Fishman and Sarah could be your cousins, if you still spoke Yiddish. But could they be if you didn't speak Yiddish any longer? The effect of the family album growing out of these photographs, even in their original appearance in the 1920s, is highly dependent on the naming, or lack thereof, of the photographic subjects.

In *Poyln*, several images and captions are worthy of close examination, as we consider the book's aspirations toward a family album through the simple act of naming. The very first personal name in *Poyln*, which appears in a series of cheder photographs, is in section 2, "Starting the Day," where it has both personal and communal implications, mediated by light and composition. The third cheder photograph (figure 6.4) flaunts the chiaroscuro effect typical of Vishniac's photographs from the decade that follows and Iudovin's (taken as part of Ansky's ethnographic expedition) from the preceding decade. According to Alexander Ivanov, Iudovin and Vishniac both worked in the pictorialist style, in order to grant photography the status of art even while marrying that art to ethnographic ambitions. About Iudovin's style, Ivanov argues:

> Iudovin often took photographs of elderly men during the expeditions. In accordance with the aesthetic of pictorialism, these are often stylized portraits in the manner of oil paintings or other graphic works. Set against a fantastical play of chiaroscuro, his images of bearded old men—handsome, wise and biblical—call to mind the works of the old masters, primarily Rembrandt.[33]

In Kacyzne's photograph of a cheder, taken in 1928 in Dlugosodlo (Bialystok province), we see two old men (one significantly older than the other) at opposite sides of the frame, and between them a table full of little boys, about five years old, seated, in caps and jackets. The older man, seated to the left and in front of the table, is dressed all in

FIGURE 6.4 Alter Kacyzne (1885–1941). *Długosiodło (Białystok province), 1928,* "Generations come, generations go: Leyzer Segal with his kheyder and his ailing father." From the Archives of the YIVO Institute for Jewish Research, New York.

white, with the exception of a knitted, peaked black skullcap on his head. He is frail and his gaze is unfocused, looking off to the right of the frame. His body, positioned sideways, with his legs slightly elevated and bent at the knees, on some kind of footstool arranged beside the children's study table, takes up half of the frame. The other man, positioned at the right of the frame, on the other side of the table, looks to the left, his gaze crisscrossing with that of the elderly man. He is dressed all in black, with a black, boxy skullcap on his head, his mouth open in speech. A child behind him peeks over his shoulder at the camera. Four children on the bench, with their backs to the camera, have turned their bodies to also look at the photographer, as do all the children on the bench facing the photographer, except those whose faces are blocked by their classmates on the opposite bench. The caption reads: "Generations come, generations go: Leyzer Segal with his kheyder and his ailing father."³⁴

The naming of the melamed, or the teacher, but not his father is significant. The cheder was probably known as "Leyzer Segal's cheder," and so, by naming him here, Kacyzne is not just naming an individual, but also a community institution. Additionally, in that act of selective naming, he channels the voices and the agency of the little boys, whose strong engagement with the photographer and the act of being photographed is expressed through their undiminished gaze. Leyzer Segal's cheder, the institution, is their cheder, so by naming their teacher, their voices are implied.

The effect of light and darkness, with the ailing elder in white, and Leyzer Segal in black, complements the caption as well. The ailing elder's outfit brightens the left side of the frame, in conjunction with a white curtain and daylight streaming in right behind him and with the four-cornered garment of a boy, worn outside his clothes across a white sleeve, right in the center of the picture. Moving your eyes to the right across the picture, it becomes much darker, culminating in the black hat and dark beard of Leyzer Segal, the black hat of the student poking his face over Segal's shoulder, and the shadows laying across Leyzer Segal's lap and bleeding under the table. The elder is like an angel in his white habitus—"going," as it were, to the next world even as he sits in the room with his son and his son's students. The teacher, on the other hand, is the epitome of doom and gloom—a figure for the difficulties of this world, or perhaps for the smaller difficulties of the little boys who exist partly in shadow and partly in light.

By naming Leyzer Segal, Kacyzne forces the viewer to alter his or her focal point. Although our eyes are naturally drawn to the whiteness of the elder and of the little boy at the center, Kacyzne, as is usual in his images, wants to draw our attention to individuals on the photograph's margins, wants the dominant perspective to sneak up from the side. Via our focus on the named Leyzer Segal, we can't help but notice the little boy looking over his shoulder. It is as if the child is photobombing the image. This child, on the other side of his teacher's darkness, is separated from the semi-lightness of his classmates, as if he has been converted in some way to the generation of adults, whose prospects are grim.

In the photograph following Leyzer Segal's (figure 6.5), another melamed is named. In it, we get a close-up, from the left, of the teacher, who occupies the entire foreground of the photograph. He holds up a shabby book in his hands, presumably a book of the Bible, based on its thickness and on the age of his students. Seated in the background of the photograph and slightly out of focus are his students, only three of them visible. Teacher and students are not at a common table like Leyzer Segal and his young students, but are seated at perpendicular *shtenders*, or reading stands. Behind the boys, aged nine or ten, is a closed door, ominously grey and broad, and in front of the boys, on the reading stands, are open books. They are looking neither at their

FIGURE 6.5 Alter Kacyzne (1885–1941), *Byale (Biała Podlaska, Lublin Province), 1926.* "The Byaler melamed, Binyomin-Hirsh the Beard. More than once his students have nailed his beard—the longest in Byale—to the table when he has dozed off. Perhaps that's why he has such wonderful, sad eyes." From the Archives of the YIVO Institute for Jewish Research, New York.

books nor at the photographer, but rather at their teacher, apprehensively. The melamed is looking out and down toward the left bottom of the frame, not into his open book at all. All are dressed in thick winter coats, buttoned to the chin, and the melamed's long, dark beard covers his lapels. Black and white are sharply contrasted in this image as well, with a white brick wall behind the melamed's black fur collar, and his skin and hands starkly white against the grayness of the reading stand and the blackness of his coat. The boys' faces pick up the white but are shadowed. The caption is as follows:

Byale (Biala Podalska, Lublin province), 1926

The Byaler melamed, Binyomin-Hirsh the Beard. More than once his students have nailed his beard—the longest in Byale—to the table when he has dozed off. Perhaps that's why he has such wonderful, sad eyes.[35]

As in the previous photograph, we see that the naming of the man is intended to identify an institution as much as to identify an individual: Binyomin-Hirsh is "The Byaler melamed." While presumably Byale had more than one melamed, it seems that he was considered an institution in and of himself. Furthermore, Kacyzne attaches his nickname, "the beard." As in the nicknames described by Kirshenblatt, this one is a tribute both to his physiognomy and to his standing in the community, as the nickname represents a consensus. His beard is the longest in Byale, apparently. Assuming Kacyzne has not observed this himself because he is not a native of Byale but just passing through to get some photographs, by thus naming him, he appears to be channeling the discourse of the townspeople. Perhaps someone told him to go take Binyomin-Hirsch the Beard's picture because he is so picturesque. The caption's climax comes in its final statement: "Perhaps that's why he has such wonderful, sad eyes." This is all Kacyzne—you do not have to be informed about Byale to see this man's soulful eyes. While the earlier part of the caption is presumably based on information that Kacyzne has received from local informants, this last part personalizes and humanizes both the photographer and the photographic subject at one and the same time.

Aside from cheder scenes, Kacyzne had a penchant for naming individuals in family groups, particularly those with close relatives in America. The final image in section 7, subtitled "Piety," was taken in Byale in 1926 (figure 6.6). It features a grandmother, a grandfather, and a very young child, perhaps three years old, sitting at a table around an alphabet primer. Each of them is gazing in a different direction, creating a triangulation of gazes: the grandmother looks at the grandfather seated to her right, the grandfather down at the child seated in his lap, and the child at the text, toward which the grandfather directs the child's eyes with a pointer. The text, the grandmother's hat, and the child's face are all illuminated in white. The grandfather's hand is at the child's elbow, holding him up, while the child, who looks exhausted (or bored to death), rests his head in the crook of his grandfather's other arm, which holds the primer. They are all seated at a well-used table whose surface

FIGURE 6.6 Alter Kacyzne (1885–1941), *Byale (Biała Podlaska, Lublin Province), 1926.* "Wolf Nachowicz, the gravedigger, teaches his grandson to read while the boy's grandmother looks on with pleasure. (The father is in America)." From the Archives of the YIVO Institute for Jewish Research, New York.

picks up the light generated by the grandmother's white cap and the text reflecting off the child's face. Just behind the grandmother's left arm is an ornate scroll-like wooden structure. At first, it looks like it might be the wooden arm of a Torah scroll, but it would be highly unusual for a Torah scroll to be sitting in the room with this family. Closer scrutiny reveals it to be the corner of a bed, and the family group is sitting at a table in front of it; just above the grandmother's right shoulder and the grandfather's left, in the space between them, is the bulk of what appears to be a feather quilt. All three figures are wearing, as in the previous cheder picture, quilted jackets, presumably to protect them from the cold house (Kacyzne seems to have gone to Byale in the wintertime). The caption says: "Wolf Nachowicz, the gravedigger, teaches his grandson to read while the boy's grandmother looks on with pleasure. (The father is in America)."[36]

As in the other images with named figures that we have just examined, only one character is named. He is also associated with his communal job—in this case, he is the community's gravedigger. It is strangely unsettling that the man in the photograph, encircled by the gaze of his wife and encircling, in turn, his beautiful grandchild with his eyes and his hand, giving him the gift of literacy, is a gravedigger. What are we to make of this conjunction of name and communal role? Without the caption, we would never know what his role in the community is, unlike other images in the volume that visually capture people at their work and need little further narrative explanation. Here, Kacyzne is gesturing to something remarkably important in our quest to understand how this ethnic album becomes a family album. There is a missing generation here: the father of the child, he offers in parentheses, is in America, and the generation now responsible for educating the child is more than several steps closer to the grave than it should be to child-rearing. To drive this point home, Kacyzne makes his named father figure, Wolf Nachowicz, a gravedigger.

There is no way of knowing whether Kacyzne's captions reflect reality or are works of fiction. In either case, the naming of a single individual in the majority of the book's portraits seems to indicate a commitment to identifying figures who operate on the edge of the familial and the ethnic. The singularity of the naming, paired with the association of the named individual with a trade, gives the image a dual purpose.

In chapter 5 we find another missing-parent image, featuring a grandmother and granddaughter in Kurtshev, Warsaw province (figure 6.7). The child, about eight years old, lays her head on her grandmother's shoulder and looks to the right of the frame. The grandmother, who looks to the left of the frame, holds her granddaughter's arm in her gnarled hands. The caption is "Mayer Gurfinkel's wife and granddaughter. Her father is in Washington; her mother is dead."[37] The named person, Mayer Gurfinkle, is not in the frame, but the caption identifies the two figures, his wife and granddaughter, in relation to him. Like the child with his grandparents learning to read, this little girl's father is in America. Her mother's death, however, explains

FIGURE 6.7 Alter Kacyzne (1885–1941), *Kurtshev (Karczew, Warsaw Province)*, "Mayer Gurfinkle's wife and granddaughter. Her father is in Washington. Her mother is dead." From the Archives of the YIVO Institute for Jewish Research, New York.

the photograph's function: it is a portrait of a missing generation, a father lost to America and a mother lost to the world. The remaining generations—grandmother and granddaughter—emphasize the gravity of the missing mother and render the missing father a sort of death as well.

A missing male family member figures prominently as well in an image of an extremely old woman in bed beside a light-filled window, one elbow supporting her head, her other hand on the pages of the book open on the windowsill. The picture was taken in Warsaw, 1925 (figure 6.8). The caption reads: "Khane Kolski, one hundred and six years old. Every evening she says vidui [a confession of sins] and eats a cookie. Her eighty year old son in America does not believe that his mother is still alive."[38] The conundrum offered by the photo is how Kacyzne knows that Khane Kolski's son does not believe she is still

FIGURE 6.8 Alter Kacyzne (1885–1941), *Varshe (Warsaw) 1925,* "Khane Kolski, one hundred and six years old. Every evening she says vidui [confession of sins] and eats a cookie. Her eighty year old son in America does not believe that his mother is still alive." From the Archives of the YIVO Institute for Jewish Research, New York.

alive. Maybe she told Kacyzne this to explain why her son seems to have suddenly stopped sending letters and funds. He certainly wouldn't write her a letter telling her he does not believe she is still alive, would he? Behind the naming of this figure and the conjecture surrounding her missing son (in America, like others we have cited) are the details, big and small, of a life, with a nightly snack balanced by a nightly expectation of death (hence the recitation of the *vidui* prayer: the final confession), the mundane pleasure of a cookie held against the monumental prospect of eternal slumber.

Khane Kolski, named here by virtue of her old age and the drama implied by her ambiguous relationship with her missing son, is one of the only named women in the volume whose name is not explicitly associated in the caption with a male relation. In one image, where a named woman is indeed associated with a male relative and the caption, unusually, names two people, we get a slightly different feeling for the role of naming in Kacyzne's oeuvre (figure 6.9). In this photo,

FIGURE 6.9 Alter Kacyzne (1885–1941), *Żelechów (Warsaw province)*, "Feyge, Motl the melamed's niece, eighty-five years old. She spins flax with her daughter." From the Archives of the YIVO Institute for Jewish Research, New York.

two elderly women, their heads modestly covered by kerchiefs, sit on a bench spinning flax; one faces toward the photographer, the other away. The undated photograph is situated in Zelechow (Warsaw province). The caption reads: "Feyge, Motl the melamed's niece, eighty-five years old. She spins flax with her daughter."[39] This caption tells us as much about the city of Zelechow as it does about Feyge and her daughter. How is that an eighty-five-year-old woman is still known as the melamed's niece? Has she not, in all her eighty-five years, earned any independent attribution? And is it possible that Motl the melamed is still alive and teaching, at an age that presumably exceeds one hundred? Or perhaps the caption tells us, as does Kirshenblatt's extended exposition, about the nature of nicknames in a particular town, in this case Zelechow. Even dead, Motl the melamed provides an identity for his niece. I wouldn't call it status, because, as we have already discussed, the literature tells us that melamedim were among the lowest of the low in traditional East European Jewish culture, teaching young children for very little pay and accorded very little respect either by their young charges or the community at large. However, as in the other named figures we have looked at, the melamed has a specific communal position, one that affords him, and even his niece, a kind of name recognition. Feyge, on the other hand, is not identified with her job in the same way that her absent uncle is; the caption's language indicates that she spins flax with her daughter, but not that she is *the* flax spinner. This may be a function of her gender—perhaps women in their town didn't possess independent professional identities.

Many other women in the book's images are named in relation to men, for example, Itzke the Glazier's wife, the Byale Rebbe's daughter, and Esther whose husband abandoned her with five children.[40] The most compelling leitmotif among named figures, however, remains the missing father. One unusual image taken in Byale in 1926 features a father and son; the father is not only present, but also the only named figure (figure 6.10). The two men, dressed identically in padded coats, sit side by side; they both have beards and wear black hats. The young one (though not so young) looks up and to his right, over his father's head. The older one looks straight at the camera, his head in his right hand, his left hand clutching his coat as if to keep it closed.

FIGURE 6.10 Alter Kacyzne (1885–1941), *Byale (Biała Podlaska, Lublin Province, 1926)*, "Father and son. To protect himself from the evil one, Leyzer Bawół, the blacksmith, will not say how old he is. Now his son does the smithing and old man has become a doctor. He sets broken arms and legs." From the Archives of the YIVO Institute for Jewish Research, New York.

As in the gravedigger portrait, the image itself gives no indication of the men's professions. The caption reads:

> Father and son. To protect himself from the Evil One, Leyzer Bawol, the blacksmith, will not say how old he is, but he must be over one hundred. Now his son does the smithing and the old man has become a doctor. He sets broken arms and legs.[41]

Though he has become the "doctor," Leyzer Bawol is still known as the town blacksmith. This image projects the story of a father and not a son, with the father's face and hand the source of light in the photograph, and the son's eyes obscured in shadows created by the angle of his head. Rather than the search for a missing father featured throughout the book, here, for once, is a "found" father, one who conceals parts of himself but is very much present and valuable within the economy of both the community and the family, as evidenced by his having passed his job down to his son while still maintaining a crucial role in the culture.

Kacyzne's unique emphasis on naming his photographs' subjects creates the resonance of a family as well as an ethnic album. At the same time, Web's decision to reinstate Kacyzne's original captions in the 1999 volume allows us to hear the peculiarities of Kacyzne's voice as he deploys it to convey the spirit of the communities he captures on film. In the quest for the man behind the camera, this is significant, because his use of free indirect discourse in his captions communicates the literary sensibility by which he most wanted to be known, as well as the unique perspective of many of his subjects.

In the first section of the book, in a 1924 photograph taken in Lublin and titled "Approaching," we see a street scene filled with people and buildings (figure 6.11). As in the other of this section's photographs,

FIGURE 6.11 Alter Kacyzne (1885–1941), *Lublin, 1924,* "The Jewish bridge (although there is no bridge)." From the Archives of the YIVO Institute for Jewish Research, New York.

Kacyzne's focus is on place, not person, and we do not get the beautiful portrait effects we have seen thus far. In this photo, only two people are facing the camera, and they are so far away that their features are indistinct; all the people have their backs turned to the camera and are walking away from the photographer, who seems to be slightly elevated, shooting, perhaps, from the window of a ground-floor apartment. The caption reads: "The Jewish bridge (although there is no bridge)."[42] Kacyzne communicates to us, his viewers, a local landmark named, in the local idiom, for something that is no longer extant, sharing both the fact of the name and the fact of the site, which are in conflict with one another. In so doing, he beautifully reflects familiarity with the discourse of the Jews in Lublin.

Part 2's final photograph, titled "Starting the Day," is undated, from Demblin (Warsaw Province) (figure 6.12). In it, we are closer to a group of people, mostly women in plaid shawls and young barefoot

FIGURE 6.12 Alter Kacyzne (1885–1941), *Demblin (Dę, Warsaw province)*, "Monday in Demblin. Make it Friday if you like." From the Archives of the YIVO Institute for Jewish Research, New York.

children, though none of their faces are distinct. Only two people, a young woman in the background on the right of the frame and a little boy just in front of her, seem to notice the camera. Everyone else is preoccupied with the baskets and carts scattered among them. The scene appears to be a market day, although Kacyzne doesn't say as much. His caption is "Monday in Demblin. Make it Friday, if you like."[43] This, it seems, is an expression of his sardonic wit that captures what he wrote to Cahan in the correspondence quoted above: that he found much of his material to be rather monotonous. Or perhaps Monday and Friday are market day in that town, rendering the days identical.

A 1927 photograph, taken in Otwock (Warsaw province), also gives Kacyzne the opportunity to articulate both the local dialect and his own sense of humor. It portrays young Orthodox boys in their four-cornered garments and skullcaps, pumping water from an enormous pump (figure 6.13). The boys—surrounded by men and older boys whose dress suggests they are peasants, yeshiva students, and businessmen—are apparently the center of some attention on the street. The caption reads: "Otwock's next generation learns how to pour water." The editor points out that "[the phrase gisn vaser—to pour water—is also used to describe a windbag.]"[44]

Several of Kacyzne's captions cite literary sources, allowing him to communicate, in another way, his affinity with literary texts and his identity as a literary persona. In these captions we find allusions to folk songs, texts by well-known writers, and even quotes from his own writing. A photograph of three girls sewing, taken in Nowy Dwor (Warsaw province, 1927), is captioned: "'Three girls are sitting and sewing.'—I. L. Peretz." (figure 6.14).[45] A photo of a Warsaw passageway, undated but identified as "the old town," in which four small, indistinct children are seated on a step (figure 6.15), quotes Kacyzne's best-known novel, *Shtarke un Shvakhe* (The Strong and the Weak, 1929–30): "Once this was the heart of Warsaw, this labyrinth of narrow alleys winding between tall, gray walls (*Shtarke un Shvakhe*)."[46] A photograph with no local or temporal attribution, of a group of children seated on the ground in a rural setting, with a religious older man standing right over them (possibly their cheder teacher?), is captioned: "Seven

FIGURE 6.13 Alter Kacyzne (1885–1941), *Otwock (Warsa Province), 1927,* "Otwock's next generation learns how to pour water." From the Archives of the YIVO Institute for Jewish Research, New York.

children sitting by a well." The editor notes that this is a quote from a Yiddish folk song (figure 6.16).[47]

Of all the images we have looked at, only one contains Kacyzne's actual name—the one with the advertisement for his literary lecture in Tshortkev. However, reading his reinstated captions alongside his images highlights his unique voice and his unique vision. He traveled across Poland taking pictures of people and places, attempting to represent them in a uniquely literary inflection that would help preserve the particular dialects and idioms of his subjects. He shared the

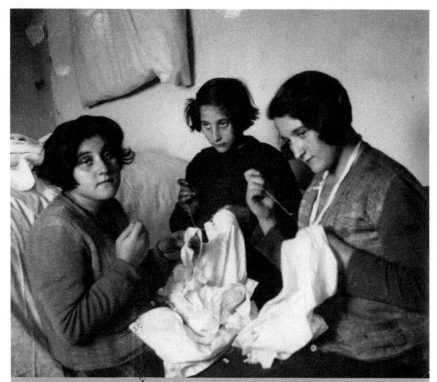

FIGURE 6.14 Alter Kacyzne (1885–1941), *Nowy Dwór (Warsaw province), 1927,* "Three girls are sitting and sewing."—I.L Peretz." From the Archives of the YIVO Institute for Jewish Research, New York.

landscape of his literary mind by framing selected photographs within the context of particular texts. As a result, the series of photographs he managed to transmit to the United States before his violent death would enable his daughter, Sulamita Kacyzne-Reale, to reconstruct a sense of her father in something of a family album even while Marek Web, the volume's editor, managed to convey the sense of an entire population across a vast territory through his framing of the photographs as "Poyln."

Kacyzne-Reale's quest for a father through language and literature in a book of images is echoed in Barbara Kirshenblatt-Gimblett's identification of a uniquely literary sensibility in her father's voice: "Mayer has a way of knowing the world that is breathtaking. He is my Diderot, Melville and Rabelais."[48] She adds:

FIGURE 6.15 Alter Kacyzne (1885–1941), *Varshe (Warsaw), the old town,* "Once this was the heart of Warsaw, this labyrinth of narrow alleys winding between tall, gray walls. (*Shtarke un shvakhe*)." From the Archives of the YIVO Institute for Jewish Research, New York.

FIGURE 6.16 Alter Kacyzne (1885–1941), "Seven children sitting by the well ..." From the Archives of the YIVO Institute for Jewish Research, New York.

> What Mayer knows he knows in relation to people. What he presents are not simple facts, they are felt facts. . . . This is a world not only to be known but also to be felt. It is the affective charge that gives to memory its luminosity.[49]

As we begin to draw this discussion to its conclusion, I would like to consider the affective relationship between image and word at the heart of these image books, infusing them with a literary sensibility that, in part, makes it possible for them to function simultaneously as family albums and ethnic albums. Mayer Kirshenblatt, according to his daughter, is a natural storyteller. For many years she encouraged him to paint scenes from his childhood before he finally agreed, at age seventy-two, to sketch his mother's kitchen. She had, for years before that, been interviewing him and recording those interviews, in the hope of writing an ethnography of the world he grew up in. When he began to paint, the project took on a vibrant life of its own. Some paintings reflected interviews she had already recorded, but others inspired further interviews or begged the expansion of existing ones. A text grew out of the conjunction of paintings and interviews, with Kirshenblatt-Gimblett helping her father to generate new text by writing key words on the top of a piece of paper and having him write, associatively, in order to flesh out the context for many of his images. The text is remarkably fluid, detailed, entertaining, and comprehensive. In it we learn about local businesses, families, food, youth groups, political movements, childhood games, religious rituals, and different types of schools, both public and religious. We learn about the destruction of the family he left behind with his emigration to Canada, and about other events that he could not possibly have witnessed, such as his own *pidyon ha-ben*, or redemption of the firstborn boy, a ritual performed when a non-priestly family's oldest child (or the firstborn of the mother) is a boy, on that child's thirtieth day of life (figure 6.17).[50] This discussion follows his discussion of his brother's circumcision ceremony. Though Kirshenblatt couldn't possibly remember his own *pidyon ha-ben*, he makes a point of re-creating what he says his own probably looked like, because this book both draws on personal memories and at the same time attempts to present a comprehensive portrait of a town and, by extension, a culture. Because a *pidyon ha-ben* and a circumcision go hand in hand in celebrating and consummating the birth of Jewish boys, he felt the need to elaborate on both.[51]

In addition to painting experiences of his own that he couldn't possibly remember, Kirshenblatt created paintings that depict members of his family undergoing experiences that he did not witness, illuminating particularly intriguing instances of crossover between the familial and the ethnic in Kirshenblatt's album. Two images, each representing the execution of members of his family and the Jewish community's expulsion from Opatow in 1942, constitute the sum total of his allusion to his family's fate in the Holocaust (figures 6.18 and 6.19). In her afterword, Kirshenblatt-Gimblett points out:

> While he says he can only paint what he remembers, his idea of
> memory is capacious enough to include legends that he heard as
> a child or read in the Apt memorial book.... He has also painted

FIGURE 6.17 Mayer Kirshenblatt (1916–2009), "Redemption of the First-born," 1993. Kirshenblatt Family Collection.

events he never witnessed but only heard about, notably the
execution of his parents' families by the Nazis, a subject he was
only able to tackle after seeing Goya's *The Shootings of the Third
of May, 1808* at the Prado.[52]

Kirshenblatt's "capacious" memory, as described by his daughter,
includes his ability to imagine the horrors of the war that he was lucky
enough to avoid. In an interesting variation on post-memory, which
within Marianne Hirsch's schema generally pertains to the experience of the second generation, Kirshenblatt is compelled, through his
imagination, to serve as an eyewitness to the massacre of his family
and to communicate that witnessing through his painting. Curiously,
he doesn't rely on other paintings or photographs of the Holocaust
to paint the executions of his family. Rather, he communicates the
singularity and personal trauma of their deaths by turning to another

FIGURE 6.18 Mayer Kirshenblatt (1916–2009), "Expulsion from Opatów: Execution of My Aunt + Family, 1941," 1997. Kirshenblatt Family Collection.

FIGURE 6.19 Mayer Kirshenblatt (1916–20009), "Execution of Grandmother on the Road to Sandomierz, 1942," June 1997. Kirshenblatt Family Collection.

massacre as his paintings' inspiration. Goya's image, *The Third of May 1808*, with a firing squad standing in close proximity to a crowd of people awaiting their own execution, seems to have helped Kirshenblatt in each of the two compositions. In the first, "Expulsion from Opatow, 1942; Execution of My Grand Aunt and Family," Kirshenblatt foregrounds the family group being executed, while the rest of the Jews in town are pushed through the space between two buildings at right angles to each other and toward a third. The plane of the painting is occupied primarily by the space of a courtyard between the two buildings, and the walls, doors, and windows of the buildings framing that space. Apt itself seems to figure as a character in the painting, as it becomes emptied of its mass of Jews, only the tail end of whom we witness being marched out. The yawning emptiness of the courtyard between the two buildings dwarfs the family group in the foreground to the right, which is being shot and seems small and pinched. As distinct from the Goya, we see here neither a pool of blood nor dead bodies falling to the ground, but we do see the shot taking place because something red and bloodlike is coming out of the gun pointed at the group, and we see a rusty smear of color just beneath the place where the bullet would presumably enter the man's back.[53]

In the image titled "Execution of Grandmother on the Road to Sandomierz, 1942," we witness the shooting of his grandmother with the same effect of the bullet flying toward her in a red rush, and the reciprocal rust color coming out of her head, where the bullet enters. Though she is on the ground, her head is still up, looking in the direction of the viewer.[54] In neither picture do we witness the actual death of the victims. Nor do we witness the aftermath of the deaths of Kirshenblatt's aunt's family or his grandmother. In both images the victims are very much alive, perhaps as he remembered them. Also in both he balances the individual victims with the group, commemorating not only his relatives' death but also the death of his entire town, thereby providing both an ethnic and a familial accounting of the massacre. His textual narration of the two images is as follows:

> The ghetto was established in 1941. It was an open ghetto in the
> sense that Jews from Apt and the environs were confined there,

but there was no wall. Yeshiye became the postman in the ghetto. When the Jews were expelled from Apt on October 20–22, 1942, Mania refused to be separated from her children and the whole family was shot in front of grandmother's house. Mania was a beautiful woman, with long blonde hair and blue eyes, like my mother and me. My grandmother was old. She was short and fat. On the march out of Apt to the labor camp in Sandomierz, she could not keep up the pace. She lagged behind, fell to the ground, and was shot on the spot. Her body was thrown onto a wagon with the corpses of other people who could not walk fast enough. Thousands of others were forced to march to the train station in Jasice and were transported to Treblinka.[55]

In his prose, Kirshenblatt names several people and several places: Yeshiye, Mania, Sandomierz, Jasice, and Treblinka. He gives us a vivid sense of Mania's physical appearance as well as that of his grandmother, and he tells us that Yeshiye served as the postman for the ghetto—in the same sense that Kacyzne shares individual's names and professional identities in order to transmit the voice of the community even as he presents individuals. The entire story of the fate of Jewish Apt during the Holocaust is compressed into one paragraph, from the ghettoization of its residents to their exile to a labor camp and their extermination. He tells us about as much as he is capable of telling us on the macro level, while providing a few humanizing details. What he knows could easily be gleaned from a history book (the evacuation and the path of those evacuated), but also from an eyewitness who watched from a distance or heard what was going on without being able to turn around and see it himself. Like such an eyewitness, he communicates that Mania's whole family was executed and that his grandmother fell down and was shot on the spot and thrown into a wagon, giving us the stories of their deaths in the broadest of terms. These broad terms are, perhaps, his way of acknowledging that he is in fact not telling the story of the Holocaust. As he says in his own words, "What I'm trying to say is: 'Hey! There was a big world out there before the holocaust.' There was a rich cultural life in Poland as I knew it at the time."[56] But to achieve the kind of comprehensiveness he seems to be aiming for, he must at least allude to the fate of the town he describes in such loving and thorough detail. Thus the broad strokes dominating these images and their descriptions reflect an awareness of his obligation to tell the story of these deaths, but a resistance to depicting them graphically.

As in our earlier discussion of *Image before My Eyes*, coedited by Kirshenblatt-Gimblett, there is a commitment to focusing on pre-Holocaust East Europe without allowing the Holocaust to become overdetermined or to back-shadow the world that came before it. However, in both works, the Holocaust does play a pivotal if brief role midway through the salvage poetic work, at its literal center. In thus situating the Holocaust, it seems that Kirshenblatt-Gimblett acknowledges the Holocaust but buries it, accentuating that although the Holocaust is part of the history of the communities she represents, it needn't frame that history nor take up a disproportionate amount of its representation.

With more than 380 images and over 400 pages of text, *They Called Me Mayer July* is a remarkable book of names and naming. It depicts the childhood of a man with at least three names—Mayer Kirshenblatt, Mayer *tamez*, and Mike Kirsch (as he comes to be known among colleagues in Canada)—but it also brings its readers into a city with street names, where each house belongs to a particular family, each courtyard is inhabited and played in by children with aunts, uncles, grandmothers, and parents, each with their own specific way of making a living, practicing Judaism, and raising their children. Kirshenblatt is careful to tell us when he doesn't know or understand something. He also tells us when he only knows something because someone else remembers it, such as the existence of a third mill, near the cemetery in Apt, owned by the Goldbergs. "But I do not remember it," he adds.[57] This book is a book as much about Apt as it is about his memory of Apt, and therefore he makes a point of telling us as much as can be known about the city and not just as much as he remembers.

In *They Called Me Mayer July*, we also hear Mayer's voice modulated at moments by Barbara's and certainly inspired by hers, in keeping with the "third voice" style explained earlier. In describing, for example, the way his mother made a soup, Kirshenblatt interjects his daughter's term for the process:

> We lived on potatoes year-round. A farmer that mother knew
> would bring potatoes directly to our house, since we bought
> them in quantity. A Jewish housewife really had to be a gourmet
> cook to prepare potatoes fifty-two different ways. When mother
> boiled potatoes, the water was not discarded. There were still a
> little starch and nourishment there. So she would make an *uge-
> brente zup*: to enhance the consistency and taste of the potato
> water: she made a dough from flour and water, rolled it into little
> crumbs, and fried them until they were an *anbren*, gave [*sic*] the
> soup color and taste; my daughter says it was basically a roux.[58]

One can imagine the many stages of discussion that went into Mayer
and Barbara's decision to keep that observation in the book. First, the
father described *ugebrente zup* as part of a larger discussion about
the types of food readily available in Apt and the different ways that
housewives found to prepare potatoes in order to make the most of
their nutritional value. Next was the description of the *anbren*, which
his daughter struggled to identify in her own culinary vocabulary, set-
tling finally on a roux. She shared this insight with her father, who
decided to include it in his text for a readership that would, like his
daughter, probably be more familiar with a roux than with *anbren*. But
he maintained his daughter's presence in his text to transmit that the
concept of the roux was her idea, not his. This, it seems to me, articulates the crux of a "third voice," wherein the voice of the father and
daughter function both together and separately to tell the story of Apt
in terms that are comprehensible to their audience.[59]

They Called Me Mayer July was conceived as the culmination of two
parallel projects—the project of the daughter anthropologist interviewing her father as a means of understanding the world that produced
him, but also the particular world he inhabited for the first nineteen
years of his life, and the project of the father finding a way to articulate his memory in an artistic medium. The visual stimulus for Mayer,
his inspiration to paint, served as the glue that bound together his
daughter Barbara's ethnographic aspirations. In her afterword to the
volume, she identifies her discovery of anthropology as an undergrad-
uate at Berkeley in 1965, where a course introduced her to a field that
"valued what was extraordinary in ordinary people, celebrated the

oldest members of a community, and appreciated their accumulated wisdom, deep memory and creative capacities late in life. This is how I discovered my own family and came to prepare for their aging."[60] Kirshenblatt-Gimblett's need to help her father claim his creative impulse and find an outlet for his memories of childhood merged with her own desire to write an ethnography of a prewar East European Jewish community. To accomplish the latter, she needed to do the former. She needed to mobilize her father in service to the production of an archive, and find a way for him to produce an archive of images to accompany the texts they were working together to create—images that would further that text, frame it, and justify it. In *They Called Me Mayer July*, Barbara Kirshenblatt-Gimblett seeks out her father, and helps him to tell both his own story and the story of Apt, turning the latter into a metonymy for the lost culture of the Jews of Poland in the aftermath of World War II. The product is a family album of an unexpected sort.

Annette Kuhn explains that she turns to her own family albums in order to better scrutinize her culture and her milieu. She calls the family album "an imagined community of nationhood that takes the family as its model."[61] The movement from family to nation, from the individual to the collective, that she describes in her work resonates with the slippage evident in Kirshenblatt-Gimblett's work between the quest for her father and the quest to describe an ethnic community. In many ways, Barbara's insistence that her father take up a paintbrush late in life, while clearly informed by his native talents and tendencies, is also informed by her anticipation of his loss. Published only two years before his death, *They Called Me Mayer July* was, indeed, a means of salvaging not only her memory of her father, but also his memories—the images that he possessed of a world and a culture long gone.

Like Roland Barthes's famous quest for an image of his mother in the aftermath of her death that would embody who she was to him, Kirshenblatt-Gimblett, by both her own and her father's reckoning, sought out her father in a picture of his mother's kitchen. This was the first painting he created (figure 6.20), and it inspired the outpouring of all his subsequent paintings. As in Barthes's *Winter Garden Photograph* of his mother as a little girl, Mayer in his *Kitchen Painting* is a little

FIGURE 6.20 Mayer Kirshenblatt (1916–2009), "Kitchen," May 1990 (one of the later kitchen paintings, not the original one). Kirshenblatt Family Collection.

boy practicing the violin at the center of the kitchen, with his mother presumably listening while cooking in the corner. It is their respective parents before they could have known them that both Kirshenblatt-Gimblett and Barthes identify as essential to understanding themselves. Clearly, a major distinction between the two is that Barthes locates this picture after his mother's death, while Kirshenblatt-Gimblett requests that her father paint this picture before his death. Their projects are clearly different. Barthes's project is to understand the nature of photography, which he attempts to better understand by seeking out his mother's essence in a photograph. Kirshenblatt-Gimblett's project, on the other hand, is to bring to fruition her work as an anthropologist and her destiny as a daughter. She wants to help her father identify that thing which will open his world to her before it is too late. Kirshenblatt-Gimblett's father's *Kitchen Painting* serves for her as Barthes's *Winter Garden Photograph* serves him.

Barthes doesn't reproduce the *Winter Garden Photograph* in *Camera Lucida*, his well-known treatise on the nature of photography, because he says its punctum—the "prick" of the photograph that causes a "wound" in its viewer—is particular to him and couldn't possibly be shared by his readers. The punctum, he claims, is never deliberately placed by the photographer nor shared by multiple viewers. In his description of the punctum, Barthes writes: "Certain details may prick me. If they do not, it is doubtless because the photographer has put them there intentionally."[62] He further rejects the possibility that anyone can plant the punctum for another person: "I dismiss all knowledge, all culture, I refuse to inherit anything from another eye than my own."[63] He concludes that "what I can name cannot really prick me."[64] According to Barthes, the punctum, therefore, is the element of a photograph that speaks to the individual viewer, beyond the photograph's context or the contextual cues gleaned by the viewer. It is that affective part of the experience of looking at a photograph that transcends history and culture, that situates photographs in the realm of the ineffable and the numinous for individual viewers.

I would argue that as visual artifacts of both an individual man and a collective culture, Kirshenblatt's paintings and Kacyzne's photographs contain punctums both for their daughters and for a collective population of American Jewish viewers. The arbitrary nature of photographs themselves helps us to understand the dynamic relationship between the "ethnic" and "familial" faces in each of the two image books we have explored in this chapter. Elizabeth Edwards points to multiple meanings to be found in the arbitrariness, or what she calls "rawness" of photographs:

> Photographs are a major historical form for the late 19th and 20th centuries and arguably we have hardly started to grasp what they are about and how to deal with their rawness. Photographs are very literally raw histories in both senses of the word—the unprocessed and the painful. Their unprocessed quality, their randomness, their minute indexicality are inherent to the medium itself. It has been suggested that anthropologists,

and for that case historians, are worried by still photography because, lacking the constraining narratives of film, still images contain too many meanings.[65]

This proliferation of meanings, the randomness of the optical unconscious as articulated by Walter Benjamin, opens photographs up to the possibility of a plurality of punctums.[66] For an American Jewish audience confronting a group of photographs such as those produced by Kacyzne and reframed by Kacyzne-Reale and Web, the infinite "recodability" of those photographs creates a new encounter with each viewing and the possibility of a new punctum. "Photographs are like monuments," says Jack Kugelmass, "they are iconic representations of other times and other places—but with a peculiar transportability. American Jews' physical tie to the Old World was fundamentally destroyed during the Holocaust, and even in America, economically mobile Jews repeatedly establish, then abandon, settlements."[67] He argues, like Annette Kuhn, that photographs allow individuals to feel they are part of a collective. They help reorient individuals to their place in a broader history. "The photo album is a trace of the past that assures us of an enduring identity, a sense of continuity in the face of change,"[68] Kugelmass affirms. Placing the photograph at an intersection of the collective and the individual, he adds, "Photographs act as a vehicle for establishing collective memory out of individual experience."[69] Elizabeth Edwards, continuing her discussion of the historical and ethnographic value of photographs, echoes this:

> Photographs operate in both private and public or personal and collective functions. This is an important distinction, because the way in which photographs can be said to move from one to the other has much to do with their reading as historical data. Images read as private are those read in a context contiguous with the life from which they are extracted: meaning and memory stay with them, as in family photographs, for example. Public photographs remove the image entirely from such a context, and meaning becomes free-floating, externally generated and read in terms of symbol and metaphor.[70]

Confronted with Kirshenblatt's images and Kacyzne's photographs, framed by their respective daughters, American Jews can approach these images of the Old Country as part of their construction of what Kugelmass has called their "ethnic patrimony." Just as the punctum of the drawings, for Barbara, and the photographs, for Sulamita, allow the images their fathers produced to constitute a family album, so too do the punctums that grow out of and around these same images for an American Jew enable an ethnic album to feel like a family album.

When you rely on photographs or memories to portray a culture, you have to work with what you happen to come across, what happens to have survived. Just as in our exploration of *Image before My Eyes* we noted that the collection must necessarily move from topic to topic in order to accommodate a rather random archive, so too are American Jews dependent on the images that are generated by artists like Kirshenblatt or photographers like Kacyzne to make sense of their own past. To a large extent our connection to those photographs feels, as Edwards would say, "random" or "free floating," with some images speaking to us in profoundly familiar ways, evoking recognition and pain, as would a punctum, and some simply speaking to us in a more generalized manner, like a studium is meant to do.

Several levels of familiarity are implicit in our encounter with these images. The Kacyzne images, as we have mentioned, have been published in the United States since the 1920s and are featured prominently, even when unattributed, in a wide variety of publications and films. The Kirshenblatt paintings are rendered in a two-dimensional folk style that also breeds a sense of recognition or familiarity. In his description of the *Winter Garden Photograph*, Barthes seeks out the "familiarity" of his mother. What he finds, though, is a mother he never knew, his mother as a child, his mother before he even existed. It is a kind of essence he finally identifies, a gesture of her hand, a look in her eye that excites him and allows him to know that he has finally found what he is looking for. This image of his mother was, like the images of Kacyzne for an American Jewish audience, an image in the archive of his mother's life. As Edwards argues, "Images in the archive can literally become re-individualized, acquiring new status through new contextual links."[71] They have, she continues, "accumulative histories that draw their significances from intersecting elements." In the case of the image books we have explored here, existing at the intersection of the family and the ethnic album, what we see is the effect of a kind of generalized and particular familiarity, a shock of personal recognition contextualized by a broader ethnic perspective.

POSTSCRIPT

Intertextuality in Post-Holocaust American Jewish Salvage Texts

How have salvage poetics become legible in the lives of American Jews beyond the pages of the texts we have looked at throughout this study?[1] In the introduction I discussed the newest *Fiddler*, the Yiddish *Fiddler*, that was a runaway hit (by Yiddish standards, of course) in 2018 and continues to this day to play to packed houses. I theorized there that *Fidler afn Dakh*, as a cornerstone of contemporary American Jewish experience, has become a familiar, accessible, framing text for Americans who are now looking for something new to connect them to their East European Jewish heritage—a Yiddish post-vernacular. Yiddish itself is far from new, but its comfortable deployment as a post-vernacular, as a language that represents a culture but is no longer governed by the normal, expected, rules of grammar and usage, is new. This process of turning to an American phenomenon (the English-language *Fiddler on the Roof*) as the frame by which to render accessible that which precedes and is implicit in it (the Yiddish language as the language spoken by the members of the culture represented in *Fiddler*) began, I would argue, in 1977 with the publication of Irving Howe's *The World of Our Fathers*, a text to which I allude in the fourth chapter of this study. In *The World of Our Fathers*, Howe attempts to delineate a genesis of American Jewish East European history that originates not in the shtetls or cities of Europe, but on the

Lower East Side of New York. For the generation of the New York Intellectuals, including Nathan Glazer, the up-and-coming sociologist who wrote *American Judaism* in 1957, from which the quote which opened this book is drawn, American Judaism was born in the streets of New York. Figures like Howe and Glazer were mostly born here, to parents from Eastern Europe, and for them the "landscape of their birthplace" (to quote the Hebrew poet Saul Tchernichowsky) was the only one that could serve as the basis for an understanding of the history of the majority of American Jews.[2] It was Yiddish on the streets of New York that compelled Irving Howe to edit his *Treasury of Yiddish Stories*, to seek out a literary precedent for the sweatshop poets of the Lower East Side, or the *Yunge*.[3] American experience of Yiddish became a new form of East European Jewish expression and served as its own unique starting point for understanding everything that came before it.

Like Howe who began with the Lower East Side as a springboard for looking backward to Europe, today, as described by Jack Wertheimer, Jews are looking at American cultural trends for ways to reach back into their own tradition. Environmentalism, for example, leads them to the traditional Jewish celebration of the trees, *Tu-B'Shvat*, the civil rights movement leads them to Passover, communities centered on healthful eating and exercise lead them back to the synagogue sanctuary where the prayers for healing, formerly an aside in the Torah reading ritual, have become a centerpiece and a focus of the service.[4] Salvage poetics are at play in this contemporary mode of ritual, practice, and Jewish identity insofar as they represent a palimpsest of tradition and modernity, a concern with accessibility and bridging. Jewish leaders today are constantly searching for ways to make Judaism relevant by starting with the present and moving backward, just like Maurice Samuel did in his address to American Jews through the medium of Sholem Aleichem, or Heschel did by attempting to give American Jews access to the culture of Talmudic study through the medium of modern Hasidic narratives. American Judaism has been involved in the creation of hybrid forms of ritual and reflection, beginning with a framework in the here and now, and injecting it with "traditional artifacts." Whereas the artifacts inserted into their hybrid frameworks in order to create folk ethnographic texts upon which we have focused in this study tended to be concrete literary, photographic, historical, and/or pictorial works, the newest, most recent model of salvage poetics can be best understood in a less artifact focused and more culturally broad sense. I have called it "hybridization." Jack Wertheimer has called it "remixing." No matter what you call it, it leads us back to one concept that long preceded the modern period and has come to define Jewish cultural transmission.

The very first idea I generally introduce in the university classes I teach on "Jewish literatures" is "intertextuality," or the invocation of one text within another. Indeed, I define Jewish literature for my students as an intertextual literature written either in a Jewish language, in a Jewish idiom, or on Jewish themes; to my mind, the intertextual component is the one that ties all other considerations together. Very few "Jewish literatures," I posit, fail to allude to earlier texts, or at the very least to textual discourses. Glückel of Hameln (1646–1724), for example, retells midrashic stories, filtered through women's early Yiddish digests of sacred texts, in her remarkable seventeenth-century ethical will.[5] Ilana Blumberg (b. 1970), in her contemporary literary autobiography *Houses of Study*, liberally invokes the book of Genesis in her reflections on Jewish women's literacy within institutions of sacred study in Jerusalem.[6] For that matter, the whole rabbinic corpus, beginning with the Mishnah and early midrash of the second century CE and continuing through the Talmud, the codes, and responsa, is intertextually based, with texts generated through commentary on other texts. The Bible itself, the foundation for the whole enterprise, is itself fundamentally intertextual, drawing on traditions in Ugaritic, Akkadian, and Sumerian literature.[7]

I would in fact reframe the scholarly and editorial act of *kinus*, or "collecting," among Jewish intellectuals at the end of the Jewish Enlightenment or at the turn of the twentieth century in terms of the place of intertextuality in the salvage poetics we have been tracing here. Bialik and Ravnitsky's *Book of Legends* (1908–11) as well as Louis Ginzburg's *Legends of the Jews* (1909), Buber's *Stories of the Hasidim* (1906–14), and S. Ansky's ethnographic expeditions between 1911 and 1914 marked a rising consciousness of the place of literary texts and intertextuality in the transmission of traditional Jewish culture at the apex of Jewish modernity. The act of gathering, translating, and disseminating sacred texts in a streamlined form with the present providing a lens and an access point to the past articulates a modern sensitivity to the continuing relevance of tradition and the necessity to redeploy it not just for historical posterity, but for cultural productivity.

"Salvaging" Jewish literary texts, be they visual or verbal, and repurposing them in order to maximize their usability among modern readers took on a life of its own in the post-Holocaust era. What had been a pressing matter of cultural preservation at the fin de siècle, and between the world wars, became urgent after the Holocaust. In fact, throughout the twentieth century, the precedent for a hybrid consciousness, a consciousness of the need to salvage artifacts for purposes of their redeployment within an "authentically" Jewish framework for modern people, remained cogent, providing a channel after the Holocaust for a uniquely modern Jewish means of coping with loss and looking toward the future. The types of intertextuality that defined different stages of Jewish literary production and consciousness extended into the post-Holocaust period in a particularly interesting form in America: a hybrid of folk-ethnographic and aesthetic aspirations and effects forged the salvage-poetic patterns we documented throughout this study.

All this is to say that my early scholarship in Modern Hebrew literature, and my upbringing in Orthodox Jewish educational environments with an emphasis on traditional Jewish textual study, unexpectedly did quite a bit to prepare me for the detour this book represents in my most recent academic work—toward an American Jewish cultural context. My background in Hebrew literature, both ancient and modern, helped me to better understand the critical ways in which intertextuality has functioned in American Jewish letters to create continuity between the pre-Holocaust period and post-Holocaust periods, between Jewish tradition and modernity, as defined by the Jewish Enlightenment as well as by the Holocaust. The texts that signified Jewish tradition shifted significantly across the geographic, temporal, and experiential abyss that separated East European Jewry from American Jewry before and after the Holocaust, with Yiddish and Hasidic texts becoming signifiers of tradition after the war, whereas before the war they were considered quite modern. Nevertheless, as I hope I have argued successfully throughout this book, those texts that served as primary textual artifacts of pre-Holocaust Jewish life in a post-Holocaust American Jewish context were, generally speaking, texts that were already self-conscious about their role in representing the demise of traditional Jewish life and the necessity for salvaging the traditional within the trappings of the modern.

The particular shape of the hybrid texts we have analyzed here is a product of a unique type of American Jewish intertextuality that resulted from the intellectual and cultural moment characterizing the immediate postwar period. *Life Is with People*, as I argued in the third chapter, couldn't have been written without the backing of the ethnographic establishment, at a liminal moment in its own development, with an emphasis on the methodologies of salvage ethnography and culture at a distance. The impulse to depict pre-Holocaust East European Jewish life in an ethnographic medium helped to channel the energies invested earlier by Maurice Samuel and Abraham Joshua Heschel, for instance, as they too authored hybrid works that relied on earlier literary texts to bolster their efforts to memorialize and describe a lost world. The crucial role played by Yiddish and Hasidic literature in the three works we explored by Samuel and Heschel as the basis for the broader folk-ethnographic constructs evident in them presents a unique intertextual self-consciousness. Irving Howe and Eliezer Greenberg, in their framing of an anthology of Yiddish fiction, also present those texts as essential to an understanding of pre-Holocaust East European Jewish culture, though in a different way. Their work, like Dawidowicz's in *The Golden Tradition* and Dobroszycki and Kirshenblatt-Gimblett's in *Image before My Eyes*, relies on the chance encounters of a scholar with archival works or artifacts and on the beautiful possibilities inherent in a broad collection of images or texts being used to construct a cultural montage.

Considering the photographs and paintings under discussion here in terms of intertextuality is also an instructive exercise. Particularly in the case of Vishniac's and Kacyzne's photographs, taken before the war for philanthropic and popular-cultural purposes, their postwar deployment acknowledges their original subject matter while heightening its ramifications. Reading the photographs as texts within their later reframings as image books allows us to consider them as texts within texts. In Vishniac's works, those reframings provide layer upon layer of textual consciousness, with his captions circling around one another, elaborating on one another, and even commenting on one another when juxtaposed across volumes. The contextualization of Kacyzne's photographs by Marek Web within the realm of "Yiddishland" and of Sulamita Kacyzne-Reale's quest for her lost father forces a reading of the photographs as texts at a nexus of ideological (in the editor's quest to use these photographs to define Yiddishland) and familial currents that speak to one another, like complementary voices: an ethnic and a family album.

The synthesis of intertextual and ethnographic concerns implicit in all the chapters of this study bring to fruition a sense of the coexistence of ethnographic and poetic impulses in modern Jewish literary works authored at the turn of the twentieth century in Hebrew and Yiddish, that I developed early on in my career, as I navigated the unique literary and cultural challenges presented by the Modern Hebrew Renaissance. In my earlier work on Dvora Baron (1887–1956), the only female fiction writer to be acknowledged in the canon of the Modern Hebrew Renaissance, I was strongly exhorted by my teachers and colleagues not to "give in" to the popular assessment of Baron as being literarily valuable only inasmuch as she gave her readers a glimpse of a forgotten corner of East European Jewish life at the turn of the twentieth century.[8] She was a literary modernist, I was taught, yet her content overshadowed her form within critical discourse, in part because she was a woman and in part because her subject matter was the East European Jewish shtetl before the Holocaust.

And indeed what drew me to Baron in the first place? Her stories gripped me because they told me about the women in the women's section listening to sermons on a cold winter afternoon, about the cakes left to cool on the windowsill, and about the reaction of mothers-in-law to the birth of a daughter. Furthermore, my own grandmothers, Holocaust survivors born and raised in Eastern Europe, were not particularly forthcoming about their lives before the war. I felt, in Baron's work, that I had found an access point to my grandmothers' lives.

After writing a book arguing for Baron's unique contribution to Hebrew modernism in order, in part, to satisfy my teachers' need to reinstate her within the canon, I asked myself whether it would be possible to reclaim Baron's content as part of a broader phenomenon in modern Hebrew and Yiddish literature from the turn of the century that didn't exclude but transcended the discourse of nationalism that largely defines critical discussions of these literatures. To what extent, I asked myself, could Baron's style be understood under the umbrella of salvage poetics, a poetic that marries literary concerns with ethnographic ones?

For those writers witnessing the demise of traditional Jewish life through modernization, migration, secularization, and ultimately the destruction of two world wars, what role did their own sense of the need to "salvage" that world play in their narrative choices? When Hebrew and Yiddish writer and critic David Frishmann (1859–1922), for example, stated that to recapture the Jewish experience in the Pale of Settlement, all Jews had to do was read the works of Mendele Moykher Sforim (S. J. Abramowitz, 1836–1917),[9] was he describing the idiosyncrasies of his own reading practices, a phenomenon unique to Mendele's writing, or something more widespread? More important, was he describing a literary style that was to become essential to the formation of modern Jewish literary experience?

In writing this book, I attempted to answer those questions. I tried to better understand what literary critics mean when they speak of "ethnographic" literary texts, and I worked to better understand a broad constellation of literary trends that seemed, to my mind, to coalesce under the heading of salvage poetics during the twentieth century. Although I did not begin this book with a commitment to investigating intertextuality within an American Jewish literary context, as the book developed, I realized that folk ethnography in the American Jewish community, just like any exploration of modern Jewish literary activity, cannot be understood without an engagement with this concept.

To return, then, to Dvora Baron, whose Hebrew stories about East European Jewish women's experience so endeared her to me, but who was read by so many early Israeli critics as "nothing more" than ethnographic, I hope that my sense of a salvage poetic in an American post-Holocaust context can recast the idea of "nothing more" than an "ethnographic" valence in literary texts. Dvora Baron, in other words, was writing before the war with an eye toward the role of her works as a kind of "photographic negative," something she actually articulates in her story "Mishpachah [Family]."[10] She thematizes the notion of return and the necessity for documentation in her Hebrew works by creating a uniquely tuned literary voice that exists both in the present of the story's telling and in the past of the story's unfolding. In a story titled "Fradel," which I pointed to in the introduction to *Intimations of Difference* as a model for how an ethnographic consciousness can be embedded in a fictional work, the eponymous protagonist goes to the ritual bath to prepare for her itinerant husband's arrival home from a business trip for a short interval. The text then shifts into a description of the institution of the *mikva* (ritual bath) for Jewish women, while framing it at the same time within the context of Fradel's intense psychological distress in the story.

The play of psychological drama and cultural description in "Fradel" epitomizes the type of "salvage poetic" I was looking for when I began this project, so many years ago. However, what I found in an American Jewish post-Holocaust context was dramatically different from what I expected to find. In the texts we explored together here, what I found was not a series of fictional texts deliberately negotiating the ethnographic and the literary in the way that Baron does in her work. Rather, I found a series of "hybrid" texts or texts that build themselves around works like those produced by Baron to create another layer of ethnographic self-consciousness. In American culture, because of the additional layer of mediation necessary for works so firmly rooted in East European Jewish culture—either because their original formulation was in Yiddish or their depiction of landscapes and institutions were so far afield from the American Jewish experience—the "hybrid" of selecting "original" artifacts from Jewish life in Eastern Europe, be they textual or photographic, and inserting them within an elaborate folk-ethnographic frame became an important means of cultural salvage.

In works like *The World of Sholem Aleichem* or *Life Is with People* and *A Treasury of Yiddish Stories*, we see an attempt to create a folk-ethnographic portrait out of the marriage of salvage aspirations and primary Yiddish literary texts that articulate a step toward modernity, not necessarily in their content but in their narratological features: in the positioning of their narrators and the self-conscious way they straddle the old and the new. In *A Vanished World* and in *The Golden Tradition*, we witness the repurposing of pre-Holocaust photographs and expository texts to illuminate not only a newly destroyed culture but also a newly destroyed sense of belonging to that culture on the parts of Roman Vishniac and Lucy Dawidowicz. In *Poyln* and *They Called Me Mayer July*, we observed the complexities of uniting a familial and an ethnic search through the deployment of pre-Holocaust memories and photographs in contemporary image books, highlighting the possibility of applying our intertextual hybrid model to visual works. Heschel's use of Hasidic anecdotes immediately after the war in his portrait of East European Jewish life in *The Earth Is the Lord's* highlights the particular needs, as he perceives them, of an American audience during a liminal moment just prior to full awareness of the extent of the Holocaust's destruction, in fact even before the liberation of Auschwitz.

In earlier stages of this project on salvage poetics I distinguished between what I called primary, secondary, and tertiary texts grappling with reconstructions of the East European Jewish world. Primary texts were those that originated in the pre-Holocaust period within the canons of traditional Jewish culture—the Torah, the Midrash, the religious texts that are so central to understanding the culture of traditional Jews. Secondary texts were those of Jewish modernity that acknowledged those earlier texts in myriad, intertextually charged ways, using them when necessary to articulate the distance between the traditional and the modern. This was the case in many of the Yiddish texts, such as those written by Mendele Moykher Sforim, who used biblical allusions to create semantic gaps between the ancient and the modern, forging a humorously self-conscious idiom that drew attention to the contemporary circumstances of East European Jews. Tertiary texts, finally, are those salvage-poetic texts that we have analyzed here. They are the texts based on the secondary salvage-poetic texts that emerged from Eastern Europe but were further mediated and modified for an audience that would have trouble accessing them in their original language or context.

Intertextual analysis, therefore, so key to my understanding of Modern Hebrew literature and so essential to the work I have done until now in that field, has taken on a new and complex importance in my exploration of the construction of post-Holocaust American Jewish folk ethnographies of pre-Holocaust East European Jewish life. How better to salvage a culture nearly wholly destroyed in the war than to identify its artifacts and build an explanatory armature around them? More important, however, in the years immediately following the war, was the urgent need to mitigate and mediate the gaps in literacy governing the American Jewish perception of pre-Holocaust East European Jewish life. How, in other words, is one to not only expose an American Jewish audience to the primary salvage texts of East European Jewry, but to translate them as well, both linguistically and culturally? In tracing the increasing prevalence of images as a kind of "new Yiddish" for American Jews, what we have observed here is the profound commitment to finding a new idiom for Jewish ethnicity in the post-Holocaust years. The farther we got from the Yiddish and Hebrew of traditional Jewish culture, the more essential it became, in Nathan Glazer's assessment, to make sure that a half-baked, illiterate religious identity did not supplant a fully fleshed out American Jewish ethnic identity, be it based in the suburbs or in the urban centers of America. Seeking out the "cultural logics" of American Jewish experience in the postwar years, wherein change is viewed as adaptive and contingent, and not necessarily fatal, through our analysis of hybrid texts based first in literature, than in photography and image, I believe we have found reason to agree with Nathan Glazer in his view that "at no point has everything been rejected at once; a kind of shifting balance has been maintained whereby each generation could relate itself meaningfully to some part of the Jewish past."[11]

NOTES

PROLOGUE: IN SEARCH OF A POSTWAR JEWISHNESS

1. Nathan Glazer, *American Judaism* (Chicago: University of Chicago Press, 1957), 132.
2. Riv Ellen Prell, "Community and the Discourse of Elegy: The Postwar Suburban Debate" in *Imagining the American Jewish Community*, ed. Jack Wertheimer (Waltham, MA: Brandeis University Press, 2007), 76.
3. Glazer, *American Judaism*, 141.
4. Ibid., 1.
5. Edward Shapiro, *A Time for Healing: American Jewry since World War II* (Baltimore: Johns Hopkins University Press, 1992), 167.
6. Prell, "Community and the Discourse of Elegy," 79.
7. Jack Wertheimer, *The New American Judaism: How Jews Practice their Religion Today* (Princeton, NJ: Princeton University Press, 2018), 18.
8. Wertheimer, *New American Judaism*, 270.
9. Ibid., 18.
10. Karen Brodkin, *How Jews Became White Folks and What that Says about Race in America* (New Brunswick, NJ: Rutgers University Press, 1998). The American Jewish move to the suburbs as a result of the professionalization of the Jews in the third generation, and their increased prosperity, has also been discussed by other scholars. See Shapiro, *Time for Healing*; Rachel Kranson, *Ambivalent Embrace: Jewish Upward Mobility in Postwar America* (Chapel Hill: University of North Carolina Press, 2017); Albert J. Gordon, *Jews in Suburbia* (Boston: Beacon Press, 1959); Oscar Handlin, *The Uprooted: The Epic Story of the Great Migrations that Made the American People* (Boston: Little, Brown and Company, 1952); Milton M. Gordon, *Assimilation in American Life: The Role*

of Race, Religion, and National Origins (New York: Oxford University Press, 1964); and Judith R. Kramer and Seymour Leventman, Children of the Gilded Ghetto: Conflict Resolution of Three Generations of American Jews (New Haven, CT: Yale University Press, 1961).

11. See Deborah Dash Moore, At Home in America: Second Generation New York Jews (New York: Columbia University Press, 1981); and Eli Lederhendler, "Domestic Virtues: Deborah Dash Moore's At Home in America and Its Historiographical Context," American Jewish History 100, no. 2 (2016): 205–19.

12. Moore, At Home, 75.

13. Brodkin, Jews Became White Folks; Deborah Dash Moore, GI Jews: How World War II Changed a Generation (Cambridge, MA: Harvard University Press, 2006).

14. Horace Kallen, "Democracy versus the Melting-Pot: A Study of American Nationality (1915)," in Theories of Ethnicity: A Classical Reader, ed. Werner Sollors (London: Macmillan, 1996), 67–92; and Horace Kallen, Culture and Democracy in the United States (New York: Boni and Liveright, 1924).

15. On George Devereux's "investiga[tion of] the contrastive and dissociative nature of ethnic behavior that is not actually prompted by any ethnic tradition but by the attempt to thwart a nonethnic otherness," see Werner Sollors, Beyond Ethnicity: Consent and Descent in American Culture (New York: Oxford University Press, 1986), 28.

16. Kranson, Ambivalent Embrace, 18.

17. Mark Zborowski and Elizabeth Herzog, Life Is with People: The Culture of the Shtetl (New York: Schocken Books, 1952); Abraham Joshua Heschel, The Earth Is the Lord's: The Inner World of the Jew in Eastern Europe (New York: Henry Schuman, 1949); and Maurice Samuel, The World of Sholem Aleichem (New York: Knopf, 1943).

18. Prell, "Community and the Discourse," 69.

19. Ibid., 82.

20. Kranson, Ambivalent Embrace, 6.

21. Ibid., 6.

22. Sollors, Beyond Ethnicity.

23. Mary Antin, The Promised Land (Boston: Houghton Mifflin Company, 1912), 1.

24. Sarah Wilson, "The Evolution of Ethnicity," ELH 76 (2009): 247–76.

AN INTRODUCTION TO SALVAGE POETICS

1. The theoretical concept of "intermediality," or the adaptation of a work from one medium to another, is well applied in this context. See Eric Mechoulan and Angela Carr, "Intermediality: An Introduction to the Arts of Transmission," *Substance* 44, no. 3 (2015): 3–18.

2. Alisa Solomon, *Wonder of Wonders: A Cultural History of Fiddler on the Roof* (New York: Metropolitan Books, 2013), 114.

3. Ibid., 117.

4. Ibid., 127, 161.

5. Ibid., 216.

6. Jonathan Freedman, *Klezmer America: Jewishness, Ethnicity and Modernity* (New York: Columbia University Press, 2008), 9.

7. Werner Sollors, *The Invention of Ethnicity* (New York: Oxford University Press, 1989), xv.

8. Joseph Berger, "How Do You Say 'Tradition' in Yiddish?," *The New York Times*, July 11, 2018.

9. Berger, "How Do You Say 'Tradition.'"

10. Alisa Solomon, "A 'Fiddler on the Roof' in Yiddish: The Way It Ought to Be," *Forward*, June 24, 2018.

11. Martin Buber, *Tales of the Hasidim: The Early Masters* (New York: Schocken Books, 1968), viii.

12. Steven T. Katz, "Dialogue and Revelation in the Thought of Martin Buber," *Religious Studies* 14, no. 1 (1978): 58–59.

13. Bialik and Ravnitsky's *Sefer ha-Aggadah* [The Book of Legends] was first published in 1908–9. See Mark W. Kiel, "Sefer ha-Aggadah: Creating a Classic Anthology," in *The Anthology in Jewish Literature*, ed. David Stern (Oxford: Oxford University Press, 2004), 226–43. M. Y. Berdischevsky collected legends from the Bible and the Talmud in a variety of different anthologies that were first published in 1904. See Zipora Kagan, "Homo Anthologicus: Micha Joseph Berdyczewski and the Anthological Genre," in Stern, *The Anthology in Jewish Literature*, 211–25. Louis Ginzberg's monumental *The Legends of the Jews*, originally published in German in 1909, an English-language anthology of biblical midrash arranged chronologically (four volumes of narrative, two volumes of footnotes, and index), was translated into English by Henrietta Szold in 1913. See Louis Ginzberg, *The Legends of the Jews* (Philadelphia: Jewish Publication Society, 1909–38). Beginning in 1906, the German Jewish philosopher Martin Buber began

to edit and publish anthologies of Hasidic stories, including a volume on Rabbi Nachman of Bratslav and the Baal Shem Tov. See Martin Buber, *Die Geschichten des Rabbi Nachman* [The Tales of Rabbi Nachman] (Frankfurt am Main: Rütten & Loening, 1906) (in German); and *Die Legende des Baal Schem* [The Legend of the Baal Shem], 2nd. ed (Frankfurt: Rütten & Loening, 1916) (in German).

14. See David Roskies, introduction to *The Dybbuk and Other Stories* (New York: Schocken Books, 1992); Gabriella Safran, *Wandering Soul: The Dybbuk's Creator, S. Ansky* (Cambridge, MA: Harvard University Press, 2010); and Gabriella Safran, Steven J. Zipperstein, and Craig Stephen Cravens, eds., *The Worlds of S. An-sky: A Russian-Jewish Intellectual at the Turn of the Century* (Stanford, CA: Stanford University Press, 2006).

15. Jeffrey Shandler, *Shtetl: A Vernacular Intellectual History* (New Brunswick, NJ: Rutgers University Press, 2014), 59–64.

16. Laurence J. Silberstein, *Martin Buber's Social and Religious Thought: Alienation and the Quest for Meaning* (New York: New York University Press, 1989), 57.

17. Ibid., 57.

18. Ibid.

19. Gershom Scholem, "Martin Buber's Hasidism: A Critique," *Commentary* 32, no. 4 (October 1, 1961): 306. See also Gershom Scholem, "Martin Buber's Conception of Judaism," in *On Jews and Judaism in Crisis: Selected Essays* (New York: Schocken Books, 1976), 126–71.

20. Martin Buber, *The Legend of the Ba'al Shem* (New York: Schocken Books, 1969), 7–8.

21. Steven E. Ascheim, *Brothers and Strangers: The East European Jew in German and German-Jewish Consciousness (1800–1923)* (Madison: University of Wisconsin Press, 1982), 208.

22. Ibid., 187.

23. Lucy Dawidowicz, "On Equal Terms: Jewish Identity in America," in *What Is the Use of Jewish History? Essays* (New York: Schocken Books, 1992), 223.

24. Martin Buber, *Hasidism and Modern Man*, ed. and trans. Maurice Friedman (New York: Harper, 1966), 51–53.

25. Laura Wexler, "What Vishniac Saw: Another Look," in *Roman Vishniac Rediscovered*, ed. Maya Benton (New York: ICP, 2015).

26. Roman Vishniac, "Commentary on the Photographs," in *A Vanished World* (New York: Farrar, Straus and Giroux), n.p. n67.

27. Shandler, *Shtetl*, 130.

28. Clifford Geertz, "Thick Description: Toward an Interpretive Theory of Culture," in *The Interpretation of Cultures: Selected Essays* (New York: Basic Books, 1973), 3–30.

29. Geertz, "Thick Description," 3–30.

30. Stephen Greenblatt and Catherine Gallagher, *Practicing New Historicism* (Chicago: University of Chicago Press, 2000).

31. Quoted in Carol S. Kessner, *The Other New York Jewish Intellectuals* (New York: New York University Press, 1994), 239. On the notion of "repurposing" earlier literature, see Shandler, *Shtetl*, 91–94.

32. Jonathan Boyarin, "Jewish Ethnography and the Question of the Book," *Anthropological Quarterly* 64, no. 1 (1991): 14–29; Harvey Goldberg, "Reflections on the Mutual Relevance of Anthropology and Judaic Studies," in *Judaism Viewed from Within and from Without* (Albany: SUNY Press, 1987), 1–43; and Geertz, *The Interpretation of Cultures*.

33. Karin Barber, *The Anthropology of Texts: Persons and Publics: Oral and Written Culture in Africa and Beyond* (Cambridge: Cambridge University Press, 2007), 154.

34. Also see Sheila Jelen, "A Treasury of Yiddish Stories: Salvage Montage and the Anti-Shtetl," in *Reconstructing the Old Country: American Jewry in the Post-Holocaust Decades*, ed. Eliyana Adler and Sheila Jelen (Detroit: Wayne State University Press, 2017), 137–51.

35. Benedict Anderson, *Imagined Communities: Reflections on the Origin and Spread of Nationalism* (London: Verso, 2006).

36. Kessner, *The Other*, 15.

37. Ibid., 231.

38. Ibid.

39. Barbara Kirshenblatt-Gimblett, "Imagining Europe," in *Divergent Jewish Cultures*, ed. Deborah Dash Moore and S. Ilan Troen (New Haven, CT: Yale University Press, 2001), 168.

40. Ibid.

41. Ibid., 155–91.

42. Ibid.

43. *Oxford English Dictionary Online*, s.v. "folklore," accessed July 21, 2019, https://www-oed-com.proxy-um.researchport.umd.edu/view/Entry/72546?redirectedFrom=folklore&.

44. Jack Kugelmass, "Jewish Icons: Envisioning the Self in Images of the Other," in *Jews and Other Differences: The New Jewish Cultural Studies*, ed.

Jonathan Boyarin and Daniel Boyarin (Minneapolis: University of Minnesota Press, 1997), 42.

45. Ibid.

46. Roland Barthes, *Camera Lucida: Reflections on Photography* (New York: Hill and Wang, 1980), 27.

47. Quoted in Elizabeth Edwards, *Raw Histories: Photographs, Anthropology and Museums* (Oxford: Berg, 2001), 10.

48. Ibid.

49. Samuel C. Heilman, *Defenders of the Faith: Inside Ultra-Orthodox Jewry* (New York: Schocken Books, 1992).

50. Janet S. Belcove-Shalin, *New World Hasidim: Ethnographic Studies of Hasidic Jews in America* (Albany: SUNY Press, 1995); and Lynn Davidman, *Becoming Un-Orthodox: Stories of Ex-Hasidic Jews* (New York: Oxford University Press, 2015).

51. See Chaya Deitsch, *Here and There: Leaving Hasidism, Keeping My Family* (New York: Schocken Books, 2015); Shulem Deen, *All Who Go Do Not Return* (Minneapolis: Graywolf Press, 2015); Leah Vincent, *Cut Me Loose: Sin and Salvation after My Ultra-Orthodox Girlhood* (New York: Penguin, 2015); Leah Lax, *Uncovered: How I Left Hasidic Life and Finally Came Home* (Phoenix: She Writes Press, 2015); Deborah Feldman, *Unorthodox: The Scandalous Rejection of My Hasidic Roots* (New York: Simon and Schuster, 2012); and Hella Winston, *Unchosen: The Hidden Lives of Hasidic Rebels* (New York: Beacon Press, 2006).

52. Lis Harris, *Holy Days: The World of a Hasidic Family* (New York: Summit Press, 1985).

53. Steven Zipperstein, "Underground Man: The Curious Case of Mark Zborowski and the Writing of a Modern Jewish Classic," *Jewish Review of Books* (Summer 2010).

54. Robert LeVine, "Culture and Personality Studies 1918–1960: Myth and History," *Journal of Personality* 69, no. 6 (December 2001): 808.

55. Ibid.

56. Georges Didi-Huberman, *Images in Spite of All: Four Photographs from Auschwitz* (Chicago: University of Chicago Press, 2008).

57. Alana Newhouse, "A Closer Reading of Roman Vishniac," *New York Times Magazine*, April 4, 2010, www.nytimes.com/2010/04/04/magazine/04shtetl-t.html.

58. Lucy Dawidowicz, *The Golden Tradition: Jewish Life and Thought in Eastern Europe* (New York: Holt, Rinehart and Winston, 1967), 6.

1. SALVAGE (SELVEDGE) TRANSLATION

1. Samuel, *World*, 26.
2. Kirshenblatt-Gimblett, "Imagining Europe," 168.
3. Solomon, *Wonder of Wonders*, 119.
4. Samuel, *World*, 20.
5. Ibid., 91.
6. Ibid., 152.
7. Ibid., 160.
8. Milton Hindus, ed., introduction to *The Worlds of Maurice Samuel: Selected Writings* (Philadelphia: Jewish Publication Society, 1977), xxi–xxiii.
9. Kwame Anthony Appiah, "Thick Translation," in *The Translation Studies Reader*, ed. Lawrence Venuti (New York: Routledge, 2000), 399.
10. Mary Louise Pratt, *Imperial Eyes: Travel Writing and Transculturation* (New York: Routledge, 2008), 8.
11. Ibid., 9.
12. Maurice Samuel, *The Gentleman and the Jew* (New York: Knopf, 1950).
13. Samuel, *World*, 7.
14. Maurice Samuel, *Little Did I Know: Recollections and Reflections* (New York: Knopf, 1963), 68.
15. Ibid., 7.
16. Robert Lynd and Helen Lynd, *Middletown: A Study in Modern American Culture* (New York: Harper and Row, 1929), 3.
17. Ibid., 6.
18. Samuel, *World*, 10–11.
19. Ibid., 11.
20. Ibid., 15.
21. Ibid., 14.
22. Ibid., 14–15.
23. Ibid., 19.
24. Erich Auerbach, *Mimesis: The Representation of Reality in Western Literature* (Princeton, NJ: Princeton University Press, 1953); and Catherine Gallagher and Stephen Greenblatt, *Practicing New Historicism* (Chicago: University of Chicago Press, 2000).
25. In all the framings of each Tevye story, for instance, Tevye calls Sholem Aleichem "Pan." See Sholem Aleichem, *Tevye the Dairyman and the Railroad Stories*, trans. Hillel Halkin (New York: Schocken Books, 1987), 3, 20, 35, 53, 82, 97, 116.

26. Maurice Samuel, *Prince of the Ghetto* (New York: Knopf, 1948), 11.
27. Ibid., 10.
28. Samuel, *World*, 84.
29. Ibid., 113.
30. Ibid.
31. Ibid., 84–85.
32. Ibid., 6.
33. See Sheila E. Jelen, "Bialik's Other Silence," *Hebrew Studies* 44 (2003): 65–86. Also Sheila E. Jelen, "Speakerly Texts and Historical Realities: Mendele's Relationship to the Revival of Hebrew Speech," in *Jewish Literature and History*, ed. Sheila E. Jelen and Eliyana R. Adler (Bethesda: University of Maryland Press, 2008), 207–21.
34. This is evident as well in the 1971 Hollywood adaptation of Sholem Aleichem's *Tevye the Milkman* stories. In that film Sholem Aleichem is replaced by the figure of the fiddler. It is the fiddler's music that accompanies the characters in the text throughout the dramas they enact, evoking the pathos and the humor elicited in the narrative text by the interaction between Sholem Aleichem and Tevye.
35. Samuel, *World*, 45.
36. Ibid., 27.
37. Gerard Genette, *Narrative Discourse: An Essay in Method* (Ithaca: Cornell University Press, 1983); and Dorrit Cohn, *Transparent Minds: Narrative Modes for Presenting Consciousness in Fiction* (Princeton, NJ: Princeton University Press, 1984).
38. Samuel, *World*, 67.
39. Ibid., 230.
40. Samuel, *Prince*, 65.
41. Lydia Liu, ed., *Tokens of Exchange: The Problem of Translation in Global Circulations* (Durham, NC: Duke University Press, 1999), 1–2.
42. Ibid.
43. Lawrence Venuti, *The Scandals of Translation: Towards an Ethics of Difference* (New York: Routledge, 1998), 11.
44. Tullio Maranhao and Bernard Streck, *Translation and Ethnography: The Anthropological Challenge of Intercultural Understanding* (Tucson: University of Arizona Press, 2003), xv.
45. Gayatri Chakavorty Spivak, "The Politics of Translation," in Venuti, *The Translation Studies Reader*, 370.

46. Sol Liptzin, *A History of Yiddish Literature* (New York: Jonathan David Publishers, 1972); and Chone Shmeruk, *Prokim fun der yidisher literatur-geshikhte* (Tel Aviv: Peretz Farlag, 1988) (in Yiddish).

47. Cynthia Ozick, "Toward a New Yiddish," in *Art and Ardor: Essays* (New York: Knopf, 1983), 151–77.

48. Ibid., 169.

49. Ozick, "Remembering Maurice Samuel," *Art and Ardor*, 213.

50. Samuel, *Prince*, 7.

51. Ibid., 9.

52. Samuel, *Little Did I Know*, 286.

53. Samuel, *World*, 3.

54. Ibid., 84.

55. Samuel, *Prince*, 8–9.

56. Ibid., 197.

57. Ibid., 154.

58. Ibid., 223.

59. Ibid., 178.

60. Ibid., 3.

61. Ibid., 15.

62. Irving Howe and Eliezer Greenberg, ed., *A Treasury of Yiddish Stories* (New York: Meridian, 1953 [Library of Congress catalogue says it was copyrighted in 1954]), 120.

63. Samuel, *Prince*, 17–18.

64. Jeffrey Shandler, *Adventures in Yiddishland: Postvernacular Language & Culture* (Berkeley: University of California Press, 2006).

65. Howe and Greenberg, *A Treasury*, 122.

66. Samuel, *Prince*, 19.

67. Y. L. Peretz, "Mesiras Nefesh," in *Ale Verk Fun Y. L. Peretz* (New York: Yiddish, 1920), 140.

68. Maurice Samuel, *In Praise of Yiddish* (New York: Cowles, 1971), 19.

69. Samuel, *In Praise of Yiddish*, 21–22.

2. SALVAGE INWARDNESS

1. Abraham Joshua Heschel, "The Eastern European Era in Jewish History," in *YIVO Annual of Jewish Social Science*, vol. 1 (New York: YIVO Institute for Jewish Research, 1946), 25.

2. Abraham Joshua Heschel, *The Earth Is the Lord's: The Inner World of the Jew in East Europe* (New York: Harper and Row, 1966), 89.

3. Jeffrey Shandler, "Heschel and Yiddish: A Struggle with Signification," *The Journal of Jewish Thought and Philosophy* 2 (1993): 259.

4. Ken Koltun-Fromm, *Imagining Jewish Authenticity: Vision and Text in American Jewish Thought* (Bloomington: Indiana University Press, 2015), 3.

5. Ibid., 53.

6. Ibid., 52.

7. Stephen S. Kayser, introduction to *Ilya Schor: Paintings on Yiddish Themes* (New York: Gallery of Jewish Art, 1947), n.p.

8. Ibid.

9. Shandler, "Heschel and Yiddish," 249.

10. Like Zborowski and Herzog, he quotes from Yiddish literature as well, though not as frequently. He draws twice on Mendele—once from his autobiography, *Shloyme Reb Hayims*, and once from *Fishke Der Krumer*.

11. Mira Schor, email message to author, February 24, 2019.

12. Ibid.

13. Ibid.

14. Sholem Aleichem, *Adventures of Mottel the Cantor's Son* (New York: Henry Schuman, 1953).

15. Schor, email message.

16. Kirshenblatt-Gimblett, "Imagining Europe," 171.

17. Heschel, *Earth Is the Lord's*, 7–8.

18. Kayser, *Paintings on Yiddish Themes*, n.p.

19. Ibid., n.p.

20. Dalia Tawil, *Life of the Old Jewish Shtetl: Paintings and Silver by Ilya Schor* (Yeshiva University Museum, 1975–76), n.p.

21. Heschel, *Earth Is the Lord's*, 50.

22. Hershel Matt, ed., "Heschel's Theology: Organized Excerpts," The Shalom Center, September 8, 2001, https://theshalomcenter.org/node/88.

23. Abraham Joshua Heschel, *God in Search of Man: A Philosophy of Judaism* (New York: Farrar, Straus and Giroux, 1977), 7–8.

24. Edward K. Kaplan, *Spiritual Radical: Abraham Joshua Heschel in America, 1940–1972* (New Haven, CT: Yale University Press, 2007), 168.

25. Mira Schor, "The Tale of the Goldsmith's Floor," *Differences: A Journal of Feminist Cultural Studies* 14, no. 3 (2003): 143.

26. Ibid., 144.

27. Tawil, *Life of the Old Jewish Shtetl*, n.p.

28. Heschel, "Eastern European Era," 103.

29. Ibid., 94–95.

30. As we saw in our discussion of Peretz's corpus, the story "Devotion unto Death" explores this theme extensively.

31. "Chelmno," Holocaust Encyclopedia, United States Holocaust Memorial Museum, accessed February 5, 2018, https://www.ushmm.org/wlc/en/article.php?ModuleId=10005194.

32. "History of YIVO," YIVO Institute for Jewish Research, accessed February 5, 2018, https://www.yivo.org/History-of-YIVO.

33. *East European Jews in Two Worlds*, ed. Deborah Dash Moore (Evanston, IL: Northwestern University Press, 1990), viii.

34. In her dissertation, "Planned Encounters: The Ethic and Aesthetic of the Hasidic Narrative," Chen Edrei, my student and colleague, theorizes the place of Hasidic hagiographies in the modern Hebrew literary canon.

35. Shandler, "Heschel and Yiddish," 275.

36. Edward K. Kaplan, "The American Mission of Abraham Joshua Heschel," in *The Americanization of the Jews*, ed. Robert Seltzer and Norman S. Cohen (New York: New York University Press 1995), 355.

37. Ibid.

38. Edward K. Kaplan and Samuel Dressner, "Heschel in Vilna," *Judaism* (June 1, 1998): 286.

39. Heschel, "Eastern European Era," 93.

40. Ibid.

41. Ibid., 101.

42. Heschel, *Earth Is the Lord's*, 92.

43. Ibid., 87.

44. Heschel, "Eastern European Era," 105.

45. Ibid., 106.

46. Heschel, *Earth Is the Lord's*, 56.

47. Heschel, "Eastern European Era," 106.

48. Ibid., 92.

49. Ibid., 96.

50. Ibid., 97.

51. Ibid., 98.

52. Ibid.

53. Ibid., 99.

54. Ibid., 100.

55. Ibid., 104.

56. Shai Held, *Abraham Joshua Heschel: The Call of Transcendence* (Blooming-ton: Indiana University Press, 2013), 17.

57. Ibid., 8.

58. Ibid.

59. William Mcdonald, "Soren Kierkegaard (1813–1855)," *Internet Encyclope-dia of Philosophy: A Peer Reviewed Academic Resource*, https://www.iep.utm .edu/kierkega/.

60. Heschel, *Earth Is the Lord's*, 56.

61. Ibid., 58–59.

62. Heschel, "Eastern European Era," 99.

63. Heschel, *Earth Is the Lord's*, 75.

64. The original three reappear in the later essay ("The Melamed and the Rich Man," "The Talmud Scholar and His Rebbe," and "Rabbi Lieber and Elijah the Prophet as told by the Baal Shem Tov").

65. Heschel, *Earth Is the Lord's*, 89.

66. Ibid., 92.

67. Ibid., 93–94.

68. Abraham Joshua Heschel, *A Passion for Truth* (Philadelphia: Jewish Publi-cation Society, 1973), xiv.

69. Ibid.

70. Ibid., 74.

71. Ibid., 79.

72. Ibid., 87.

73. Ibid., 94.

74. Arthur Green, "Abraham Joshua Heschel: Recasting Hasidism for Mod-erns," *Modern Judaism* 29, no. 1 (February 2009): 63.

75. Shandler, "Heschel and Yiddish," 245–99.

76. Annette Aronowicz, "Heschel's Yiddish Kotsk: Some Reflections on Inwardness," in *Abraham Joshua Heschel: Philosophy, Theology and Inter-religious Dialogue*, ed. Stanislaw Krajewski and Adam Lipszyc (Wiesbaden: Harrasowitz Verlag, 2009), 112.

77. Ibid.

78. Morris M. Faierstein, "Abraham Joshua Heschel and the Holocaust," *Mod-ern Judaism* 19, no. 3 (October 1999): 259.

79. Ibid.

80. Kaplan, "American Mission," 358.

81. Ibid., 359.

3. SALVAGE LITERARY INFERENCE

1. Zborowski and Herzog, *Life Is with People*, 25.
2. Ibid.
3. Barbara Kirshenblatt-Gimblett, introduction to Zborowski and Herzog, *Life Is with People*, ix.
4. Ibid., 50.
5. Ibid., 225.
6. Ibid.
7. Ibid., 226.
8. Ibid., 229.
9. On types in early modernist literature, see George Lukacs, *Studies in European Realism* (New York: Grosset and Dunlap, 1964) and *History and Class Consciousness: Studies in Marxist Dialectics* (Cambridge, MA: MIT Press, 1971).
10. Zborowski and Herzog, *Life Is with People*, 25.
11. Moshe Decter, "The Old Country Way of Life: The Rediscovery of the Shtetl," *Commentary* (June 1952): 604.
12. Zborowski and Herzog, *Life Is with People*, 25.
13. Authored by Rabbi Jacob ben Isaac Ashkenazi of Janow Poland in the seventeenth century, the oldest extant edition of the *Tzena U'rena* is from 1622, published in Hanau. Named for a verse in the Song of Songs (3:11)—"O maidens of Zion go forth and gaze [*Tzena U'rena*]"—the book was nevertheless designated by the author for both men and women. As stipulated in his introduction: "This work aims to enable men and women . . . to understand the word of God in simple language." See Chava Turniansky, "Ze'enah U-Re'enah," *The Encyclopedia of Jewish Women*, https://jwa.org/encyclopedia/article/zeenah-u-reenah.
14. Authored by Elia Levita Bakhur in 1507–8, the *Bovo Bukh* was a very popular chivalric romance, written in Yiddish. See Elia Levita Bakhur, *Bovo Bukh*, trans. Jerry C. Smith (n.p.: Fenestra Books, 2003). On early Yiddish literature, see Jeremy Dauber, *Antonio's Devils: Writers of the Jewish Enlightenment and the Birth of Modern Hebrew and Yiddish Literature* (Palo Alto, CA: Stanford University Press, 2004).
15. Zborowski and Herzog, *Life Is with People*, 126.
16. Ibid., 127.

17. Jonathan Boyarin, *The Ethnography of Reading* (Berkeley: University of California Press, 1993).

18. Zborowski and Herzog, *Life Is with People*, 91.

19. Ibid., 93.

20. Ibid., 96.

21. Ibid., 97.

22. Richard Handler, "Ruth Benedict and the Modernist Sensibility," in *Modernist Anthropology: From Fieldwork to Text*, ed. Marc Manganaro (Princeton, NJ: Princeton University Press, 1990), 163.

23. Kirshenblatt-Gimblett, introduction to Zborowski and Herzog, *Life Is with People*, xxxiii.

24. Ibid.

25. Zborowski and Herzog, *Life Is with People*, ix.

26. Kirshenblatt-Gimblett, "Imagining Europe," 165.

27. Ibid.

28. Zborowski and Herzog, *Life Is with People*, 30

29. Ibid., 105.

30. Ibid., 427.

31. Ibid., 262–63.

32. Ibid., 263.

33. Barbara Tedlock, "From Participant Observation to the Observation of Participation: The Emergence of Narrative Ethnography," *Journal of Anthropological Research* 47, no. 1 (Spring 1991): 69–94.

34. For a discussion of the history of the place of representing the world "as it is" in modern Hebrew letters, see Sheila Jelen, "Things as They Are: The Mimetic Imperative," in *Intimations of Difference: Dvora Baron in the Modern Hebrew Renaissance* (Syracuse, NY: Syracuse University Press, 2007).

35. Ruth Benedict, *Patterns of Culture* (New York: Houghton Mifflin, 1934).

36. Kirshenblatt-Gimblett, introduction to Zborowski and Herzog, *Life Is with People*, ix.

37. Margaret Mead and Rhoda Métraux, eds., *The Study of Culture at a Distance* (Chicago: University of Chicago Press, 1953), 3.

38. Zborowski and Herzog, *Life Is with People,* xxvii.

39. Mead and Métraux, *Study of Culture*, 3.

40. Kirshenblatt-Gimblett, "Imagining Europe," 166.

41. Zborowski and Herzog, *Life Is with People*, 25.

42. Ibid., 238.

43. *Galitsianers* were Jews from Galicia instead of Lithuania. There were two types of East European Jews in popular culture, differing in their diet, their Yiddish and their personalities—among many other things.

44. Zborowski and Herzog, *Life Is with People*, 230.
45. Margaret Mead, "We Are All Third Generation," in *Keep Your Powder Dry: An Anthropologist Looks at America* (Freeport, NY: Books for Libraries Press, 1971), 17–33.
46. Zborowski and Herzog, *Life Is with People*, 232.
47. Robert Redfield, "The Folk Society," *The American Journal of Sociology* 32, no. 4 (1947): 294.
48. Zborowski and Herzog, *Life Is with People*, 426
49. Handler, "Ruth Benedict," 163.
50. Ibid., 169–70.
51. Franz Boas, "An Anthropologist's Credo," *The Nation* (August 27, 1938), 203.
52. Ibid.
53. Benedict, *Patterns of Culture*, 2–3.
54. Handler, "Ruth Benedict," 173.

4. SALVAGE MONTAGE

1. Irving Howe, *A Margin of Hope* (San Diego: Harcourt Brace Javonovich, 1982), 261
2. Lucjan Dobroszycki and Barbara Kirshenblatt-Gimblett, *Image before My Eyes: A Photographic History of Jewish Life in Poland 1864–1939* (New York: Schocken Books, 1977), xiv.
3. Dawidowicz, *Golden Tradition*, 6.
4. Miriam Heywood, "True Images: Metaphor, Metonymy and Montage in Proust and Goddard," *Paragraph* 33, no. 1 (2010): 44.
5. Ibid., 38.
6. Alexandra Wettlaufer, "Ruskin and Laforgue: Visual-Verbal Dialectics and the Poetics/Politics of Montage," *Comparative Literature Studies* 32, no. 4 (1995): 524.
7. Ibid., 533.
8. Georges Didi-Huberman, *Images in Spite of All: Four Photographs from Auschwitz* (Chicago: University of Chicago Press, 2004).
9. I thank the anonymous reader from Wayne State University Press for providing this definition of the Sonderkommando in his review of this essay. My original, more concise definition was deemed "irksomely simplistic," therefore I have opted to use the reader's expanded definition in light of the gravity of the subject matter under discussion.

10. Didi-Huberman, *Images*, 120.
11. Ibid.
12. Ibid., 121.
13. Ibid., 120.
14. Ibid., 20.
15. Ibid., 22.
16. Ibid., 25. See also Giorgio Agamben, *Remnants of Auschwitz: The Witness and the Archive* (New York: Zone Books, 1999).
17. Didi-Huberman, *Images*, 98–99.
18. David Margolick, "Dr. Lucjan Dobroszycki, 70; Wrote of Doomed Polish Jews," *New York Times*, October 26, 1995, www.nytimes.com/1995/10/26/nyregion/dr-lucjan-dobroszycki-70-wrote-of-doomed-polish-jews.html.
19. "Eliezer Greenberg Dead at 80," *Jewish Telegraphic Agency*, June 7, 1977, www.jta.org/1977/06/07/archive/eliezer-greenberg-dead-at-80.
20. Jerome Badanes and Joshua Waletzky, *Image before My Eyes* (New York: YIVO Institute for Jewish Research, 1980).
21. Howe, *Margin of Hope*, 137.
22. On the history of the Chelm folk story and the reactions, in the press, of the Chelm community, see Itzik Gottesman, *Defining the Yiddish Nation: The Jewish Folklorists of Poland* (Detroit: Wayne State University Press, 2003), 49, 64–65.
23. Howe and Greenberg, *A Treasury*, 1.
24. Ibid., 4.
25. Ibid.
26. Ibid., 5.
27. Tawil, *Life of the Old Jewish Shtetl*, n.p.
28. Howe and Greenberg, *A Treasury*, 6.
29. Ibid.
30. Ibid., 7.
31. Ibid., 187–92.
32. Ibid., 205–13.
33. Ibid., 206.
34. Ibid., 210–11.
35. Ibid., 211.
36. Ibid., 213–19.
37. Ibid., 219.
38. Ibid., 275–79.
39. Ibid., 279.

40. Michael André Bernstein, *Foregone Conclusions: Against Apocalyptic History* (Berkeley: University of California Press, 1994).

41. Roland Barthes, *Camera Lucida*, 96. "In front of the photograph of my mother as a child, I tell myself: she is going to die. I shudder, like Winnicott's psychotic patient over a catastrophe which has already occurred. Whether or not the subject is already dead, every photograph is this catastrophe."

42. Indeed, in a recent discussion of Mark Zborowski, Steve Zipperstein has reread *Life Is with People* as similarly specious with regard to its presentation of the shtetl. Zborowski, he argues, a Soviet spy, was not the shtetl "insider" that Margaret Mead had imagined when she had hired him to write the book. Rather, he came from a large city and was profoundly suspicious of the shtetl as a backwater and religiously moribund place. In his citation of a transcript wherein Zborowski and Mead and their team were trying to find a unifying idea around which to organize their portrait of East European Jewish life, he identifies the moment when Zborowski argues that traditional Jewish life is a spiritual, and not a physical, entity. The shtetl, therefore, as the organizing principle for the book, serves as just that: an organizing principle, not an accurate representation of a locale and its culture. Kirshenblatt-Gimblett points out Mead's role in the construction of the literary shtetl to compensate for Zborowski's claim about the lack of a physical locus for their study. See Steven J. Zipperstein, "Underground Man: The Curious Case of Mark Zborowski and the Writing of a Modern Jewish Classic," *Jewish Review of Books* (Summer 2010), jewishreviewofbooks.com/articles/275/underground-man-the-curious -case-of-mark-zborowski-and-the-writing-of-a-modern-jewish-classic/. Also see Kirshenblatt-Gimblett, introduction to *Life Is With People*.

43. Dawidowicz, *What Is the Use*, xvi.

44. Ibid., 5.

45. Ibid.

46. Ibid., 7.

47. Dawidowicz, *Golden Tradition*, 5.

48. Ibid.

49. Ibid., 6.

50. Ibid., 88.

51. Dawidowicz, *What Is the Use*, 224.

52. Ibid., 223.

53. On Jewish autobiography as a sign of Jewish modernity, see Marcus Moseley, *Being for Myself Alone: Origins of Jewish Autobiography* (Stanford, CA: Stanford University Press, 2005).

54. See Hirsz Abramowicz, *Profiles of a Lost World: Memoirs of East European Jewish Life before World War II*, ed. Jeffrey Shandler and Dina Abramowicz (Detroit: Wayne State University Press, 1999).

55. Lucy Dawidowicz, *From That Place and Time: A Memoir 1938–1947* (New York: Norton, 1989), 202.

56. Dawidowicz, *What Is the Use*, 24.

57. Dawidowicz provides an extensive background on Vilna in her memoir. See *From That Place*, 28–50.

58. On Shatzky, see his entry in Dawidowicz, *Golden Tradition*, 263–69, as well as her allusions to him in *From That Place*, 11–13.

59. For a description of the Aspirantur program, see Dawidowicz, *From That Place*, 77–100.

60. Dawidowicz, *What Is the Use*, 24.

61. Ibid., 25.

62. On Birnbaum, see Dawidowicz, *Golden Tradition*, 213–22, and *What Is the Use*, 231–32.

63. Bernard Malamud, "The Magic Barrel," in *The Stories of Bernard Malamud* (New York: Farrar, Straus and Giroux, 1983), 134.

64. Lucy Dawidowicz, *The Jewish Presence* (New York: Holt, Reinhart and Winston, 1977), 46–57.

65. Dawidowicz, *From That Place*, 113.

66. Ibid., 107.

67. Dawidowicz, *Golden Tradition*, 305.

68. Ibid., 415.

69. Ibid.

70. Ibid., 422, 426.

71. Ibid., 254.

72. On Weinreich and other leaders of YIVO, see Lucy Dawidowicz, *From That Place*, 77–100. On Weinreich's flight from Europe in parallel to Dawidowicz's, see Dawidowicz, *From That Place*, 186–203.

73. Howe, *Margin of Hope*, 133.

74. Dobroszycki and Kirshenblatt-Gimblett, *Image before My Eyes*, xiii.

75. Badanes and Waletzky, *Image*.

76. Barthes, *Camera Lucida*, 96.

77. W. J. T. Mitchell, *Picture Theory: Essays on Verbal and Visual Representation* (Chicago: University of Chicago Press, 1994).

78. Ibid., 289.

79. Ibid., 292.

80. Ibid.

81. Ibid., 297.

82. Ibid., 298.

83. Dobroszycki and Kirshenblatt-Gimblett, *Image before My Eyes*, 175–77.

84. Ibid., 215.

85. Ibid., 184.

86. Ibid., 176.

87. Ibid., 67–68.

88. Ibid., 152.

89. Although it should be noted that since this is a Vishniac photo and a Vishniac caption, as we will discuss in chapter 5, it is quite possible that Vishniac invented this fate for Rabbi Eisenberg. While it is safe to presume that Eisenberg died in the war, Vishniac may not necessarily have known the details.

90. Moi Ver [Moshe Vorobeichic] and Zalman Shneour, *The Ghetto Lane in Vilna* (Zurich: O Fussli, 1931).

91. Carol Zemel, "Imagining the Shtetl: Diaspora Culture, Photography and Eastern European Jews," in *Diaspora and Visual Culture*, ed. Nicholas Mirzoeff (New York: Routledge, 2000), 193–206.

5. AUTO-ETHNOGRAPHIC SALVAGE

1. I am grateful to Maya Benton of the International Center of Photography (ICP) and to the executors of the Vishniac Foundation for their careful reading of this chapter. Their corrections and comments were extremely valuable and made a significant contribution to this chapter's final version.

2. Elie Wiesel, foreword to *A Vanished World*, by Roman Vishniac (New York: Farrar, Straus and Giroux, 1983), n.p.

3. Barthes, *Camera Lucida*.

4. Roman Vishniac, *Polish Jews: A Pictorial Record* (New York: Schocken Books, 1947), 30.

5. Ibid., 31.

6. Ibid.

7. Roman Vishniac, *A Vanished World* (New York: Farrar, Straus and Giroux), 2.

8. Vishniac, "Commentary," n.p.

9. For a discussion of the genesis of Vishniac's corpus of photographs on East European Jewry, see the chronology for Vishniac's life and work posted on the ICP website: vishniac.icp.org/chronology.

10. Maya Benton, "Vishniac on Assignment," in *Roman Vishniac Rediscovered*, ed. Maya Benton (New York: International Center of Photography, 2015), 109.

11. Jeffrey Shandler, "Behold a Vanished World," in Benton, *Roman Vishniac Rediscovered*, 135.

12. Eddy Portnoy, "Vishniac and the Yiddish Press," in Benton, *Roman Vishniac Rediscovered*, 116. For a discussion of Vishniac's *A Pictorial Visit to the Jewish Children in Poland*, see Benton, "Vishniac on Assignment," in Benton, *Roman Vishniac Rediscovered*, 112–13. *A Pictorial Visit to the Jewish Children in Poland,* as described by Benton, like *Polish Jews* and *A Vanished World*, contains photographs exclusively by Vishniac (of children selected from his series of photographs taken on JDC trips). It also, like *A Vanished World*, features a series of lengthy captions narrating those photographs. These captions, however, are purely descriptive, and not reflexive. While it would be interesting to conjecture as to why a book written in 1938 would not display the auto-ethnographic impulse displayed by a book from 1983, suffice it to say that Vishniac's post-Holocaust production, especially nearly four decades after the war, may possess a salvage poetic sensibility that the earlier work did not. Since my focus in this study is on the forging of a popular American post-Holocaust cultural discourse about pre-Holocaust East European Jewry, however, I will not be discussing *A Pictorial Visit*. Both *Polish Jews* and *A Vanished World* were readily available publications, broadly reviewed and widely seen. Unfortunately, *A Pictorial Visit to the Jewish Children in Poland* was only recently found. It did not contribute in any significant way to the construction of a popular folk ethnography.

13. Another reason I have chosen to focus on *A Vanished World* and *Polish Jews* to the exclusion of Vishniac's other publications is that these are monographs focused on his photographs alone. While Vishniac hand selected over a hundred images (as opposed to the thirty-one that appear in *Polish Jews*) for Abramovitch's 1947 *The Vanished World*, he did not have the opportunity to frame them as a single oeuvre as he did in his own 1983 *A Vanished World*. Even in *Polish Jews*, which also presents a streamlined

narrative constituted exclusively by Vishniac's own photographs, Vishniac neither selected nor captioned its images—indeed an editor at Schocken Books did so. For our purposes, *Polish Jews* is useful as a contrast and complement to *A Vanished World*; with the help of *Polish Jews* we will focus our discussion on *A Vanished World*, which represents the culmination of Vishniac's agency as a photographer as well as a narrator.

14. James Buzard, "On Auto-ethnographic Authority," *Yale Journal of Criticism* 16, no. 1 (Spring 2003): 73.

15. These approximately 300 nonscience images were published from more than 10,000 negatives, shot from the 1920s to the 1950s. The science negatives, shot from the 1920s through the 1980s number more than 20,000. Between 500 and 1,000 of those have been published.

16. The exhibit opened in New York City, and traveled to Fort Lauderdale, Amsterdam, Paris, Warsaw, Houston, San Francisco. An opening in London took place in 2018. (Thank you to Maya Benton for this information.)

17. Bernadette Van Woerkom, "A Radically Different Style: Jewish Pioneers in the Dutch Polder," in Benton, *Roman Vishniac Rediscovered*, 193–97.

18. Two photographs from Berlin that appear in *A Vanished World* feature Vishniac's daughter, Mara, in 1933. The first is in front of posters for the November 12 plebiscite. The second is in front of a store window displaying the tools necessary to measure the cranium in order to establish Aryan credentials. Vishniac, *Vanished*, 15–16.

19. David Shneer, "Russian Émigré in Berlin," in Benton, *Roman Vishniac Rediscovered*, 55–60; Ute Eskildsen, "The Strolling Observer," in Benton, *Roman Vishniac Rediscovered*, 43–50.

20. Atina Grossman and Avinoam Patt, "Vishniac and the Surviving Remnant," in Benton, *Roman Vishniac Rediscovered*, 205–10; Daniella Doron, "Lives Reborn: Vishniac's Photographs of Displaced Persons Camps in France," in Benton, *Roman Vishniac Rediscovered*, 211–12; and Steven Hoelscher, "A Landscape of Ruins: Roman Vishniac's Return to Postwar Berlin," in Benton, *Roman Vishniac Rediscovered*, 213–18.

21. Deborah Dash Moore, "Roman Vishniac's New York," in Benton, *Roman Vishniac Rediscovered*, 275–82; Hasia Diner, "The Jewish Child in New York," in Benton, *Roman Vishniac Rediscovered*, 283–88; Yue Ma and Herb Tam, "Vishniac's Chinatown," in Benton, *Roman Vishniac Rediscovered*,

289–92; and Eddy Portnoy, "From the Shtetl to Burlesque," in Benton, *Roman Vishniac Rediscovered*, 293–96.

22. Norman Barker, "The Curious Microscopist," in Benton, *Roman Vishniac Rediscovered*, 297–304; and Cornell Capa and Michael Edelson, *The Concerns of Roman Vishniac: Man, Nature and Science* (New York: The Jewish Museum of New York, 1971).

23. Benton, introduction to *Roman Vishniac Rediscovered*, 12. There she articulates the goal of her volume and of the exhibit she curated on which the volume is based: "*Roman Vishniac Rediscovered* provides a comprehensive reappraisal of Vishniac's total photographic output."

24. Kacyzne died on July 7, 1941, when he was marched to the Jewish cemetery in Tarnopol, Ukraine, along with a group of others and died there after many hours of torture and beatings. Kipnis died in 1942 of a stroke in the Warsaw ghetto shortly before his wife, Zimra, was deported to Treblinka, where she was killed. Alter Kacyzne, *Poyln* (New York: Metropolitan Books, Henry Holt, 1999), xxii, and Teresa Smiechekowska, "City and Eyes: Menachem Kipnis' Photographs," *Jewish Historical Institute*, January 9, 2014, www.jhi.pl/en/blog/2014-01-09-city-and-eyes-menachem-kipnis-s-photographs.

25. Buzard, "On Auto-ethnographic Authority," 61.

26. Carlo Ginzburg, "Just One Witness," in *Probing the Limits of Representation: Nazism and the Final Solution,* ed. Saul Friedlander (Cambridge, MA: Harvard University Press, 1992), 82–96.

27. Laura Hobson Faure, "Taking a Closer Look at Vishniac in France," in Benton, *Roman Vishniac Rediscovered*, 199–204; Eugene Kinkead, "Profiles: The Tiny Landscape," *The New Yorker*, June 25 and July 2, 1955.

28. Wiesel, foreword to *Vanished*, n.p.

29. Maya Balakirsky Katz, *The Visual Culture of Chabad* (Cambridge: Cambridge University Press, 2010), 1.

30. Kinkead, "Tiny Landscape," 32.

31. "As Russian as he was, Vishniac was also Jewish and had witnessed how the collapse of Russian society and European society more broadly in the wake of the war, had unleased a violent anti-semitism in earlier days . . . Those who had ended up in Berlin had formed one of the most vibrant, albeit short lived émigré Jewish communities in the world." See David Shneer, "Russian Émigré in Berlin," in Benton, *Roman Vishniac Rediscovered*, 56.

32. In contrast to many of the Jews involved in that exodus, Vishniac's family was fortunate to be living in Wilmersdorf, a Berlin neighborhood highly populated by affluent Russian Jews, not in the Jewish ghetto. vishniac.icp .org/chronology.

33. Aschheim, *Brothers and Strangers*, 11.

34. Ibid., 12.

35. Ibid., 31.

36. Ibid., 37.

37. Ibid.

38. Ibid.

39. According to Steven Ascheim, the moving force behind the Volksheim was Siegfried Lehmann (1892–1958). Based on socialist ideas and youth culture ideologies, the first public talk given at the Volksheim was titled "Judaism and Socialism." Aschheim, *Brothers and Strangers*, 194.

40. Aschheim, *Brothers and Strangers*, 194.

41. Dan Laor, "Agnon in Germany 1912–1924: A Chapter of a Biography," *AJS Review* 18, no. 1 (1993): 75–93.

42. Gershom Sholem, "Reflections on S. Y. Agnon," *Commentary* 44 (December 1967): 59–66.

43. David Shneer, "Russian Émigré," in Benton, *Roman Vishniac Rediscovered*, 8.

44. Roman Vishniac, preface to *A Vanished World* (New York: Farrar, Straus and Giroux).

45. Laura Wexler aptly terms this rhetoric of prophecy in Vishniac's writings "proleptic memory," which she defines as "memory ahead of itself—attempting to thrust the images of the present forward into the future." See Laura Wexler, "What Vishniac Saw: Another Look," in Benton, *Roman Vishniac Rediscovered*, 32.

46. It would be hard to argue that Vishniac was influenced by *The Face of East European Jewry* as much as he became aware of it in the course of his documentary commission for the JDC and entered into an aesthetic dialogue with it. Aesthetically, Vishniac was influenced by the Russian Constructivist Movement and other articulations of the avant garde in the early part of the twentieth century. Maya Benton, phone conversation with the author, September 27, 2017.

47. Arnold Zweig, *The Face of East European Jewry*, ed. and trans. Noah Isenberg (Berkeley: University of California Press, 2004), ix–xxvii.

48. Ibid., ix–xxvii.

49. Ibid.

50. Kinkead, "Tiny Landscape," 33.

51. For introductions to Sander, see August Sander, *Citizens of the 20th Century: Portrait Photographs 1892–1952* (Cambridge, MA: MIT Press, 1986) and *Men without Masks: Faces of Germany 1910–1938* (Greenwich, CT: New York Graphic Society, 1973).

52. Zweig, *Face*, 1.

53. Ibid.

54. Ibid., 1–28.

55. Carol Zemel draws attention to this parallel in a chapter on Roman Vishniac "Zchor: Roman Vishniac's eulogy of East European Jews" in *Looking Jewish: Visual Culture and Modern Diaspora* (Bloomington: Indiana University Press, 2015), 90–94. She attributes this insight to Maya Benton, who wrote about this in her unpublished master's thesis: "Framing the Ostjuden: Mythologies of the East European Jew in Herman Struck's Drawings and Roman Vishniac's Photographs" (MA thesis, University of London, Courtland Institute of Art, 2003).

56. According to Maya Benton, Vishniac's JDC images were reproduced on charity collection boxes (tzedakah cans) in Paris. Benton, phone conversation.

57. Not to be mistaken for the ghettos established throughout Europe for the Jews during the war. However, Wilson's adoption of this rhetoric is a good example of the kind of back-shadowing that situates pre-Holocaust aesthetic works within a post-Holocaust historical consciousness.

58. Edmund Wilson, "Polish Jews," *The New Yorker*, July 22, 1947, 79.

59. Roman Vishniac, preface to *Polish Jews: A Pictorial Record* (New York: Schocken Books, 1947), n.p.

60. Maya Benton has conjectured that the absence of attribution to Vishniac in this brief review may have inspired him to insert himself all the more intensively into the narrative surrounding subsequent publications, such as *A Vanished World*.

61. Capa and Edelson, *The Concerns of Roman Vishniac,* 9.

62. Ibid.

63. Ibid.

64. Ibid.

65. Ibid.

66. Wiesel, foreword to *Vanished*, n.p.

67. Ibid.

68. Ibid.

69. Ibid.

70. Elie Wiesel, *Night* (New York: Hill and Wang, 2006).

71. Wiesel, foreword to *Vanished*, n.p.

72. Vishniac, "Commentary," n.p.

73. Ibid.

74. Ibid.

75. Ibid.

76. Ibid.

77. Walter Benjamin, "The Work of Art in the Age of Mechanical Reproduction," in *Illuminations* (London: Fontana, 1973), 217–64.

78. Quoted in W. J. T. Mitchell, "The Photographic Essay: Four Case Studies," in *Picture Theory: Essays on Verbal and Visual Representation* (Chicago: University of Chicago Press, 1994), 281.

79. Quoted in Mitchell, *Picture Theory*, 290.

80. W. G. Sebald, *Austerlitz* (New York: Random House, 2001); and Ronit Matalon, *The One Facing Us* (New York: Metropolitan Books, 1998).

81. John Berger and Jean Mohr, *Another Way of Telling* (New York: Pantheon, 1982), 91.

82. Ibid.

83. W. J. T Mitchell, *What Do Pictures Want? The Lives and Loves of Images* (Chicago: University of Chicago Press, 2005), 33.

84. Barthes, *Camera Lucida*, 26–27.

6. PATRONYMIC SALVAGE

1. Mayer Kirshenblatt and Barbara Kirshenblatt-Gimblett, *They Called Me Mayer July: Painted Memories of a Jewish Childhood in Poland before the Holocaust* (Berkeley: University of California Press, 2007), 1.

2. Kirshenblatt-Gimblett, "A Daughter's Afterword," in *They Called Me Mayer July*, 369.

3. Nakhman Blitz, "The Martyrdom of Alter Kacyzne," *Dos Naye Lebn*, no. 10, 1945 (in Yiddish).

4. Marek Web, introduction to *Poyln: Jewish Life in the Old Country*, by Alter Kacyzne (New York: Metropolitan Books, 1999), xxi–xxii.

5. Web, "Acknowledgements," in Kacyzne, *Poyln*, ix.

6. For example, in a well-known photographic album published as early as 1947 by Raphael Abramovitch with images from the YIVO Archives, we can see many of Kacyzne's photographs, mostly unattributed. See Raphael Abramovitch, *The Vanished World* (New York: Forward Association, 1947).

7. For a definition of Yiddishland, see Shandler, "Imagining Yiddishland," in *Adventures in Yiddishland,* 31–58.

8. Web, introduction to *Poyln*, xi.

9. Kugelmass, "Jewish Icons."

10. Edwards, *Raw Histories*, 18.

11. Kirshenblatt and Kirshenblatt-Gimblett, *They Called*, 5.

12. Ibid., 2.

13. Web, introduction to *Poyln*, xvii.

14. Kacyzne was inspired by Peretz to move to Warsaw and become a Yiddish writer. He also became a protégé of Ansky, writing the 1937 screenplay for *The Dybbuk* and becoming his literary executor. One can see the relationship between his photographic project and that undertaken by Ansky and his nephew Iudovin, who served as the official photographer for Ansky's ethnographic expedition, in Kacyzne's emphasis on laborers and his black-and-white portraiture.

15. Lucjan Dobroszycki and Barbara Kirshenblatt-Gimblett, in their introduction to *Image before My Eyes*, make this argument. See Dobroszycki and Kirshenblatt-Gimblett, *Image before My Eyes*, 26.

16. Web, introduction to *Poyln*, xvi.

17. Ibid., xxii.

18. Ibid., xvii.

19. Kacyzne, *Poyln*, 29.

20. Kugelmass, "Jewish Icons," 31.

21. Pierre Bourdieau, *Photography: A Middle Brow Art* (Stanford, CA: Stanford University Press, 1990), 31–38; Susan Sontag, *On Photography* (New York: Picador, 1977), 16.

22. Annette Kuhn, *Family Secrets: Acts of Memory and Imagination* (London: Verso, 2002), 1–24; Marianne Hirsch, *Family Frames: Photography,*

Narrative and Postmemory (Cambridge, MA: Harvard University Press, 1997), 7–15.

23. Ibid., 7–15.
24. Barthes, *Camera Lucida*, 89.
25. Sontag, *On Photography*, 9.
26. Barthes, *Camera Lucida*, 26–27.
27. Kirshenblatt and Kirshenblatt-Gimblett, *They Called*, 28.
28. Ibid., 30.
29. Ibid., 15.
30. Web, introduction to *Poyln*, xxii.
31. *Forward*, June 6, 1926, YIVO Archive.
32. *Forward*, December 19, 1926, YIVO Archive.
33. Eugene M. Avrutin, Valerii Dymshits, Alexander Ivanov, Alexander Lvov, Harriet Murav, and Alla Sokolova, *Photographing the Jewish Nation: Pictures from S. Ansky's Ethnographic Expeditions* (Waltham, MA: Brandeis University Press, 2009), 33.
34. Kacyzne, *Poyln*, 26.
35. Ibid., 27.
36. Ibid., 150.
37. Ibid., 102.
38. Ibid., 104.
39. Ibid., 69.
40. Ibid., 106, 96, 70.
41. Ibid., 77.
42. Ibid., 11.
43. Ibid., 34.
44. Ibid., 22.
45. Ibid., 45.
46. Ibid., 110.
47. Ibid., 113.
48. Kirshenblatt and Kirshenblatt-Gimblett, *They Called*, 372.
49. Ibid., 374.
50. Ibid., 192.
51. Ibid., 190–92.
52. Ibid., 376.
53. Ibid., 170.
54. Ibid.

55. Ibid., 171.
56. Ibid., 353.
57. Ibid., 42.
58. Ibid., 97.
59. In a similar instance, when Kirshenblatt describes a special kind of cake made from cookie dough that was served at his brother's circumcision ceremony, he says that the cookie was decorated with Maczek: "tiny balls of multicolored sugar, were sprinkled over the whole thing. (My daughter says they are called sprinkles, hundreds and thousands, or nonpareils in English)." Kirshenblatt and Kirshenblatt-Gimblett, *They Called*, 90.
60. Ibid., 361.
61. Kuhn, *Family Secrets*, 99.
62. Barthes, *Camera Lucida*, 47.
63. Ibid., 51.
64. Ibid.
65. Edwards, *Raw Histories*, 5.
66. Benjamin, "Work of Art," 217–64.
67. Kugelmass, "Jewish Icons," 45.
68. Ibid.
69. Ibid.
70. Edwards, *Raw Histories*, 8.
71. Ibid., 13.

POSTSCRIPT: INTERTEXTUALITY IN POST-HOLOCAUST AMERICAN JEWISH SALVAGE TEXTS

1. I thank the anonymous reader who formulated this excellent question and suggested that I address it in the conclusion to this book.
2. Saul Tschernikhowsky, "ha-Adam Eino Ele Tavnit Moldadeto" [Man Is Nothing but the Landscape of His Birthplace], Ben-Yehuda, https://benyehuda.org/tchernichowsky/haadam-eino-ela.html.
3. On the American Yiddish poets, see Benjamin and Barbara Harshav, *American Yiddish Poetry: A Bilingual Anthology* (Stanford, CA: Stanford University Press, 2007).
4. Wertheimer, *New American Judaism*, 43–49.
5. Glüekel of Hameln, *The Memoirs of Gluckel of Hameln*, trans. Marvin Lowenthal (New York: Schocken Books, 1987).

6. Ilana Blumberg, *Houses of Study: A Jewish Woman among Books* (Lincoln: University of Nebraska Press, 2007).

7. My thanks to Daniel Frese, of the University of Kentucky, for his assistance in formulating this.

8. Sheila Jelen, *Intimations of Difference: Dvora Baron in the Modern Hebrew Renaissance* (Syracuse, NY: Syracuse University Press, 2007).

9. David Frishmann (1859–1922) famously wrote of Shalom Yaakov Abramowitz, or Mendele Mokher Sforim (1835–1917): "Let's imagine for example that some terrible flood came and erased every bit of that world from the earth, along with the memory of that world, until there was not one single sign of that life left and by chance all that remained was *The Book of Beggars*, *The Vale of Tears*, *The Travels of R. Benjamin the Third* and *Of Bygone Days*, along with his small sketches and stories, then there is no doubt on the basis of these sketches the critic could recreate the street life of the Jews in the Russian shtetl totally accurately." David Frishmann, "Mendele Mokher Sforim," in *Kol Kitve David Frishmann* [Collected Works of David Frishmann] (Warsaw: Lilly Frischmann, 1931), 6:76.

10. Dvora Baron, "Family," in *The First Day and Other Stories*, ed. and trans. Chana Kronfeld and Naomi Seidman (Berkeley: University of California Press, 2001).

11. Glazer, *American Judaism*, 140.

WORKS CITED

Abramovitch, Raphael. *The Vanished World*. New York: Forward Association, 1947.

Abramowicz, Hirsz. *Profiles of a Lost World: Memoirs of East European Jewish Life before World War II*. Edited by Jeffrey Shandler and Dina Abramowicz. Detroit: Wayne State University Press, 1999.

Agamben, Giorgio. *Remnants of Auschwitz: The Witness and the Archive*. New York: Zone Books, 1999.

Anderson, Benedict. *Imagined Communities: Reflections on the Origins and Spread of Nationalism*. New York: Verso, 1991.

Antin, Mary. *The Promised Land*. Boston: Houghton Mifflin, 1912.

Aronowicz, Annette. "Heschel's Yiddish Kotsk: Some Reflections on Inwardness." In *Abraham Joshua Heschel: Philosophy, Theology and Interreligious Dialogue*, edited by Stanislaw Krajewski and Adam Lipszyc, 112–21. Wiesbaden: Harrasowitz Verlag, 2009.

Appiah, Kwame Anthony. "Thick Translation." In *The Translation Studies Reader*, edited by Lawrence Venuti, 331–43. New York: Routledge, 2000.

Ascheim, Steven E. *Brothers and Strangers: The East European Jew in German and German-Jewish Consciousness (1800–1923)*. Madison: University of Wisconsin Press, 1982.

Auerbach, Erich. *Mimesis: The Representation of Reality in Western Literature*. Princeton, NJ: Princeton University Press, 1953.

Avrutin, Eugene M., Valerii Dymshits, Alexander Ivanov, Alexander Lvov, Harriet Murav, and Alla Sokolova. *Photographing the Jewish Nation: Pictures from S. Ansky's Ethnographic Expeditions*. Waltham, MA: Brandeis University Press, 2009.

Badanes, Jerome, and Joshua Waletzky. *Image before My Eyes*. New York: YIVO Institute for Jewish Research, 1980.

Bakhur, Elia Levita. *Bovo Bukh*. Translated by Jerry C. Smith. N.p.: Fenestra Books, 2003.

Barthes, Roland. *Camera Lucida*. New York: Hill and Wang, 1981.

Barber, Karin. *The Anthropology of Texts: Persons and Publics: Oral and Written Culture in Africa and Beyond*. Cambridge: Cambridge University Press, 2007.

Barker, Norman. "The Curious Microscopist." In Benton, *Roman Vishniac Rediscovered*, 297–304.

Baron, Dvora. *The First Day and Other Stories*. Edited and translated by Chana Kronfeld and Naomi Seidman. Berkeley: University of California Press, 2001.

Barthes, Roland. *Camera Lucida: Reflections on Photography*. New York: Hill and Wang, 1980.

Belcove-Shalin, Janet S. *New World Hasidim: Ethnographic Studies of Hasidic Jews in America*. Albany: SUNY Press, 1995.

Benedict, Ruth. *Patterns of Culture*. New York: Houghton Mifflin, 1934.

Benjamin, Walter. "The Work of Art in the Age of Mechanical Reproduction." In *Illuminations*, 217–264. London: Fontana, 1973.

Benton, Maya. *Framing the Ostjuden: Mythologies of the East European Jew in Herman Struck's Drawings and Roman Vishniac's Photographs*. MA thesis, University of London, Courtland Institute of Art, 2003.

——, ed. *Roman Vishniac Rediscovered*. New York: International Center of Photography, 2015.

Berger, John, and Jean Mohr. *Another Way of Telling*. New York: Pantheon, 1982.

Bernstein, Michael André. *Foregone Conclusions: Against Apocalyptic History*. Berkeley: University of California Press, 1994.

Blitz, Nakhman. "The Martyrdom of Alter Kacyzne." *Dos Naye Lebn*, no. 10, 1945. In Yiddish.

Blumberg, Ilana. *Houses of Study: A Jewish Woman among Books*. Lincoln: University of Nebraska Press, 2007.

Boas, Franz. "An Anthropologist's Credo." *The Nation*. August 27, 1938, 201–204.

Bourdieau, Pierre. *Photography: A Middle Brow Art*. Stanford, CA: Stanford University Press, 1990.

Boyarin, Jonathan. *The Ethnography of Reading*. Berkeley: University of California Press, 1993.

——. "Jewish Ethnography and the Question of the Book." *Anthropological Quarterly* 64, no. 1 (1991): 14–29.

Brodkin, Karen. *How Jews Became White Folks and What that Says About Race in America*. New Brunswick, NJ: Rutgers University Press, 1998.

Buber, Martin. *Die Legende des Baal Schem* [The Legend of the Baal Shem]. 2nd. ed Frankfurt: Rütten & Loening, 1916. In German.

———. *Die Geschichten des Rabbi Nachman* [The Tales of Rabbi Nachman]. Frankfurt am Main: Rütten & Loening, 1906. In German.

———. *Hasidism and Modern Man*. Edited and translated by Maurice Friedman. New York: Harper, 1966.

———. *Tales of the Hasidim: The Early Masters*. New York: Schocken Books, 1968.

———. *The Legend of the Ba'al Shem*. New York: Schocken Books, 1969.

Buzard, James. "On Auto-ethnographic Authority." *Yale Journal of Criticism* 16, no. 1 (Spring 2003): 61–91.

Capa, Cornell, and Michael Edelson. *The Concerns of Roman Vishniac: Man, Nature and Science*. New York: The Jewish Museum of New York, 1971.

Chakavorty Spivak, Gayatri. "The Politics of Translation." In *The Translation Studies Reader*, edited by Lawrence Venuti, 312–30. New York: Routledge, 2000.

Clifford, James, George E. Marcus, and Kim Fortun. *Writing Culture: The Poetics and Politics of Ethnography*. Berkeley: University of California Press, 1986.

Dash Moore, Deborah. *At Home in America: Second Generation New York Jews*. New York: Columbia University Press, 1981.

———, ed. *East European Jews in Two Worlds*. Evanston, IL: Northwestern University Press, 1990.

———. "Roman Vishniac's New York." In Benton, *Roman Vishniac Rediscovered*, 275–82.

Dauber, Jeremy. *Antonio's Devils: Writers of the Jewish Enlightenment and the Birth of Modern Hebrew and Yiddish Literature*. Palo Alto, CA: Stanford University Press, 2004.

Davidman, Lynn. *Becoming Un-Orthodox: Stories of Ex-Hasidic Jews*. New York: Oxford University Press, 2015.

Dawidowicz, Lucy. *What Is the Use of Jewish History? Essays*. New York: Schocken Books, 1992.

———. *The Golden Tradition: Jewish Life and Thought in Eastern Europe*. New York: Holt, Rinehart and Winston, 1967.

———. *From That Place and Time: A Memoir 1938–1947*. New York: Norton, 1989.

———. *The Jewish Presence*. New York: Holt, Reinhart and Winston, 1977.

Decter, Moshe. "The Old Country Way of Life: The Rediscovery of the Shtetl." *Commentary* (June 1952): 600–604.

Deen, Shulem. *All Who Go Do Not Return*. Minneapolis: Graywolf Press, 2015.

Deitsch, Chaya. *Here and There: Leaving Hasidism, Keeping My Family*. New York: Schocken Books, 2015.

Didi-Huberman, Georges. *Images in Spite of All: Four Photographs from Auschwitz*. Chicago: University of Chicago Press, 2008.

Diner, Hasia. "The Jewish Child in New York." In Benton, *Roman Vishniac Rediscovered* 283–88.

Dobroszycki, Lucjan, and Barbara Kirshenblatt-Gimblett. *Image before My Eyes: A Photographic History of Jewish Life in Poland 1864–1939*. New York: Schocken Books, 1977.

Doron, Daniella. "Lives Reborn: Vishniac's Photographs of Displaced Persons Camps in France." In Benton, *Roman Vishniac Rediscovered*, 211–12.

Edwards, Elizabeth. *Raw Histories: Photographs, Anthropology and Museums*. Oxford: Berg, 2001.

"Eliezer Greenberg Dead at 80." *Jewish Telegraphic Agency*. June 7, 1977. www .jta.org/1977/06/07/archive/eliezer-greenberg-dead-at-80.

Eskildsen, Ute. "The Strolling Observer." In Benton, *Roman Vishniac Rediscovered*, 43–50.

Feldman, Deborah. *Unorthodox: The Scandalous Rejection of My Hasidic Roots*. New York: Simon and Schuster, 2012.

Forward. June 6, 1926. YIVO Archive.

Forward. December 19, 1926. YIVO Archive.

Franzos, Karl Emil. *Aus Halb-Asien: Culturbilder aus Galizian, der Bukowina, Südrussland un Rumänien*. Berlin: Duncker and Humboldt, 1876.

Frishmann, David. "Mendele Mokher Sforim." In *Kol Kitve David Frishmann* [Collected Works of David Frishmann], 6:76. Warsaw: Lilly Frischmann, 1931.

Geertz, Clifford. *The Interpretation of Cultures*. New York: Basic Books, 1973.

Ginzburg, Carlo. "Just One Witness." In *Probing the Limits of Representation: Nazism and the Final Solution*, edited by Saul Friedlander, 82–96. Cambridge, MA: Harvard University Press, 1992.

Ginzberg, Louis. *The Legends of the Jews*. Philadelphia: Jewish Publication Society, 1909–38.

Glazer, Nathan. *American Judaism*. Chicago: University of Chicago Press, 1957.

Goldberg, Harvey. "Reflections on the Mutual Relevance of Anthropology and Judaic Studies." In *Judaism Viewed from Within and from Without*, 1–43. Albany: SUNY Press, 1987.

Gordon, Albert J. *Jews in Suburbia*. Boston: Beacon Press, 1959.

Gordon, Milton M. *Assimilation in American Life: The Role of Race, Religion and National Origins*. New York: Oxford, 1964.

Gottesman, Itzik. *Defining the Yiddish Nation: The Jewish Folklorists of Poland*. Detroit: Wayne State University Press, 2003.

Green, Arthur. "Abraham Joshua Heschel: Recasting Hasidism for Moderns." *Modern Judaism* 29, no. 1 (February 2009): 62–79.

Greenblatt, Stephen, and Catherine Gallagher. *Practicing New Historicism*. Chicago: University of Chicago Press, 2000.

Grossman, Atina, and Avinoam Patt. "Vishniac and the Surviving Remnant." In Benton, *Roman Vishniac Rediscovered*, 205–10.

Handler, Richard. "Ruth Benedict and the Modernist Sensibility." In *Modernist Anthropology: From Fieldwork to Text*, edited by Marc Manganaro, 163–82. Princeton, NJ: Princeton University Press, 1990.

Handlin, Oscar. *The Uprooted: The Epic Story of the Great Migrations that Made the American People*. Boston: Little, Brown and Company, 1952.

Harris, Lis. *Holy Days: The World of a Hasidic Family*. New York: Summit Press, 1985.

Heilman, Samuel C. *Defenders of the Faith: Inside Ultra-Orthodox Jewry*. New York: Schocken Books, 1992.

Held, Shai. *Abraham Joshua Heschel: The Call of Transcendence*. Bloomington: Indiana University Press, 2013.

Heschel, Abraham Joshua. *A Passion for Truth*. Philadelphia: Jewish Publication Society, 1973.

———. *The Earth Is the Lord's: The Inner World of the Jew in Eastern Europe*. New York: Henry Schuman, 1949.

———. *God in Search of Man: A Philosophy of Judaism*. New York: Farrar, Straus and Giroux, 1977.

———. "The Eastern European Era in Jewish History." In *YIVO Annual of Jewish Social Science*, vol. 1, 86–106. New York: YIVO Institute for Jewish Research, 1946.

Heywood, Miriam. "True Images: Metaphor, Metonymy and Montage in Proust and Goddard." *Paragraph* 33, no. 1 (2010): 37–51.

Hindus, Milton, ed. Introduction to *The Worlds of Maurice Samuel: Selected Writings*. Philadelphia: Jewish Publication Society, 1977.

Hirsch, Marianne. *Family Frames: Photography, Narrative and Postmemory*. Cambridge, MA: Harvard University Press, 1997.

—— Faure, Laura Hobson. "Taking a Closer Look at Vishniac in France." In Benton, *Roman Vishniac Rediscovered*, 199–204.

Hoelscher, Steven. "A Landscape of Runs: Roman Vishniac's Return to Postwar Berlin." In Benton, *Roman Vishniac Rediscovered*, 213–18.

Howe, Irving, and Eliezer Greenberg, eds. *A Treasury of Yiddish Stories*. New York: Meridian, 1954.

Howe, Irving. *A Margin of Hope*. San Diego: Harcourt Brace Javonovich, 1982.

Jelen, Sheila E. "A Treasury of Yiddish Stories: Salvage Montage and the Anti-Shtetl." In *Reconstructing the Old Country: American Jewry in the Post-Holocaust Decades*, edited by Eliyana Adler and Sheila Jelen, 137–51. Detroit: Wayne State University Press, 2017.

——. "Bialik's Other Silence." *Hebrew Studies* 44 (2003): 65–86.

——. "Speakerly Texts and Historical Realities: Mendele's Relationship to the Revival of Hebrew Speech." In *Jewish Literature and History*, edited by Sheila E. Jelen and Eliyana R. Adler, 207–21. Bethesda: University of Maryland Press, 2008.

——. "Things as they Are: The Mimetic Imperative." In *Intimations of Difference: Dvora Baron in the Modern Hebrew Renaissance*, 51–78. Syracuse, NY: Syracuse University Press, 2007.

Kallen, Horace. "Democracy versus the Melting-Pot: A Study of American Nationality (1915)." In *Theories of Ethnicity: A Classical Reader*, edited by Werner Sollors, 67–92. London: Macmillan, 1996.

Kallen, Horace. *Culture and Democracy in the United States*. New York: Boni and Liveright, 1924.

Kaplan, Edward K. "The American Mission of Abraham Joshua Heschel." In *The Americanization of the Jews*, edited by Robert Seltzer and Norman S. Cohen, 355–74. New York: New York University Press, 1995.

——. *Spiritual Radical: Abraham Joshua Heschel in America, 1940–1972*. New Haven, CT: Yale University Press, 2007.

Kaplan, Edward K., and Samuel Dressner. "Heschel in Vilna." *Judaism* (June 1, 1998): 278–95.

Kacyzne, Alter. *Poyln*. New York: Metropolitan Books, Henry Holt, 1999.

Katz, Maya Balakirsky. *The Visual Culture of Chabad*. Cambridge: Cambridge University Press, 2010.

Katz, Steven T. "Dialogue and Revelation in the Thought of Martin Buber." *Religious Studies* 14, no. 1 (1978): 57–68.

Kayser, Stephen S. Introduction to *Ilya Schor: Paintings on Yiddish Themes*. New York: Gallery of Jewish Art, 1947.

Kessner, Carol S. *The Other New York Jewish Intellectuals*. New York: New York University Press, 1994.

Kinkead, Eugene. "Profiles: The Tiny Landscape." *The New Yorker* (June 25 and July 2, 1955): 31–56.

Kirshenblatt, Mayer, and Barbara Kirshenblatt-Gimblett. *They Called Me Mayer July: Painted Memories of a Jewish Childhood in Poland before the Holocaust*. Berkeley: University of California Press, 2007.

Kirshenblatt-Gimblett, Barbara. "Imagining Europe." In *Divergent Jewish Cultures*, edited by Deborah Dash Moore and S. Ilan Troen, 168. New Haven, CT: Yale University Press, 2001.

Koltun-Fromm, Ken. *Imagining Jewish Authenticity: Vision and Text in American Jewish Thought*. Bloomington: Indiana University Press, 2015.

Kramer, Judith R., and Seymour Leventman. *Children of the Gilded Ghetto: Conflict Resolution of Three Generations of American Jews*. New Haven, CT: Yale University Press, 1961.

Kranson, Rachel. *Ambivalent Embrace: Jewish Upward Mobility in Postwar America*. Chapel Hill: University of North Carolina Press, 2017.

Kugelmass, Jack. "Jewish Icons: Envisioning the Self in Images of the Other." In *Jews and Other Differences: The New Jewish Cultural Studies*, edited by Jonathan Boyarin and Daniel Boyarin, 30–53. Minneapolis: University of Minnesota Press, 1997.

Kuhn, Annette. *Family Secrets: Acts of Memory and Imagination*. London: Verso, 2002.

Laor, Dan. "Agnon in Germany 1912–1924: A Chapter of a Biography." *AJS Review* 18, no. 1 (1993): 75–93.

Lax, Leah. *Uncovered: How I Left Hasidic Life and Finally Came Home*. Phoenix: She Writes Press, 2015.

Lederhendler, Eli. "Domestic Virtues: Deborah Dash Moore's At Home in America and its Historiographical Context." *American Jewish History* 100, no. 2 (2016): 205–19.

Liptzin, Sol. *A History of Yiddish Literature*. New York: Jonathan David Publishers, 1972.

Liu, Lydia, ed. *Tokens of Exchange: The Problem of Translation in Global Circulations*. Durham, NC: Duke University Press, 1999.

LeVine, Robert. "Culture and Personality Studies 1918–1960: Myth and History." *Journal of Personality* 69, no. 6 (December 2001): 803–18.

Lowenthal, Marvin, trans. *The Memoirs of Gluckel of Hameln*. New York: Schocken Books, 1987.

Lukacs, George. *Studies in European Realism*. New York: Grosset and Dunlap, 1964.

——. *History and Class Consciousness: Studies in Marxist Dialectics*. Cambridge, MA: MIT Press, 1971.

Lynd, Robert, and Helen Lynd. *Middletown: A Study in Modern American Culture*. New York: Harper and Row, 1929.

Ma, Yue, and Herb Tam. "Vishniac's Chinatown." In Benton, *Roman Vishniac Rediscovered*, 289–92.

Malamud, Bernard. "The Magic Barrel." In *The Stories of Bernard Malamud*, 124–43. New York: Farrar, Straus and Giroux, 1983.

Maranhao, Tullio, and Bernard Streck. *Translation and Ethnography: The Anthropological Challenge of Intercultural Understanding*. Tucson: University of Arizona Press, 2003.

Margolick, David. "Dr. Lucjan Dobroszycki, 70; Wrote of Doomed Polish Jews." *New York Times*. October 26, 1995. www.nytimes.com/1995/10/26/nyregion/dr-lucjan-dobroszycki-70-wrote-of-doomed-polish-jews.html.

Matalon, Ronit. *The One Facing Us*. New York: Metropolitan Books, 1998.

Matt, Hershel, ed., "Heschel's Theology: Organized Excerpts." The Shalom Center, September 8, 2001. https://theshalomcenter.org/node/88.

Mead, Margaret. "We Are All Third Generation." In *Keep Your Powder Dry: An Anthropologist Looks at America*, 17–33. Freeport, NY: Books for Libraries Press, 1971.

Mead, Margaret, and Rhoda Métraux, eds. *The Study of Culture at a Distance*. Chicago: University of Chicago Press, 1953.

Mitchell, W. J. T. *Picture Theory: Essays on Verbal and Visual Representation*. Chicago: University of Chicago Press, 1994.

——. *What Do Pictures Want? The Lives and Loves of Images*. Chicago: University of Chicago Press, 2005.

Moseley, Marcus. *Being for Myself Alone: Origins of Jewish Autobiography*. Stanford, CA: Stanford University Press, 2005.

Newhouse, Alana. "A Closer Reading of Roman Vishniac." *New York Times Magazine*. April 4, 2010. www.nytimes.com/2010/04/04/magazine/04shtetl-t.html.

Ozick, Cynthia. *Art and Ardor: Essays*. New York: Knopf, 1983.

Peretz, Y. L. "Mesiras Nefesh." In *Ale Verk Fun Y. L. Peretz*, vol. VII, 135–84. New York: Yiddish, 1920.

Portnoy, Eddy. "From the Shtetl to Burlesque." In Benton, *Roman Vishniac Rediscovered*, 293–96.

———. "Vishniac and the Yiddish Press." In Benton, *Roman Vishniac Rediscovered*, 129–33.

Pratt, Mary Louise. *Imperial Eyes: Travel Writing and Transculturation*. New York: Routledge, 2008.

Prell, Riv Ellen. "Community and the Discourse of Elegy: The Postwar Suburban Debate." In *Imagining the American Jewish Community*, edited by Jack Wertheimer, 67–92. Waltham, MA: Brandeis University Press, 2007.

Rabinowitz, S. J. [Sholem Aleichem]. *Adventures of Mottel the Cantor's Son*. New York: Henry Schuman, 1953.

———. *Tevye the Dairyman and the Railroad Stories*. Translated by Hillel Halkin. New York: Schocken Books, 1987.

Redfield, Robert. "The Folk Society." *The American Journal of Sociology* 32, no. 4 (1947): 293–308.

Roskies, David. Introduction to *The Dybbuk and Other Writings*, xi–xxxvi. New York: Schocken Books, 1992.

Safran, Gabriella. *Wandering Soul: The Dybbuk's Creator, S. Ansky*. Cambridge, MA: Harvard University Press, 2010.

Safran, Gabriella, Steven J. Zipperstein, and Craig Stephen Cravens, eds. *The Worlds of S. An-sky: A Russian-Jewish Intellectual at the Turn of the Century*. Stanford, CA: Stanford California Press, 2006.

Samuel, Maurice. *The Gentleman and the Jew*. New York: Knopf, 1950.

———. *In Praise of Yiddish*. New York: Cowles, 1971.

———. *Little Did I Know: Recollections and Reflections*. New York: Knopf, 1963.

———. *Prince of the Ghetto*. New York: Knopf, 1948.

———. *The World of Sholem Aleichem*. New York: Knopf, 1943.

Sander, August. *Citizens of the 20th Century: Portrait Photographs 1892–1952*. Cambridge, MA: MIT Press, 1986.

———. *Men without Masks: Faces of Germany 1910–1938*. Greenwich, CT: New York Graphic Society, 1973.

Scholem, Gershom. "Martin Buber's Conception of Judaism." In *On Jews and Judaism in Crisis: Selected Essays*, 126–71. New York: Schocken Books, 1976.

———. "Martin Buber's Hasidism: A Critique." *Commentary* 32, no. 4 (October 1, 1961): 304–16.

———. "Reflections on S. Y. Agnon." *Commentary* 44 (December 1967): 59–66.

Schor, Mira. "The Tale of the Goldsmith's Floor." *Differences: A Journal of Feminist Cultural Studies* 14, no. 3 (2003): 136–61.

Sebald, W. G. *Austerlitz*. New York: Random House, 2001.

Shandler, Jeffrey. *Adventures in Yiddishland: Postvernacular Language & Culture*. Berkeley: University of California Press, 2006.

———. "Behold a Vanished World." In Benton, *Roman Vishniac Rediscovered*, 135–38.

———. "Heschel and Yiddish: A Struggle with Signification." *The Journal of Jewish Thought and Philosophy* 2 (1993): 245–99.

———. *Shtetl: A Vernacular Intellectual History*. New Brunswick, NJ: Rutgers University Press, 2014.

Shapiro, Edward. *A Time for Healing: American Jewry since World War II*. Baltimore: Johns Hopkins University Press, 1992.

Shmeruk, Chone. *Prokim fun der yidisher literatur-geshikhte*. Tel Aviv: Peretz Farlag, 1988. In Yiddish.

Shneer, David. "Russian Émigré in Berlin." In Benton, *Roman Vishniac Rediscovered*, 55–60.

Silberstein, Laurence J. *Martin Buber's Social and Religious Thought: Alienation and the Quest for Meaning*. New York: New York University Press, 1989.

Smiechekowska, Teresa. "City and Eyes: Menachem Kipnis' Photographs." Jewish Historical Institute. January 9, 2014. www.jhi.pl/en/blog/2014-01 -09-city-and-eyes-menachem-kipnis-s-photographs.

Sollors, Werner. *Beyond Ethnicity: Consent and Descent in American Culture*. New York: Oxford University Press, 1986.

———. *The Invention of Ethnicity*. New York: Oxford University Press, 1991.

Solomon, Alisa. *Wonder of Wonders: A Cultural History of Fiddler on the Roof*. New York: Metropolitan Books, 2013.

Sontag, Susan. *On Photography*. New York: Picador, 1977.

Stern, David. *The Anthology in Jewish Literature*. Oxford: Oxford University Press, 2004.

Tawil, Dalia. *Life of the Old Jewish Shtetl: Paintings and Silver by Ilya Schor*. Yeshiva University Museum, 1975–76.

Tedlock, Barbara. "From Participant Observation to the Observation of Partic-
    ipation: The Emergence of Narrative Ethnography." *Journal of Anthropo-
    logical Research* 47, no. 1 (Spring 1991): 69–94.

Tschernikhowsky, Saul "ha-Adam Eino Ele Tavnit Moldadeto" [Man Is Noth-
    ing but the Landscape of His Birthplace]. Ben-Yehuda. https://benyehuda
    .org/tchernichowsky/haadam-eino-ela.html.

Turniansky, Chava. "Ze'enah U-Re'enah." *The Encyclopedia of Jewish Women.*
    https://jwa.org/encyclopedia/article/zeenah-u-reenah.

Van Woerkom, Bernadette. "A Radically Different Style: Jewish Pioneers in the
    Dutch Polder." In Benton, *Roman Vishniac Rediscovered,* 193–97.

Venuti, Lawrence. *The Scandals of Translation: Towards an Ethics of Difference.*
    New York: Routledge, 1998.

Ver, Moi, and Zalman Shneour. *The Ghetto Lane in Vilna.* Zurich: O Fussli,
    1931.

Vincent, Leah. *Cut Me Loose: Sin and Salvation after My Ultra-Orthodox Girl-
    hood.* New York: Penguin, 201.

Vishniac, Roman. *A Vanished World.* New York: Farrar, Straus and Giroux,
    1983.

———. *Polish Jews: A Pictorial Record.* New York: Schocken Books, 1947.

Web, Marek. Introduction to *Poyln: Jewish Life in the Old Country,* by Alter
    Kacyzne, xxi–xxii. New York: Metropolitan Books, 1999.

Wettlaufer, Alexandra. "Ruskin and Laforgue: Visual-Verbal Dialectics and
    the Poetics/Politics of Montage." *Comparative Literature Studies* 32, no. 4
    (1995): 514–35.

Wexler, Laura. "What Vishniac Saw: Another Look." In Benton, *Roman Vishniac
    Rediscovered,* 31–39.

Wiesel, Elie. Foreword to *A Vanished World,* by Roman Vishniac, n.p. New
    York: Farrar, Straus and Giroux, 1983.

———. *Night.* New York: Hill and Wang, 2006.

Wilson, Edmund. "Polish Jews." *The New Yorker* (July 22, 1947): 79.

Wilson, Sarah. "The Evolution of Ethnicity." *ELH* 76 (2009): 247–76.

Winston, Hella. *Unchosen: The Hidden Lives of Hasidic Rebels.* New York: Bea-
    con Press, 2006.

Zborowski, Mark, and Elizabeth Herzog. *Life Is with People: The Culture of the
    Shtetl.* New York: Schocken Books, 1952; 1995.

Zemel, Carol. "Imagining the Shtetl: Diaspora Culture, Photography and
    Eastern European Jews." In *Diaspora and Visual Culture,* edited by Nicho-
    las Mirzoeff, 193–206. New York: Routledge, 2000.

——. "Zchor: Roman Vishniac's Eulogy of East European Jews." In *Shaping Losses: Cultural Memory and the Holocaust*, 75–86. Urbana: University of Illinois Press, 2001.

Zipperstein, Steven J. "Underground Man: The Curious Case of Mark Zborowski and the Writing of a Modern Jewish Classic." *Jewish Review of Books* (Summer 2010), jewishreviewofbooks.com/articles/275/underground-man-the-curious-case-of-mark-zborowski-and-the-writing-of-a-modern-jewish-classic/.

INDEX